**Nominated for 3 EISNER AWARDS including
Best New Series and Best Ongoing Series**

**Featured on the Best of the Year List
for The Village Voice, IGN and The Oregonian**

"Incredibly fun and ridiculously addictive. . . A roller-coaster ride through a library, weaving famous authors and characters into a tale of mystery that is, at once, oddly familiar yet highly original."
-USA TODAY.COM

"Casually literate and intelligent, engrossing from the first page, THE UNWRITTEN is a gem of a conspiracy story with enough metafictional layers to launch a thesis or two."
-SCRIPPS HOWARD NEWS SERVICE

"A taut thriller that slyly plays off the real-world mania for imaginary ones . . .
Carey has not only created a brisk and addictive story, sketched with crafty allusions to classic literature, but also neatly subverted the celebrity-worship manias of fantasy fandom and questioned the very nature of storytelling itself."
- PUBLISHERS WEEKLY

"A High-Minded Literary Hodgepodge-with Wizards!"
-PORTLAND MERCURY

"A top-tier reading experience."
- IGN

"Fascinating."
- BOSTON HERALD

"Everything I love about comics, period."
- AIN'T IT COOL NEWS

"Favorite book of the year."
- NEWSARAMA

the **unwritten**
INSIDE MAN

Karen Berger SVP-Executive Editor
Pornsak Pichetshote Editor-Original Series
Bob Harras Group Editor-Collected Editions
Robbin Brosterman Design Director-Books
Louis Prandi Art Director

DC COMICS

Diane Nelson President
Dan DiDio and Jim Lee Co-Publishers
Geoff Johns Chief Creative Officer
Patrick Caldon EVP-Finance and Administration
John Rood EVP-Sales, Marketing and Business Development
Amy Genkins SVP-Business and Legal Affairs
Steve Rotterdam SVP-Sales and Marketing
John Cunningham VP-Marketing
Terri Cunningham VP-Managing Editor
Alison Gill VP-Manufacturing
David Hyde VP-Publicity
Sue Pohja VP-Book Trade Sales
Alysse Soll VP-Advertising and Custom Publishing
Bob Wayne VP-Sales
Mark Chiarello Art Director

THE UNWRITTEN: INSIDE MAN
Published by DC Comics. Cover and compilation
Copyright © 2010 Mike Carey and Peter Gross.
All Rights Reserved. Originally published in single
magazine form as THE UNWRITTEN 6-12. Copyright
© 2009, 2010 Mike Carey and Peter Gross. All Rights
Reserved. VERTIGO and all characters, their distinctive
likenesses and related elements featured in this
publication are trademarks of DC Comics. The stories,
characters and incidents featured in this publication are
entirely fictional. DC Comics does not read or accept
unsolicited submissions of ideas, stories or artwork.
DC Comics, 1700 Broadway, New York, NY 10019.
A Warner Bros. Entertainment Company. Printed in
Canada. First Printing. ISBN: 978-1-4012-2873-6

SUSTAINABLE
FORESTRY
INITIATIVE
Certified Chain of Custody
Promoting Sustainable
Forest Management
www.sfiprogram.org
Fiber used in this product line meets the
sourcing requirements of the SFI program.
www.sfiprogram.org PWC-SFICOC-260

the UnWritten

Inside Man

Mike Carey & Peter Gross Script - Story - Art   Jimmy Broxton Finishes – Jud Stiss

Kurt Huggins Zelda Devon Finishes – Eliza Mae Hertford's Willowbank Tales

Chris Chuckry Jeanne McGee Kurt Huggins Zelda Devon Colorists

Todd Klein Letterer Yuko Shimizu Cover Artist

THE UNWRITTEN created by Gross and Carey

Introduction

The Unwritten is Mike Carey and Peter Gross writing literature, in two different ways. Firstly, in that, for instance, the story of a French regional prison governor who loves his fantasy-prone children is not one that sits within a genre. It's the sort of thing, like the existential plight of Tommy Taylor, one would expect from a novel found in the middle of the book store, not at the frayed edges where books whose characters live within sets of reader expectations hang out. There's no format: the stories here all contribute to a bigger tale, but we're not waiting to see what our hero and his friends will get up to on their quest this issue. They might not be in it. Or they might be, but it might not be about them. Carey and his co-plotter/artist have created a literary playground for themselves out of thin air. There's a central mystery about what's going on, but the digressions and notes in the margin are just as interesting.

This is almost an anthology, of stories bound together purely by theme. But it's such a huge and compelling theme that there's no good reason why anyone should ever want that mystery to be solved.

That's the second way they're writing literature: obviously, they're writing *about* it.

They want to show us the gravitational distortion of reality by fiction. For instance, when our heroes encounter a phantom version of Nazi brutality, they just about ignore it initially, the *Raiders of the Lost Ark* or *Cabaret* theme musics probably playing somewhere in their unconscious. They're not too perturbed by it: they think they've seen this, that they know what this is. It's to the creators' credit that they find a new way, with the tale of *Jud Süss*, to shock us with the fascists' own distortion of reality and text. The background radiation of *The Unwritten*, as seen in internet forum and blog snippets, is a psychotic real world one degree more

hysterical than our own, weighed down by fiction, shaped by it almost to eschaton, or as science fiction writers would have it, to the point of singularity. The title of the series itself might refer not to something that hasn't been done, but to something that's being undone, a tapestry that's being unpicked.

The Unwritten also uses the language of magic to talk about literature. *Willowbank Tales* exists not only to have fun with sweary rabbits, but to describe the negative space within stories in a magical/psychological way. That space is represented by a literal vault of the unconscious. (I'm sure we might soon meet a madwoman in an attic.) *Jud Süss* is rendered into a cosmic monster, something out of H.P. Lovecraft or P.J. Hammond. A missing creator writes between the lines in novels, in the details. That feels like something a schizophrenic might tell you. Narrative equals consciousness equals magical power equals political power, an

equation which feels instinctively true, which might even define existence.

Amongst all this, Carey and Gross don't neglect character. 'Mr. Bun felt like a clock that has been over-wound.' A horrible fate for those undeserving of it that doesn't feel like something one would normally find in fiction, but that instead speaks of reality. An untrustworthy but charming fellow traveller who's actually a writer himself, but never quite describes himself as such.

As I said: doing literature while talking about it. It's like we're watching them pull themselves up into the air by their bootstraps.

Paul Cornell

Paul Cornell is a Hugo award-nominated writer whose television credits include Dr. Who, Primeval, *and* Pulse.

The Fall of Tom Taylor???
POSTED: Wednesday, October 21 @ 12:00 am

Now how art thou fallen from Heaven, oh Tom Taylor, son of the morning!

Don't get me wrong. I know these are hard times for all quasi-celebrities, with the public attention span running shorter than ever; and the wise old proverb tells us that there's no such thing as bad publicity. But I think our boy Thomas is testing that theory to the limits.

Tom's claim to fame was always a little dubious, to be honest. Okay, so his father wrote the most popular series of books the publishing world has ever seen: and yes, Tom shares a name (more or less) with the young wizard who stars in those books, Tommy Taylor™. But really, Tom is not that interesting a guy, and his sole contribution to the legend was to earn a meager crust on the fan circuit signing his father's books.

Then he hit the news when an earnest young lady challenged him at a convention, claiming that most of the documentation relating to Tom's so-called life is forged. Cue howls of outrage, crazed denunciations, burnings in effigy — and then, more surprising, the emergence of a cult who believe that Tom IS Tommy, the word made flesh, a multiplatform savior for a media-saturated age.

That might have been something of a happy ending, if Tom hadn't then gone to the Villa Diodati — the last place where his famous father was seen alive — and (allegedly) slaughtered half a dozen people in an insane and possibly drug-fueled orgy of violence.

What else? Mysterious cabals? Shadowy assassins? Unconfirmed reports that a winged cat was seen flying over Geneva on the day of the killings? The rumor mill runs on hard fuel, kiddies. It can't grind smoke.

This entry was posted on Wednesday, October 14 at 12:00 am. Tags: **Celebrity, Pop Culture, Arts and Life.** You can skip to the end and leave a response. Commenters must abide by the forum's Rules and Regulations.

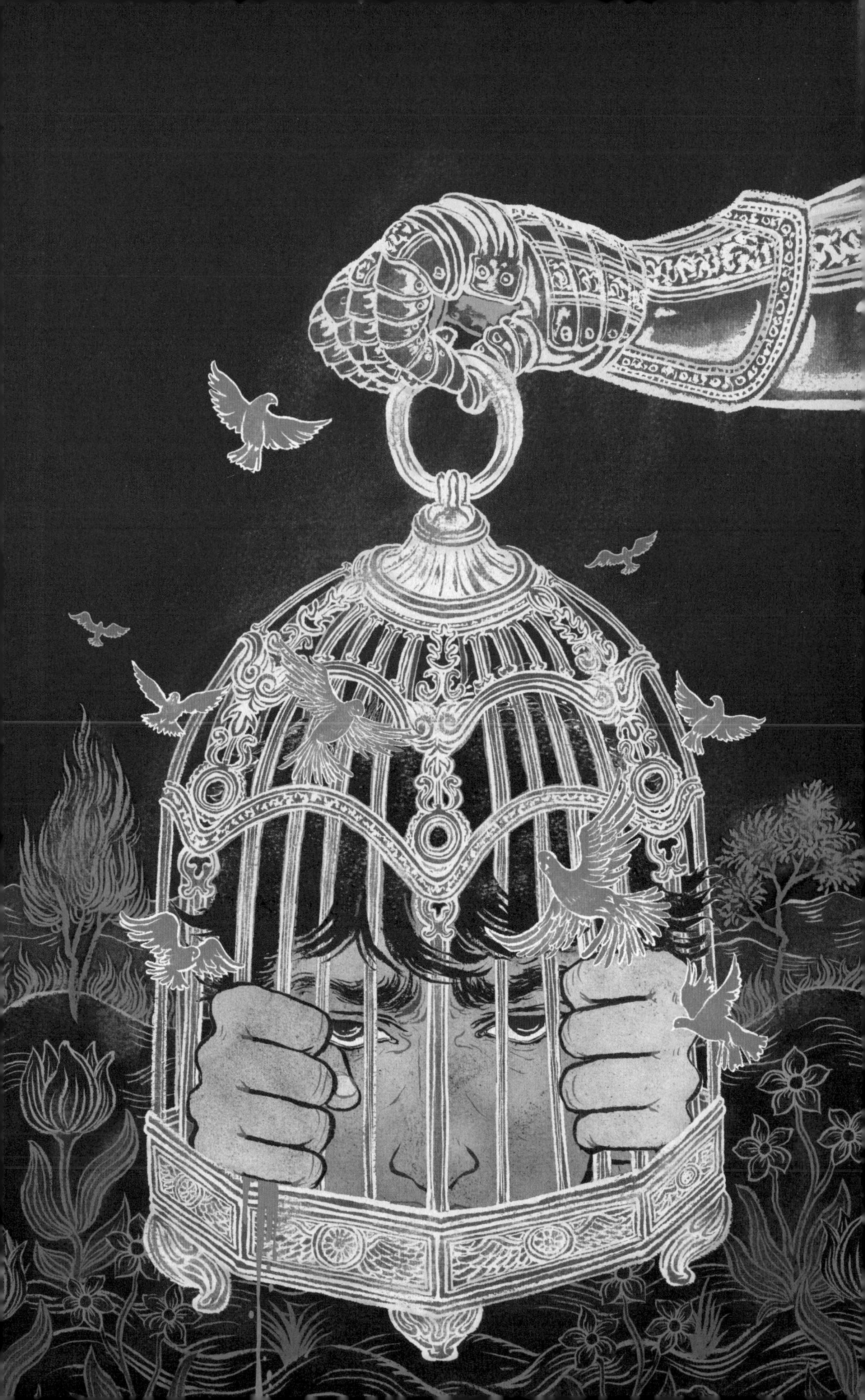

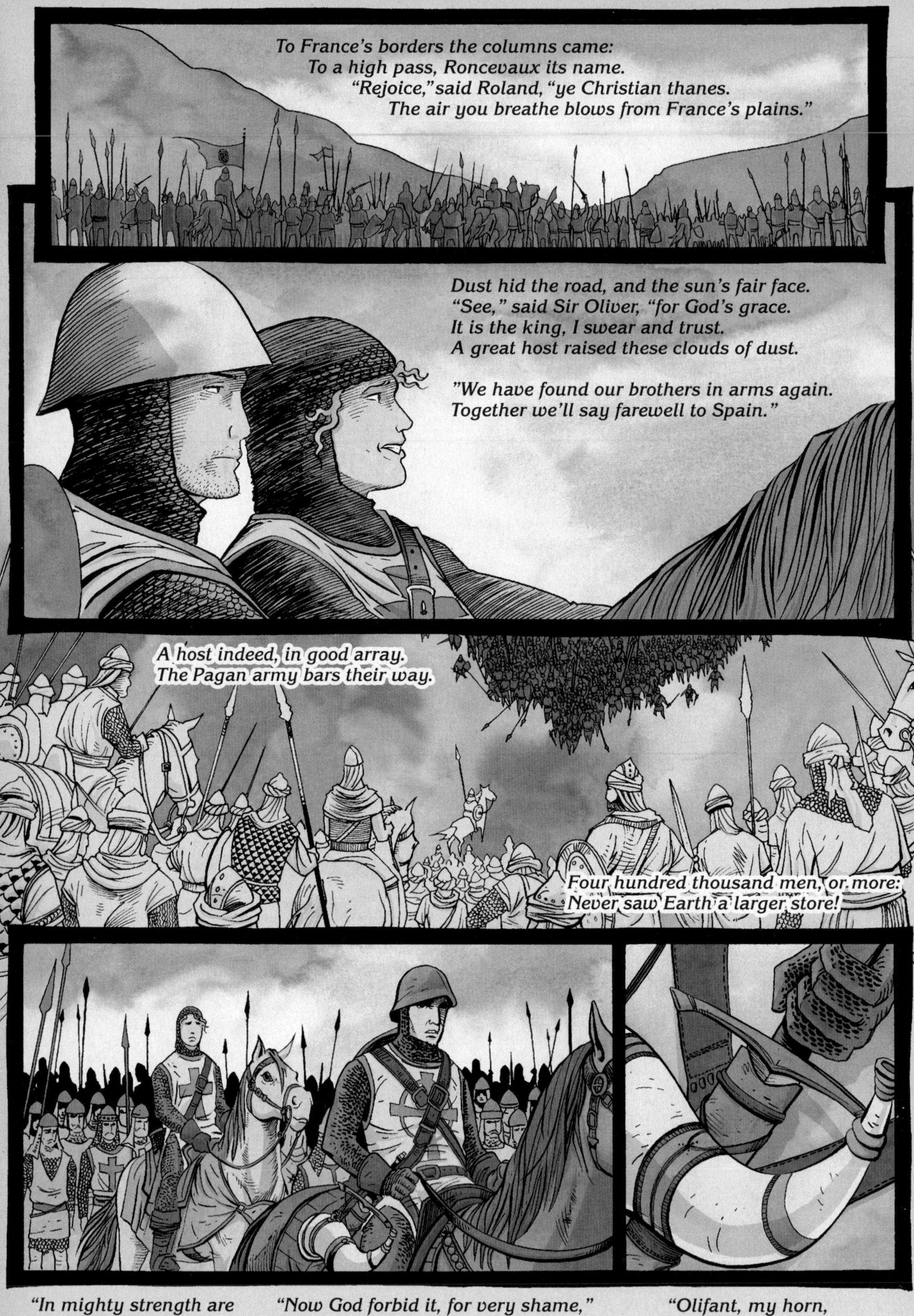
To France's borders the columns came:
To a high pass, Roncevaux its name.
"Rejoice," said Roland, "ye Christian thanes.
The air you breathe blows from France's plains."
Dust hid the road, and the sun's fair face.
"See," said Sir Oliver, "for God's grace.
It is the king, I swear and trust.
A great host raised these clouds of dust.
"We have found our brothers in arms again.
Together we'll say farewell to Spain."
A host indeed, in good array.
The Pagan army bars their way.
Four hundred thousand men, or more:
Never saw Earth a larger store!

"In mighty strength are
the Heathen crew,"
Oliver said, "and our
knights are few.
Roland, I beg you,
sound your horn.
The king will hear,
and his host return."

"Now God forbid it, for very shame,"
Said Roland. "I would be to blame
If out of fear I called the king,
His arm to bend, his aid to bring.

"Olifant, my horn,
shall here abide,
Untouched, unsounded
at my side."

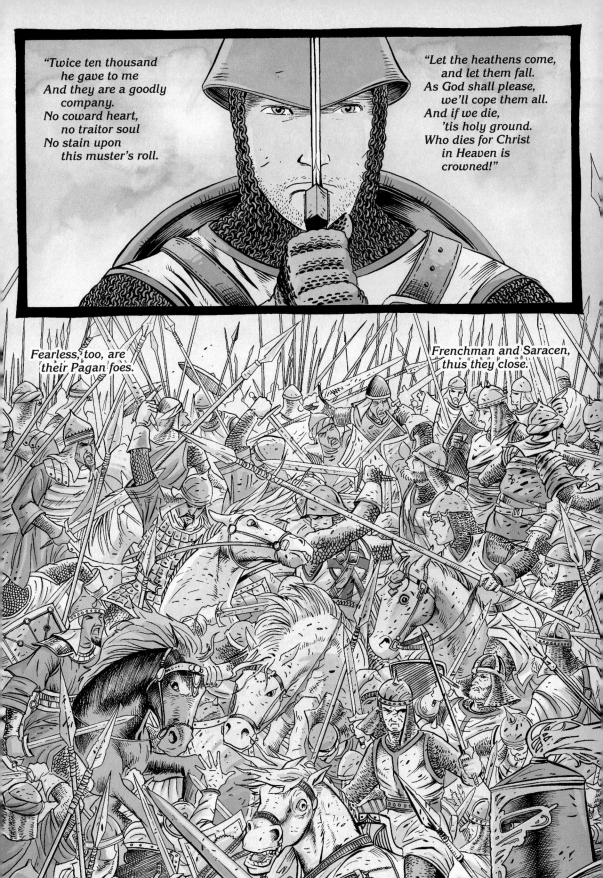

"Twice ten thousand
    he gave to me
And they are a goodly
    company.
No coward heart,
    no traitor soul
No stain upon
    this muster's roll.

"Let the heathens come,
    and let them fall.
As God shall please,
    we'll cope them all.
And if we die,
    'tis holy ground.
Who dies for Christ
    in Heaven is
    crowned!"

Fearless, too, are
    their Pagan foes.

Frenchman and Saracen,
    thus they close.

INSIDE MAN

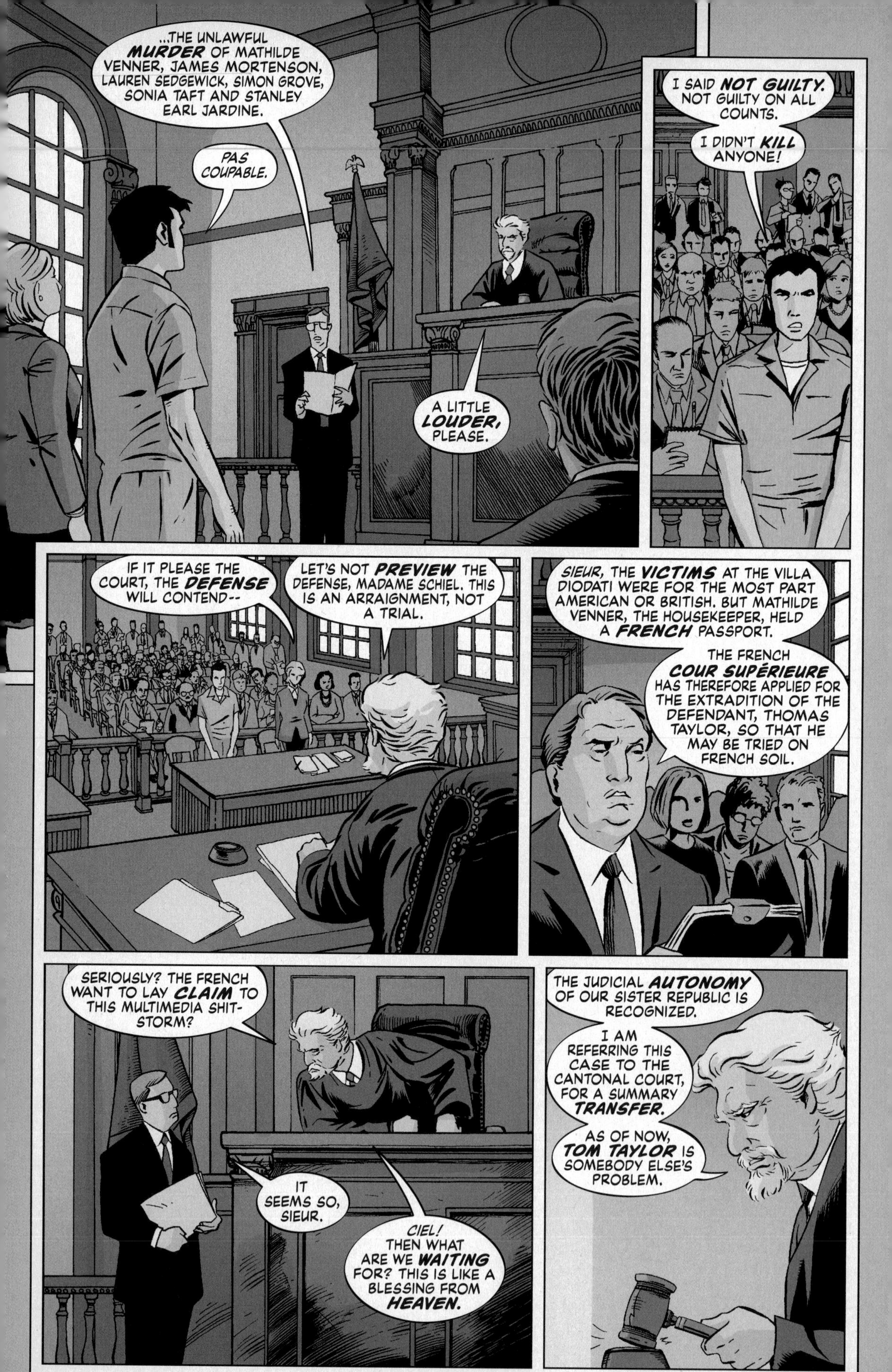
...THE UNLAWFUL MURDER OF MATHILDE VENNER, JAMES MORTENSON, LAUREN SEDGEWICK, SIMON GROVE, SONIA TAFT AND STANLEY EARL JARDINE.
PAS COUPABLE.
A LITTLE LOUDER, PLEASE.
I SAID NOT GUILTY. NOT GUILTY ON ALL COUNTS.
I DIDN'T KILL ANYONE!
IF IT PLEASE THE COURT, THE DEFENSE WILL CONTEND--
LET'S NOT PREVIEW THE DEFENSE, MADAME SCHIEL. THIS IS AN ARRAIGNMENT, NOT A TRIAL.
SIEUR, THE VICTIMS AT THE VILLA DIODATI WERE FOR THE MOST PART AMERICAN OR BRITISH. BUT MATHILDE VENNER, THE HOUSEKEEPER, HELD A FRENCH PASSPORT.
THE FRENCH COUR SUPÉRIEURE HAS THEREFORE APPLIED FOR THE EXTRADITION OF THE DEFENDANT, THOMAS TAYLOR, SO THAT HE MAY BE TRIED ON FRENCH SOIL.
SERIOUSLY? THE FRENCH WANT TO LAY CLAIM TO THIS MULTIMEDIA SHIT-STORM?
IT SEEMS SO, SIEUR.
CIEL! THEN WHAT ARE WE WAITING FOR? THIS IS LIKE A BLESSING FROM HEAVEN.
THE JUDICIAL AUTONOMY OF OUR SISTER REPUBLIC IS RECOGNIZED.
I AM REFERRING THIS CASE TO THE CANTONAL COURT, FOR A SUMMARY TRANSFER.
AS OF NOW, TOM TAYLOR IS SOMEBODY ELSE'S PROBLEM.

Dr. Swann Cares about YOU

ONLINE PSYCHIATRIC HELP FROM A CERTIFIED PROFESSIONAL

Home | Help Me | Helped | Special Features | Store

GO!

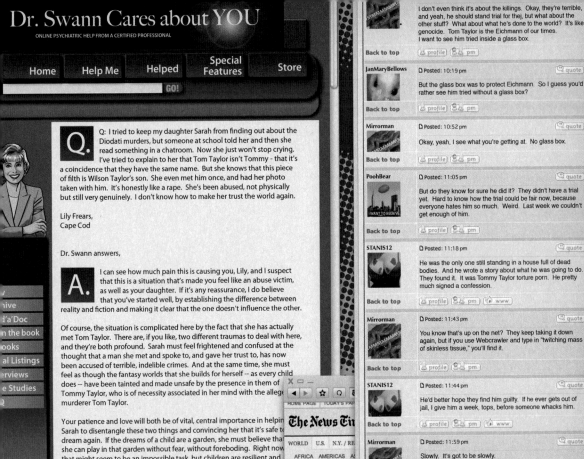

Q. Q: I tried to keep my daughter Sarah from finding out about the Diodati murders, but someone at school told her and then she read something in a chatroom. Now she just won't stop crying. I've tried to explain to her that Tom Taylor isn't Tommy - that it's a coincidence that they have the same name. But she knows that this piece of filth is Wilson Taylor's son. She even met him once, and had her photo taken with him. It's honestly like a rape. She's been abused, not physically but still very genuinely. I don't know how to make her trust the world again.

Lily Frears,
Cape Cod

Dr. Swann answers,

A. I can see how much pain this is causing you, Lily, and I suspect that this is a situation that's made you feel like an abuse victim, as well as your daughter. If it's any reassurance, I do believe that you've started well, by establishing the difference between reality and fiction and making it clear that the one doesn't influence the other.

Of course, the situation is complicated here by the fact that she has actually met Tom Taylor. There are, if you like, two different traumas to deal with here, and they're both profound. Sarah must feel frightened and confused at the thought that a man she met and spoke to, and gave her trust to, has now been accused of terrible, indelible crimes. And at the same time, she must feel as though the fantasy worlds that she builds for herself -- as every child does -- have been tainted and made unsafe by the presence in them of Tommy Taylor, who is of necessity associated in her mind with the allege murderer Tom Taylor.

Your patience and love will both be of vital, central importance in helpin Sarah to disentangle these two things and convincing her that it's safe t dream again. If the dreams of a child are a garden, she must believe tha she can play in that garden without fear, without foreboding. Right now that might seem to be an impossible task, but children are resilient and they can recover fully from terrible psychic harm.

I'm going to divide this process into three phases, and take you through the key factors belonging to each of

ive
'a'Doc
n the book
ooks
al Listings
erviews
e Studies

I don't even think it's about the killings. Okay, they're terrible, and yeah, he should stand trial for thej, but what about the other stuff? What about what he's done to the world? It's like genocide. Tom Taylor is the Eichmann of our times. I want to see him tried inside a glass box.

Back to top | profile | pm

JanMaryBellows — Posted: 10:19 pm — quote

But the glass box was to protect Eichmann. So I guess you'd rather see him tried without a glass box?

Back to top | profile | pm

Mirrorman — Posted: 10:52 pm — quote

Okay, yeah, I see what you're getting at. No glass box.

Back to top | profile | pm

PoohBear — Posted: 11:05 pm — quote

I WANT TO BELIEVE

But do they know for sure he did it? They didn't have a trial yet. Hard to know how the trial could be fair now, because everyone hates him so much. Weird. Last week we couldn't get enough of him.

Back to top | profile | pm

STANIS12 — Posted: 11:18 pm — quote

He was the only one still standing in a house full of dead bodies. And he wrote a story about what he was going to do. They found it. It was Tommy Taylor torture porn. He pretty much signed a confession.

Back to top | profile | pm | www

Mirrorman — Posted: 11:43 pm — quote

You know that's up on the net? They keep taking it down again, but if you use Webcrawler and type in "twitching mass of skinless tissue," you'll find it.

Back to top | profile | pm

STANIS12 — Posted: 11:44 pm — quote

He'd better hope they find him guilty. If he ever gets out of jail, I give him a week, tops, before someone whacks him.

Back to top | profile | pm | www

Mirrorman — Posted: 11:59 pm — quote

Slowly. It's got to be slowly.

---

http://www.peruugle.com/search/Tommy+Taylor+Switzerla

Journalist and environmentalist George Monbiot said at the so-called End-of-the-World Summit in Patagonia that the time for implementing phased and relatively painless measures to control climate change had come and gone. "It's a question, now, of how hard we hit the wall." he said. "It's difficult not to despair when we see how many last chances have been squandered by . . .

AdventAssociation - The ALMANACs

Librarian Offers to Testify
LazaroWeekly - 38 minutes ago
Derek Winters, librarian at London's University College, has come forward to talk about his own encounter with Tom Taylor - a scant day before the Villa Diodati murder spree. Winters claims that Tom Taylor came to the College library in search of fictional characters from several Dickens novels, all of whom he claimed to have met. "It was . . .

Policeman in Diodati Case Hospitalized
ParallelPress - 4 hours ago
A twice-decorated police officer, Louis Pagnol, has been hospitalized for stress after taking part in the murder investigation at the Villa Diodati. Pagnol became increasingly disturbed by the horrendous sights at the Villa, his superior officer, Assistant Commissioner Félis Rousse, has said in a prepared statement: He began to behave aberrantly and to report visual hallucinations. Colleagues removed him from the scene shortly after the arrest of Tom Taylor, during which he claimed to have seen a flying . . .

Is There a Fourteenth Tommy Taylor Novel?
TeaRooms - 8 hours ago

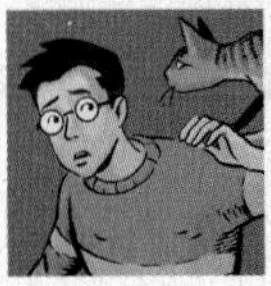

Speculation mounted yesterday that the renewal by Queensbury Publishing of the copyright protections on existing Tommy Taylor properties, and their extension to territories such as China and Southeast Asia, was a preemptive action designed to prevent pirates and counterfeiters from profiting when a fourteenth Tommy Taylor novel is announced later this year. Editor Ernie Cole refused to respond to questions about whether he has been in contact with missing author Wilson Taylor, and whether Queensbury had received . . .

all 2,759 news articles >>

"Kill with Kindness" Lecturer Dismissed
PanWNews - 4 hours ago
An academic who suggested that cities and even local communities should be set euthanasia targets in order to cut the global population back to nineteenth century levels has lost his position at the UK's Durham University. Lawrence Ivens claimed that runaway population growth was the biggest threat to the world's future, and insisted that his radical solution posed no ethical problems. "All societies have culled their populations when they had to," an unrepentant Ivens argued yesterday. "And killing a loved one can actually be an experience that brings you closer . . .

The News Ti

HOME PAGE | TODAY'S PA

WORLD | U.S. | N.Y. / RE

AFRICA | AMERICAS | A

Come to Judgment

By VINCENT J. HAMMER

SIGN IN TO E-MAIL
PRINT
REPRINTS
SHARE
ARTICLE TOOLS SPONSORED BY

Controversy continues to surround the murders at the Villa Diodati in Geneva, and the subsequent police investigation. Diehard Tom Taylor supporters claim that the evidence which led to Taylor's arrest was circumstantial at best, and that the police have failed to follow up on reported sightings of another man in the vicinity of the Villa in the immediate run-up to the brutal killings.

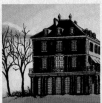

The Villa Diodati became a true site of gothic horror this past week.

But as the forum for Taylor's trial shifts from Switzerland to France, fewer and fewer voices seem to be raised in his support. Local chapters of the Tommy Taylor Fan Club throughout Europe and America have ritually "divorced" themselves from the troubled celebrity, many of them tearing out Taylor's autograph from treasured copies of his father's best-selling novels.

Even more extreme responses have come from other sources - including a record number of direct threats to Taylor's life from outraged former fans, some of which are under active investigation by the police.

Taylor's aberrant behavior in the past few weeks has been seen by many as a response to an incident at London's recent TommyCon. Taylor was confronted by a graduate student who accused him of not being who he claims to be, asserting that most of the documents proving his identity are forged.

Taylor went to ground, but was pursued wherever he went by enraged and disillusioned readers of the beloved novels. He was then hospitalized after an incident in which he was kidnapped by an obsessive fan dressed as Tommy Taylor's fictional nemesis, Count Ambrosio. The incident culminated in the detonation of a nail bomb, killing Taylor's stalker but leaving him unharmed - a fact which caused some to hail Taylor as the living incarnation of his fictional counterpart: "Tommy Taylor made flesh." Some even hailed him as a messiah.

Few, however, would endorse those judgments now, as Taylor perpares to stand trial on six counts of murder. The bloody rampage at the Villa Diodati has silenced most of those voices which previously

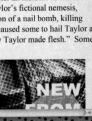

NEW

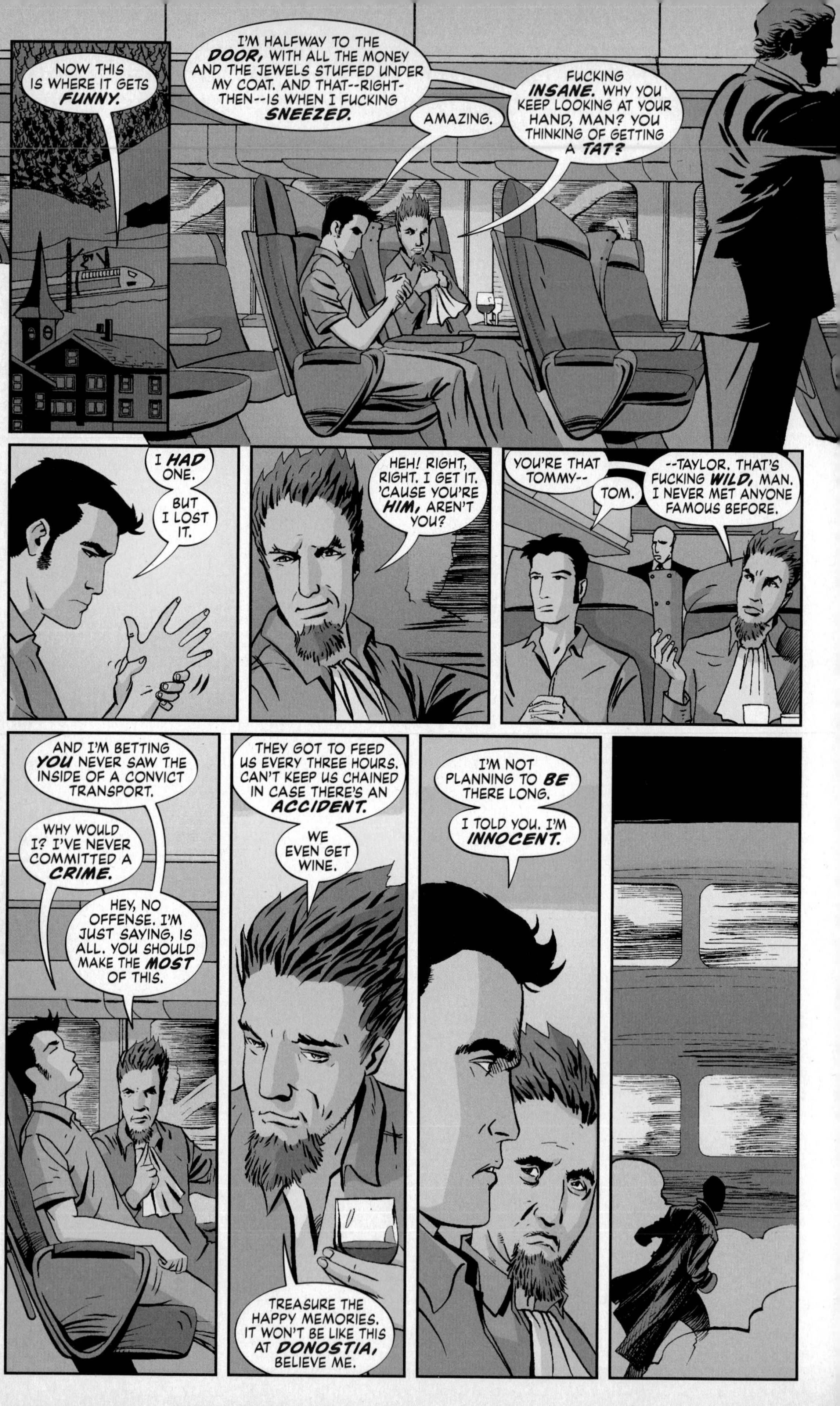
NOW THIS IS WHERE IT GETS FUNNY.
I'M HALFWAY TO THE DOOR, WITH ALL THE MONEY AND THE JEWELS STUFFED UNDER MY COAT. AND THAT--RIGHT-THEN--IS WHEN I FUCKING SNEEZED.
AMAZING.
FUCKING INSANE. WHY YOU KEEP LOOKING AT YOUR HAND, MAN? YOU THINKING OF GETTING A TAT?
I HAD ONE.
BUT I LOST IT.
HEH! RIGHT, RIGHT. I GET IT. 'CAUSE YOU'RE HIM, AREN'T YOU?
YOU'RE THAT TOMMY--
TOM.
--TAYLOR. THAT'S FUCKING WILD, MAN. I NEVER MET ANYONE FAMOUS BEFORE.
AND I'M BETTING YOU NEVER SAW THE INSIDE OF A CONVICT TRANSPORT.
WHY WOULD I? I'VE NEVER COMMITTED A CRIME.
HEY, NO OFFENSE. I'M JUST SAYING, IS ALL. YOU SHOULD MAKE THE MOST OF THIS.
THEY GOT TO FEED US EVERY THREE HOURS. CAN'T KEEP US CHAINED IN CASE THERE'S AN ACCIDENT.
WE EVEN GET WINE.
TREASURE THE HAPPY MEMORIES. IT WON'T BE LIKE THIS AT DONOSTIA, BELIEVE ME.
I'M NOT PLANNING TO BE THERE LONG.
I TOLD YOU. I'M INNOCENT.

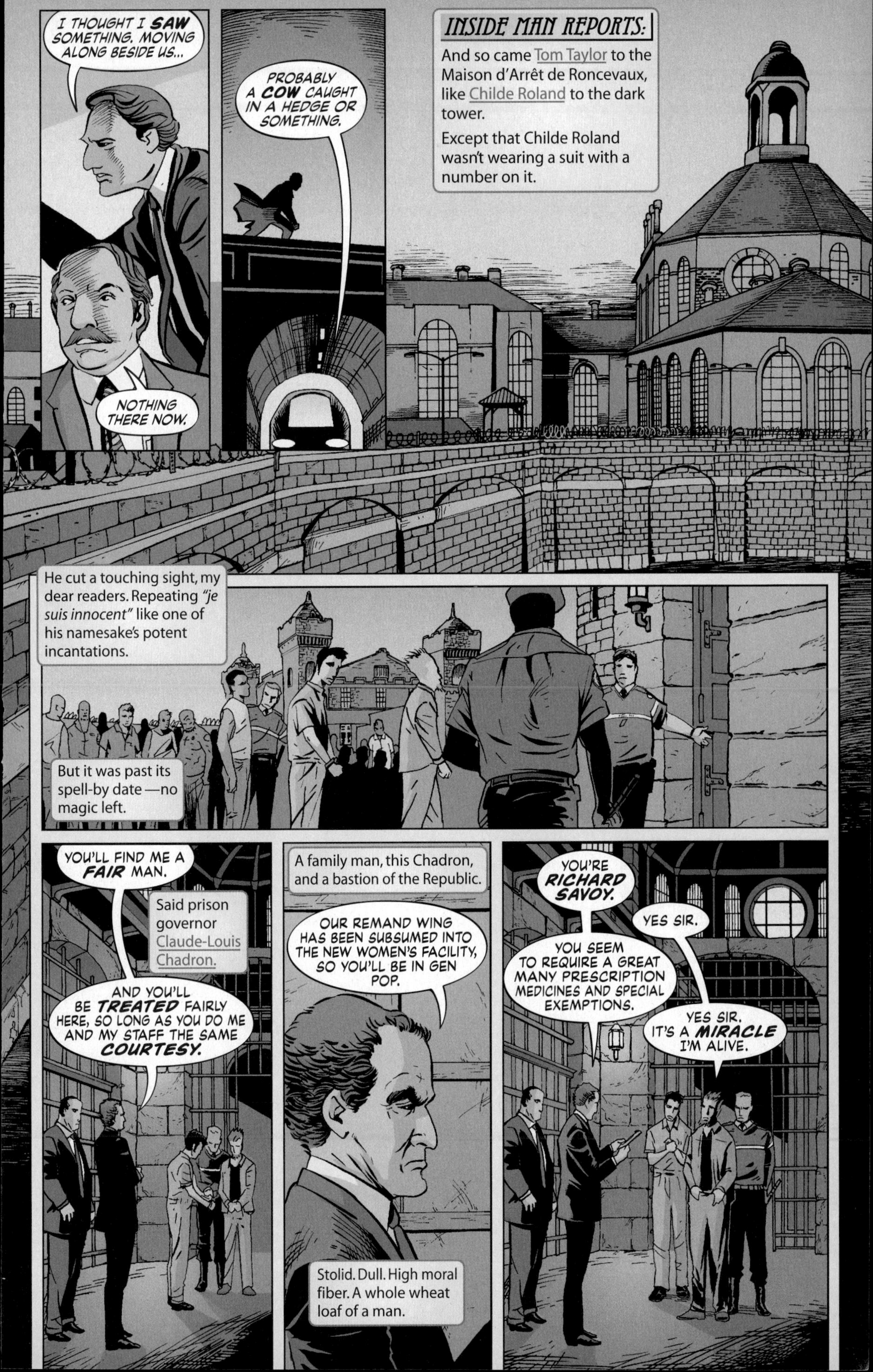
I THOUGHT I SAW SOMETHING. MOVING ALONG BESIDE US...
NOTHING THERE NOW.
PROBABLY A COW CAUGHT IN A HEDGE OR SOMETHING.
INSIDE MAN REPORTS:
And so came Tom Taylor to the Maison d'Arrêt de Roncevaux, like Childe Roland to the dark tower.
Except that Childe Roland wasn't wearing a suit with a number on it.
He cut a touching sight, my dear readers. Repeating "je suis innocent" like one of his namesake's potent incantations.
But it was past its spell-by date—no magic left.
YOU'LL FIND ME A FAIR MAN.
Said prison governor Claude-Louis Chadron.
AND YOU'LL BE TREATED FAIRLY HERE, SO LONG AS YOU DO ME AND MY STAFF THE SAME COURTESY.
A family man, this Chadron, and a bastion of the Republic.
OUR REMAND WING HAS BEEN SUBSUMED INTO THE NEW WOMEN'S FACILITY, SO YOU'LL BE IN GEN POP.
Stolid. Dull. High moral fiber. A whole wheat loaf of a man.
YOU'RE RICHARD SAVOY.
YES SIR.
YOU SEEM TO REQUIRE A GREAT MANY PRESCRIPTION MEDICINES AND SPECIAL EXEMPTIONS.
YES SIR. IT'S A MIRACLE I'M ALIVE.

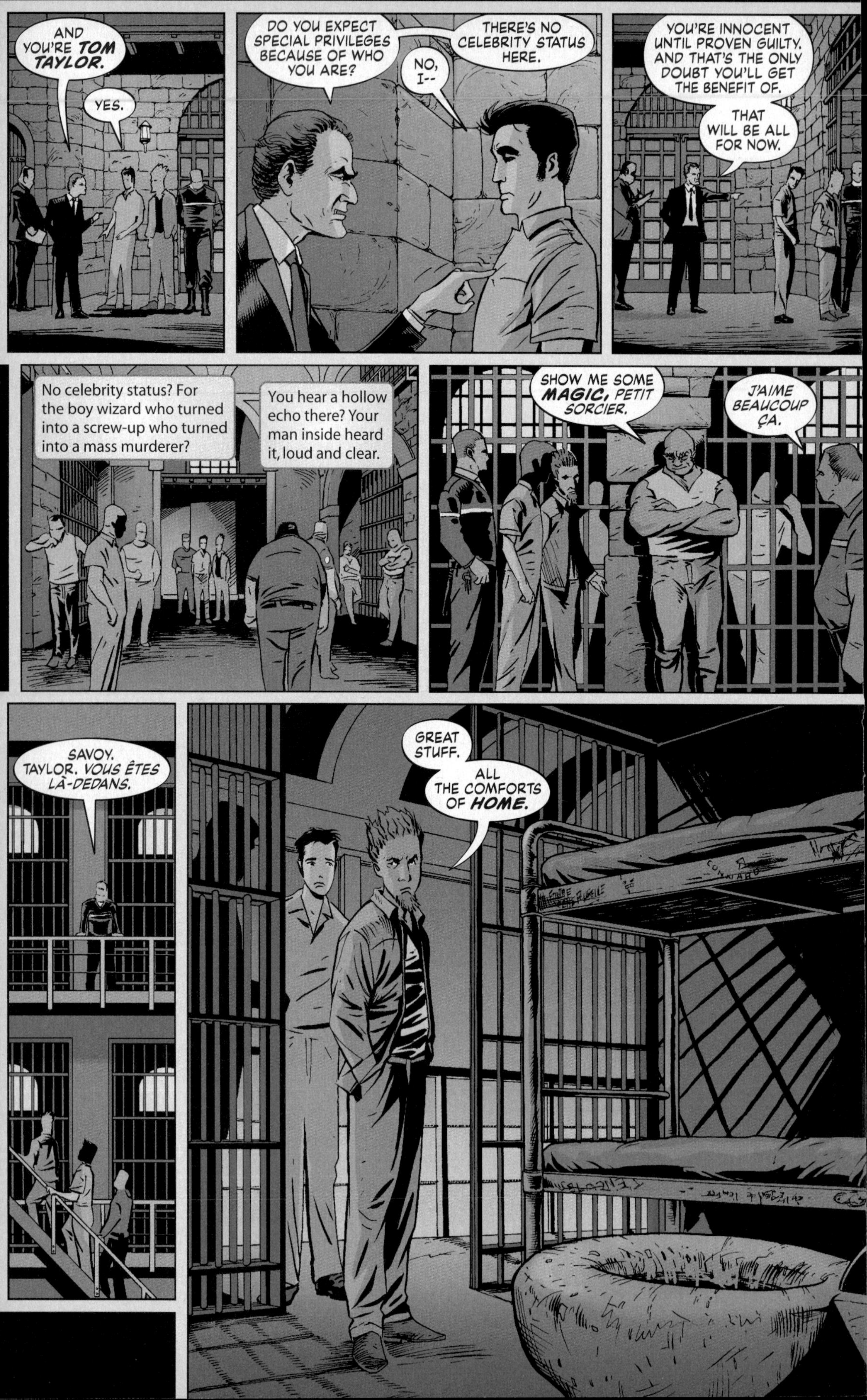
AND YOU'RE TOM TAYLOR.
YES.
DO YOU EXPECT SPECIAL PRIVILEGES BECAUSE OF WHO YOU ARE?
NO, I--
THERE'S NO CELEBRITY STATUS HERE.
YOU'RE INNOCENT UNTIL PROVEN GUILTY. AND THAT'S THE ONLY DOUBT YOU'LL GET THE BENEFIT OF.
THAT WILL BE ALL FOR NOW.
No celebrity status? For the boy wizard who turned into a screw-up who turned into a mass murderer?
You hear a hollow echo there? Your man inside heard it, loud and clear.
SHOW ME SOME MAGIC, PETIT SORCIER.
J'AIME BEAUCOUP ÇA.
SAVOY. TAYLOR. VOUS ÊTES LÀ-DEDANS.
GREAT STUFF.
ALL THE COMFORTS OF HOME.

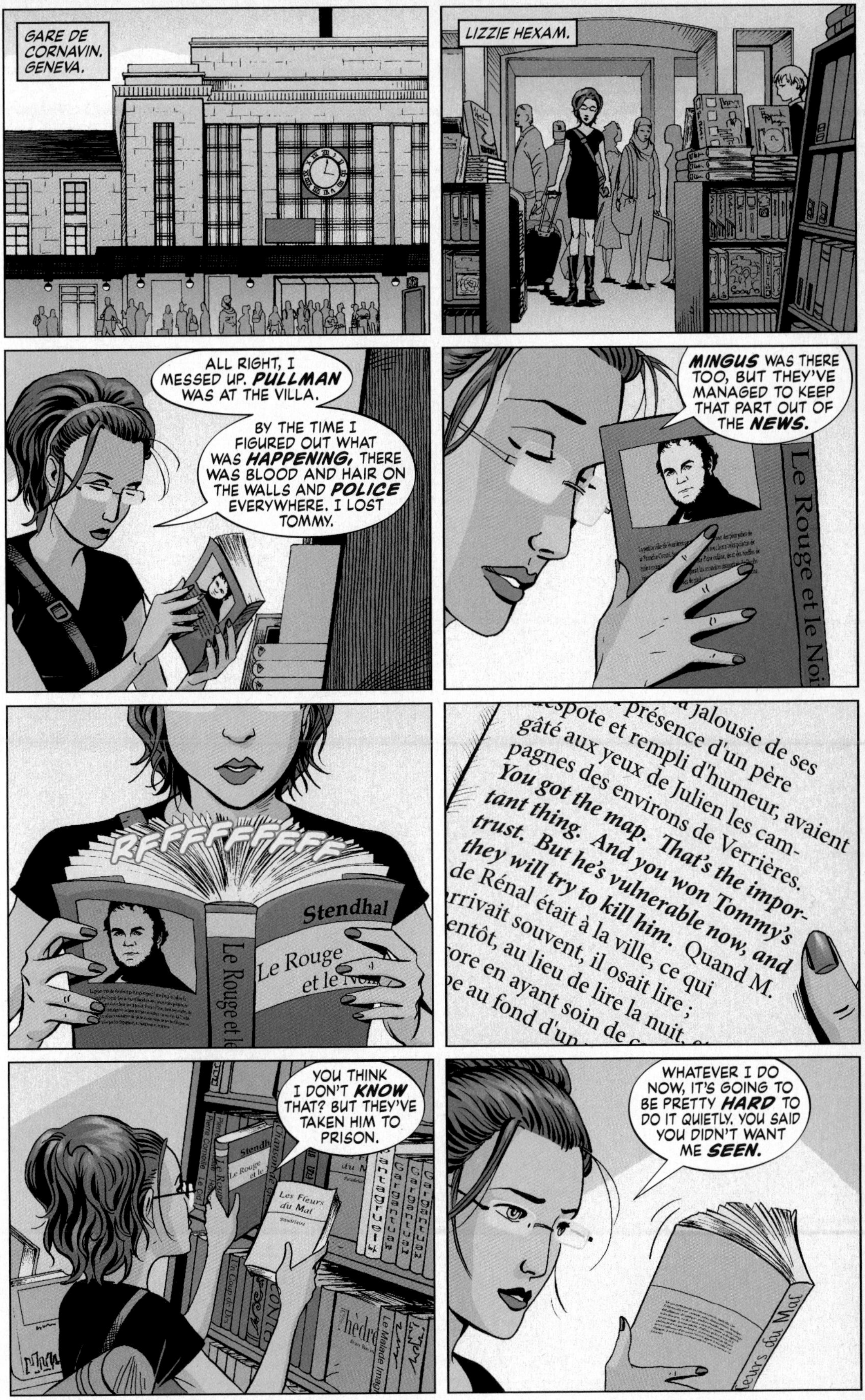
GARE DE CORNAVIN. GENEVA.
LIZZIE HEXAM.
ALL RIGHT, I MESSED UP. PULLMAN WAS AT THE VILLA.
BY THE TIME I FIGURED OUT WHAT WAS HAPPENING, THERE WAS BLOOD AND HAIR ON THE WALLS AND POLICE EVERYWHERE. I LOST TOMMY.
MINGUS WAS THERE TOO, BUT THEY'VE MANAGED TO KEEP THAT PART OUT OF THE NEWS.
Le Rouge et le Noi
RFFFFFFFFF
Stendhal
Le Rouge et le Noir
présence d'un père
jalousie de ses
spote et rempli d'humeur, avaient
gâté aux yeux de Julien les cam-
pagnes des environs de Verrières.
You got the map. That's the important thing. And you won Tommy's
trust. But he's vulnerable now, and
they will try to kill him. Quand M.
de Rénal était à la ville, ce qui
rrivait souvent, il osait lire ;
entôt, au lieu de lire la nuit,
ore en ayant soin de
be au fond d'un
YOU THINK I DON'T KNOW THAT? BUT THEY'VE TAKEN HIM TO PRISON.
Les Fleurs du Mal
Gargantua
WHATEVER I DO NOW, IT'S GOING TO BE PRETTY HARD TO DO IT QUIETLY. YOU SAID YOU DIDN'T WANT ME SEEN.

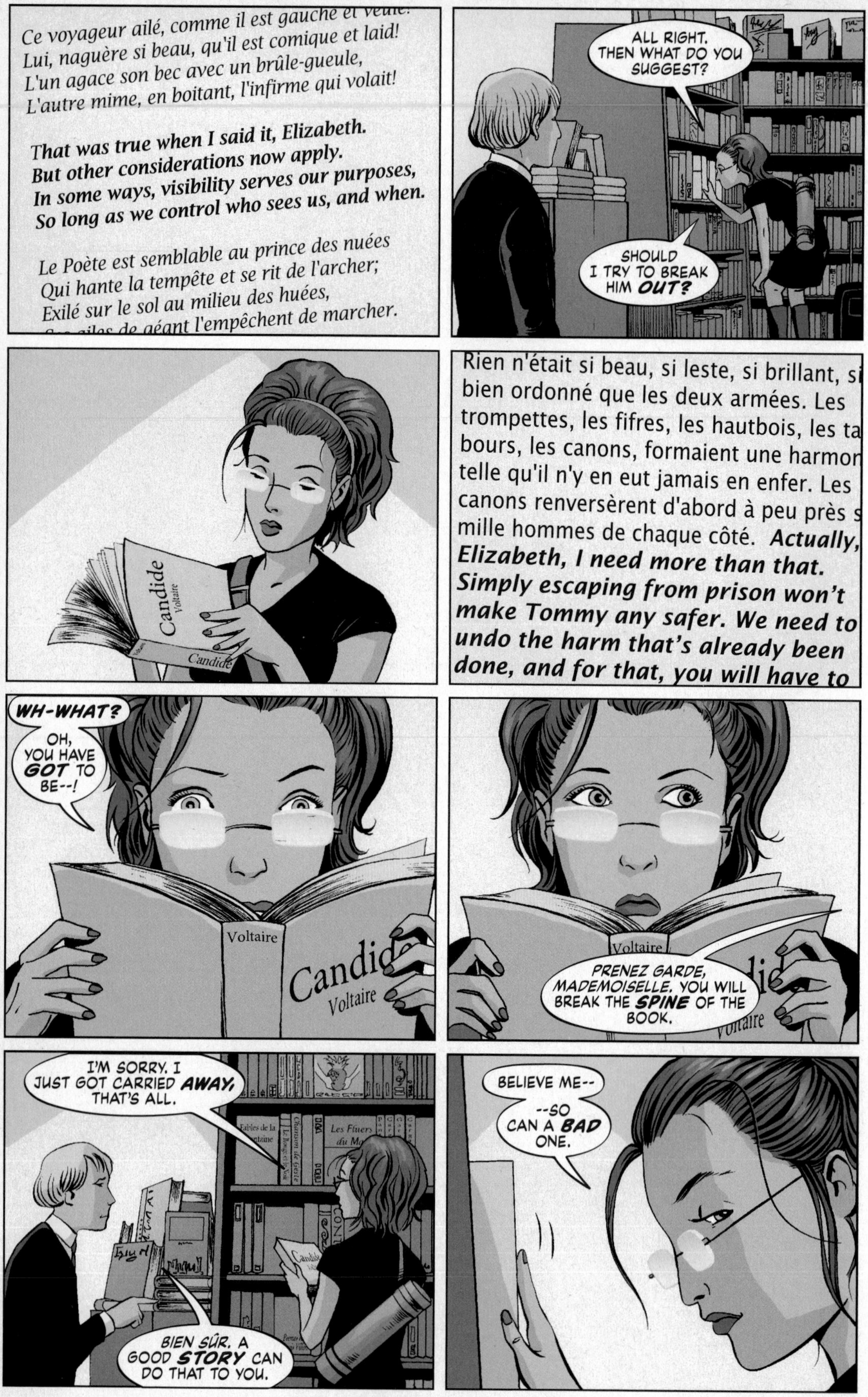

Ce voyageur ailé, comme il est gauche et veule!
Lui, naguère si beau, qu'il est comique et laid!
L'un agace son bec avec un brûle-gueule,
L'autre mime, en boitant, l'infirme qui volait!
That was true when I said it, Elizabeth. But other considerations now apply. In some ways, visibility serves our purposes, So long as we control who sees us, and when.
Le Poète est semblable au prince des nuées
Qui hante la tempête et se rit de l'archer;
Exilé sur le sol au milieu des huées,
géant l'empêchent de marcher.
ALL RIGHT. THEN WHAT DO YOU SUGGEST?
SHOULD I TRY TO BREAK HIM OUT?
Candide
Voltaire
Rien n'était si beau, si leste, si brillant, si bien ordonné que les deux armées. Les trompettes, les fifres, les hautbois, les ta bours, les canons, formaient une harmon telle qu'il n'y en eut jamais en enfer. Les canons renversèrent d'abord à peu près s mille hommes de chaque côté. Actually, Elizabeth, I need more than that. Simply escaping from prison won't make Tommy any safer. We need to undo the harm that's already been done, and for that, you will have to
WH-WHAT?
OH, YOU HAVE GOT TO BE--!
Voltaire
Candide
Voltaire
PRENEZ GARDE, MADEMOISELLE. YOU WILL BREAK THE SPINE OF THE BOOK.
I'M SORRY. I JUST GOT CARRIED AWAY. THAT'S ALL.
BIEN SÛR. A GOOD STORY CAN DO THAT TO YOU.
BELIEVE ME--
--SO CAN A BAD ONE.

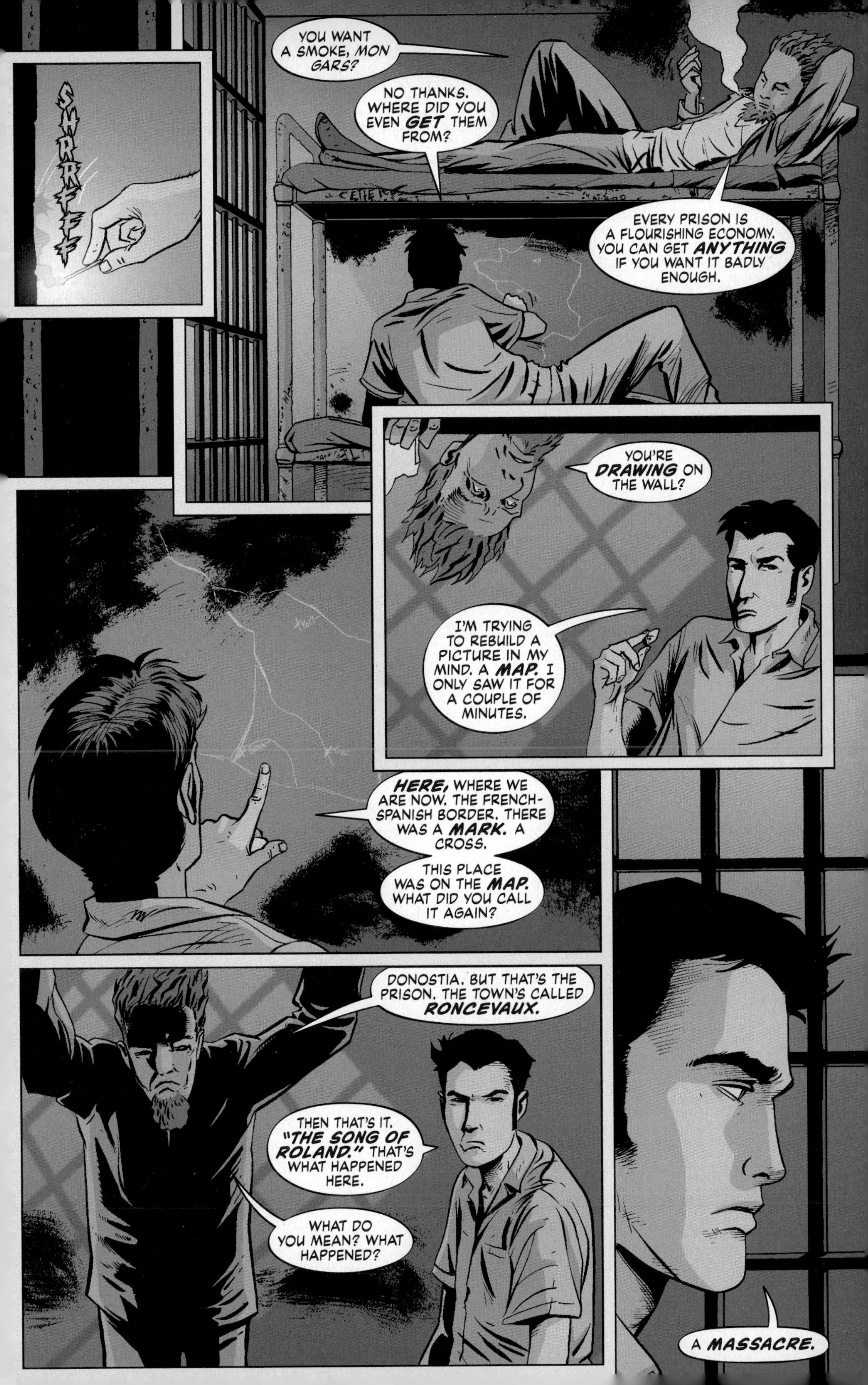
SHRRFFF
YOU WANT A SMOKE, MON GARS?
NO THANKS. WHERE DID YOU EVEN GET THEM FROM?
EVERY PRISON IS A FLOURISHING ECONOMY. YOU CAN GET ANYTHING IF YOU WANT IT BADLY ENOUGH.
YOU'RE DRAWING ON THE WALL?
I'M TRYING TO REBUILD A PICTURE IN MY MIND. A MAP. I ONLY SAW IT FOR A COUPLE OF MINUTES.
HERE, WHERE WE ARE NOW. THE FRENCH-SPANISH BORDER. THERE WAS A MARK. A CROSS.
THIS PLACE WAS ON THE MAP. WHAT DID YOU CALL IT AGAIN?
DONOSTIA. BUT THAT'S THE PRISON. THE TOWN'S CALLED RONCEVAUX.
THEN THAT'S IT. "THE SONG OF ROLAND." THAT'S WHAT HAPPENED HERE.
WHAT DO YOU MEAN? WHAT HAPPENED?
A MASSACRE.

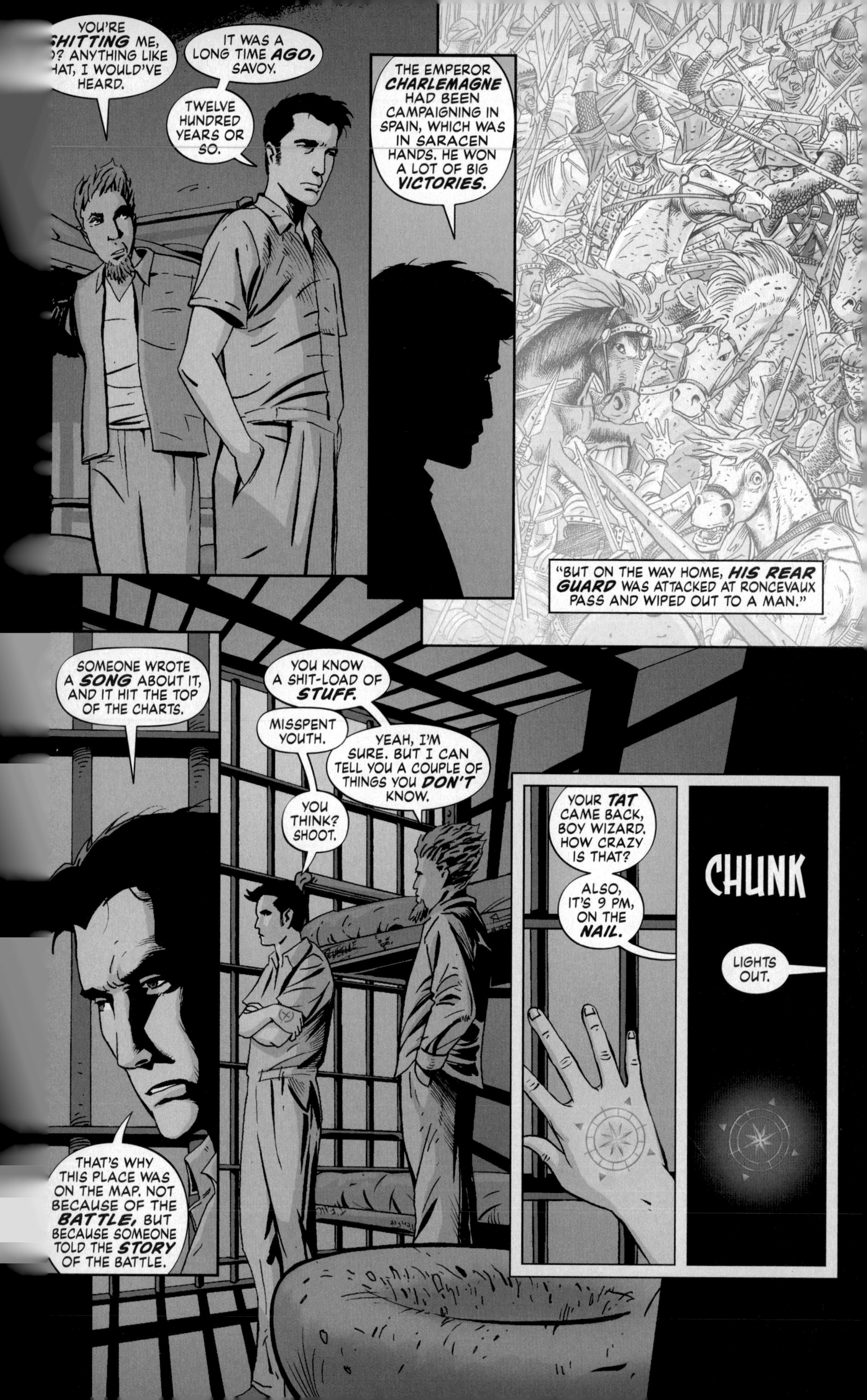
YOU'RE SHITTING ME, ?? ANYTHING LIKE THAT, I WOULD'VE HEARD.
IT WAS A LONG TIME AGO, SAVOY.
TWELVE HUNDRED YEARS OR SO.
THE EMPEROR CHARLEMAGNE HAD BEEN CAMPAIGNING IN SPAIN, WHICH WAS IN SARACEN HANDS. HE WON A LOT OF BIG VICTORIES.
"BUT ON THE WAY HOME, HIS REAR GUARD WAS ATTACKED AT RONCEVAUX PASS AND WIPED OUT TO A MAN."
SOMEONE WROTE A SONG ABOUT IT, AND IT HIT THE TOP OF THE CHARTS.
THAT'S WHY THIS PLACE WAS ON THE MAP. NOT BECAUSE OF THE BATTLE, BUT BECAUSE SOMEONE TOLD THE STORY OF THE BATTLE.
YOU KNOW A SHIT-LOAD OF STUFF.
MISSPENT YOUTH.
YEAH, I'M SURE. BUT I CAN TELL YOU A COUPLE OF THINGS YOU DON'T KNOW.
YOU THINK? SHOOT.
YOUR TAT CAME BACK, BOY WIZARD. HOW CRAZY IS THAT?
ALSO, IT'S 9 PM, ON THE NAIL.
CHUNK
LIGHTS OUT.

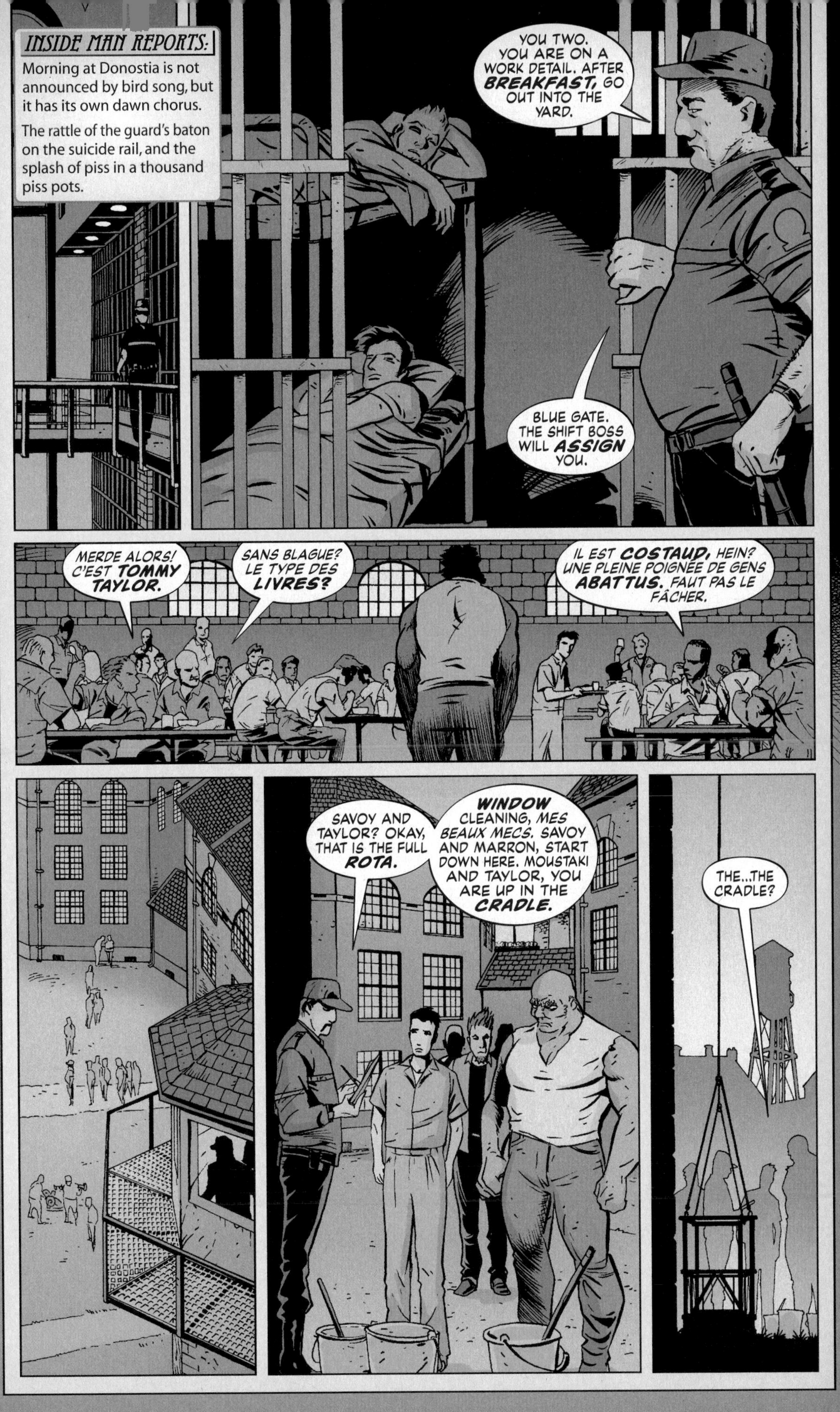
INSIDE MAN REPORTS:
Morning at Donostia is not announced by bird song, but it has its own dawn chorus.
The rattle of the guard's baton on the suicide rail, and the splash of piss in a thousand piss pots.
YOU TWO. YOU ARE ON A WORK DETAIL. AFTER BREAKFAST, GO OUT INTO THE YARD.
BLUE GATE. THE SHIFT BOSS WILL ASSIGN YOU.
MERDE ALORS! C'EST TOMMY TAYLOR.
SANS BLAGUE? LE TYPE DES LIVRES?
IL EST COSTAUD, HEIN? UNE PLEINE POIGNÉE DE GENS ABATTUS. FAUT PAS LE FÂCHER.
SAVOY AND TAYLOR? OKAY, THAT IS THE FULL ROTA.
WINDOW CLEANING, MES BEAUX MECS. SAVOY AND MARRON, START DOWN HERE. MOUSTAKI AND TAYLOR, YOU ARE UP IN THE CRADLE.
THE...THE CRADLE?

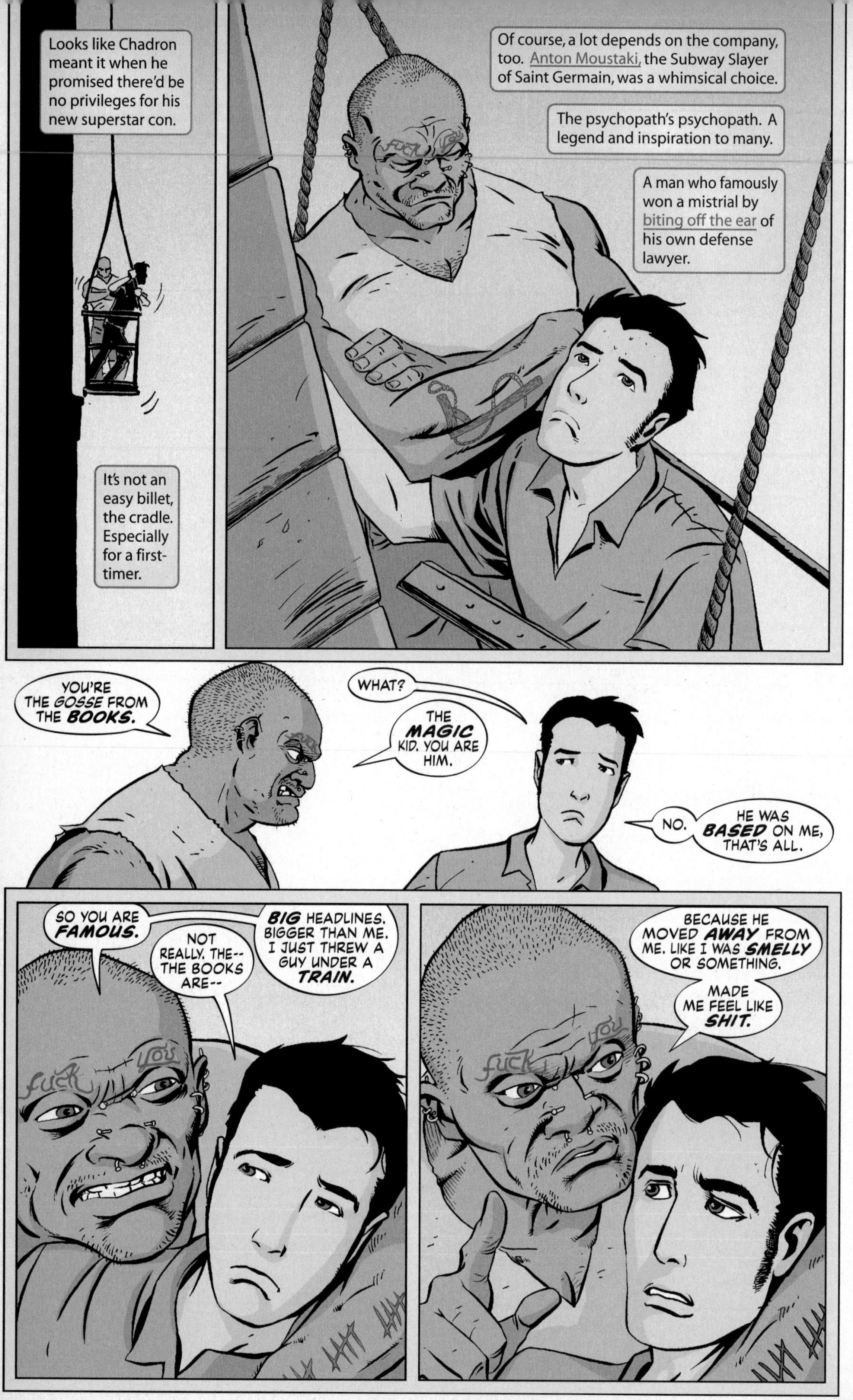
Looks like Chadron meant it when he promised there'd be no privileges for his new superstar con.
It's not an easy billet, the cradle. Especially for a first-timer.
Of course, a lot depends on the company, too. Anton Moustaki, the Subway Slayer of Saint Germain, was a whimsical choice.
The psychopath's psychopath. A legend and inspiration to many.
A man who famously won a mistrial by biting off the ear of his own defense lawyer.
YOU'RE THE GOSSE FROM THE BOOKS.
WHAT?
THE MAGIC KID. YOU ARE HIM.
NO.
HE WAS BASED ON ME, THAT'S ALL.
SO YOU ARE FAMOUS.
NOT REALLY. THE-- THE BOOKS ARE--
BIG HEADLINES. BIGGER THAN ME. I JUST THREW A GUY UNDER A TRAIN.
BECAUSE HE MOVED AWAY FROM ME. LIKE I WAS SMELLY OR SOMETHING.
MADE ME FEEL LIKE SHIT.

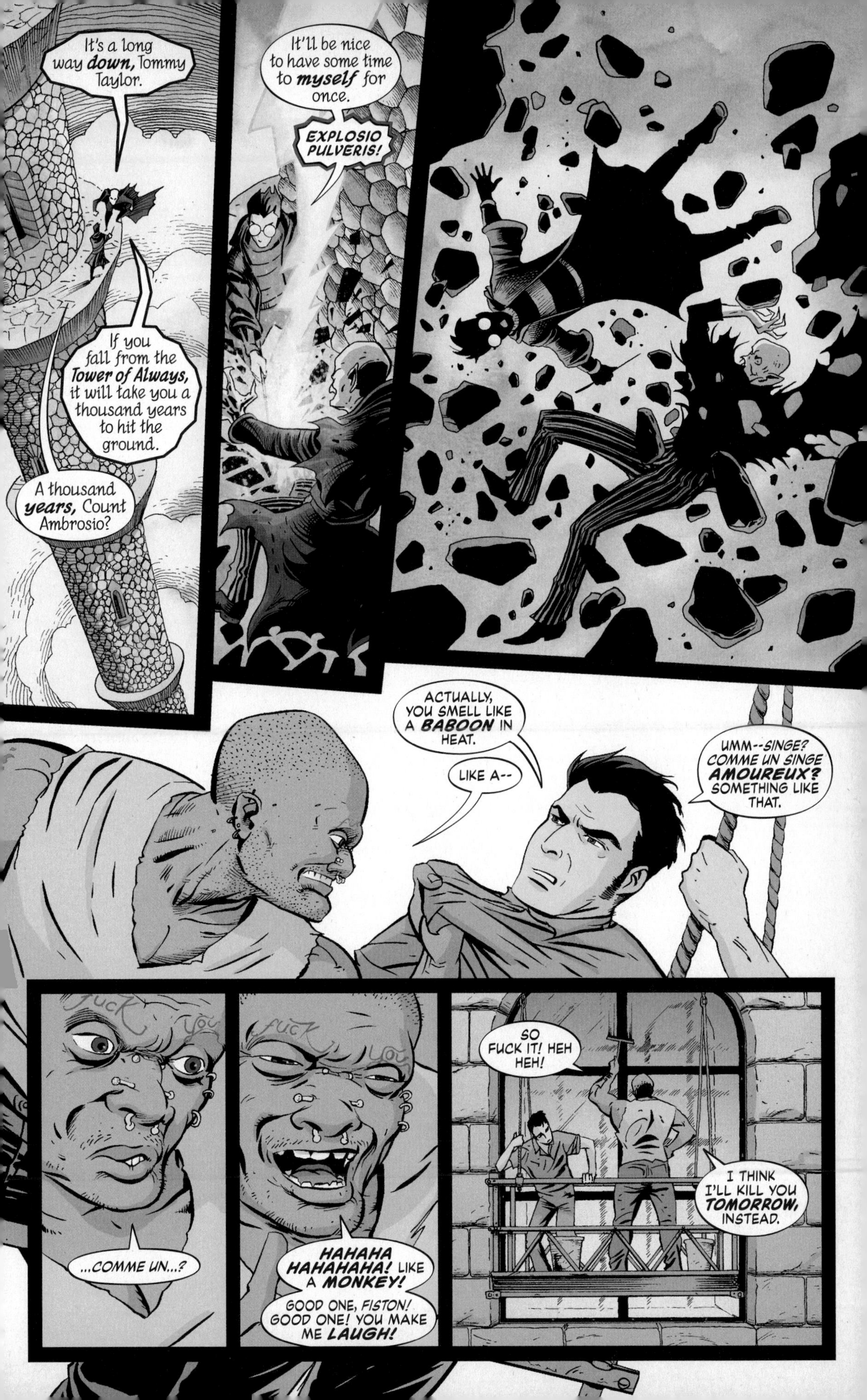

It's a long way down, Tommy Taylor.
If you fall from the Tower of Always, it will take you a thousand years to hit the ground.
A thousand years, Count Ambrosio?
It'll be nice to have some time to myself for once.
EXPLOSIO PULVERIS!
ACTUALLY, YOU SMELL LIKE A BABOON IN HEAT.
LIKE A--
UMM--SINGE? COMME UN SINGE AMOUREUX? SOMETHING LIKE THAT.
...COMME UN...?
HAHAHA HAHAHAHA! LIKE A MONKEY!
GOOD ONE, FISTON! GOOD ONE! YOU MAKE ME LAUGH!
SO FUCK IT! HEH HEH!
I THINK I'LL KILL YOU TOMORROW, INSTEAD.

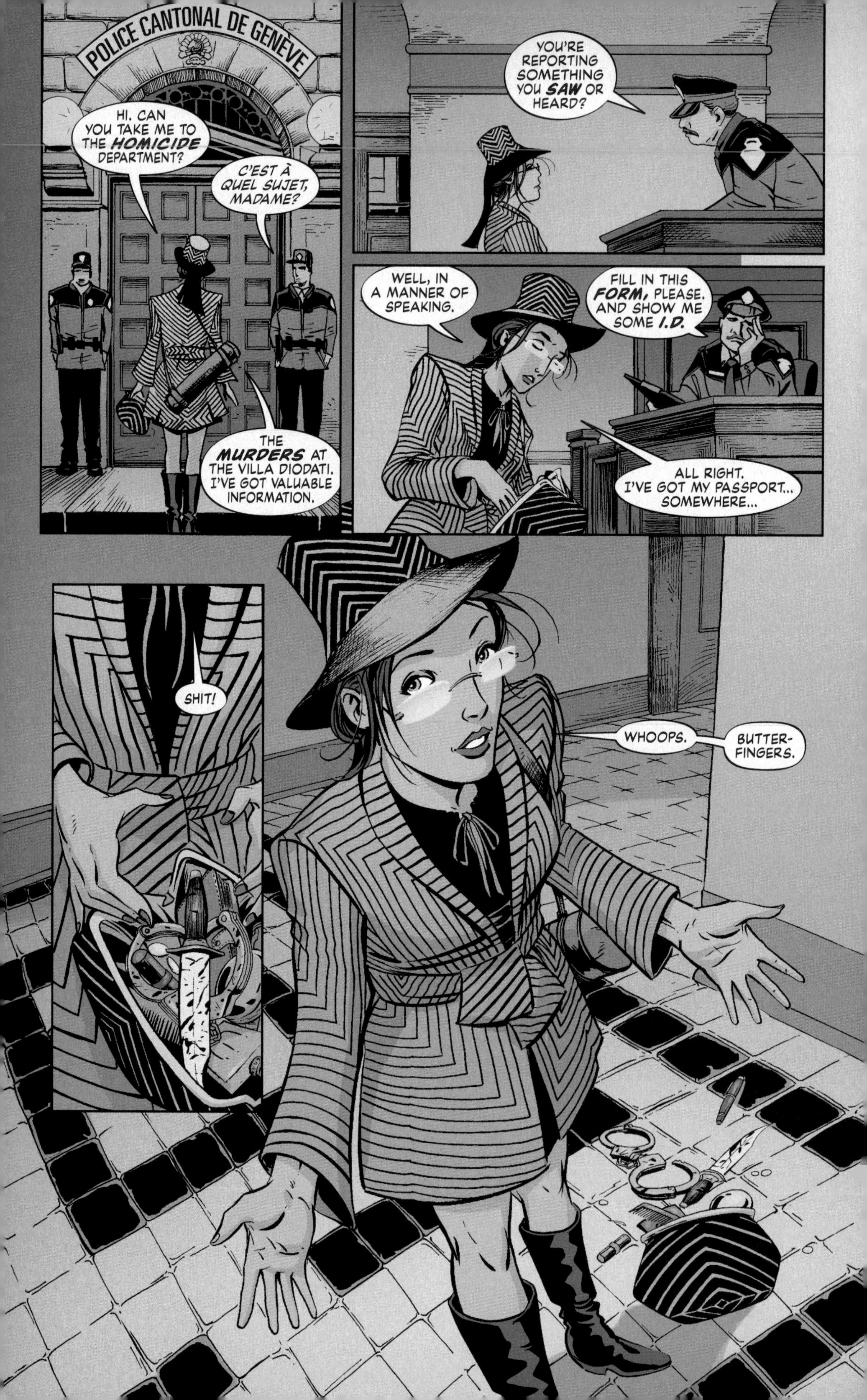
POLICE CANTONAL DE GENÈVE
HI. CAN YOU TAKE ME TO THE HOMICIDE DEPARTMENT?
C'EST À QUEL SUJET, MADAME?
THE MURDERS AT THE VILLA DIODATI. I'VE GOT VALUABLE INFORMATION.
YOU'RE REPORTING SOMETHING YOU SAW OR HEARD?
WELL, IN A MANNER OF SPEAKING.
FILL IN THIS FORM, PLEASE. AND SHOW ME SOME I.D.
ALL RIGHT. I'VE GOT MY PASSPORT... SOMEWHERE...
SHIT!
WHOOPS.
BUTTER-FINGERS.

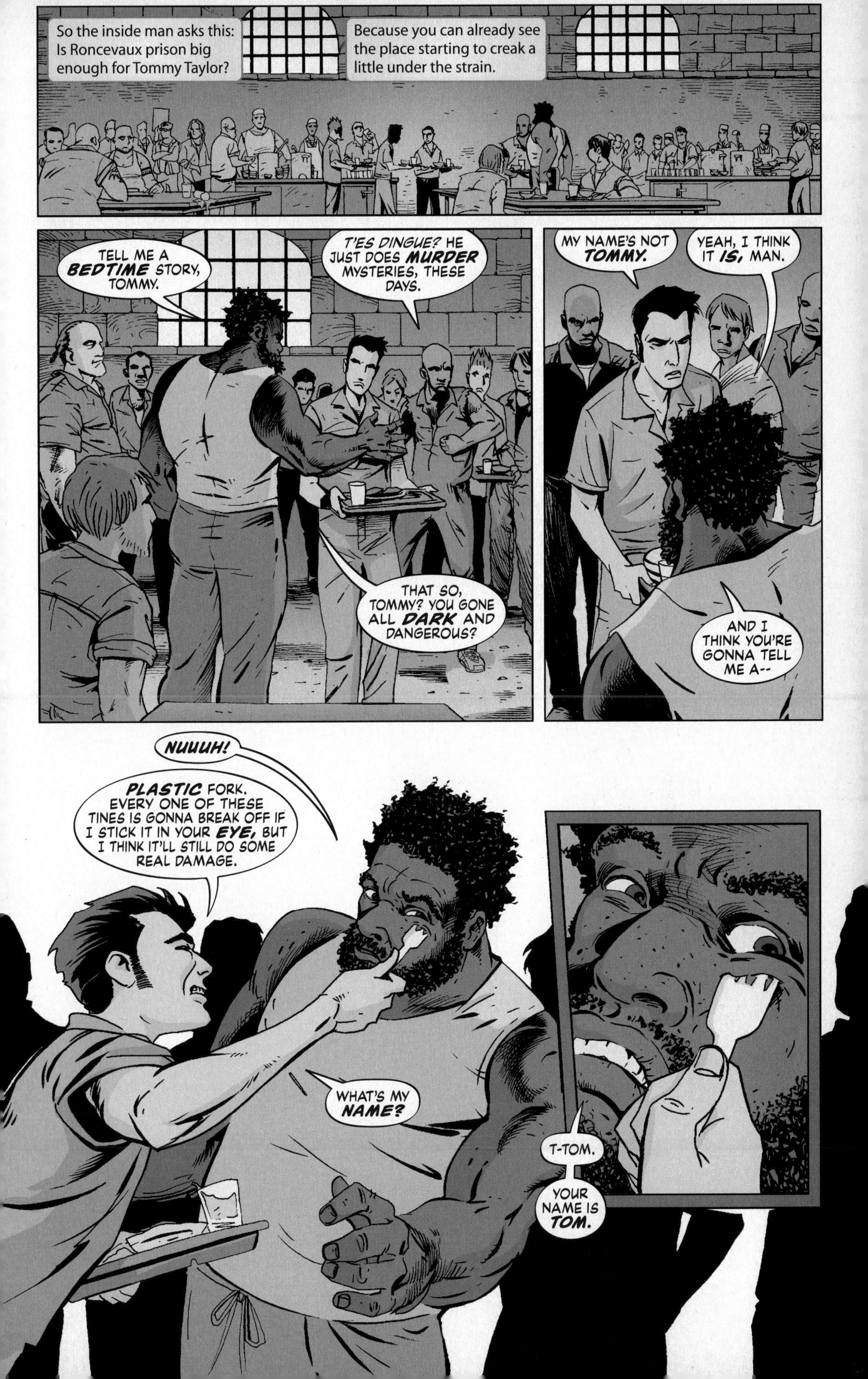
So the inside man asks this: Is Roncevaux prison big enough for Tommy Taylor?
Because you can already see the place starting to creak a little under the strain.
TELL ME A BEDTIME STORY, TOMMY.
T'ES DINGUE? HE JUST DOES MURDER MYSTERIES, THESE DAYS.
THAT SO, TOMMY? YOU GONE ALL DARK AND DANGEROUS?
MY NAME'S NOT TOMMY.
YEAH, I THINK IT IS, MAN.
AND I THINK YOU'RE GONNA TELL ME A--
NUUUH!
PLASTIC FORK. EVERY ONE OF THESE TINES IS GONNA BREAK OFF IF I STICK IT IN YOUR EYE, BUT I THINK IT'LL STILL DO SOME REAL DAMAGE.
WHAT'S MY NAME?
T-TOM.
YOUR NAME IS TOM.

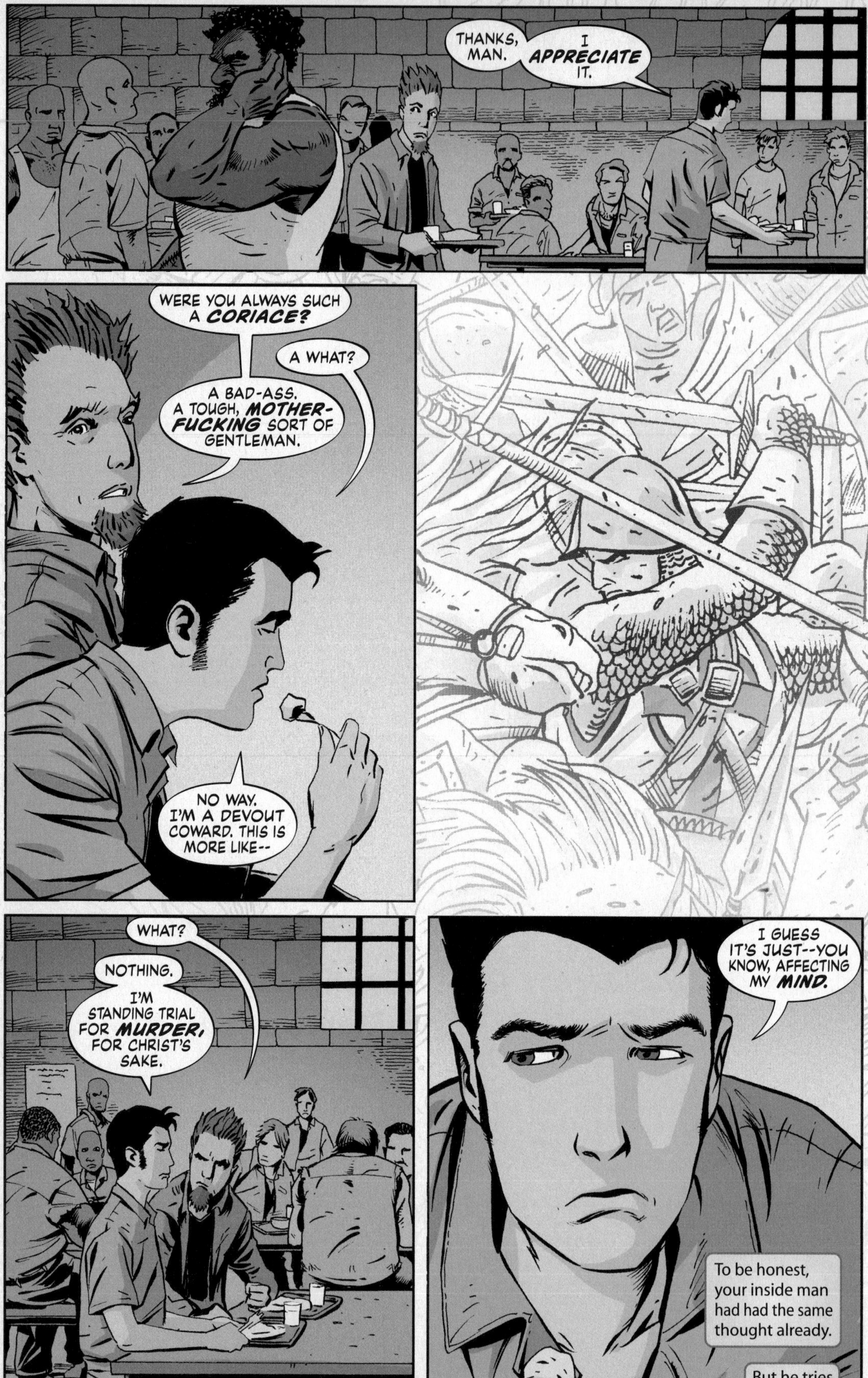
THANKS, MAN.
I APPRECIATE IT.
WERE YOU ALWAYS SUCH A CORIACE?
A WHAT?
A BAD-ASS. A TOUGH, MOTHER-FUCKING SORT OF GENTLEMAN.
NO WAY. I'M A DEVOUT COWARD. THIS IS MORE LIKE--
WHAT?
NOTHING.
I'M STANDING TRIAL FOR MURDER, FOR CHRIST'S SAKE.
I GUESS IT'S JUST--YOU KNOW, AFFECTING MY MIND.
To be honest, your inside man had had the same thought already.
But he tries never to prejudge.

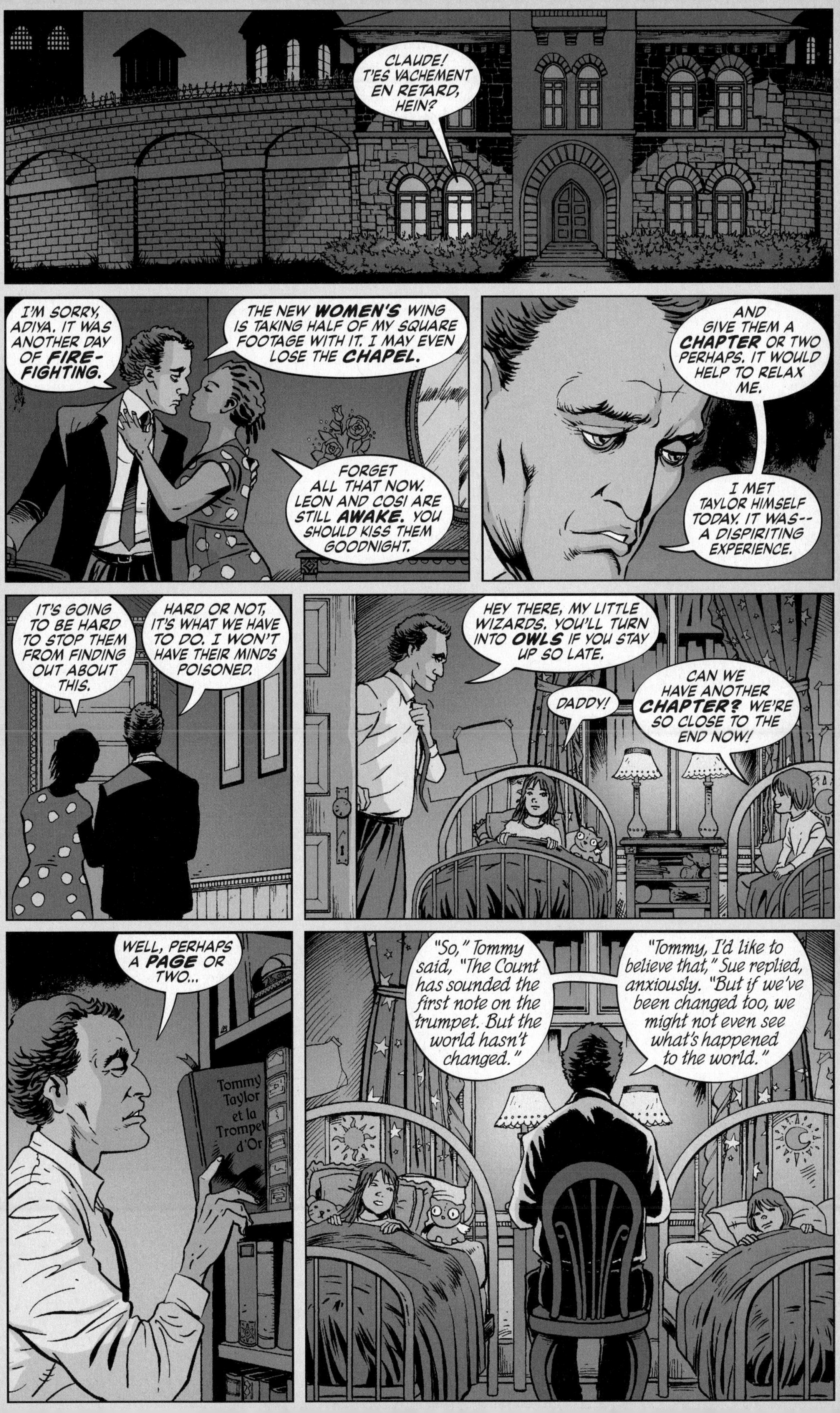
CLAUDE! T'ES VACHEMENT EN RETARD, HEIN?
I'M SORRY, ADIYA. IT WAS ANOTHER DAY OF **FIRE-FIGHTING.**
THE NEW **WOMEN'S** WING IS TAKING HALF OF MY SQUARE FOOTAGE WITH IT. I MAY EVEN LOSE THE **CHAPEL.**
FORGET ALL THAT NOW. LEON AND COSI ARE STILL **AWAKE.** YOU SHOULD KISS THEM GOODNIGHT.
AND GIVE THEM A **CHAPTER** OR TWO PERHAPS. IT WOULD HELP TO RELAX ME.
I MET TAYLOR HIMSELF TODAY. IT WAS-- A DISPIRITING EXPERIENCE.
IT'S GOING TO BE HARD TO STOP THEM FROM FINDING OUT ABOUT THIS.
HARD OR NOT, IT'S WHAT WE HAVE TO DO. I WON'T HAVE THEIR MINDS POISONED.
HEY THERE, MY LITTLE WIZARDS. YOU'LL TURN INTO **OWLS** IF YOU STAY UP SO LATE.
DADDY!
CAN WE HAVE ANOTHER **CHAPTER?** WE'RE SO CLOSE TO THE END NOW!
WELL, PERHAPS A **PAGE** OR TWO...
Tommy Taylor et la Trompet d'Or
"So," Tommy said, "The Count has sounded the first note on the trumpet. But the world hasn't changed."
"Tommy, I'd like to believe that," Sue replied, anxiously. "But if we've been changed too, we might not even see what's happened to the world."

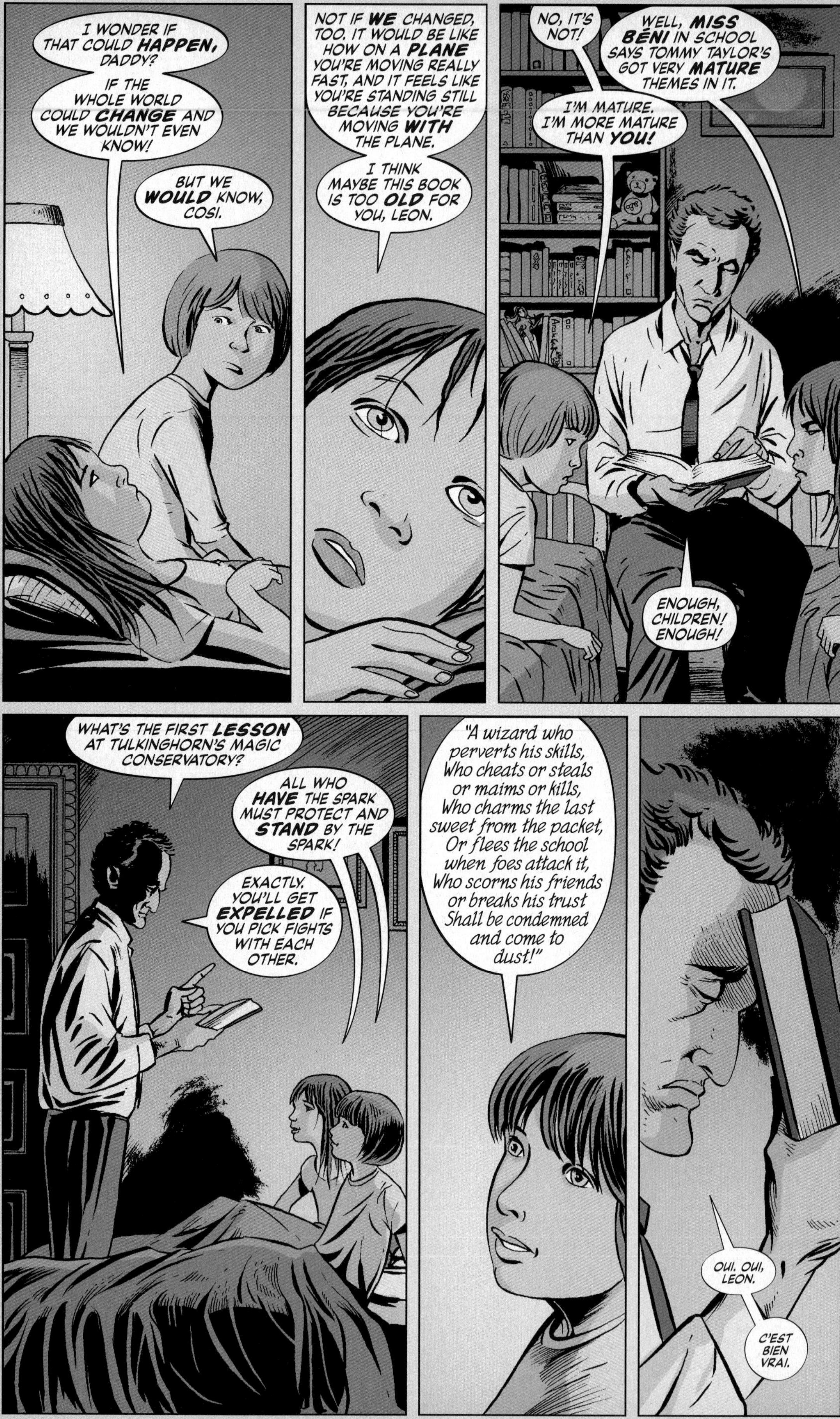
I WONDER IF THAT COULD HAPPEN, DADDY?
IF THE WHOLE WORLD COULD CHANGE AND WE WOULDN'T EVEN KNOW!
BUT WE WOULD KNOW, COSI.
NOT IF WE CHANGED, TOO. IT WOULD BE LIKE HOW ON A PLANE YOU'RE MOVING REALLY FAST, AND IT FEELS LIKE YOU'RE STANDING STILL BECAUSE YOU'RE MOVING WITH THE PLANE.
I THINK MAYBE THIS BOOK IS TOO OLD FOR YOU, LEON.
NO, IT'S NOT!
WELL, MISS BÉNI IN SCHOOL SAYS TOMMY TAYLOR'S GOT VERY MATURE THEMES IN IT.
I'M MATURE. I'M MORE MATURE THAN YOU!
ENOUGH, CHILDREN! ENOUGH!
WHAT'S THE FIRST LESSON AT TULKINGHORN'S MAGIC CONSERVATORY?
ALL WHO HAVE THE SPARK MUST PROTECT AND STAND BY THE SPARK!
EXACTLY. YOU'LL GET EXPELLED IF YOU PICK FIGHTS WITH EACH OTHER.
"A wizard who perverts his skills, Who cheats or steals or maims or kills, Who charms the last sweet from the packet, Or flees the school when foes attack it, Who scorns his friends or breaks his trust Shall be condemned and come to dust!"
OUI. OUI, LEON.
C'EST BIEN VRAI.

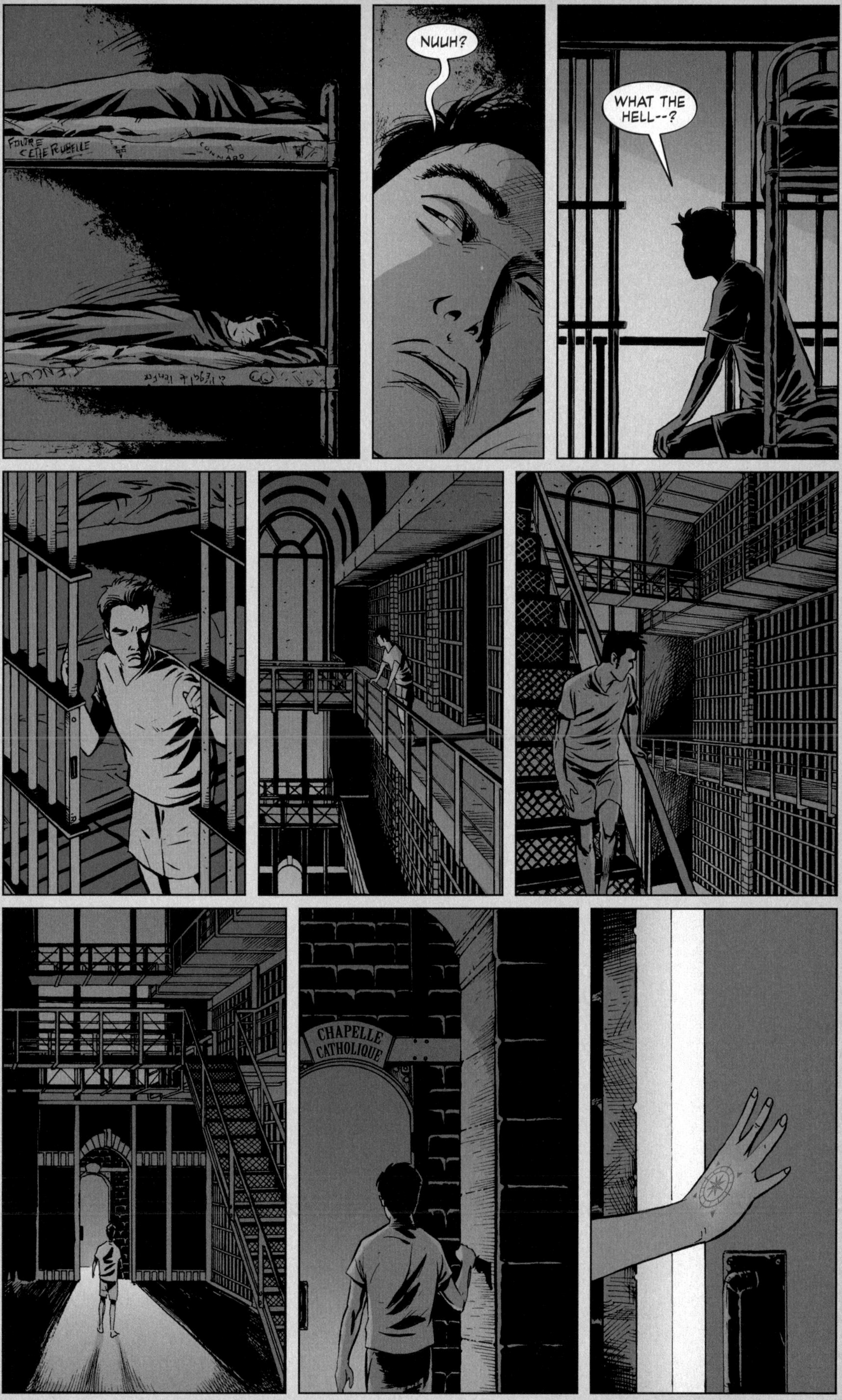
FOUTRE CETTE POUBELLE
CONNARD
NUUH?
WHAT THE HELL--?
CHAPELLE CATHOLIQUE

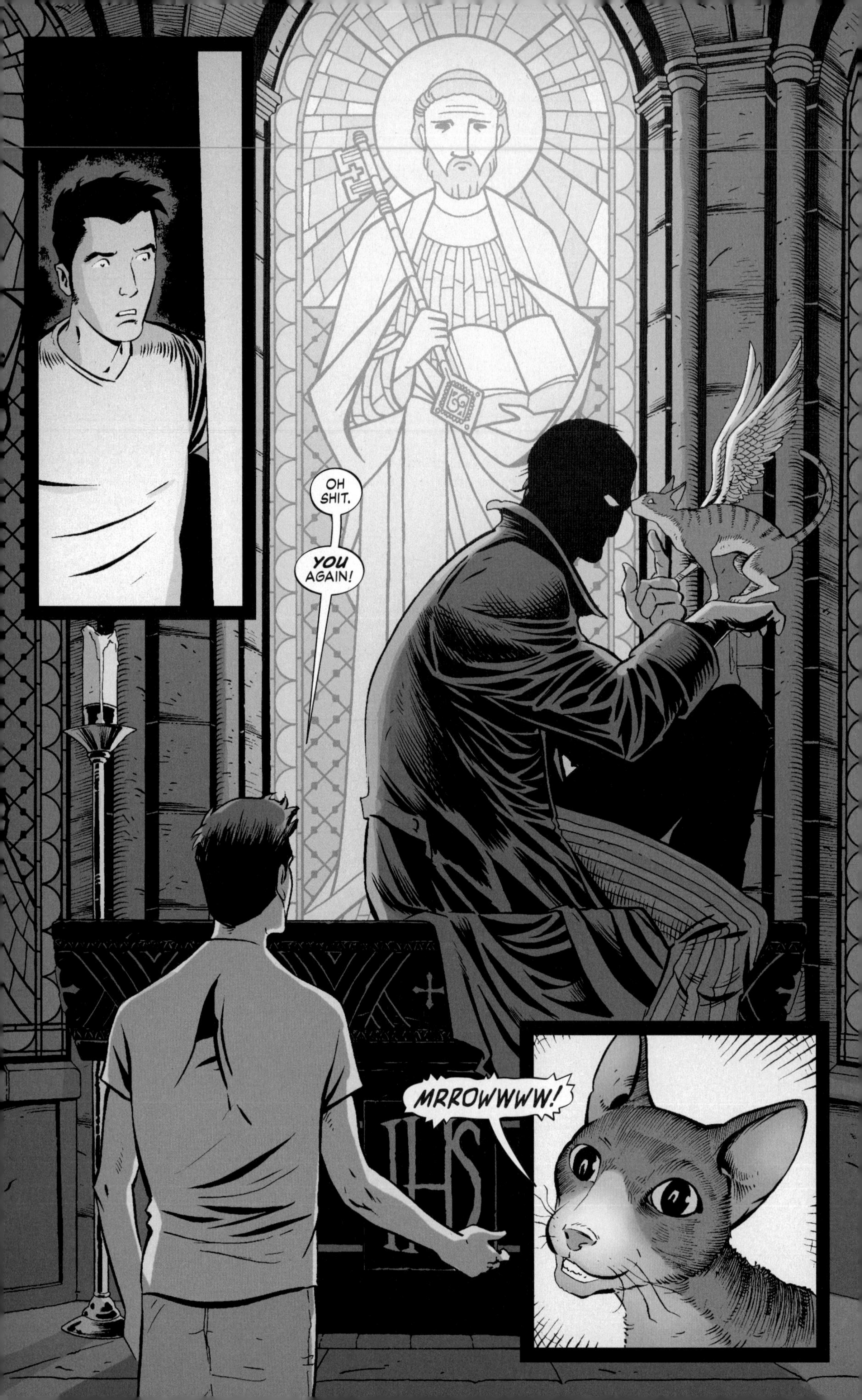
OH SHIT.
YOU AGAIN!
MRROWWWW!

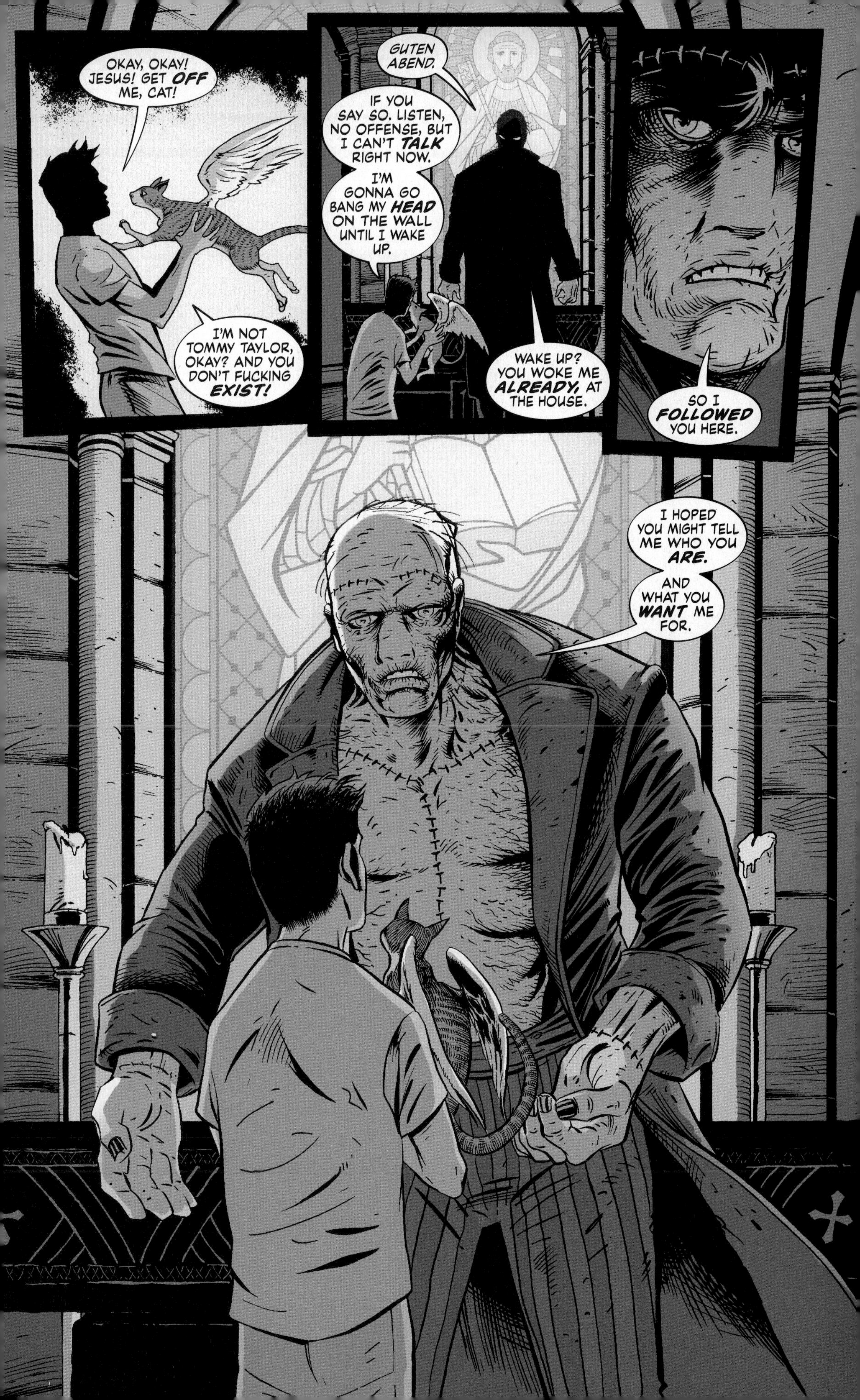
OKAY, OKAY! JESUS! GET OFF ME, CAT!
I'M NOT TOMMY TAYLOR, OKAY? AND YOU DON'T FUCKING EXIST!
GUTEN ABEND.
IF YOU SAY SO. LISTEN, NO OFFENSE, BUT I CAN'T TALK RIGHT NOW.
I'M GONNA GO BANG MY HEAD ON THE WALL UNTIL I WAKE UP.
WAKE UP? YOU WOKE ME ALREADY, AT THE HOUSE.
SO I FOLLOWED YOU HERE.
I HOPED YOU MIGHT TELL ME WHO YOU ARE.
AND WHAT YOU WANT ME FOR.

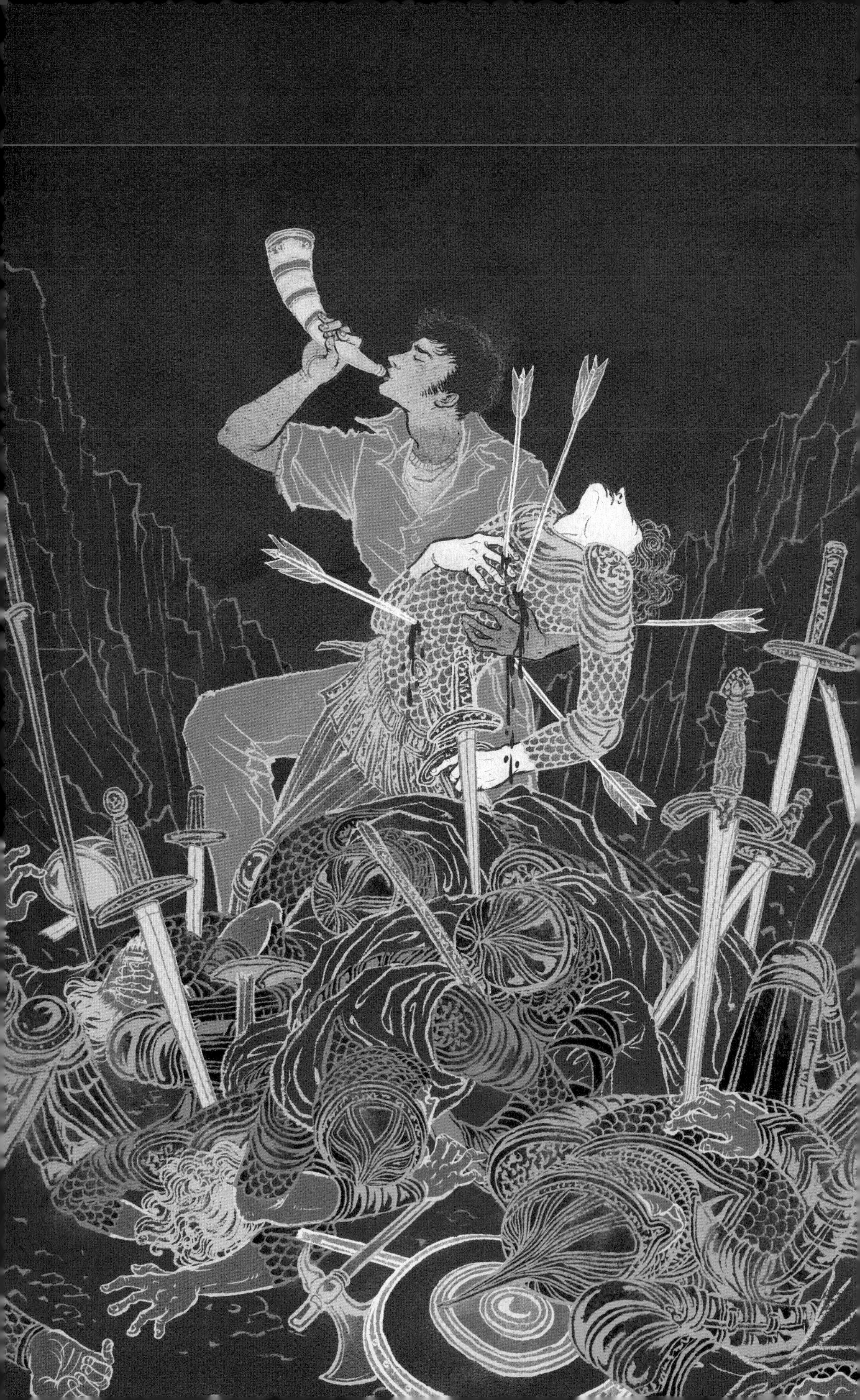

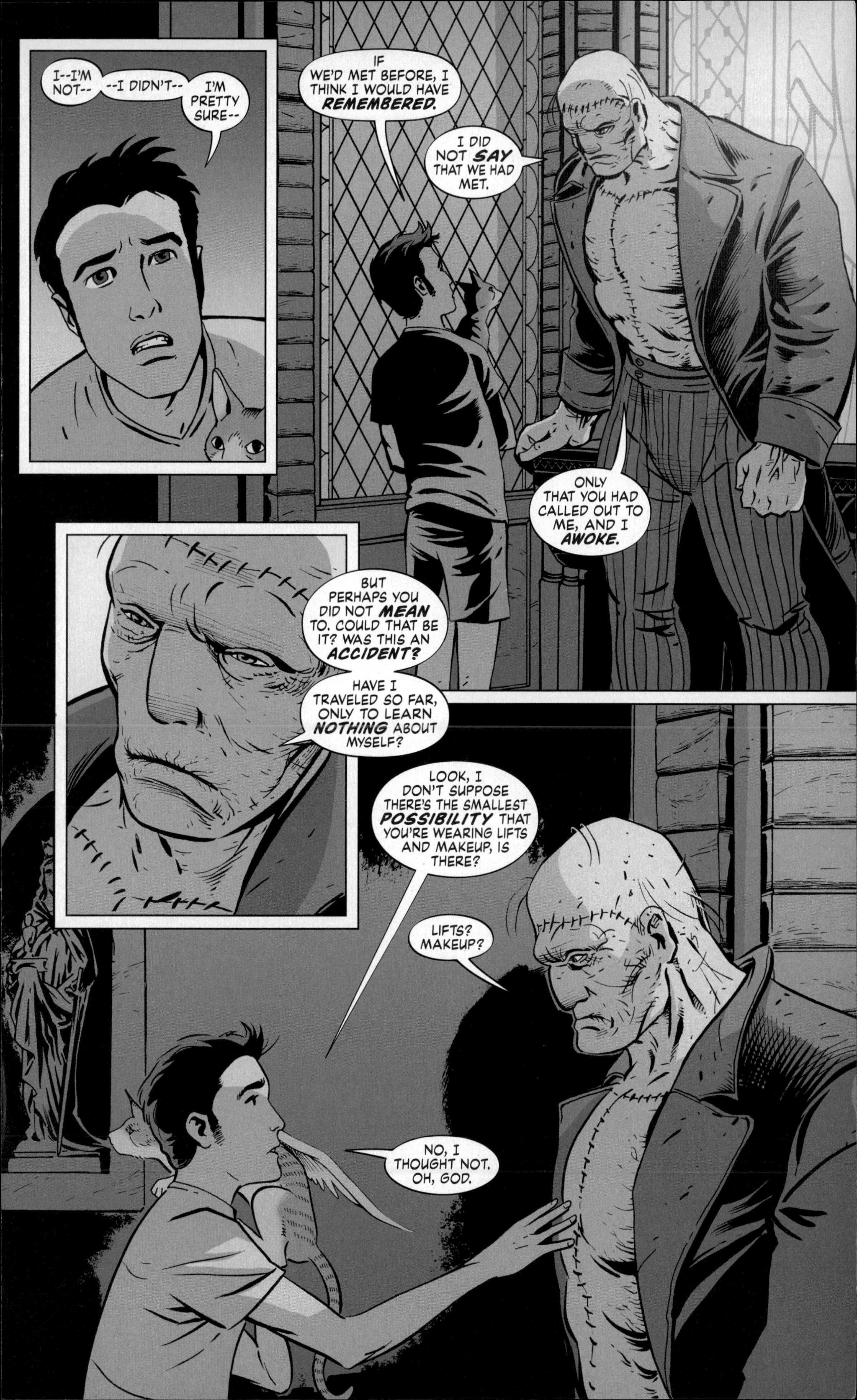
I--I'M NOT--
--I DIDN'T--
I'M PRETTY SURE--
IF WE'D MET BEFORE, I THINK I WOULD HAVE REMEMBERED.
I DID NOT SAY THAT WE HAD MET.
ONLY THAT YOU HAD CALLED OUT TO ME, AND I AWOKE.
BUT PERHAPS YOU DID NOT MEAN TO. COULD THAT BE IT? WAS THIS AN ACCIDENT?
HAVE I TRAVELED SO FAR, ONLY TO LEARN NOTHING ABOUT MYSELF?
LOOK, I DON'T SUPPOSE THERE'S THE SMALLEST POSSIBILITY THAT YOU'RE WEARING LIFTS AND MAKEUP, IS THERE?
LIFTS? MAKEUP?
NO, I THOUGHT NOT. OH, GOD.

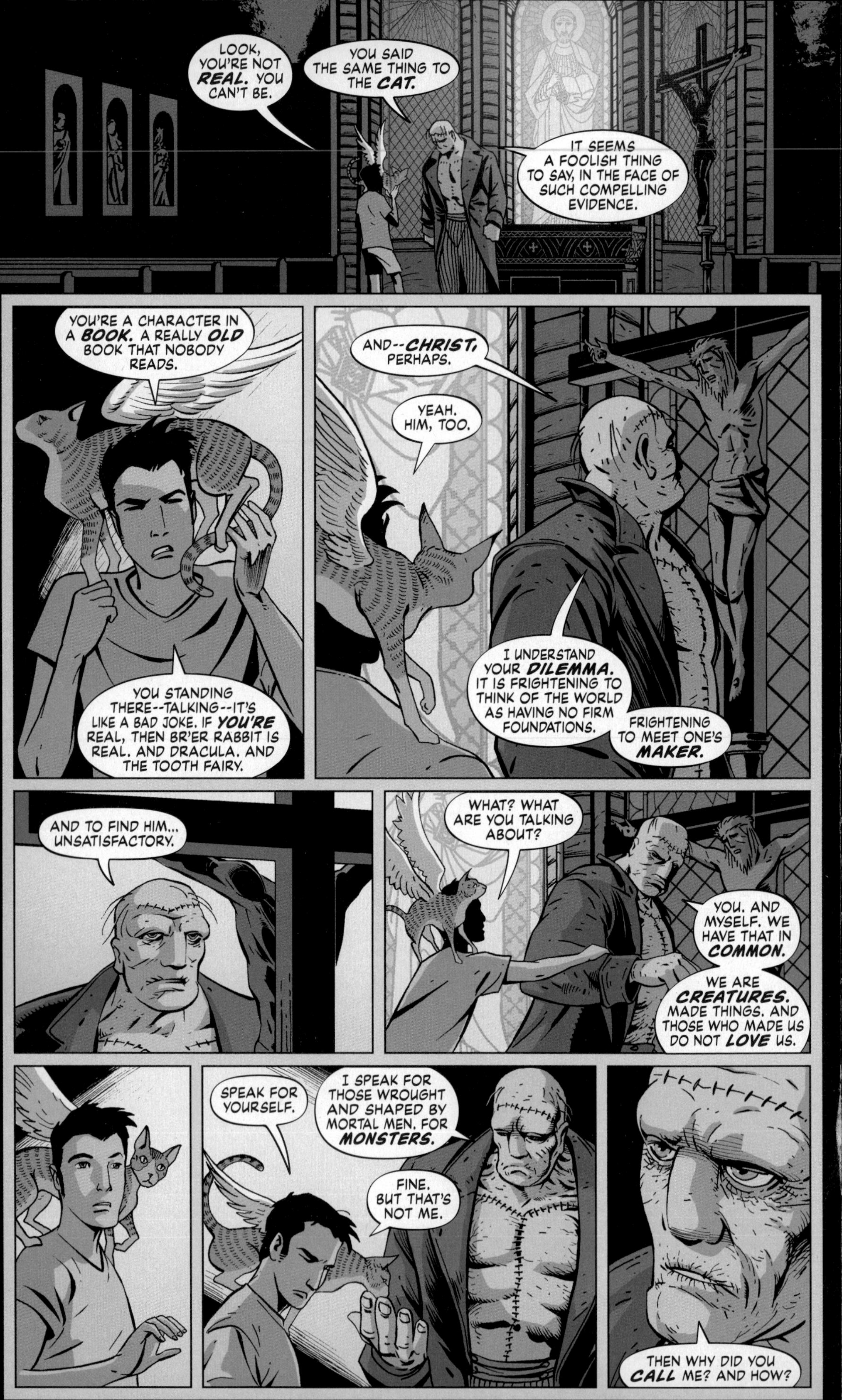

LOOK, YOU'RE NOT REAL. YOU CAN'T BE.
YOU SAID THE SAME THING TO THE CAT.
IT SEEMS A FOOLISH THING TO SAY, IN THE FACE OF SUCH COMPELLING EVIDENCE.
YOU'RE A CHARACTER IN A BOOK. A REALLY OLD BOOK THAT NOBODY READS.
YOU STANDING THERE--TALKING--IT'S LIKE A BAD JOKE. IF YOU'RE REAL, THEN BR'ER RABBIT IS REAL. AND DRACULA. AND THE TOOTH FAIRY.
AND--CHRIST, PERHAPS.
YEAH. HIM, TOO.
I UNDERSTAND YOUR DILEMMA. IT IS FRIGHTENING TO THINK OF THE WORLD AS HAVING NO FIRM FOUNDATIONS.
FRIGHTENING TO MEET ONE'S MAKER.
AND TO FIND HIM... UNSATISFACTORY.
WHAT? WHAT ARE YOU TALKING ABOUT?
YOU. AND MYSELF. WE HAVE THAT IN COMMON.
WE ARE CREATURES. MADE THINGS. AND THOSE WHO MADE US DO NOT LOVE US.
SPEAK FOR YOURSELF.
I SPEAK FOR THOSE WROUGHT AND SHAPED BY MORTAL MEN. FOR MONSTERS.
FINE. BUT THAT'S NOT ME.
THEN WHY DID YOU CALL ME? AND HOW?

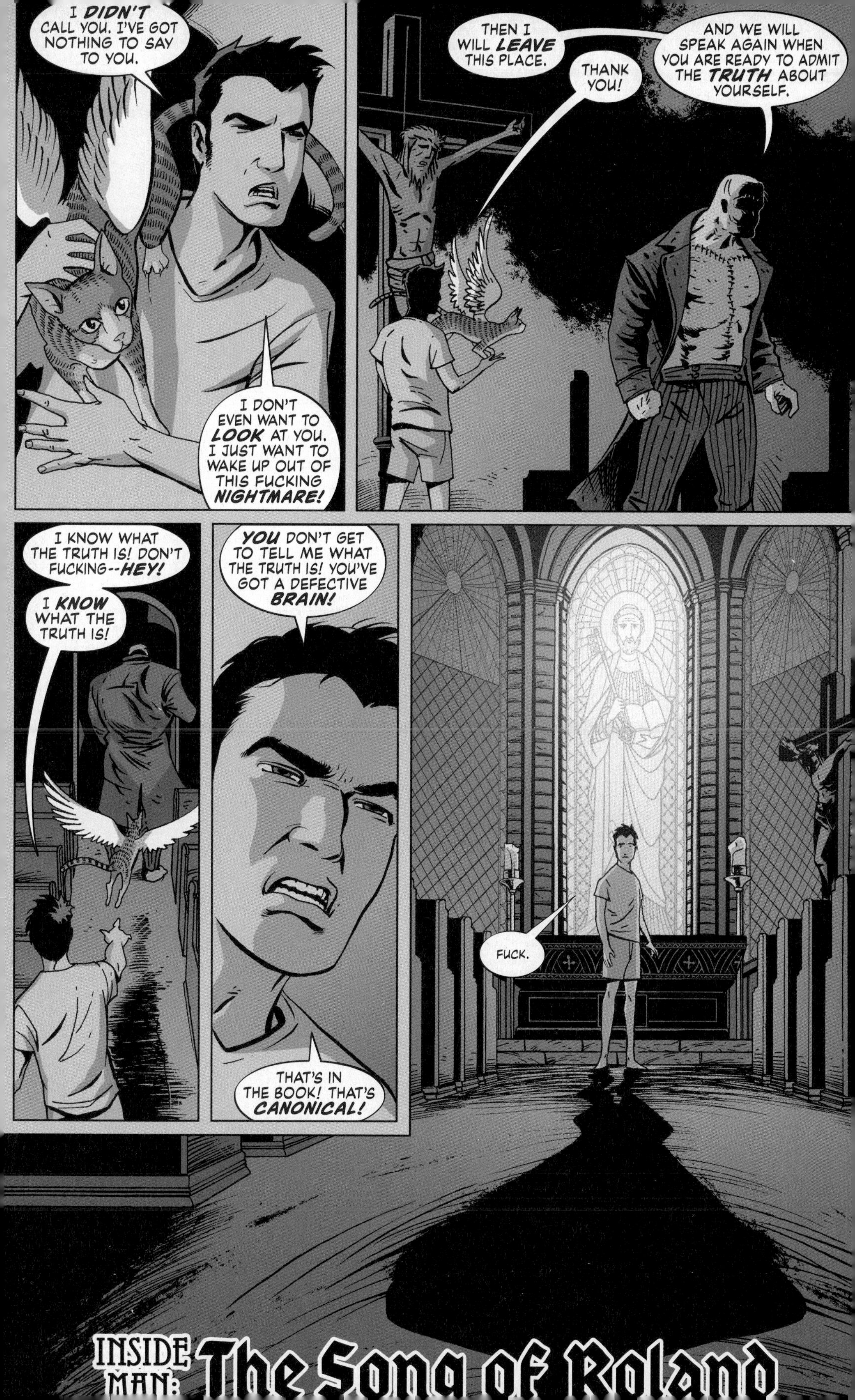
I DIDN'T CALL YOU. I'VE GOT NOTHING TO SAY TO YOU.
I DON'T EVEN WANT TO LOOK AT YOU. I JUST WANT TO WAKE UP OUT OF THIS FUCKING NIGHTMARE!
THEN I WILL LEAVE THIS PLACE.
AND WE WILL SPEAK AGAIN WHEN YOU ARE READY TO ADMIT THE TRUTH ABOUT YOURSELF.
THANK YOU!
I KNOW WHAT THE TRUTH IS! DON'T FUCKING--HEY!
I KNOW WHAT THE TRUTH IS!
YOU DON'T GET TO TELL ME WHAT THE TRUTH IS! YOU'VE GOT A DEFECTIVE BRAIN!
THAT'S IN THE BOOK! THAT'S CANONICAL!
FUCK.
INSIDE MAN: The Song of Roland

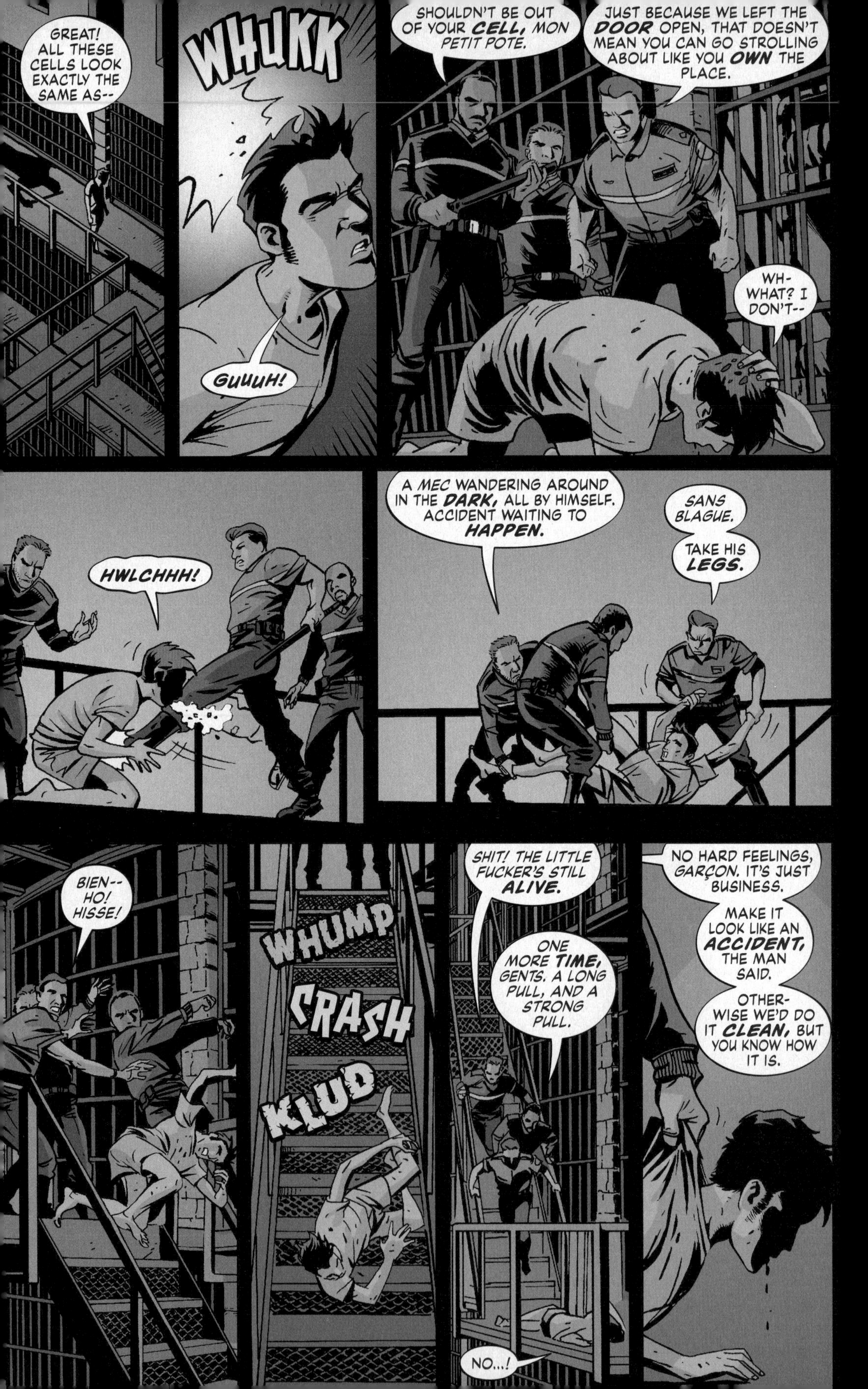
GREAT! ALL THESE CELLS LOOK EXACTLY THE SAME AS--
WHUKK
GUUUH!
SHOULDN'T BE OUT OF YOUR CELL, MON PETIT POTE.
JUST BECAUSE WE LEFT THE DOOR OPEN, THAT DOESN'T MEAN YOU CAN GO STROLLING ABOUT LIKE YOU OWN THE PLACE.
WH-WHAT? I DON'T--
HWLCHHH!
A MEC WANDERING AROUND IN THE DARK, ALL BY HIMSELF. ACCIDENT WAITING TO HAPPEN.
SANS BLAGUE.
TAKE HIS LEGS.
BIEN-- HO! HISSE!
WHUMP
CRASH
KLUD
SHIT! THE LITTLE FUCKER'S STILL ALIVE.
ONE MORE TIME, GENTS. A LONG PULL, AND A STRONG PULL.
NO...!
NO HARD FEELINGS, GARÇON. IT'S JUST BUSINESS.
MAKE IT LOOK LIKE AN ACCIDENT, THE MAN SAID.
OTHER-WISE WE'D DO IT CLEAN, BUT YOU KNOW HOW IT IS.

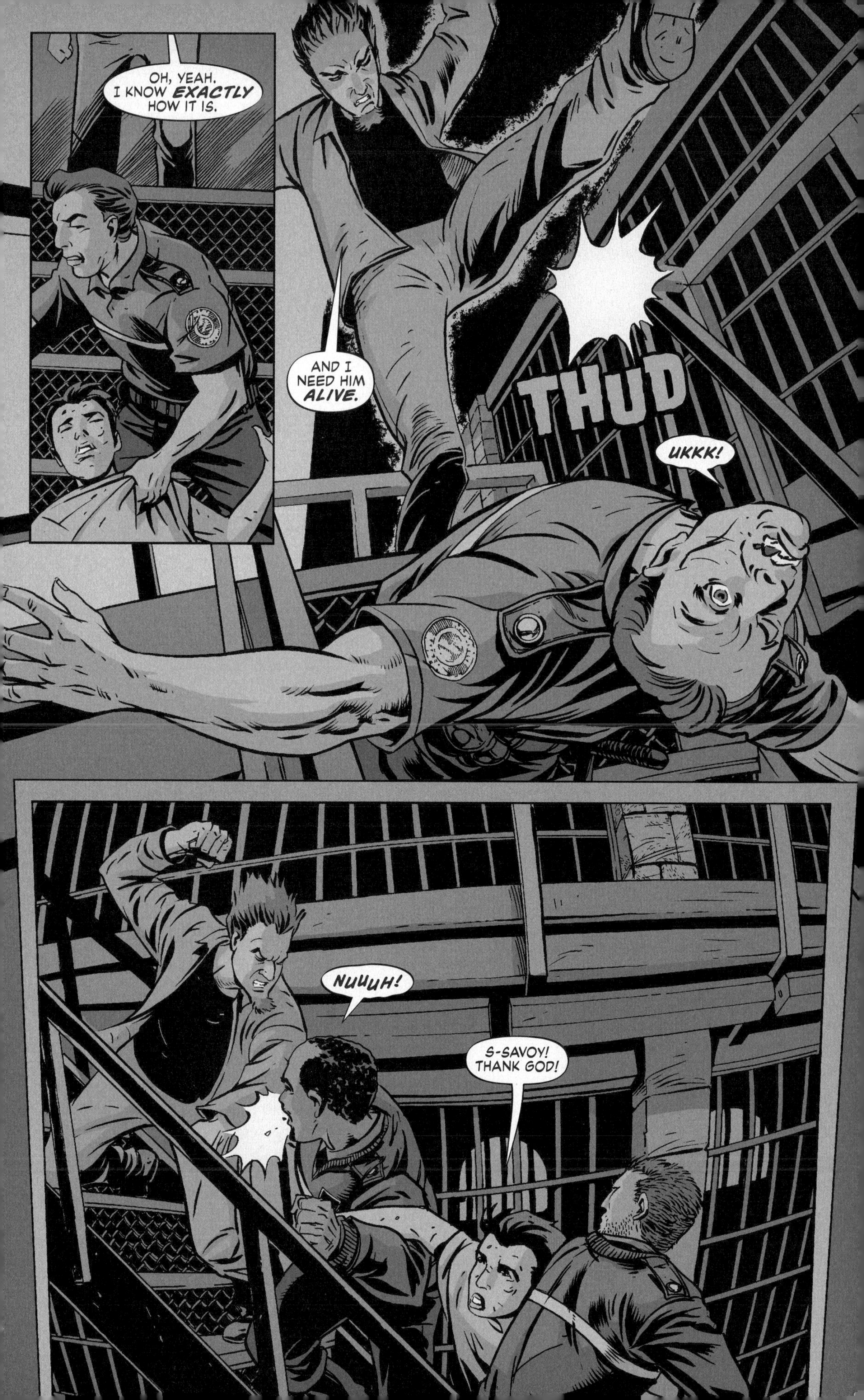
OH, YEAH. I KNOW EXACTLY HOW IT IS.
AND I NEED HIM ALIVE.
THUD
UKKK!
NUUUH!
S-SAVOY! THANK GOD!

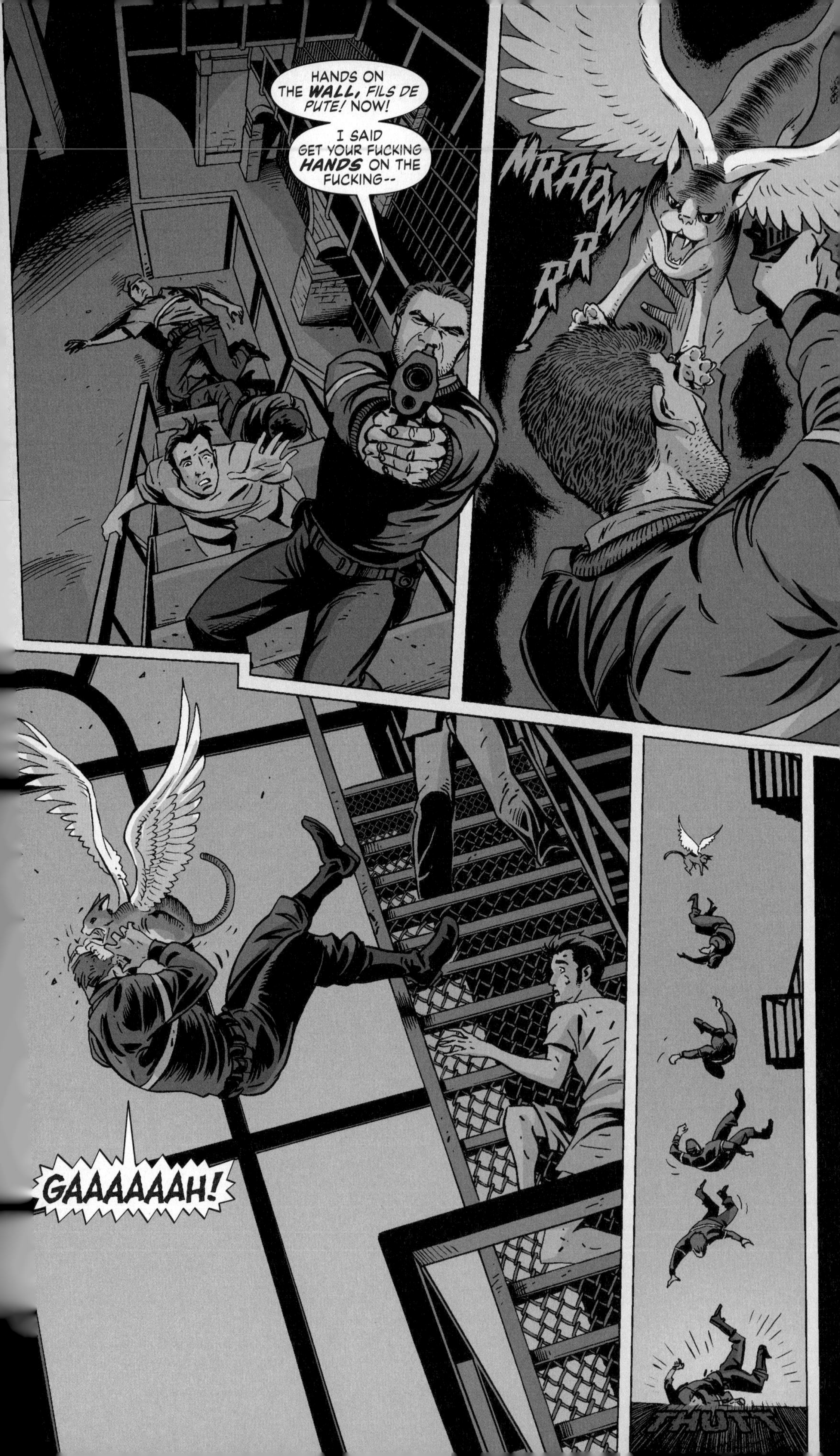
HANDS ON THE WALL, FILS DE PUTE! NOW!
I SAID GET YOUR FUCKING HANDS ON THE FUCKING--
MRAOWRRR
GAAAAAAH!
THUTT

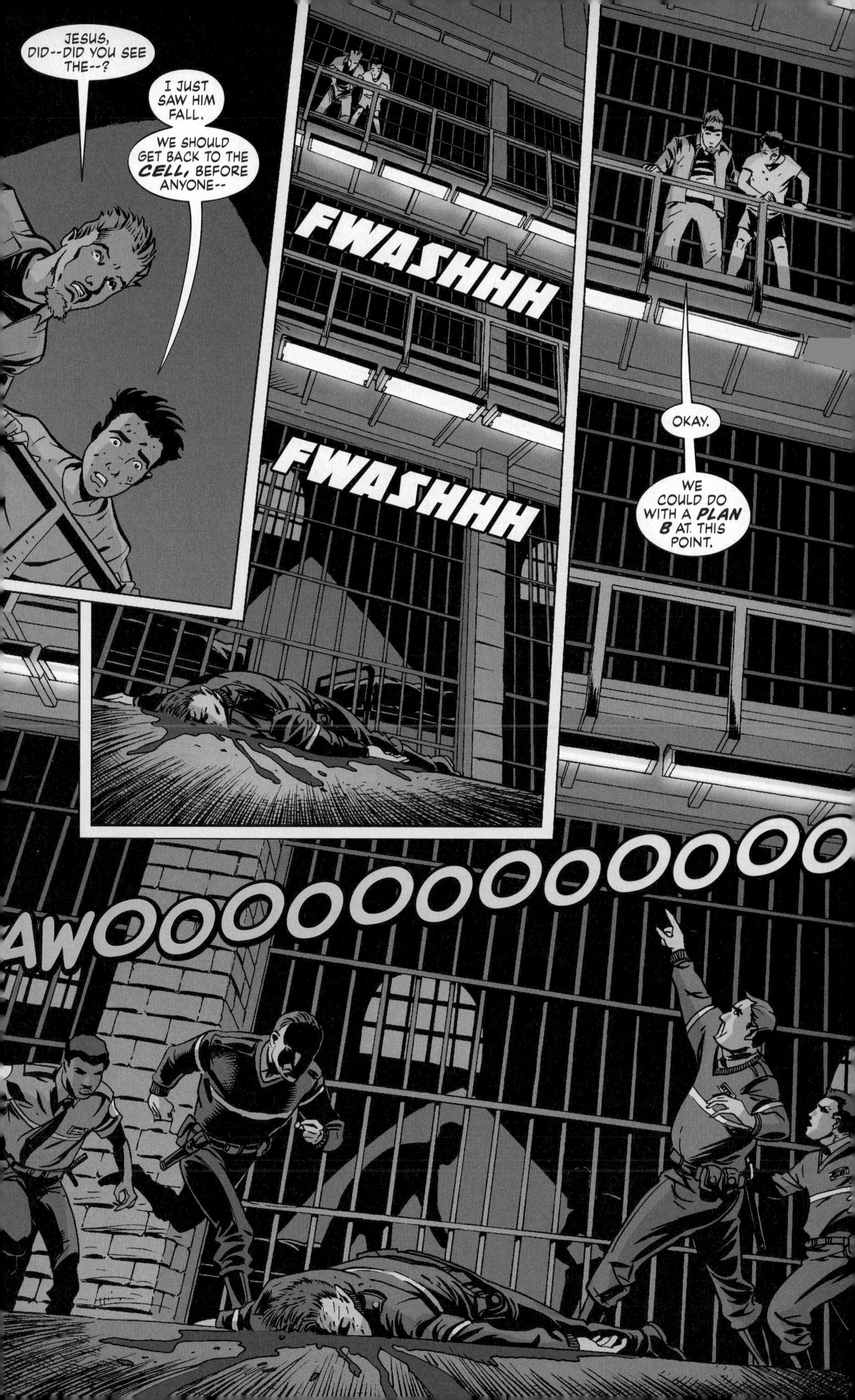
JESUS, DID--DID YOU SEE THE--?
I JUST SAW HIM FALL.
WE SHOULD GET BACK TO THE CELL, BEFORE ANYONE--
FWASHHH
FWASHHH
OKAY.
WE COULD DO WITH A PLAN B AT THIS POINT.
AWOOOOOOOOOOOOOOO

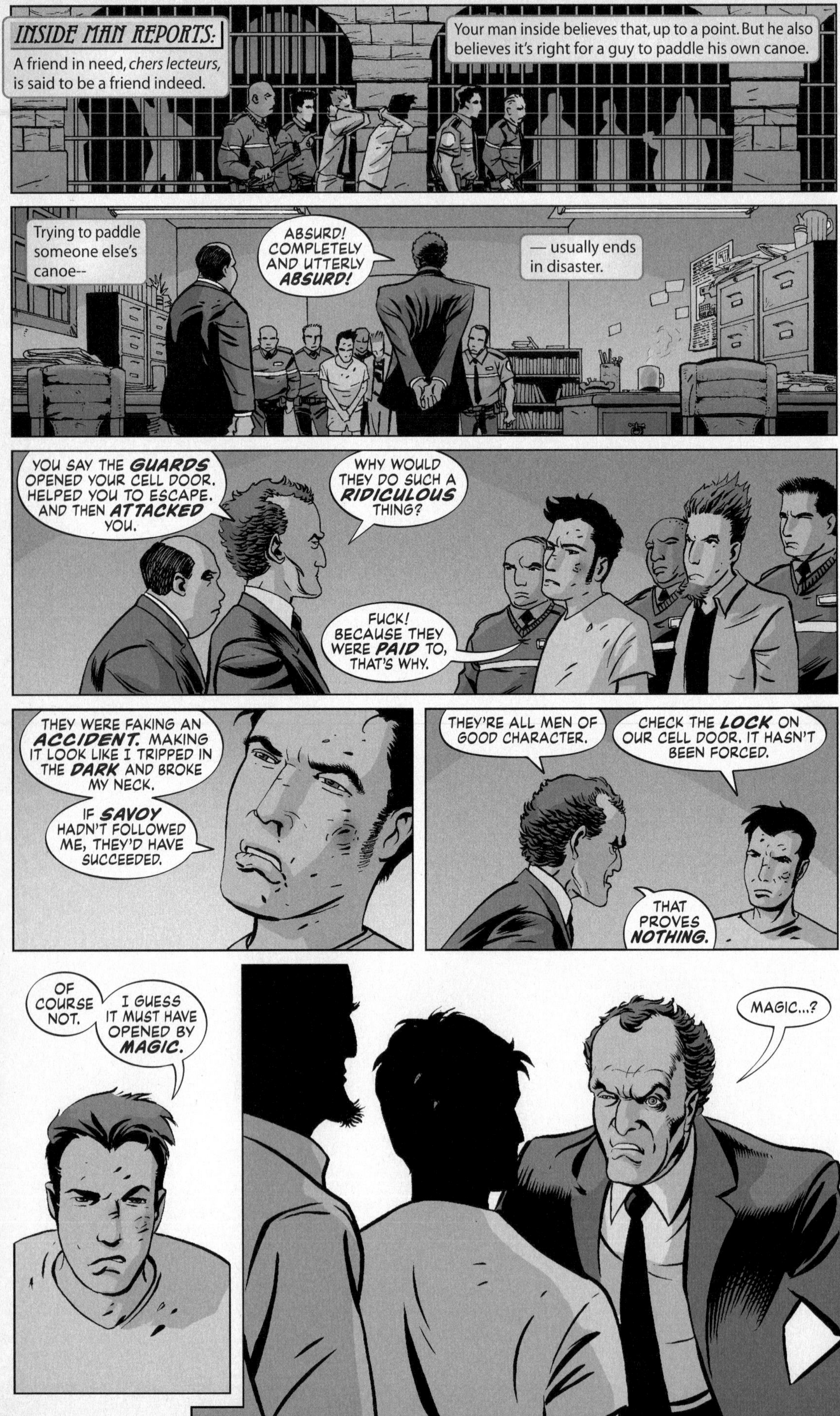
INSIDE MAN REPORTS:
A friend in need, *chers lecteurs,* is said to be a friend indeed.
Your man inside believes that, up to a point. But he also believes it's right for a guy to paddle his own canoe.
Trying to paddle someone else's canoe--
ABSURD! COMPLETELY AND UTTERLY ABSURD!
— usually ends in disaster.
YOU SAY THE GUARDS OPENED YOUR CELL DOOR. HELPED YOU TO ESCAPE. AND THEN ATTACKED YOU.
WHY WOULD THEY DO SUCH A RIDICULOUS THING?
FUCK! BECAUSE THEY WERE PAID TO, THAT'S WHY.
THEY WERE FAKING AN ACCIDENT. MAKING IT LOOK LIKE I TRIPPED IN THE DARK AND BROKE MY NECK.
IF SAVOY HADN'T FOLLOWED ME, THEY'D HAVE SUCCEEDED.
THEY'RE ALL MEN OF GOOD CHARACTER.
CHECK THE LOCK ON OUR CELL DOOR. IT HASN'T BEEN FORCED.
THAT PROVES NOTHING.
OF COURSE NOT.
I GUESS IT MUST HAVE OPENED BY MAGIC.
MAGIC...?

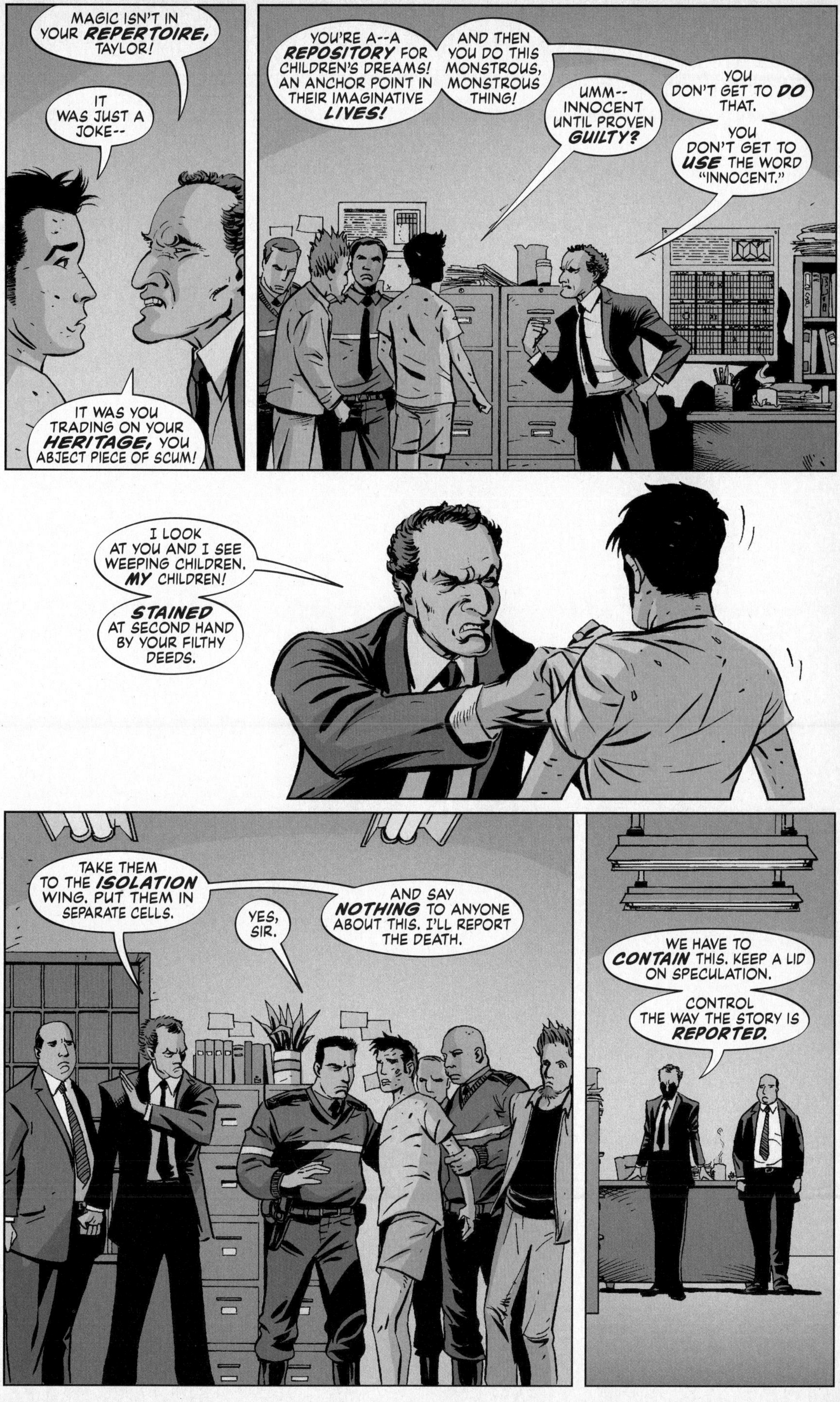
MAGIC ISN'T IN YOUR REPERTOIRE, TAYLOR!
IT WAS JUST A JOKE--
IT WAS YOU TRADING ON YOUR HERITAGE, YOU ABJECT PIECE OF SCUM!
YOU'RE A--A REPOSITORY FOR CHILDREN'S DREAMS! AN ANCHOR POINT IN THEIR IMAGINATIVE LIVES!
AND THEN YOU DO THIS MONSTROUS, MONSTROUS THING!
UMM-- INNOCENT UNTIL PROVEN GUILTY?
YOU DON'T GET TO DO THAT.
YOU DON'T GET TO USE THE WORD "INNOCENT."
I LOOK AT YOU AND I SEE WEEPING CHILDREN. MY CHILDREN!
STAINED AT SECOND HAND BY YOUR FILTHY DEEDS.
TAKE THEM TO THE ISOLATION WING. PUT THEM IN SEPARATE CELLS.
YES, SIR.
AND SAY NOTHING TO ANYONE ABOUT THIS. I'LL REPORT THE DEATH.
WE HAVE TO CONTAIN THIS. KEEP A LID ON SPECULATION.
CONTROL THE WAY THE STORY IS REPORTED.

NEWS | POLITICS | OPINIONS | BUSINESS | LOCAL | SPORTS | ARTS

SEARCH: go

Thursday

MYSTERIOUS DEATH AT DONOSTIA

Donostia prison, in Southern France, is in the news again today after a guard suffered a fatal fall from an internal walkway. The prison was already under a media spotlight because celebrity murder suspect Tom Taylor is currently being held on remand there, pending trial for the Villa Diodati slayings.

The guard, Martin Busquel, 34, apparently tripped and fell over a safety rail while conducting his ordinary nightly rounds. A press release from prison governor Claude-Louis Chadron emphasized that there are no suspicious circumstances and consequently no need for an external investigation. Local news feeds, however, were reporting before the death was announced that two other guards on the same night shift were admitted to nearby Bois-Terrière Hospital with facial and abdominal injuries.

Donostia seems to have courted controversy many times in recent months. The opening of the new women's wing has unrolled amid accusations from human rights groups that overcrowding at the prison has now reached crisis proportions. The Ministry for the Interior has denied this, stating that Donostia adheres to official guidelines which guarantee every prisoner 30 cubic meters of living space.

Governor Chadron himself has only recently returned from a leave of absence which some allege was to allow him to be treated for work-related stress and depression. If so, he must have wished that Tom Taylor has remained in Switzerland rather than being extradited to

Dr. Swann Cares about YOU

ONLINE PSYCHIATRIC HELP FROM A CERTIFIED PROFESSIONAL

Home | Help Me | Helped | Special Features | Store

GO!

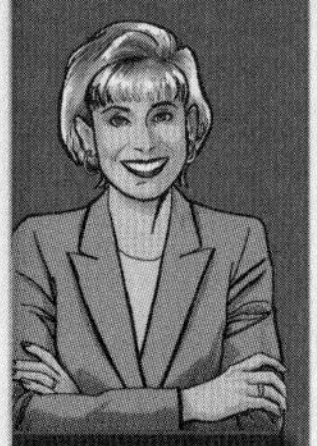

New
Archive
Find'a'Doc
Be in the book
E-Books
Local Listings
Interviews
Case Studies
FAQ

Tommy Taylor Syndrome

by Doctor Pauline Swann

If the health of the human collective unconscious can be measured by our dreams, we're in a pretty bad state right now. Six patients in four days have mentioned end-of-the-world dreams in their regular sessions with me. Apocalyptic imagery pr angels and trumpets, books with seven seals, great beasts and women clad in the su And one surprise guest star: Tommy Taylor.

There are, I suppose, plenty of very good reasons why people should feel pessimisti about the immediate future. The past year has seen the twenty-first century's first pandemic, the near-collapse of the world's economies and the news that the most pessimistic forecasts about global warming were still understating the direness of t problem.

But why Tommy Taylor?

The answer to that is a complex one, and it points to the vital importance of story in lives. Ask anyone about *Tommy Taylor and the Cave of Silence*, the first novel in Wils Taylor's modern masterpiece, and they'll instantly be able to tell you where and wh they first read it - or when it was read to them, if like me they encountered it first as bedtime story administered in always-too-small doses by indulgent parents.

So Tommy Taylor is emblematic of our childhood: an uncomplicated and sinless ple that was amazingly intense, and spreads its light around the whole of our interior landscape.

Except that the light has been extinguished, or polluted by the lurid red glow of the Diodati murders. It's as though a partner has been unfaithful to us, or we've been estranged from one of our children. The psychic trauma is no less real because it sp from an imaginary source. We're all of us sick, and the name of our sickness is Tommy Taylor.

The cure, surely, is to wean ourselves from this dependency. We have to move into post-Tommy state of mental health and resilience - a project that will be difficult, bu

http://www.InsideMan.blogtronic.com/PRISONDIARY

SEARCH BLOG | Next Bl

PRISON DIARY

INSIDE MAN REPORTS

WEDNESDAY

Day 1

Z-list celebrity, media whipping boy, suspected savior and now convict.

Tom Taylor's first day at Donostia was a fairly memorable one. Whether he's the cold-hearted killer his enemies make him out to be, or the victim of circumstances painted by his few remaining fans, he certainly made an impression here in the arse end of the correctional system, where liberty, equality and fraternity are someone else's problems.

Claude-Louis, our beloved governor, decided to avoid any possible suggestion of favoritism by giving poor Tom the shittiest job in the whole jail - up in the cradle, chipping out old mortar from Donostia's crumbling brickwork so B wing can be repainted and survive another winter.

Eighty feet off the ground, with only Anton "Subway Slayer" Moustaki for company, Tom must have been reflecting on how fleeting fame is, and how fickle the adoration of the sweaty masses. Last week his name was in the prayers of the emotionally retarded of all ages, from Silken Samarkand to Cedared wherever-the-fuck. Today he can't scrape up the change to buy a smoke (one euro or a tenth of a blow-job at Donostia prices).

Night fell, and the cell doors slammed. What did Tom Taylor dream about, as he lay

ARCHIVES

Swordsman55 — Posted: 1:03 am — quote

I don't care what the papers say. Tom is Tommy. He didn't do those things.

Back to top

SweetSueSparrow — Posted: 1:10 am — quote

Someone did. If it wasn't him, he really worked hard to make it look like it was.

Back to top

ZFACTOR — Posted: 1:12 am — quote

There was meant to be another guy at the villa. Some witnesses said that anyway. I think I read that.

Back to top

SweetSueSparrow — Posted: 1:20 am — quote

But the descriptions were all over the place. Someone even said his hand wasn't real, or he had like a wooden glove on or something.

Back to top

Swordsman55 — Posted: 1:38 pm — quote

Tom is Tommy.

Back to top

SweetSueSparrow — Posted: 1:43 pm — quote

Yeah that's the answer to everything Swordsman. Thanks.

Back to top

Related Searches: Tommy Taylor, Wilson Taylor, Replica Wands, Golden Trumpet, Tim Hunter, Cosplay Robes, Virgin

All items | Auctions only | InstaBuy only — **14,281 results found for Tom Taylor memorabilia**

Sort by: Best Match

	Current Price	You Have
Signed Convention Programme: TommyCon 2006 INSCRIBED "TO SARAH, HOPE THE MAGIC STAYS WITH YOU FOREVER." OWNER NO LONGER WANTS OR NEEDS — InstaBuy	$5	<1m
Death Row Tom. Lmtd edition resin figure set: 136/500 SEND TOM TAYLOR TO THE ELECTRIC CHAIR, GUILLOTINE OR LETHAL CHAMBER: A DIFFERENT EXECUTION EVERY DAY. — 62 Bids	$612.00	6m
Complete set of Tommy Taylor Novels ALL 1st EDITIONS EXCEPT FOR Tommy Taylot and the Glass Sword, 3rd PRINTING. ALL SIGNED BY TOM TAYLOR. — 14 Bids	$178.32	7m

TV, Movie & Character Toys (456)

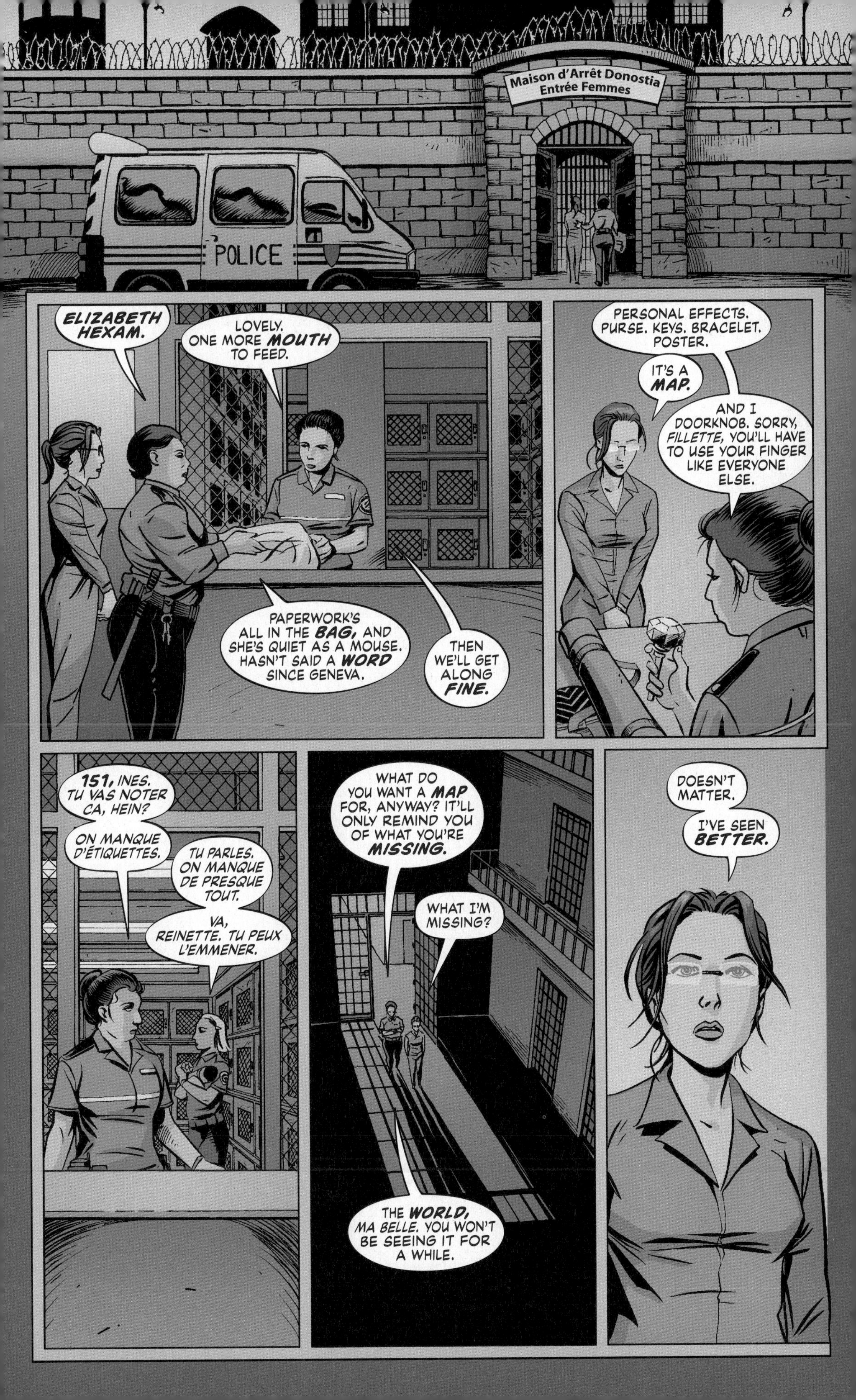
Maison d'Arrêt Donostia
Entrée Femmes
POLICE
ELIZABETH HEXAM.
LOVELY. ONE MORE MOUTH TO FEED.
PAPERWORK'S ALL IN THE BAG, AND SHE'S QUIET AS A MOUSE. HASN'T SAID A WORD SINCE GENEVA.
THEN WE'LL GET ALONG FINE.
PERSONAL EFFECTS. PURSE. KEYS. BRACELET. POSTER.
IT'S A MAP.
AND I DOORKNOB. SORRY, FILLETTE, YOU'LL HAVE TO USE YOUR FINGER LIKE EVERYONE ELSE.
151, INES. TU VAS NOTER CA, HEIN?
ON MANQUE D'ÉTIQUETTES.
TU PARLES. ON MANQUE DE PRESQUE TOUT.
VA, REINETTE. TU PEUX L'EMMENER.
WHAT DO YOU WANT A MAP FOR, ANYWAY? IT'LL ONLY REMIND YOU OF WHAT YOU'RE MISSING.
WHAT I'M MISSING?
THE WORLD, MA BELLE. YOU WON'T BE SEEING IT FOR A WHILE.
DOESN'T MATTER.
I'VE SEEN BETTER.

The isolation wing at Donostia isn't as bad as it sounds. Okay, the cell is a box, the cots have no mattress or blankets, and the temperature is a bracing 10 degrees.

But the peace and quiet let a man catch up with his work.

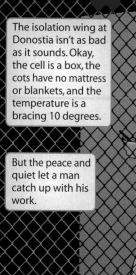

I'M REALLY **SORRY** I GOT YOU INTO THIS, SAVOY.

At least, intermittently.

YOU DIDN'T. I GOT **MYSELF** INTO IT.

I DIDN'T **HAVE** TO FOLLOW YOU, DID I? AND I DIDN'T HAVE TO STEP INTO THAT **PORK ROAST.**

IT'S TOO BAD THE GUY **FELL,** BUT FUCK IT. IF ANYONE'S TO BLAME HERE, IT'S **ME,** FOR NOT KEEPING UP MY PROFESSIONAL STANDARDS.

PROFESSIONAL **STANDARDS?** YOU'RE AN ARMED ROBBER.

TOM, DO YOU BELIEVE **EVERYTHING** YOU'RE TOLD?

THEY BROUGHT ME DOWN FROM **GENEVA** WITH YOU. BUNKED ME IN WITH YOU. EVEN LET ME KEEP MY **PHONE.** YOU DIDN'T THINK THAT WAS STRANGE AT ALL?

I **PAY** FOR ALL THIS. OR AT LEAST, THE COMPANY THAT HOSTS MY **BLOG** DOES.

THE GUARDS POCKET A NICE LITTLE BONUS, AND I GET EXCLUSIVE ACCESS.

I'M A **JOURNALIST,** MAN.

AND YOU'RE THE **STORY.**

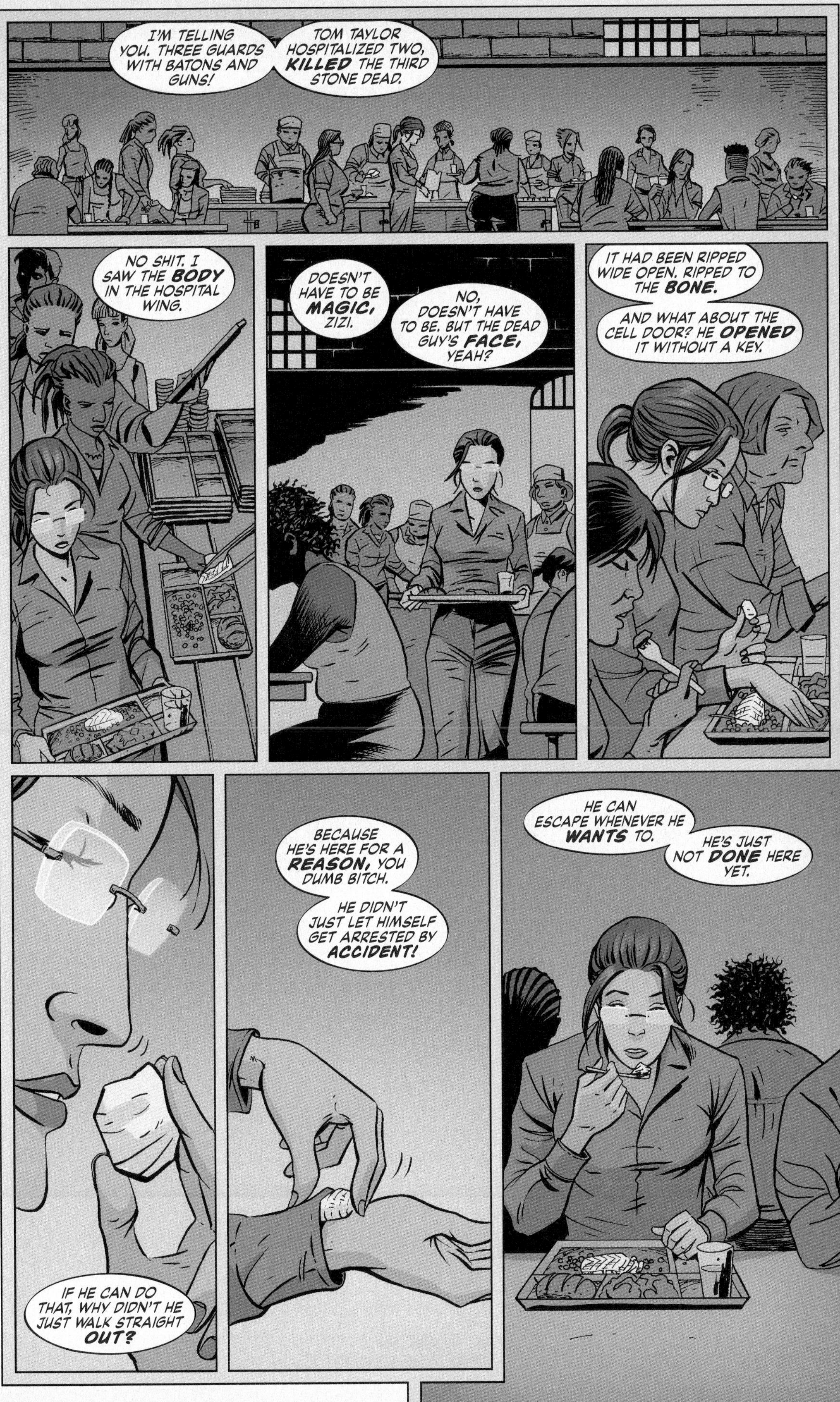
I'M TELLING YOU. THREE GUARDS WITH BATONS AND GUNS!
TOM TAYLOR HOSPITALIZED TWO, KILLED THE THIRD STONE DEAD.
NO SHIT. I SAW THE BODY IN THE HOSPITAL WING.
DOESN'T HAVE TO BE MAGIC, ZIZI.
NO, DOESN'T HAVE TO BE. BUT THE DEAD GUY'S FACE, YEAH?
IT HAD BEEN RIPPED WIDE OPEN. RIPPED TO THE BONE.
AND WHAT ABOUT THE CELL DOOR? HE OPENED IT WITHOUT A KEY.
IF HE CAN DO THAT, WHY DIDN'T HE JUST WALK STRAIGHT OUT?
BECAUSE HE'S HERE FOR A REASON, YOU DUMB BITCH.
HE DIDN'T JUST LET HIMSELF GET ARRESTED BY ACCIDENT!
HE CAN ESCAPE WHENEVER HE WANTS TO.
HE'S JUST NOT DONE HERE YET.

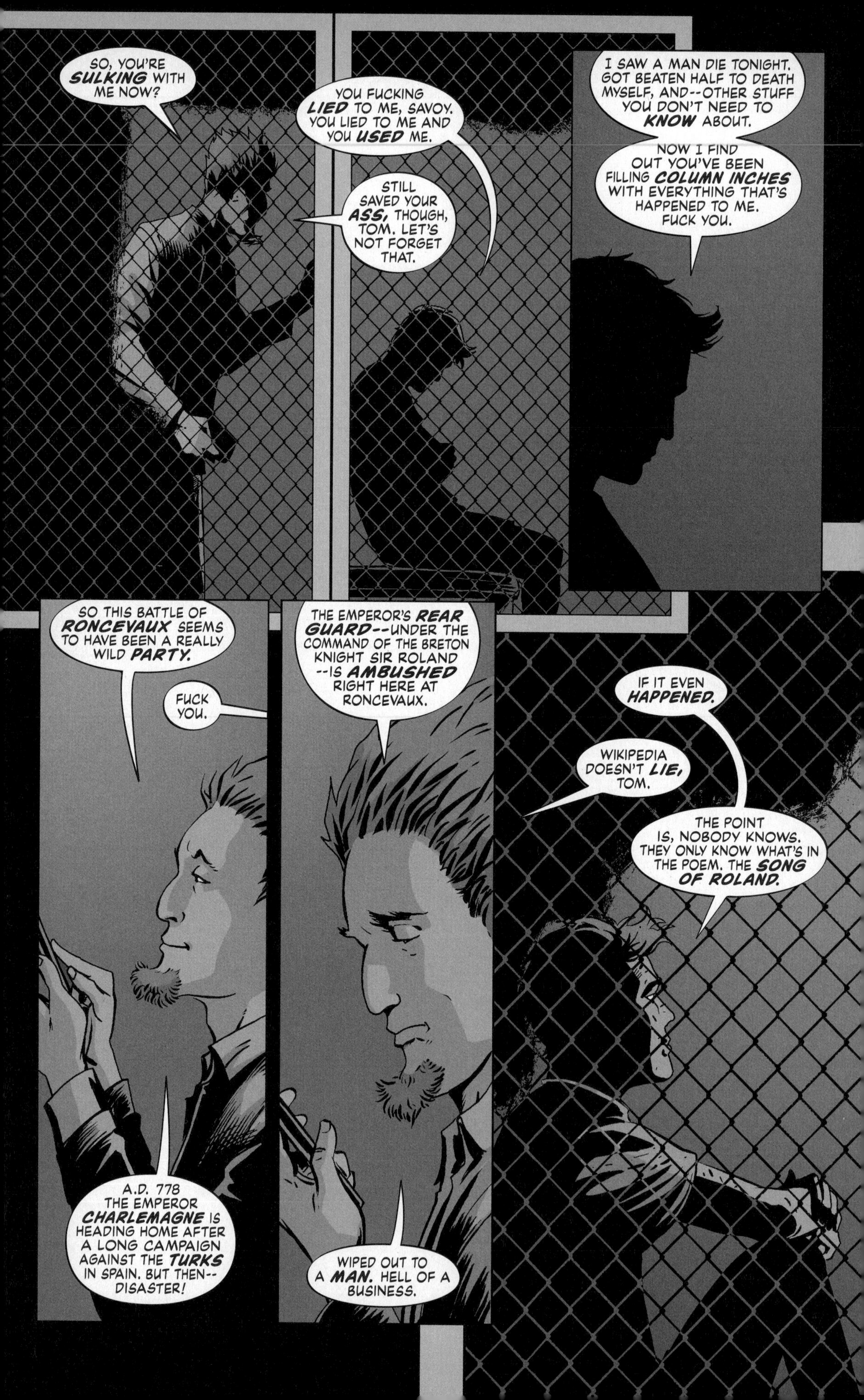
SO, YOU'RE SULKING WITH ME NOW?
YOU FUCKING LIED TO ME, SAVOY. YOU LIED TO ME AND YOU USED ME.
STILL SAVED YOUR ASS, THOUGH, TOM. LET'S NOT FORGET THAT.
I SAW A MAN DIE TONIGHT. GOT BEATEN HALF TO DEATH MYSELF, AND--OTHER STUFF YOU DON'T NEED TO KNOW ABOUT.
NOW I FIND OUT YOU'VE BEEN FILLING COLUMN INCHES WITH EVERYTHING THAT'S HAPPENED TO ME. FUCK YOU.
SO THIS BATTLE OF RONCEVAUX SEEMS TO HAVE BEEN A REALLY WILD PARTY.
FUCK YOU.
A.D. 778 THE EMPEROR CHARLEMAGNE IS HEADING HOME AFTER A LONG CAMPAIGN AGAINST THE TURKS IN SPAIN. BUT THEN--DISASTER!
THE EMPEROR'S REAR GUARD--UNDER THE COMMAND OF THE BRETON KNIGHT SIR ROLAND--IS AMBUSHED RIGHT HERE AT RONCEVAUX.
WIPED OUT TO A MAN. HELL OF A BUSINESS.
IF IT EVEN HAPPENED.
WIKIPEDIA DOESN'T LIE, TOM.
THE POINT IS, NOBODY KNOWS. THEY ONLY KNOW WHAT'S IN THE POEM. THE SONG OF ROLAND.

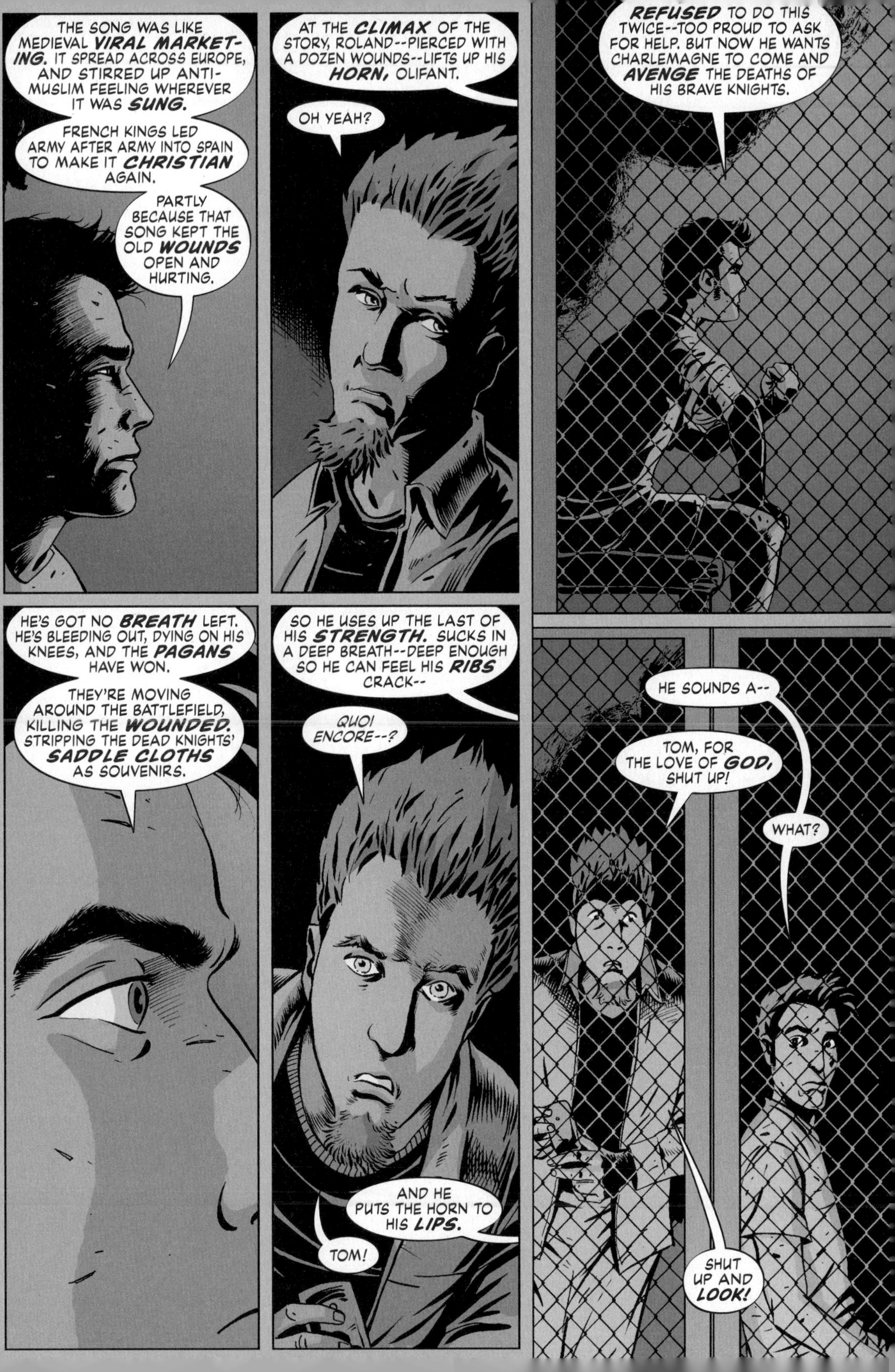
THE SONG WAS LIKE MEDIEVAL VIRAL MARKETING. IT SPREAD ACROSS EUROPE, AND STIRRED UP ANTI-MUSLIM FEELING WHEREVER IT WAS SUNG.
FRENCH KINGS LED ARMY AFTER ARMY INTO SPAIN TO MAKE IT CHRISTIAN AGAIN.
PARTLY BECAUSE THAT SONG KEPT THE OLD WOUNDS OPEN AND HURTING.
AT THE CLIMAX OF THE STORY, ROLAND--PIERCED WITH A DOZEN WOUNDS--LIFTS UP HIS HORN, OLIFANT.
OH YEAH?
REFUSED TO DO THIS TWICE--TOO PROUD TO ASK FOR HELP. BUT NOW HE WANTS CHARLEMAGNE TO COME AND AVENGE THE DEATHS OF HIS BRAVE KNIGHTS.
HE'S GOT NO BREATH LEFT. HE'S BLEEDING OUT, DYING ON HIS KNEES, AND THE PAGANS HAVE WON.
THEY'RE MOVING AROUND THE BATTLEFIELD, KILLING THE WOUNDED. STRIPPING THE DEAD KNIGHTS' SADDLE CLOTHS AS SOUVENIRS.
SO HE USES UP THE LAST OF HIS STRENGTH. SUCKS IN A DEEP BREATH--DEEP ENOUGH SO HE CAN FEEL HIS RIBS CRACK--
QUOI ENCORE--?
AND HE PUTS THE HORN TO HIS LIPS.
TOM!
HE SOUNDS A--
TOM, FOR THE LOVE OF GOD, SHUT UP!
WHAT?
SHUT UP AND LOOK!

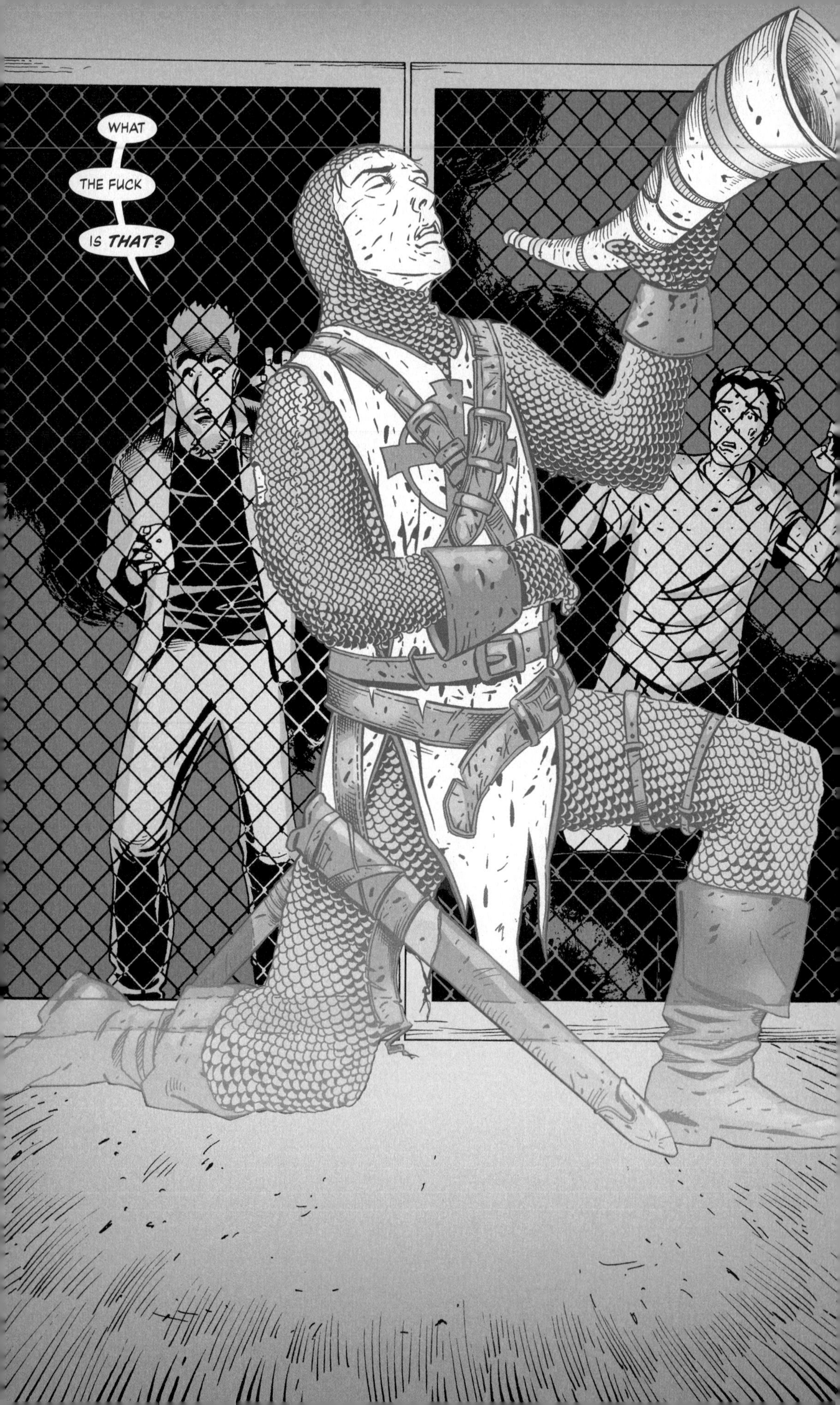
WHAT
THE FUCK
IS THAT?

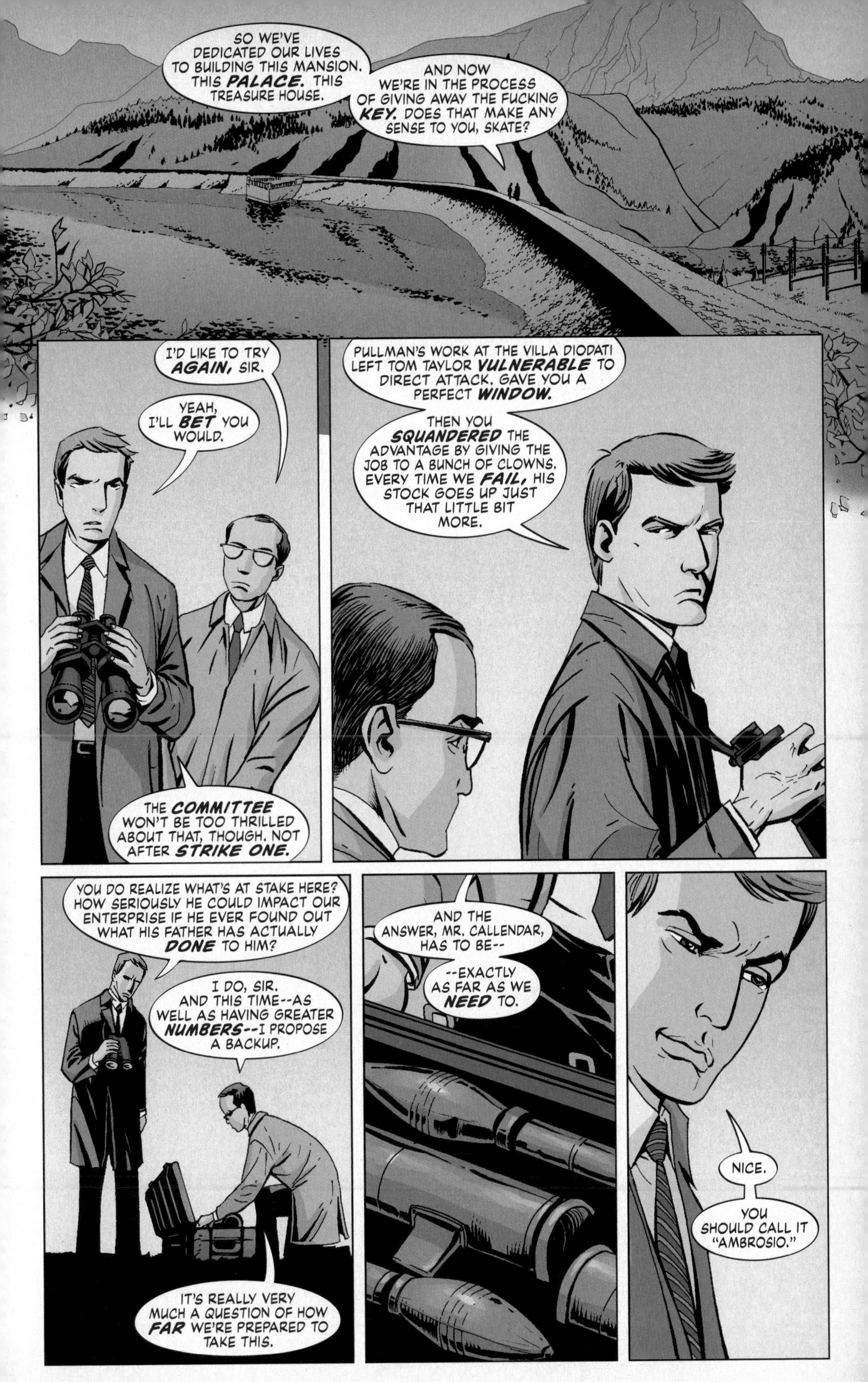
SO WE'VE DEDICATED OUR LIVES TO BUILDING THIS MANSION. THIS PALACE. THIS TREASURE HOUSE.
AND NOW WE'RE IN THE PROCESS OF GIVING AWAY THE FUCKING KEY. DOES THAT MAKE ANY SENSE TO YOU, SKATE?
I'D LIKE TO TRY AGAIN, SIR.
YEAH, I'LL BET YOU WOULD.
THE COMMITTEE WON'T BE TOO THRILLED ABOUT THAT, THOUGH. NOT AFTER STRIKE ONE.
PULLMAN'S WORK AT THE VILLA DIODATI LEFT TOM TAYLOR VULNERABLE TO DIRECT ATTACK. GAVE YOU A PERFECT WINDOW.
THEN YOU SQUANDERED THE ADVANTAGE BY GIVING THE JOB TO A BUNCH OF CLOWNS. EVERY TIME WE FAIL, HIS STOCK GOES UP JUST THAT LITTLE BIT MORE.
YOU DO REALIZE WHAT'S AT STAKE HERE? HOW SERIOUSLY HE COULD IMPACT OUR ENTERPRISE IF HE EVER FOUND OUT WHAT HIS FATHER HAS ACTUALLY DONE TO HIM?
I DO, SIR. AND THIS TIME--AS WELL AS HAVING GREATER NUMBERS--I PROPOSE A BACKUP.
IT'S REALLY VERY MUCH A QUESTION OF HOW FAR WE'RE PREPARED TO TAKE THIS.
AND THE ANSWER, MR. CALLENDAR, HAS TO BE--
--EXACTLY AS FAR AS WE NEED TO.
NICE.
YOU SHOULD CALL IT "AMBROSIO."

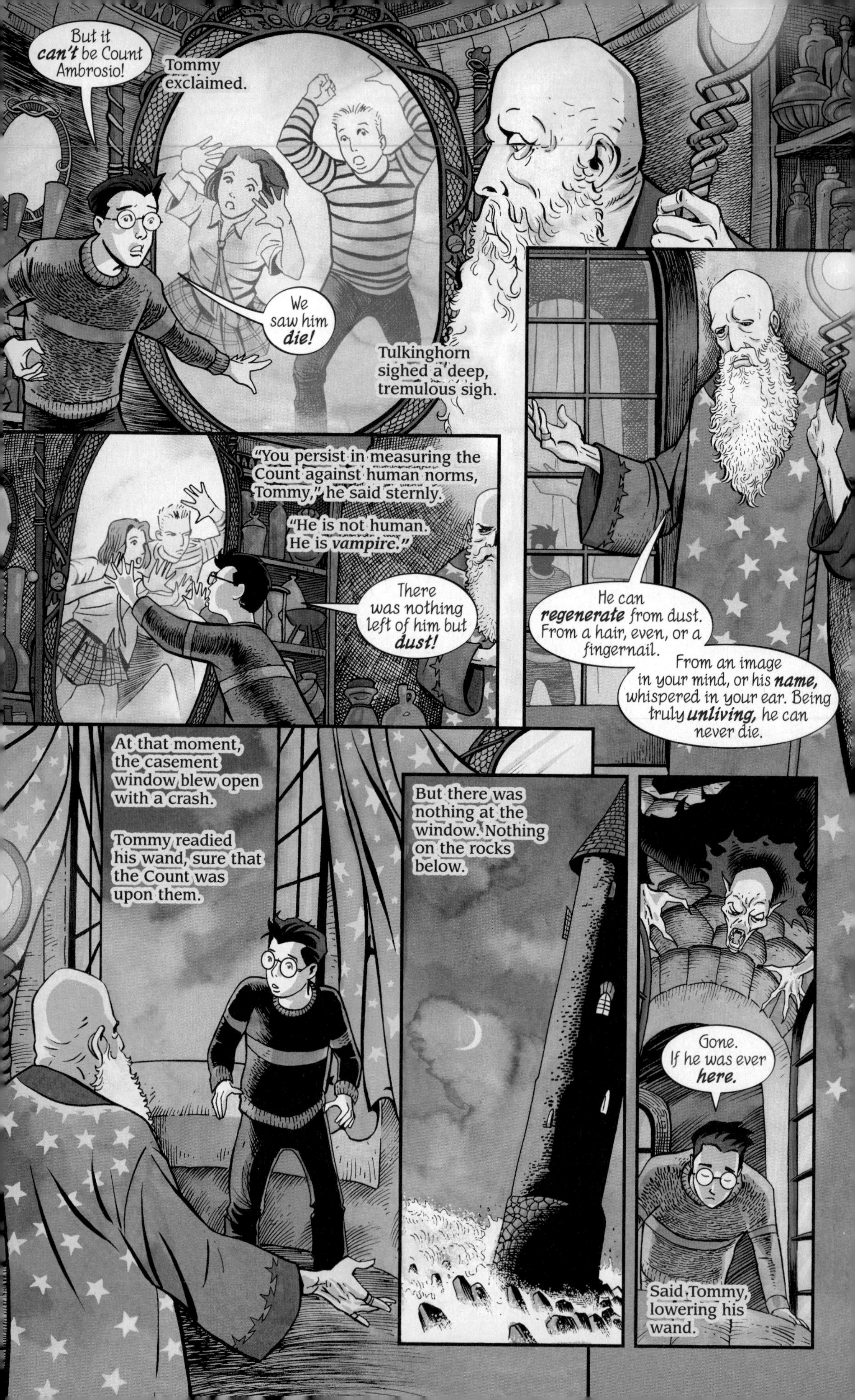
But it can't be Count Ambrosio!
Tommy exclaimed.
We saw him die!
Tulkinghorn sighed a deep, tremulous sigh.
"You persist in measuring the Count against human norms, Tommy," he said sternly.
"He is not human. He is vampire."
There was nothing left of him but dust!
He can regenerate from dust. From a hair, even, or a fingernail.
From an image in your mind, or his name, whispered in your ear. Being truly unliving, he can never die.
At that moment, the casement window blew open with a crash.
Tommy readied his wand, sure that the Count was upon them.
But there was nothing at the window. Nothing on the rocks below.
Gone. If he was ever here.
Said Tommy, lowering his wand.

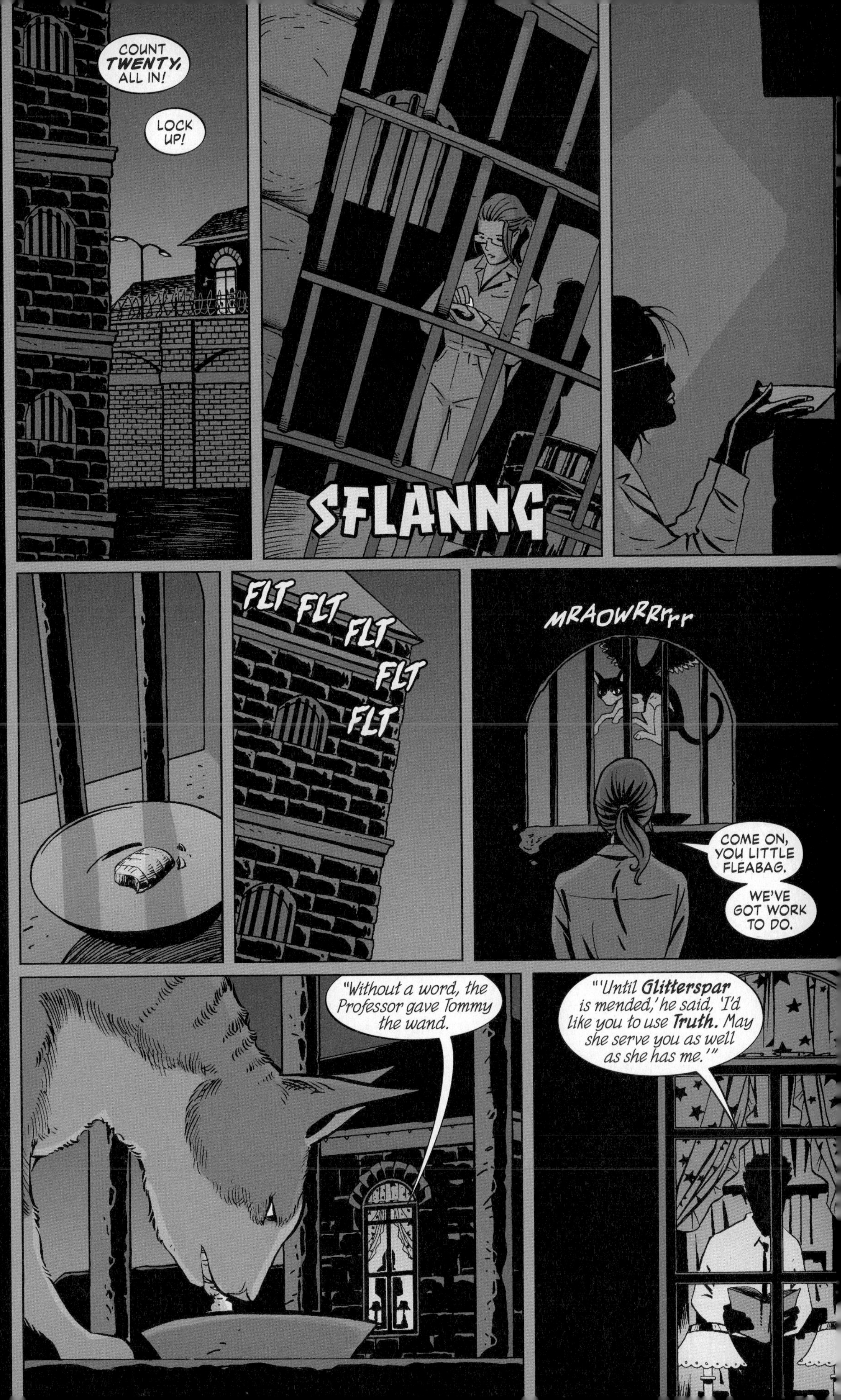
COUNT TWENTY, ALL IN!
LOCK UP!
SFLANNG
FLT FLT FLT FLT FLT
MRAOWRrrrr
COME ON, YOU LITTLE FLEABAG.
WE'VE GOT WORK TO DO.
"Without a word, the Professor gave Tommy the wand.
"'Until Glitterspar is mended,' he said, 'I'd like you to use Truth. May she serve you as well as she has me.'"

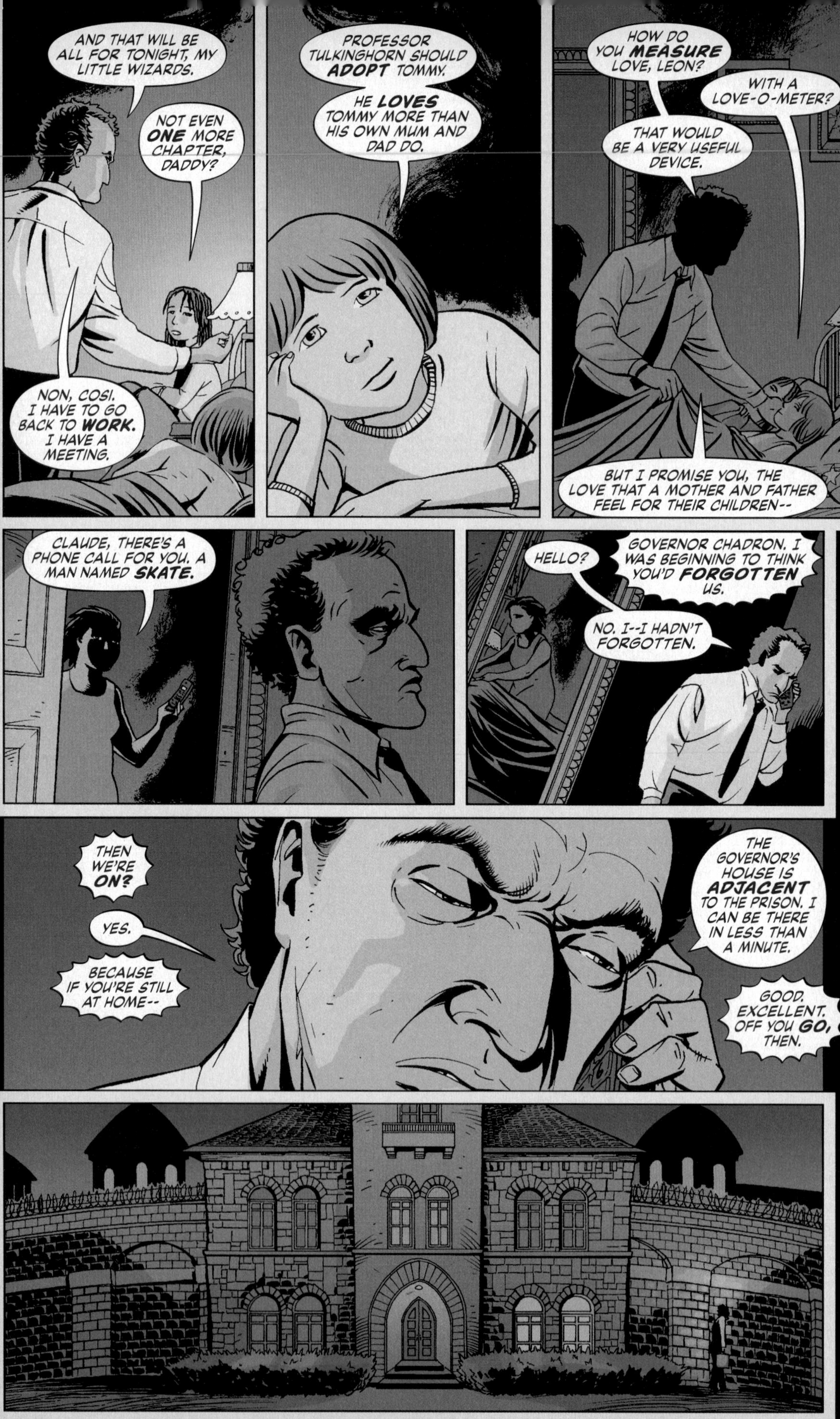
AND THAT WILL BE ALL FOR TONIGHT, MY LITTLE WIZARDS.
NOT EVEN ONE MORE CHAPTER, DADDY?
NON, COSI. I HAVE TO GO BACK TO WORK. I HAVE A MEETING.
PROFESSOR TULKINGHORN SHOULD ADOPT TOMMY.
HE LOVES TOMMY MORE THAN HIS OWN MUM AND DAD DO.
HOW DO YOU MEASURE LOVE, LEON?
WITH A LOVE-O-METER?
THAT WOULD BE A VERY USEFUL DEVICE.
BUT I PROMISE YOU, THE LOVE THAT A MOTHER AND FATHER FEEL FOR THEIR CHILDREN--
CLAUDE, THERE'S A PHONE CALL FOR YOU. A MAN NAMED SKATE.
HELLO?
GOVERNOR CHADRON. I WAS BEGINNING TO THINK YOU'D FORGOTTEN US.
NO. I--I HADN'T FORGOTTEN.
THEN WE'RE ON?
YES.
BECAUSE IF YOU'RE STILL AT HOME--
THE GOVERNOR'S HOUSE IS ADJACENT TO THE PRISON. I CAN BE THERE IN LESS THAN A MINUTE.
GOOD. EXCELLENT. OFF YOU GO, THEN.

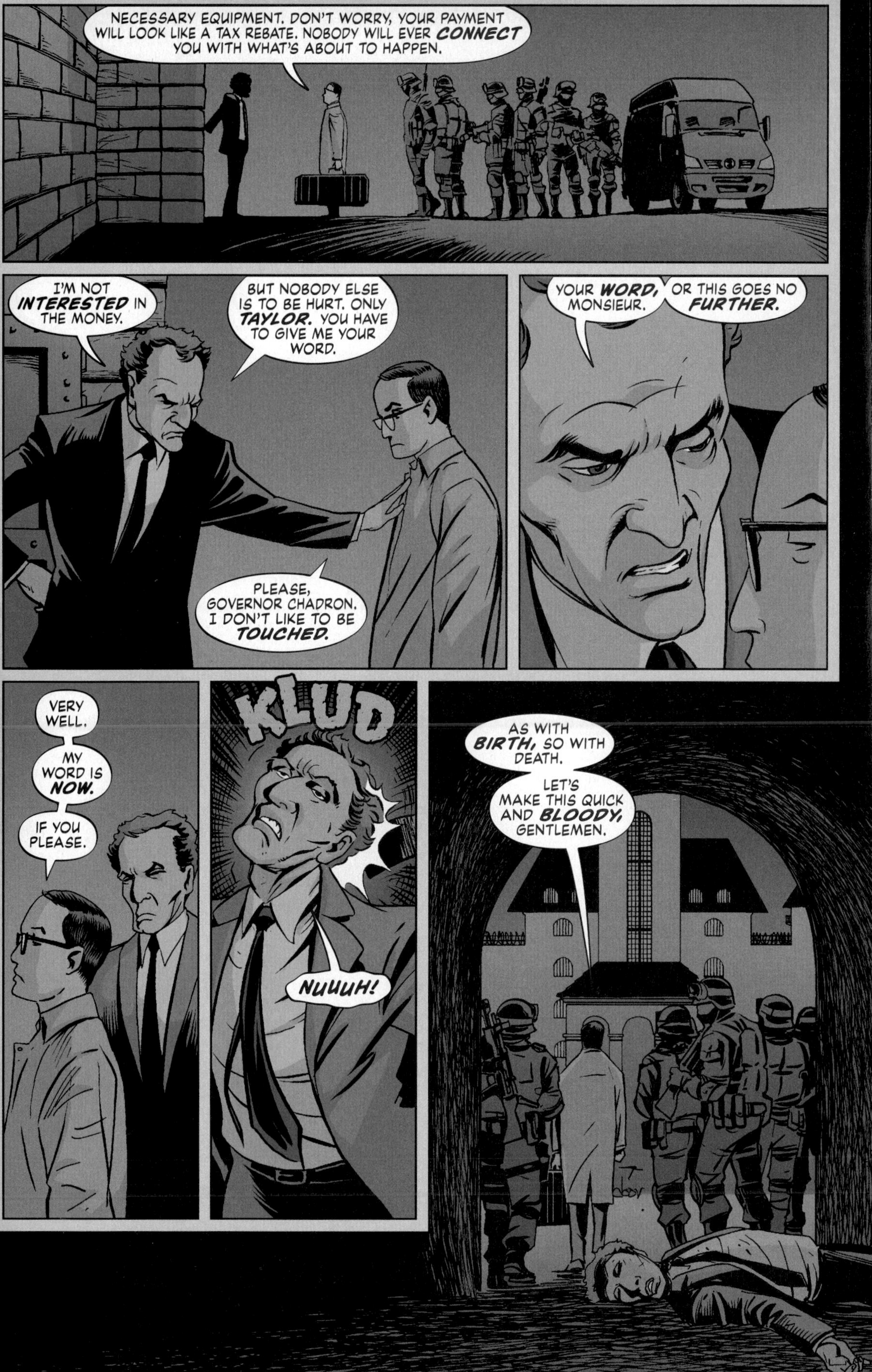
NECESSARY EQUIPMENT. DON'T WORRY, YOUR PAYMENT WILL LOOK LIKE A TAX REBATE. NOBODY WILL EVER CONNECT YOU WITH WHAT'S ABOUT TO HAPPEN.
I'M NOT INTERESTED IN THE MONEY.
BUT NOBODY ELSE IS TO BE HURT. ONLY TAYLOR. YOU HAVE TO GIVE ME YOUR WORD.
PLEASE, GOVERNOR CHADRON. I DON'T LIKE TO BE TOUCHED.
YOUR WORD, MONSIEUR.
OR THIS GOES NO FURTHER.
VERY WELL.
MY WORD IS NOW.
IF YOU PLEASE.
KLUD
NUUUH!
AS WITH BIRTH, SO WITH DEATH.
LET'S MAKE THIS QUICK AND BLOODY, GENTLEMEN.

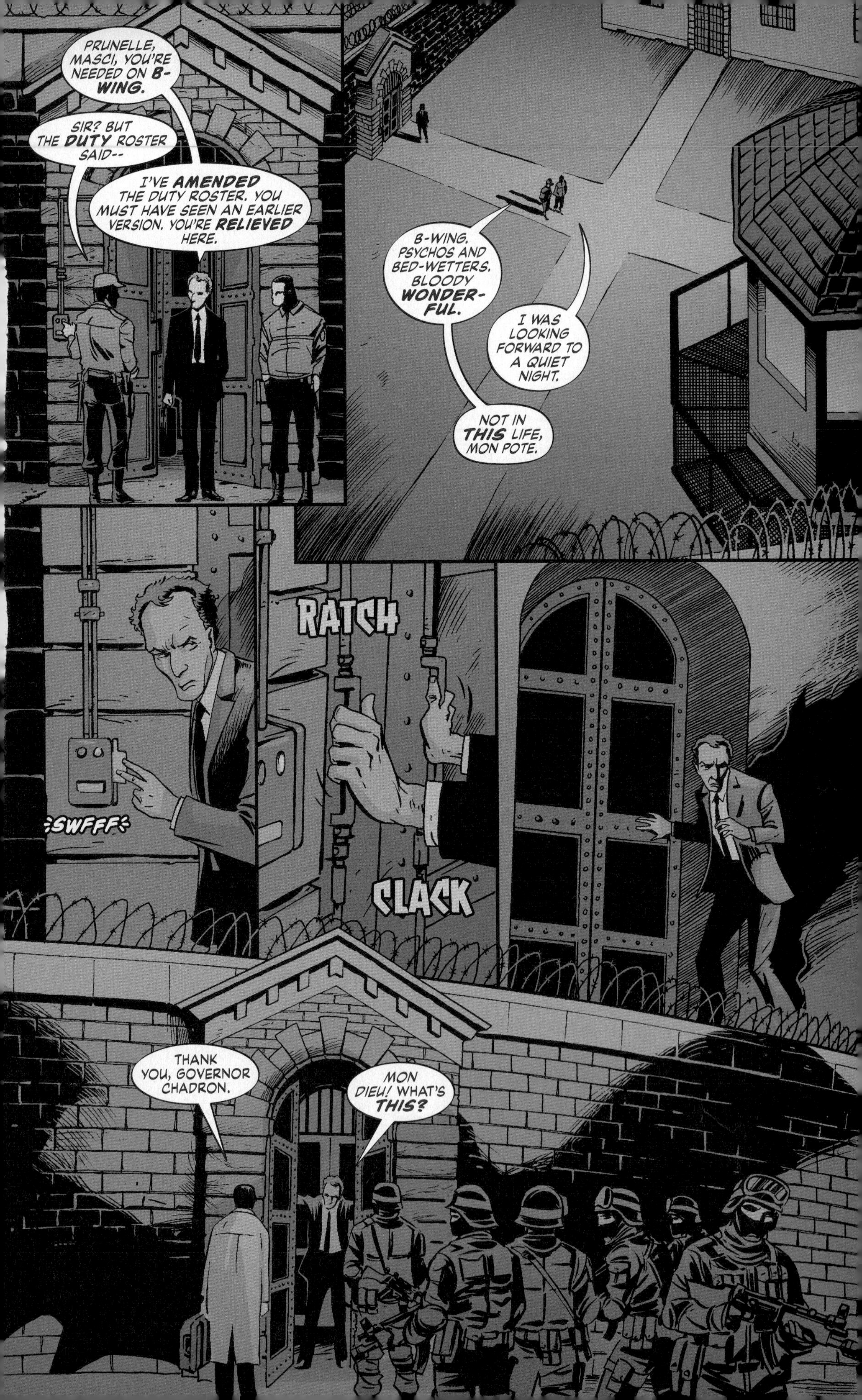
PRUNELLE, MASCI, YOU'RE NEEDED ON B-WING.
SIR? BUT THE DUTY ROSTER SAID--
I'VE AMENDED THE DUTY ROSTER. YOU MUST HAVE SEEN AN EARLIER VERSION. YOU'RE RELIEVED HERE.
B-WING. PSYCHOS AND BED-WETTERS. BLOODY WONDER-FUL.
I WAS LOOKING FORWARD TO A QUIET NIGHT.
NOT IN THIS LIFE, MON POTE.
SWFFF
RATCH
CLACK
THANK YOU, GOVERNOR CHADRON.
MON DIEU! WHAT'S THIS?

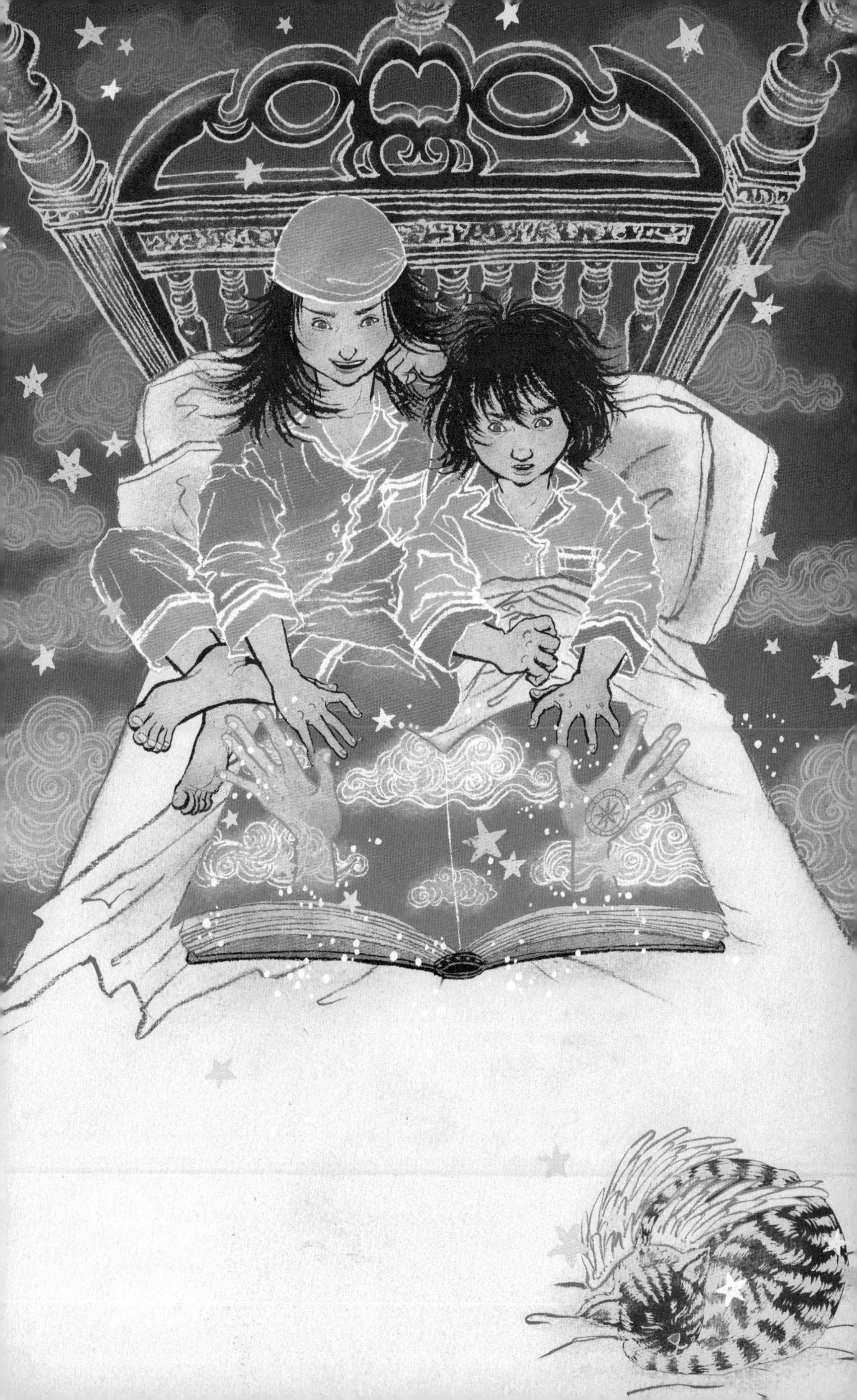

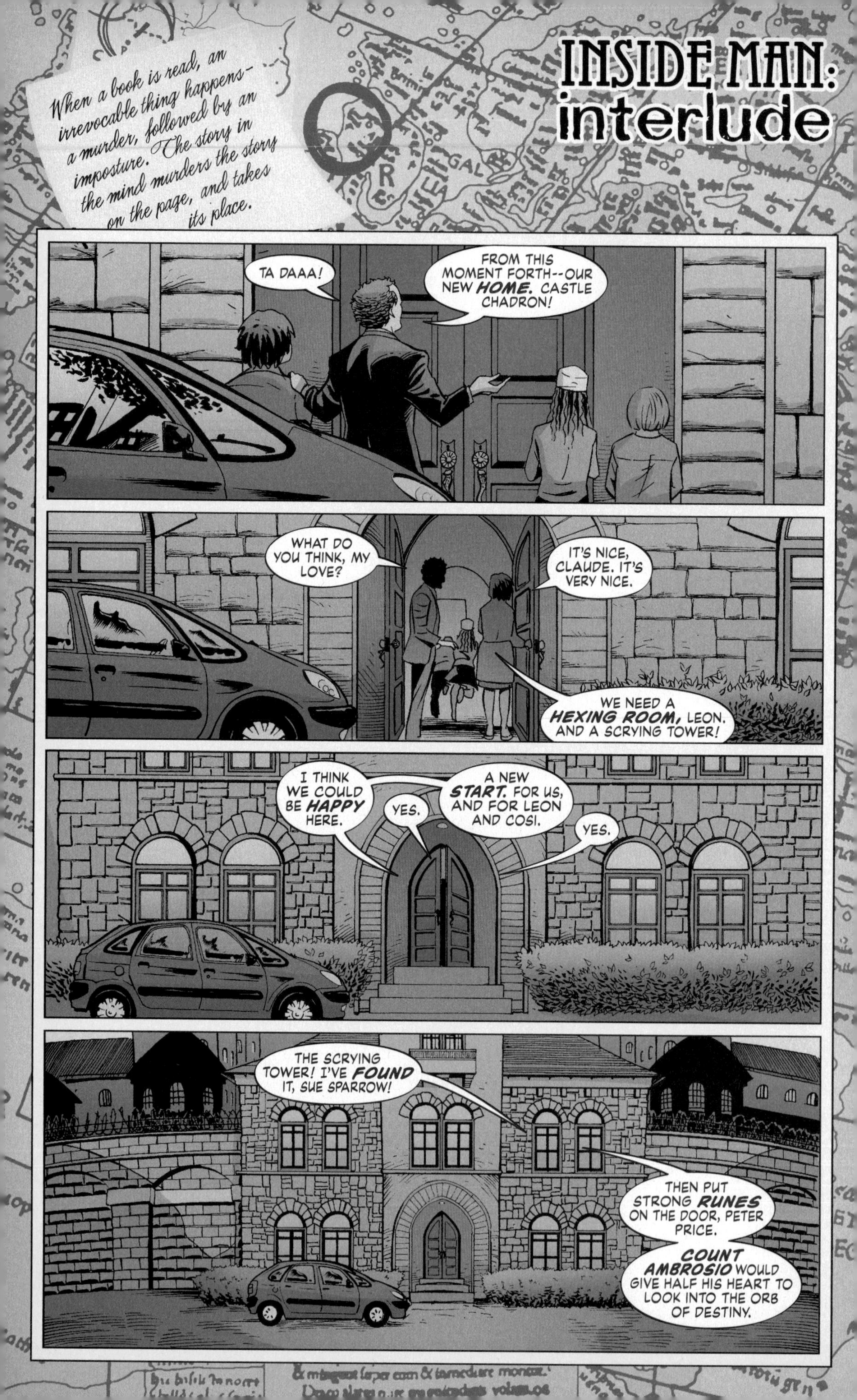
INSIDE MAN: interlude
When a book is read, an irrevocable thing happens– a murder, followed by an imposture. The story in the mind murders the story on the page, and takes its place.
TA DAAA!
FROM THIS MOMENT FORTH--OUR NEW HOME. CASTLE CHADRON!
WHAT DO YOU THINK, MY LOVE?
IT'S NICE, CLAUDE. IT'S VERY NICE.
WE NEED A HEXING ROOM, LEON. AND A SCRYING TOWER!
I THINK WE COULD BE HAPPY HERE.
YES.
A NEW START. FOR US, AND FOR LEON AND COSI.
YES.
THE SCRYING TOWER! I'VE FOUND IT, SUE SPARROW!
THEN PUT STRONG RUNES ON THE DOOR, PETER PRICE.
COUNT AMBROSIO WOULD GIVE HALF HIS HEART TO LOOK INTO THE ORB OF DESTINY.

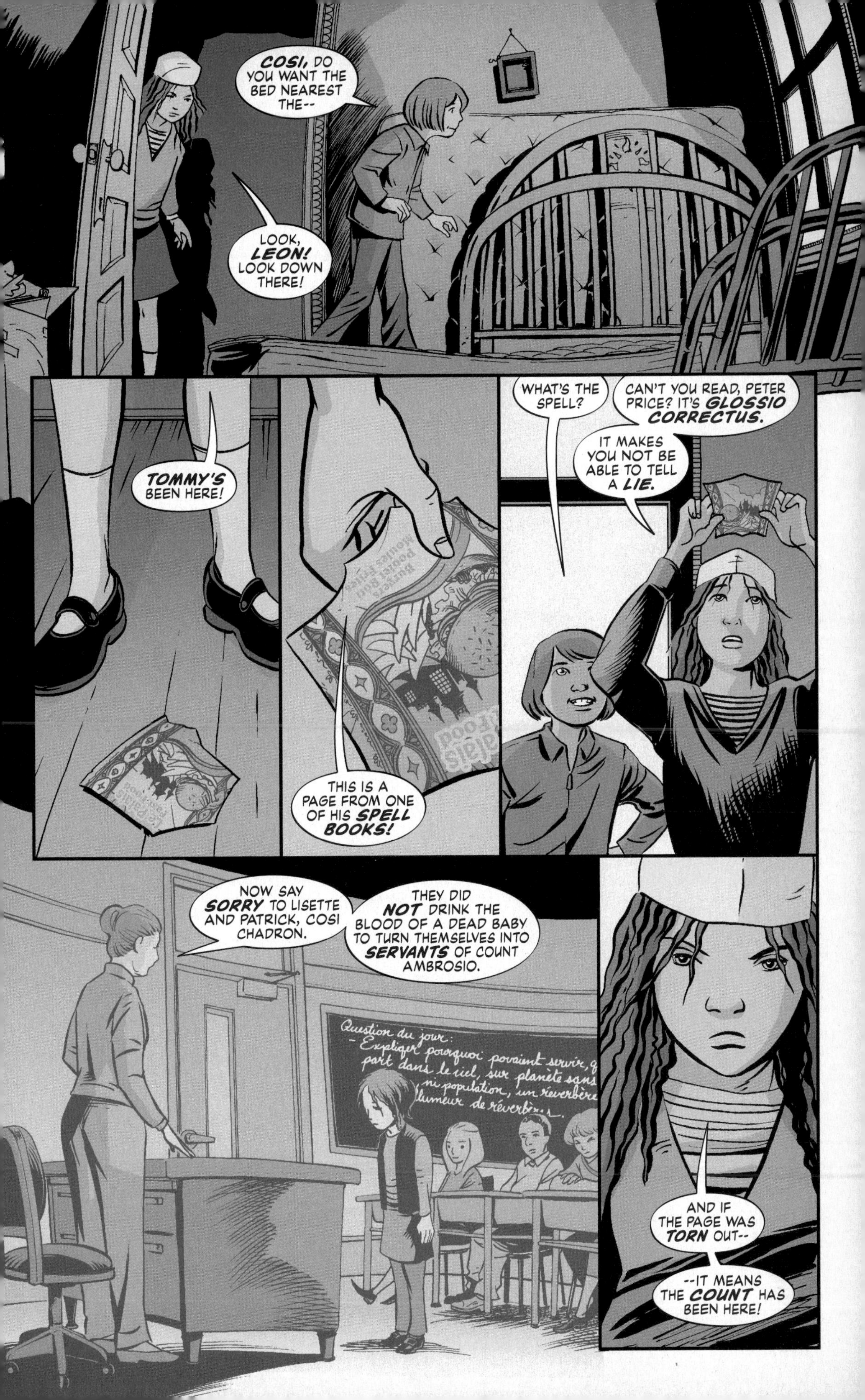
COSI, DO YOU WANT THE BED NEAREST THE--
LOOK, LEON! LOOK DOWN THERE!
TOMMY'S BEEN HERE!
THIS IS A PAGE FROM ONE OF HIS SPELL BOOKS!
WHAT'S THE SPELL?
CAN'T YOU READ, PETER PRICE? IT'S GLOSSIO CORRECTUS.
IT MAKES YOU NOT BE ABLE TO TELL A LIE.
NOW SAY SORRY TO LISETTE AND PATRICK, COSI CHADRON.
THEY DID NOT DRINK THE BLOOD OF A DEAD BABY TO TURN THEMSELVES INTO SERVANTS OF COUNT AMBROSIO.
Question du jour:
AND IF THE PAGE WAS TORN OUT--
--IT MEANS THE COUNT HAS BEEN HERE!

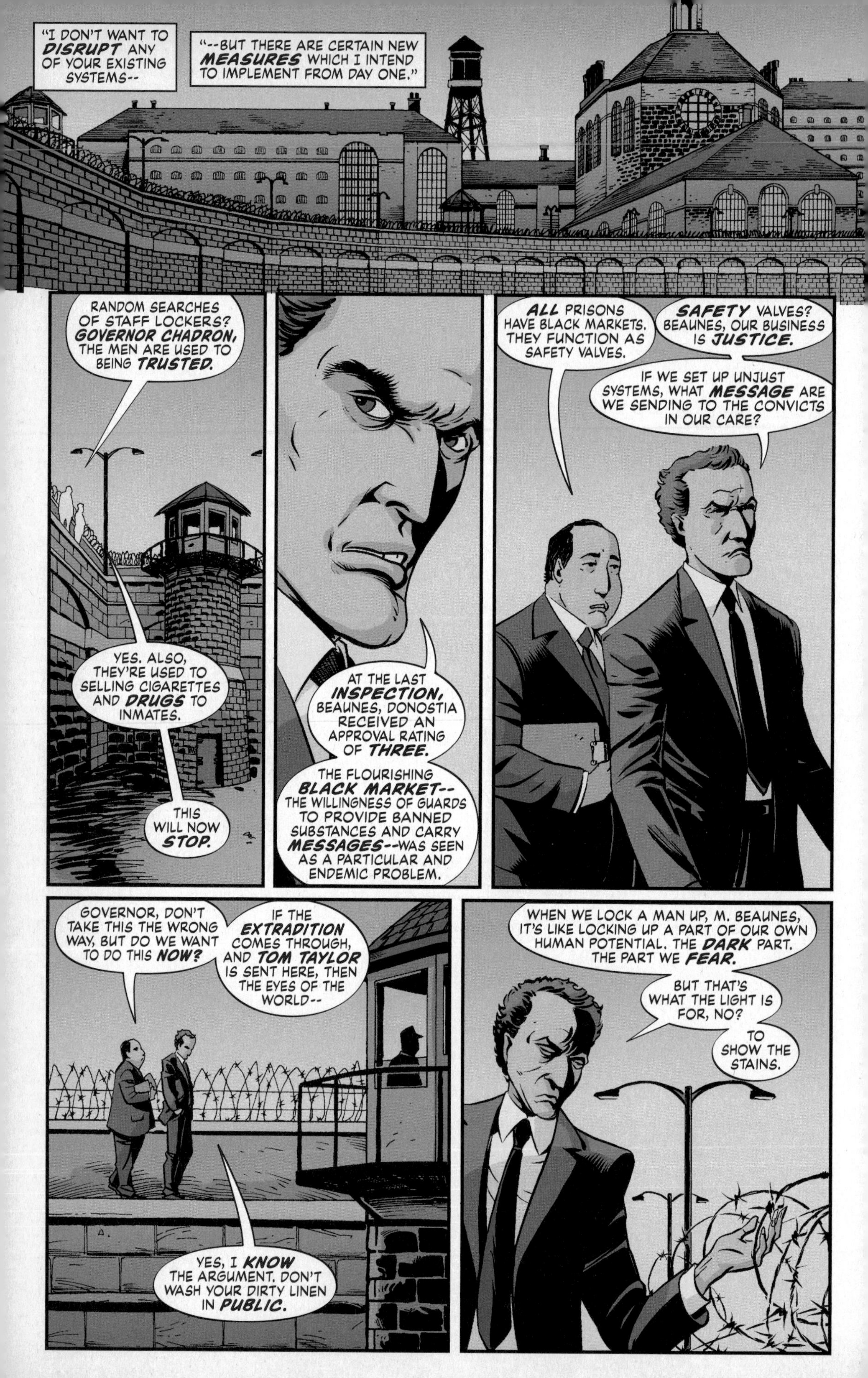
"I DON'T WANT TO DISRUPT ANY OF YOUR EXISTING SYSTEMS--
"--BUT THERE ARE CERTAIN NEW MEASURES WHICH I INTEND TO IMPLEMENT FROM DAY ONE."
RANDOM SEARCHES OF STAFF LOCKERS? GOVERNOR CHADRON, THE MEN ARE USED TO BEING TRUSTED.
YES. ALSO, THEY'RE USED TO SELLING CIGARETTES AND DRUGS TO INMATES.
THIS WILL NOW STOP.
AT THE LAST INSPECTION, BEAUNES, DONOSTIA RECEIVED AN APPROVAL RATING OF THREE.
THE FLOURISHING BLACK MARKET-- THE WILLINGNESS OF GUARDS TO PROVIDE BANNED SUBSTANCES AND CARRY MESSAGES--WAS SEEN AS A PARTICULAR AND ENDEMIC PROBLEM.
ALL PRISONS HAVE BLACK MARKETS. THEY FUNCTION AS SAFETY VALVES.
SAFETY VALVES? BEAUNES, OUR BUSINESS IS JUSTICE.
IF WE SET UP UNJUST SYSTEMS, WHAT MESSAGE ARE WE SENDING TO THE CONVICTS IN OUR CARE?
GOVERNOR, DON'T TAKE THIS THE WRONG WAY, BUT DO WE WANT TO DO THIS NOW?
IF THE EXTRADITION COMES THROUGH, AND TOM TAYLOR IS SENT HERE, THEN THE EYES OF THE WORLD--
YES, I KNOW THE ARGUMENT. DON'T WASH YOUR DIRTY LINEN IN PUBLIC.
WHEN WE LOCK A MAN UP, M. BEAUNES, IT'S LIKE LOCKING UP A PART OF OUR OWN HUMAN POTENTIAL. THE DARK PART. THE PART WE FEAR.
BUT THAT'S WHAT THE LIGHT IS FOR, NO?
TO SHOW THE STAINS.

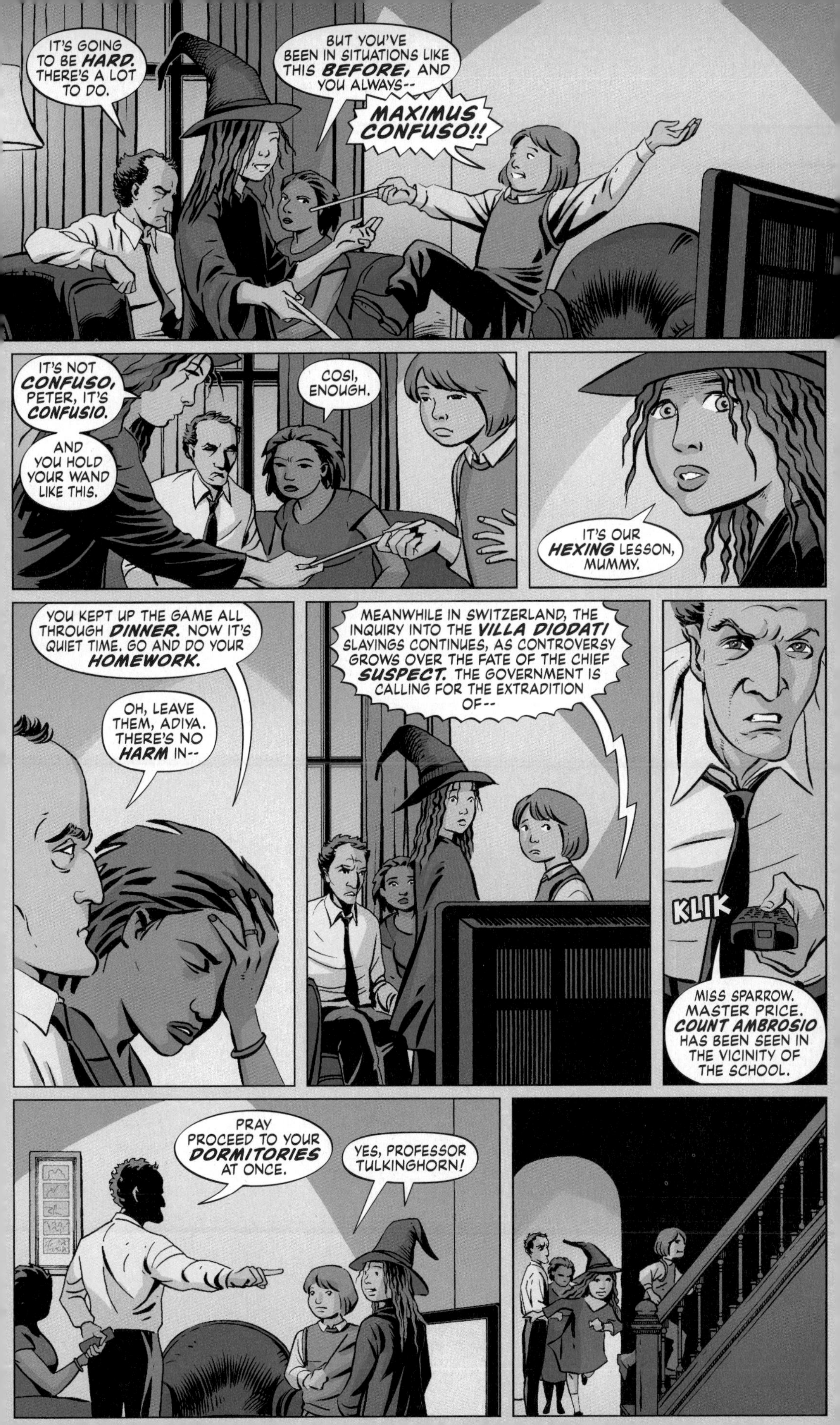
IT'S GOING TO BE HARD. THERE'S A LOT TO DO.
BUT YOU'VE BEEN IN SITUATIONS LIKE THIS BEFORE, AND YOU ALWAYS--
MAXIMUS CONFUSO!!
IT'S NOT CONFUSO, PETER, IT'S CONFUSIO.
AND YOU HOLD YOUR WAND LIKE THIS.
COSI, ENOUGH.
IT'S OUR HEXING LESSON, MUMMY.
YOU KEPT UP THE GAME ALL THROUGH DINNER. NOW IT'S QUIET TIME. GO AND DO YOUR HOMEWORK.
OH, LEAVE THEM, ADIYA. THERE'S NO HARM IN--
MEANWHILE IN SWITZERLAND, THE INQUIRY INTO THE VILLA DIODATI SLAYINGS CONTINUES, AS CONTROVERSY GROWS OVER THE FATE OF THE CHIEF SUSPECT. THE GOVERNMENT IS CALLING FOR THE EXTRADITION OF--
KLIK
MISS SPARROW. MASTER PRICE. COUNT AMBROSIO HAS BEEN SEEN IN THE VICINITY OF THE SCHOOL.
PRAY PROCEED TO YOUR DORMITORIES AT ONCE.
YES, PROFESSOR TULKINGHORN!

...--INVESTIGATING OFFICERS HAVE AS YET COME FORWARD WITH NO EXPLANATION AS TO WHY TOM TAYLOR SHOULD HAVE EMBARKED ON THIS MURDER SPREE. THE VICTIMS APPEAR TO HAVE BEEN STRANGERS, BOTH TO HIM AND TO EACH OTHER.

IS IT TRUE? IS HE COMING TO *DONOSTIA?* YOUR SECRETARY, MME GILBERT, SAID--

YES. IT'S TRUE.

HE'LL ARRIVE ON *MONDAY.*

I'LL TREAT HIM THE SAME AS *ANYONE,* OF COURSE.

I'D INFINITELY PREFER NOT TO SULLY MY *HANDS* WITH HIM, BUT I'LL DO MY JOB.

HE'S ONLY ON *REMAND,* CLAUDE. THERE'S BEEN NO TRIAL.

OF COURSE. AND SOME CLEVER LAWYER COULD GET HIM OFF ON A DIMINISHED *CAPACITY* PLEA.

BUT THE EVIDENCE--HIS FINGERPRINTS, THE CALL TO THE POLICE--ADMITS NO DOUBT.

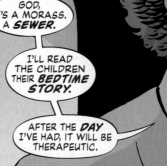

GOD, IT'S A MORASS. A *SEWER.*

I'LL READ THE CHILDREN THEIR *BEDTIME STORY.*

AFTER THE *DAY* I'VE HAD, IT WILL BE THERAPEUTIC.

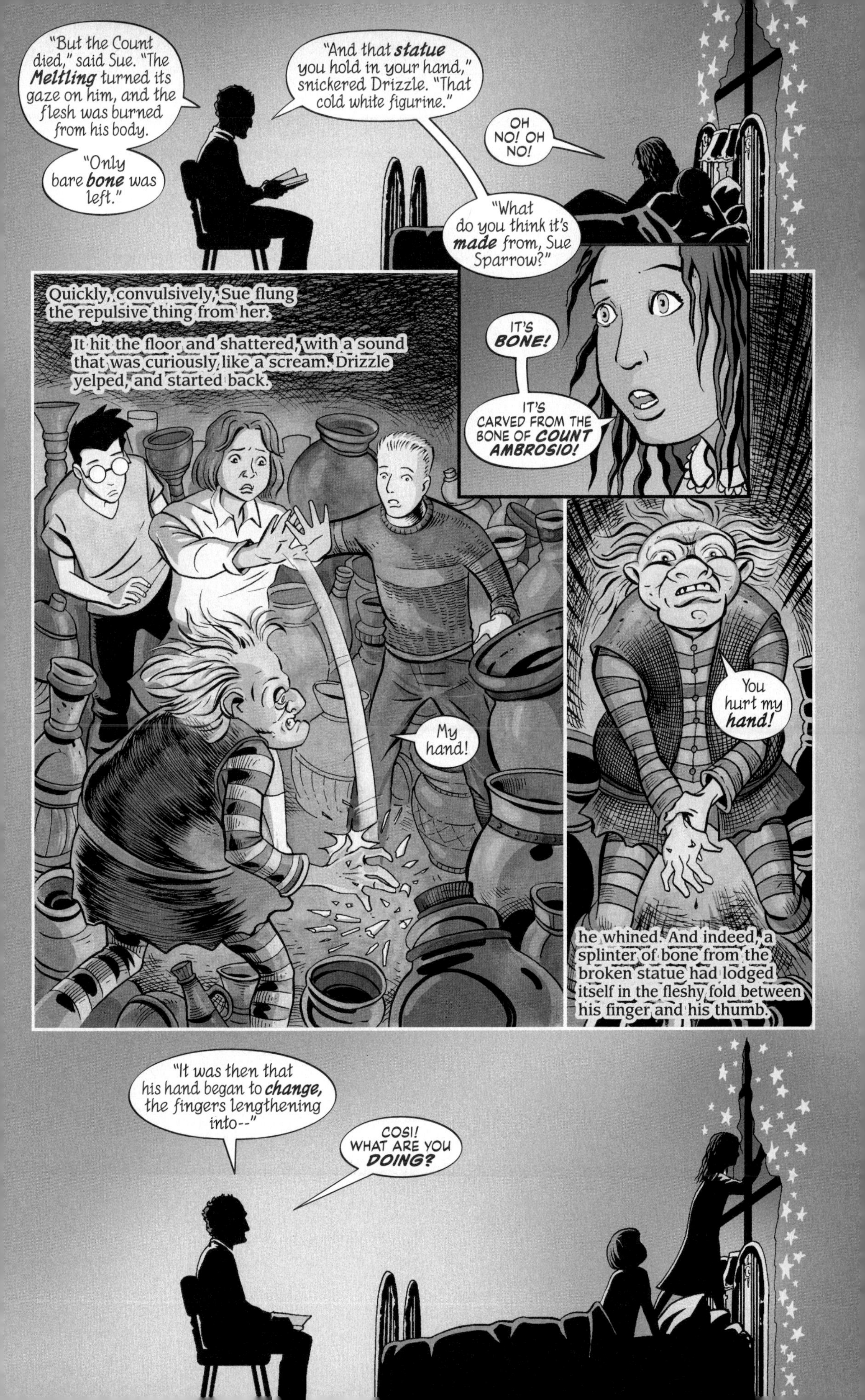
"But the Count died," said Sue. "The Meltling turned its gaze on him, and the flesh was burned from his body.
"Only bare bone was left."
"And that statue you hold in your hand," snickered Drizzle. "That cold white figurine."
OH NO! OH NO!
"What do you think it's made from, Sue Sparrow?"
IT'S BONE!
IT'S CARVED FROM THE BONE OF COUNT AMBROSIO!
Quickly, convulsively, Sue flung the repulsive thing from her.
It hit the floor and shattered, with a sound that was curiously like a scream. Drizzle yelped, and started back.
My hand!
You hurt my hand!
he whined. And indeed, a splinter of bone from the broken statue had lodged itself in the fleshy fold between his finger and his thumb.
"It was then that his hand began to change, the fingers lengthening into--"
COSI! WHAT ARE YOU DOING?

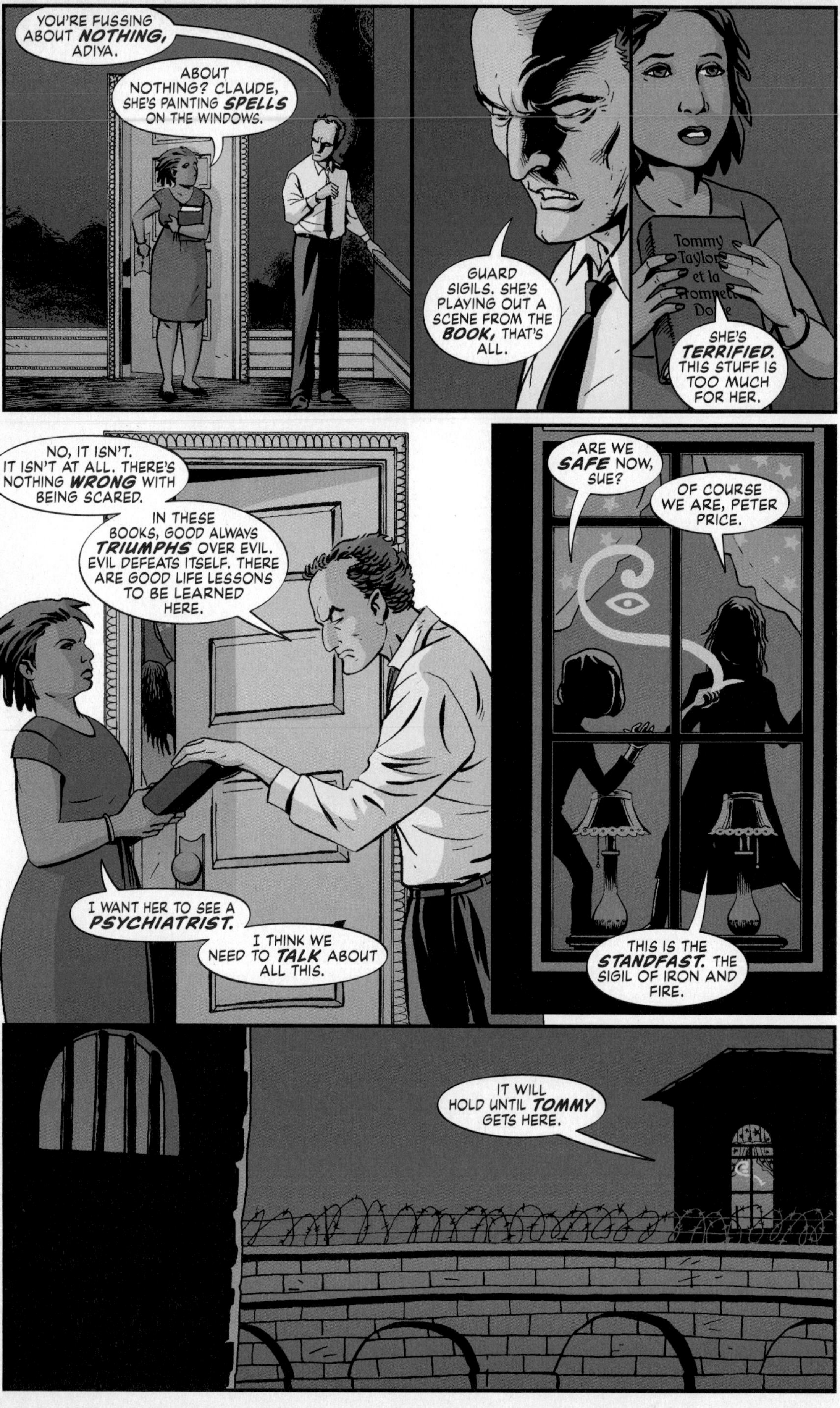
YOU'RE FUSSING ABOUT NOTHING, ADIYA.
ABOUT NOTHING? CLAUDE, SHE'S PAINTING SPELLS ON THE WINDOWS.
GUARD SIGILS. SHE'S PLAYING OUT A SCENE FROM THE BOOK, THAT'S ALL.
Tommy Taylor et la Trompette Dorée
SHE'S TERRIFIED. THIS STUFF IS TOO MUCH FOR HER.
NO, IT ISN'T. IT ISN'T AT ALL. THERE'S NOTHING WRONG WITH BEING SCARED.
IN THESE BOOKS, GOOD ALWAYS TRIUMPHS OVER EVIL. EVIL DEFEATS ITSELF. THERE ARE GOOD LIFE LESSONS TO BE LEARNED HERE.
I WANT HER TO SEE A PSYCHIATRIST.
I THINK WE NEED TO TALK ABOUT ALL THIS.
ARE WE SAFE NOW, SUE?
OF COURSE WE ARE, PETER PRICE.
THIS IS THE STANDFAST. THE SIGIL OF IRON AND FIRE.
IT WILL HOLD UNTIL TOMMY GETS HERE.

Iran Defies Nuclear Ban... | Toxic Waste Kills 400 Afer Record Spill... | Stem Cell Disaster: Who is Blame...
BIG NEWS: Tom Taylor accomplice... | BW Sues Start-up Publi... | New Tea Discovered in A... | FEED HISTORY

The POSTnation

When all else fails, read everything.

HOME | BREAKING NEWS | POLITICS | BUSINESS | WORLD | MEDIA | TECHNOLOGY | ENTERTAINMENT
ARTS | LIVING | STYLE | VIDEO | BLOGS | LINKS

When a Book Becomes a Disease:
Dr. Pauline Swann and Tommy Taylor

filed by: Barb. G. Celaeno

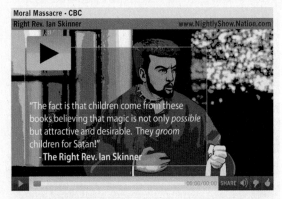

Moral Massacre - CBC
Right Rev. Ian Skinner
www.NightlyShow.Nation.com
"The fact is that children come from these books believing that magic is not only *possible* but attractive and desirable. They *groom* children for Satan!"
- The Right Rev. Ian Skinner
00:00/00:00
SHARE

Moral Massacre - CBC
Lewis Hale, anthropologist
www.NightlyShow.Nation.com
"Most audiences, for most of human history, haven't *distinguished* between stories and spells. To describe something in words was to summon it, or bind it, or call on its *power*."
- Lewis Hale
00:00/00:00
SHARE

Watch all your favorite late-night shows at NightlyShow.Nation

On CBC's Moral Massacre debate show, broadcast last night at 9.00pm EST, Dr. Pauline Swann astonished the studio audience and her fellow guests by asserting that Tommy Taylor now constitutes a nationwide – perhaps a global – mental health problem.

Dr. Swann, a noted psychotherapist, has already published three books discussing the links between modern culture and mental health. Now, in *The Poisoned Well*, she turns her theory of cultural bootstrapping on the biggest media target of all: the lovable boy wizard whose exploits have been read by more than a third of humanity.

"Karl Jung suggested that there's a collective human unconscious," Swann said. "An under-mind that feeds all our myths, all our deepest instincts. That's always been true. But in an age of mass culture, we can actually write to the under-mind. Our virally spreading fictions embed themselves in the collective unconscious of humanity and change it."

Swann's work remains controversial. Her most notorious case study – a drawing of Mickey Mouse by a blind autistic child in Peru – has been challenged as a possible fake.

Last night's debate, though, centered on the Tommy Taylor books, and the extent to which the actions of Tom Taylor, the real-life model for their fictional hero, have "poisoned the well" of children's imaginations. Reference was made to the blood-bath at the Villa Diodati, which occurred after the publication of Swann's book but seems to provide striking support for her thesis.

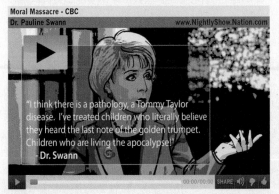

Watch complete episode at NightlyShow.Nation

Moral Massacre - CBC
Dr. Pauline Swann
www.NightlyShow.Nation.com
"I think there is a pathology, a Tommy Taylor disease. I've treated children who literally believe they heard the last note of the golden trumpet. Children who are living the apocalypse!"
- Dr. Swann
00:00/00:00
SHARE

Moral Massacre - CBC
Maria Korglas, author
www.NightlyShow.Nation.com
"Children will 'literally believe' anything while the book is in their hands. That's the derivation of the word 'literally.' That's what literature is for. *Incarnation*."
- Maria Korglas
00:00/00:00
SHARE

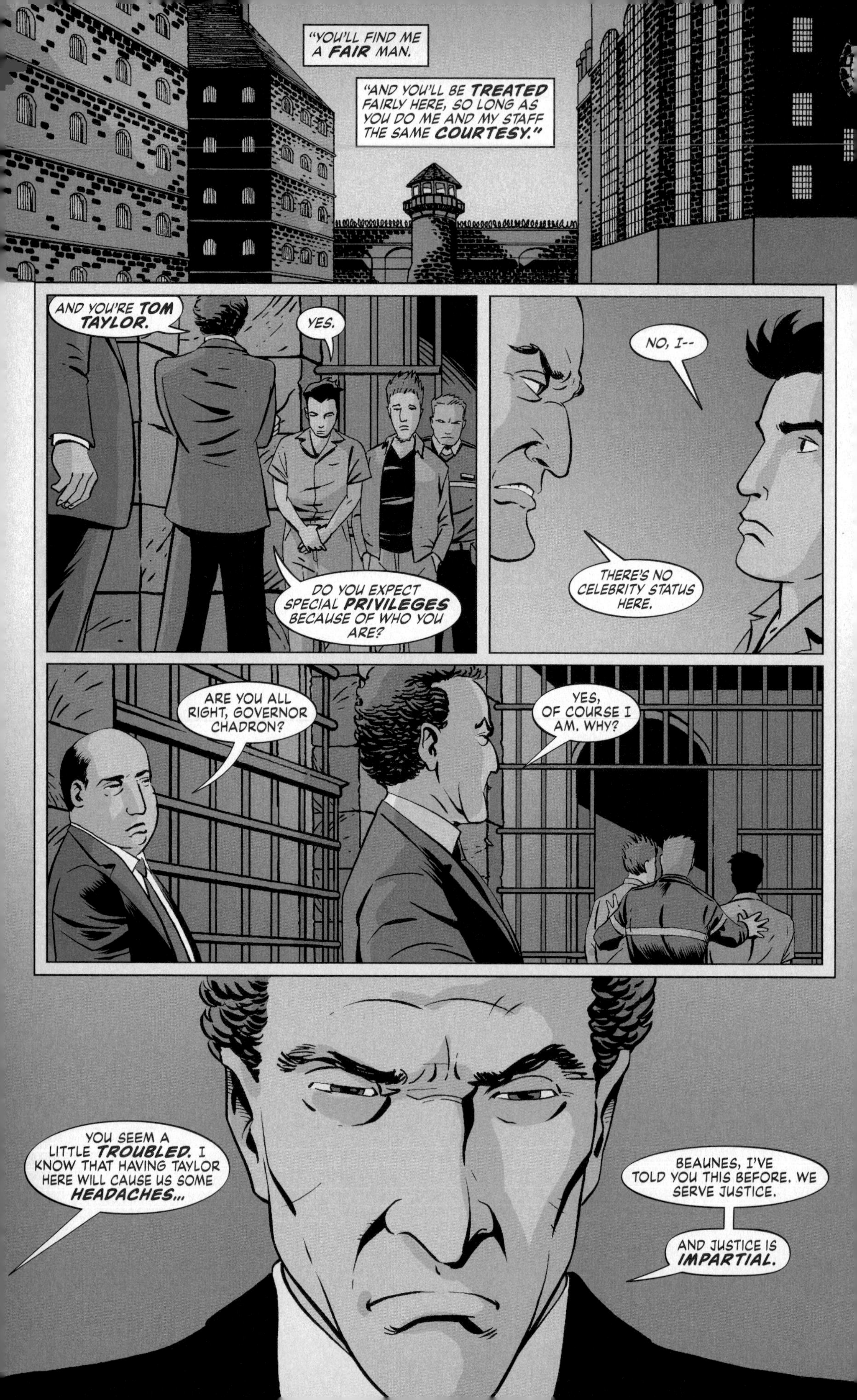
"YOU'LL FIND ME A FAIR MAN.
"AND YOU'LL BE TREATED FAIRLY HERE, SO LONG AS YOU DO ME AND MY STAFF THE SAME COURTESY."
AND YOU'RE TOM TAYLOR.
YES.
DO YOU EXPECT SPECIAL PRIVILEGES BECAUSE OF WHO YOU ARE?
NO, I--
THERE'S NO CELEBRITY STATUS HERE.
ARE YOU ALL RIGHT, GOVERNOR CHADRON?
YES, OF COURSE I AM. WHY?
YOU SEEM A LITTLE TROUBLED. I KNOW THAT HAVING TAYLOR HERE WILL CAUSE US SOME HEADACHES...
BEAUNES, I'VE TOLD YOU THIS BEFORE. WE SERVE JUSTICE.
AND JUSTICE IS IMPARTIAL.

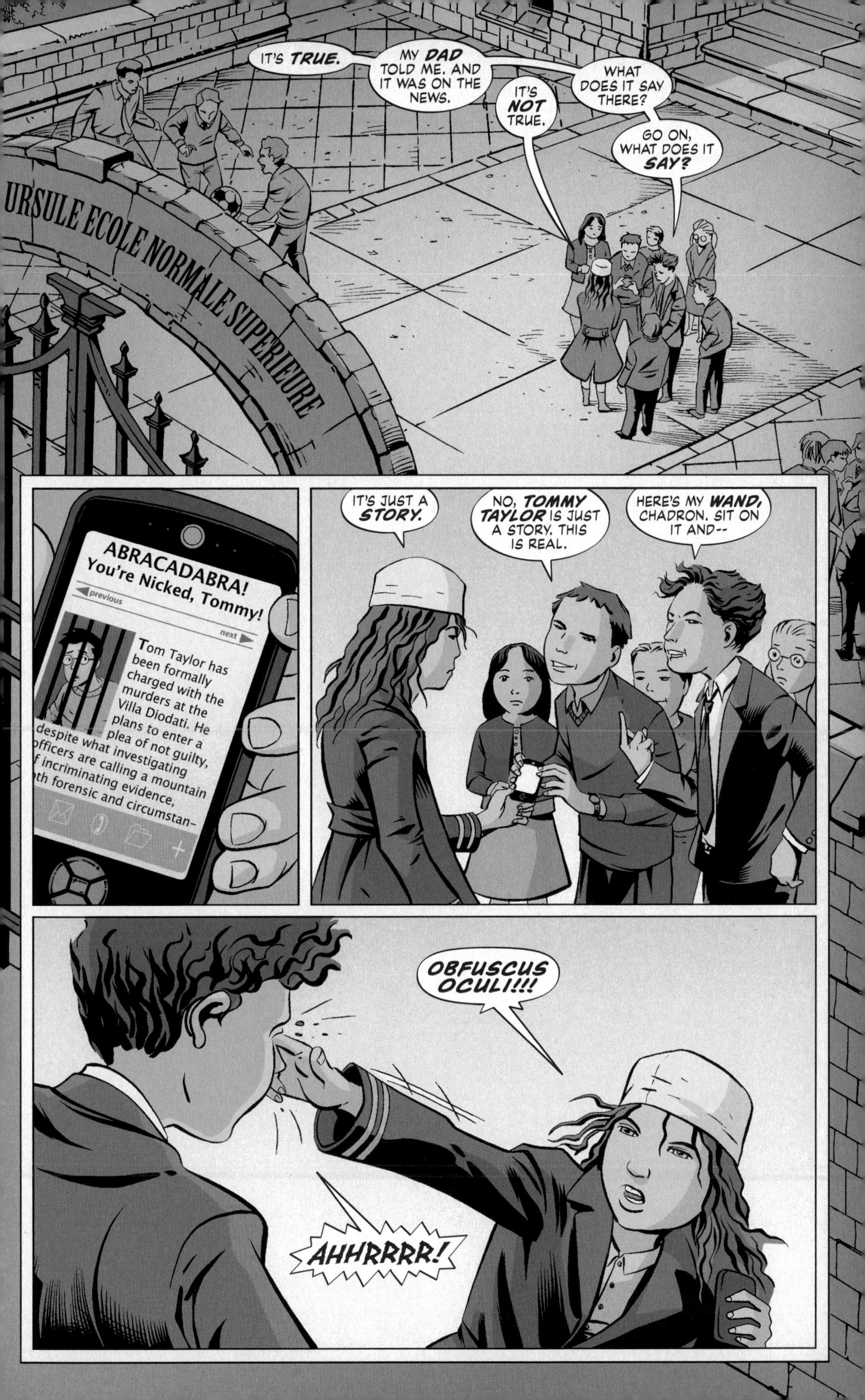
IT'S TRUE.
MY DAD TOLD ME. AND IT WAS ON THE NEWS.
IT'S NOT TRUE.
WHAT DOES IT SAY THERE?
GO ON, WHAT DOES IT SAY?
URSULE ECOLE NORMALE SUPERIEURE
ABRACADABRA! You're Nicked, Tommy!
previous
next
Tom Taylor has been formally charged with the murders at the Villa Diodati. He plans to enter a plea of not guilty, despite what investigating officers are calling a mountain of incriminating evidence, both forensic and circumstan-
IT'S JUST A STORY.
NO, TOMMY TAYLOR IS JUST A STORY. THIS IS REAL.
HERE'S MY WAND, CHADRON. SIT ON IT AND--
OBFUSCUS OCULI!!!
AHHRRRR!

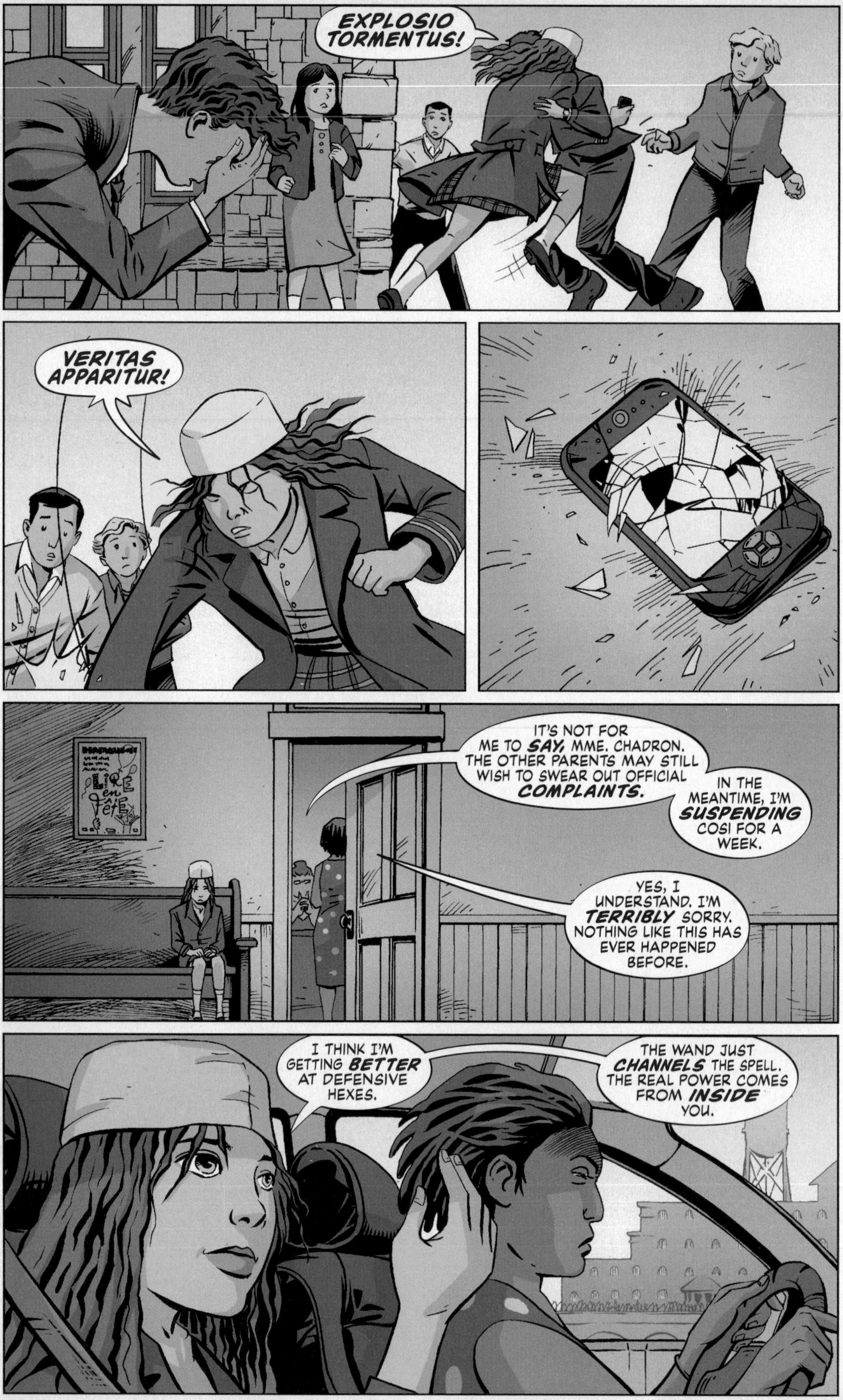
EXPLOSIO TORMENTUS!
VERITAS APPARITUR!
IT'S NOT FOR ME TO SAY, MME. CHADRON. THE OTHER PARENTS MAY STILL WISH TO SWEAR OUT OFFICIAL COMPLAINTS.
IN THE MEANTIME, I'M SUSPENDING COSI FOR A WEEK.
YES, I UNDERSTAND. I'M TERRIBLY SORRY. NOTHING LIKE THIS HAS EVER HAPPENED BEFORE.
I THINK I'M GETTING BETTER AT DEFENSIVE HEXES.
THE WAND JUST CHANNELS THE SPELL. THE REAL POWER COMES FROM INSIDE YOU.

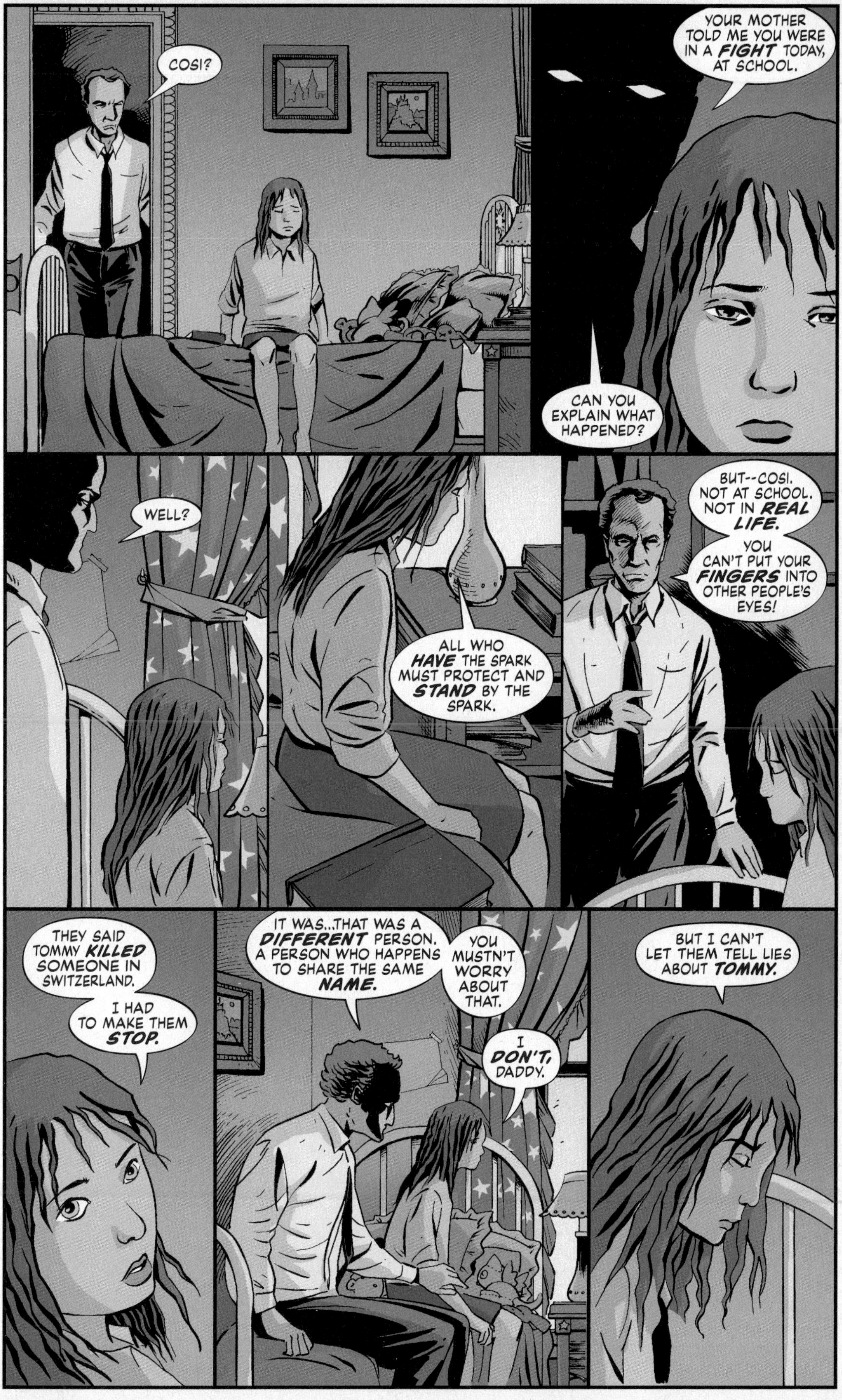
COSI?
YOUR MOTHER TOLD ME YOU WERE IN A FIGHT TODAY, AT SCHOOL.
CAN YOU EXPLAIN WHAT HAPPENED?
WELL?
ALL WHO HAVE THE SPARK MUST PROTECT AND STAND BY THE SPARK.
BUT--COSI. NOT AT SCHOOL. NOT IN REAL LIFE.
YOU CAN'T PUT YOUR FINGERS INTO OTHER PEOPLE'S EYES!
THEY SAID TOMMY KILLED SOMEONE IN SWITZERLAND.
I HAD TO MAKE THEM STOP.
IT WAS...THAT WAS A DIFFERENT PERSON. A PERSON WHO HAPPENS TO SHARE THE SAME NAME.
YOU MUSTN'T WORRY ABOUT THAT.
I DON'T, DADDY.
BUT I CAN'T LET THEM TELL LIES ABOUT TOMMY.

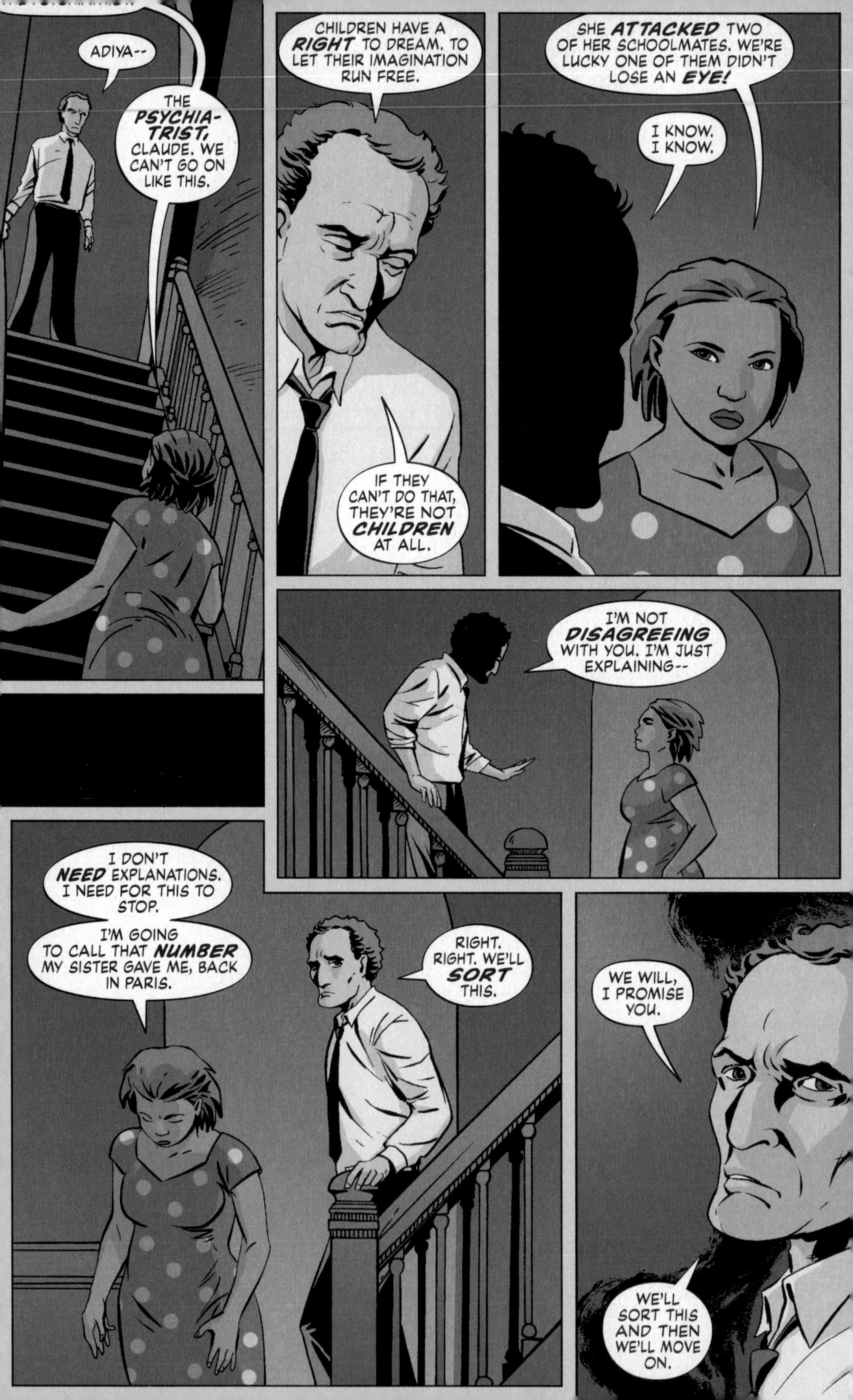
ADIYA--
THE PSYCHIATRIST, CLAUDE. WE CAN'T GO ON LIKE THIS.
CHILDREN HAVE A RIGHT TO DREAM. TO LET THEIR IMAGINATION RUN FREE.
IF THEY CAN'T DO THAT, THEY'RE NOT CHILDREN AT ALL.
SHE ATTACKED TWO OF HER SCHOOLMATES. WE'RE LUCKY ONE OF THEM DIDN'T LOSE AN EYE!
I KNOW. I KNOW.
I'M NOT DISAGREEING WITH YOU. I'M JUST EXPLAINING--
I DON'T NEED EXPLANATIONS. I NEED FOR THIS TO STOP.
I'M GOING TO CALL THAT NUMBER MY SISTER GAVE ME, BACK IN PARIS.
RIGHT. RIGHT. WE'LL SORT THIS.
WE WILL, I PROMISE YOU.
WE'LL SORT THIS AND THEN WE'LL MOVE ON.

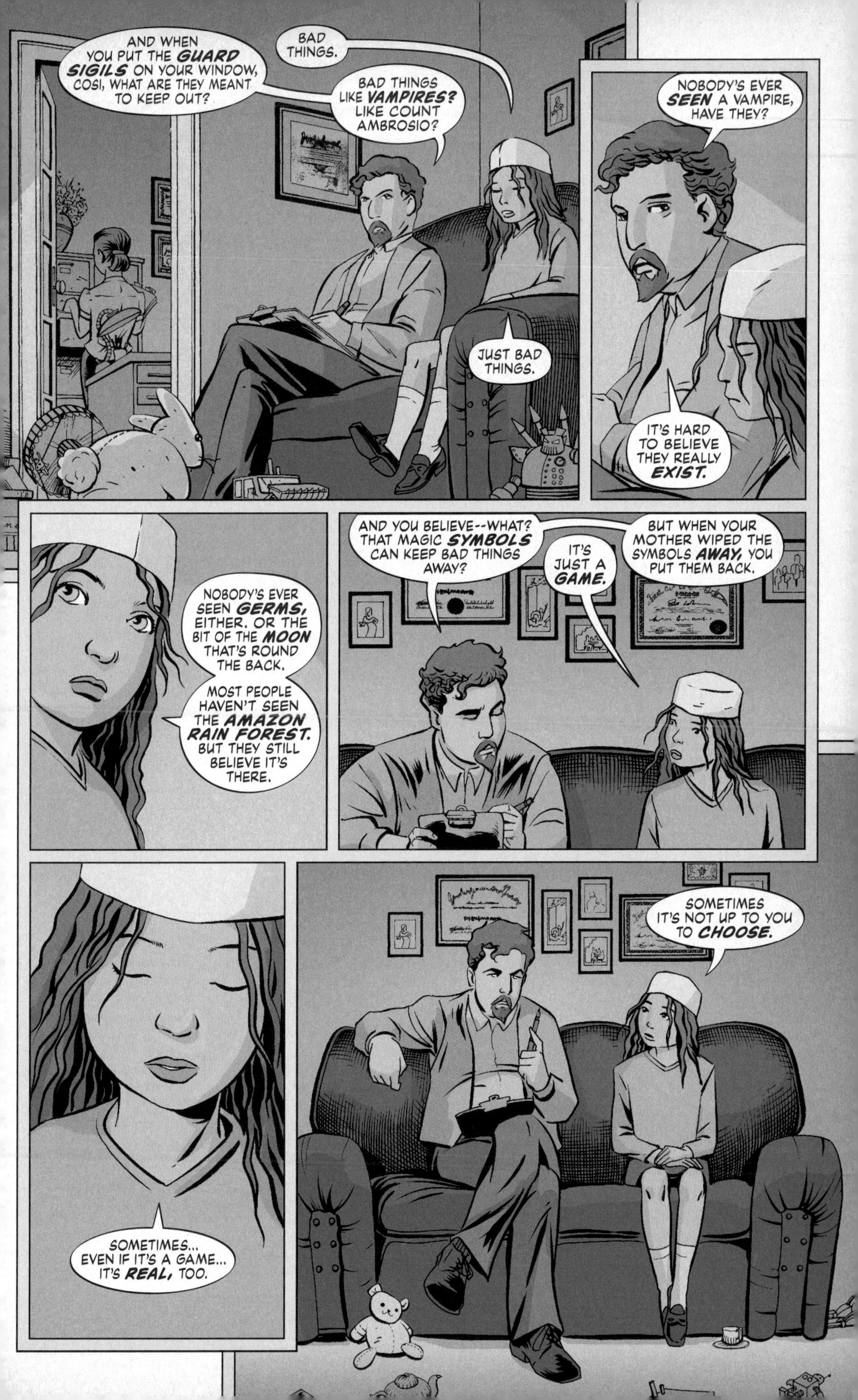
AND WHEN YOU PUT THE GUARD SIGILS ON YOUR WINDOW, COSI, WHAT ARE THEY MEANT TO KEEP OUT?
BAD THINGS.
BAD THINGS LIKE VAMPIRES? LIKE COUNT AMBROSIO?
JUST BAD THINGS.
NOBODY'S EVER SEEN A VAMPIRE, HAVE THEY?
IT'S HARD TO BELIEVE THEY REALLY EXIST.
NOBODY'S EVER SEEN GERMS, EITHER. OR THE BIT OF THE MOON THAT'S ROUND THE BACK.
MOST PEOPLE HAVEN'T SEEN THE AMAZON RAIN FOREST. BUT THEY STILL BELIEVE IT'S THERE.
AND YOU BELIEVE--WHAT? THAT MAGIC SYMBOLS CAN KEEP BAD THINGS AWAY?
IT'S JUST A GAME.
BUT WHEN YOUR MOTHER WIPED THE SYMBOLS AWAY, YOU PUT THEM BACK.
SOMETIMES... EVEN IF IT'S A GAME... IT'S REAL, TOO.
SOMETIMES IT'S NOT UP TO YOU TO CHOOSE.

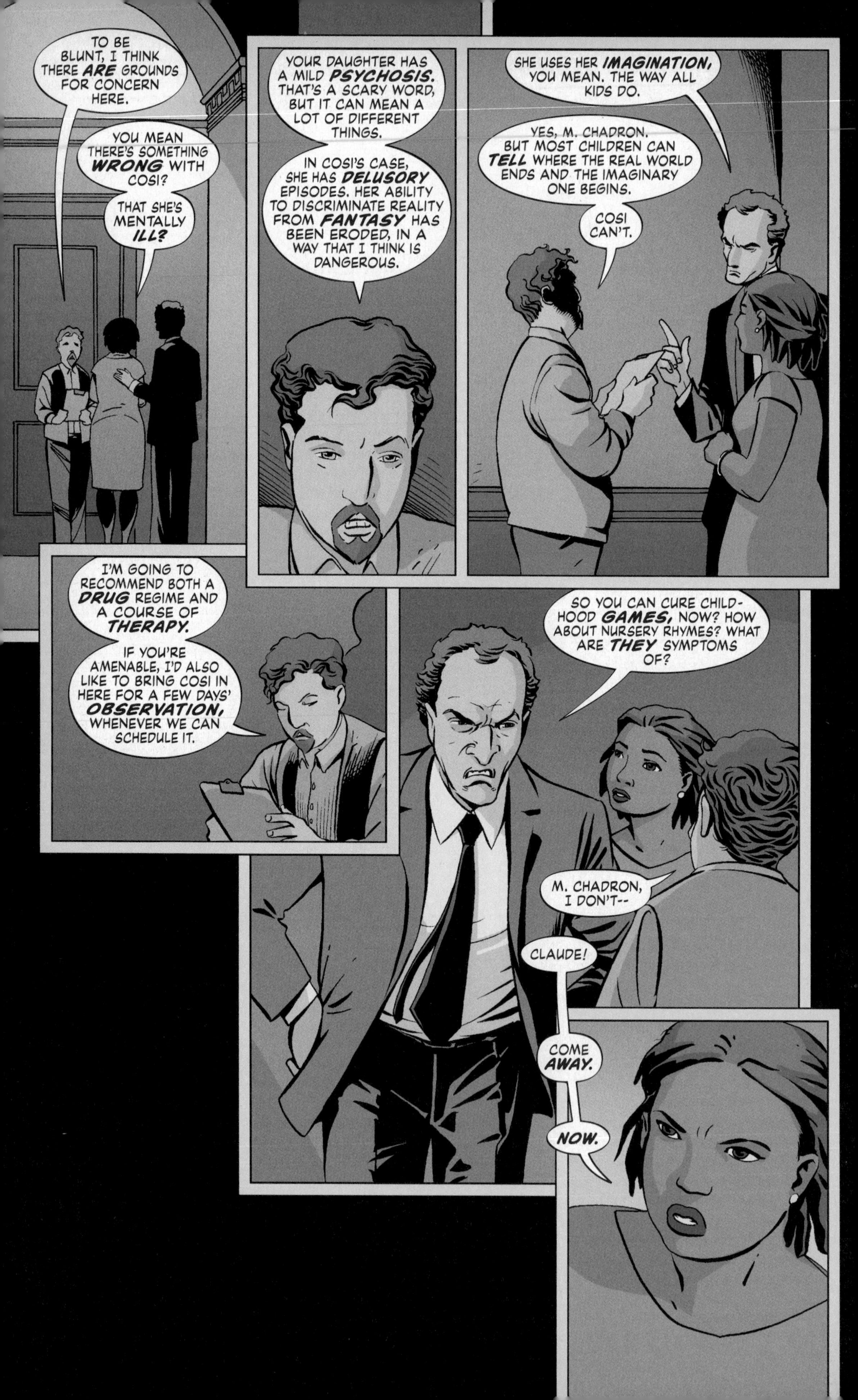
TO BE BLUNT, I THINK THERE ARE GROUNDS FOR CONCERN HERE.
YOU MEAN THERE'S SOMETHING WRONG WITH COSI?
THAT SHE'S MENTALLY ILL?
YOUR DAUGHTER HAS A MILD PSYCHOSIS. THAT'S A SCARY WORD, BUT IT CAN MEAN A LOT OF DIFFERENT THINGS.
IN COSI'S CASE, SHE HAS DELUSORY EPISODES. HER ABILITY TO DISCRIMINATE REALITY FROM FANTASY HAS BEEN ERODED, IN A WAY THAT I THINK IS DANGEROUS.
SHE USES HER IMAGINATION, YOU MEAN. THE WAY ALL KIDS DO.
YES, M. CHADRON. BUT MOST CHILDREN CAN TELL WHERE THE REAL WORLD ENDS AND THE IMAGINARY ONE BEGINS.
COSI CAN'T.
I'M GOING TO RECOMMEND BOTH A DRUG REGIME AND A COURSE OF THERAPY.
IF YOU'RE AMENABLE, I'D ALSO LIKE TO BRING COSI IN HERE FOR A FEW DAYS' OBSERVATION, WHENEVER WE CAN SCHEDULE IT.
SO YOU CAN CURE CHILDHOOD GAMES, NOW? HOW ABOUT NURSERY RHYMES? WHAT ARE THEY SYMPTOMS OF?
M. CHADRON, I DON'T--
CLAUDE!
COME AWAY.
NOW.

YOU DID THIS.

WHAT?

YOU *ENCOURAGE* HER, EVERY TIME. YOU PLAY ALONG. "I AM YOUR BELOVED *HEADMASTER!*"

YOU PUT THIS *GARBAGE* IN HER HEAD, AND NOW IT'S MADE HER SICK.

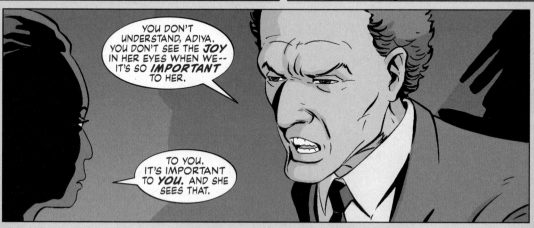

YOU DON'T UNDERSTAND, ADIYA. YOU DON'T SEE THE *JOY* IN HER EYES WHEN WE-- IT'S SO *IMPORTANT* TO HER.

TO YOU. IT'S IMPORTANT TO *YOU.* AND SHE SEES THAT.

AND NOW THAT TAYLOR BOY IS IN YOUR PRISON, CHARGED WITH TERRIBLE CRIMES.

I'LL *DEAL* WITH THAT.

OF COURSE YOU WILL, CLAUDE. IT'S IN YOUR *JOB* DESCRIPTION.

BUT IT'S NOT IN *HERS.*

SHE'S ONLY IN THIS STATE BECAUSE OF YOU.

I--I THINK PERHAPS I'LL *WALK* BACK. I NEED--

I NEED TO *THINK.*

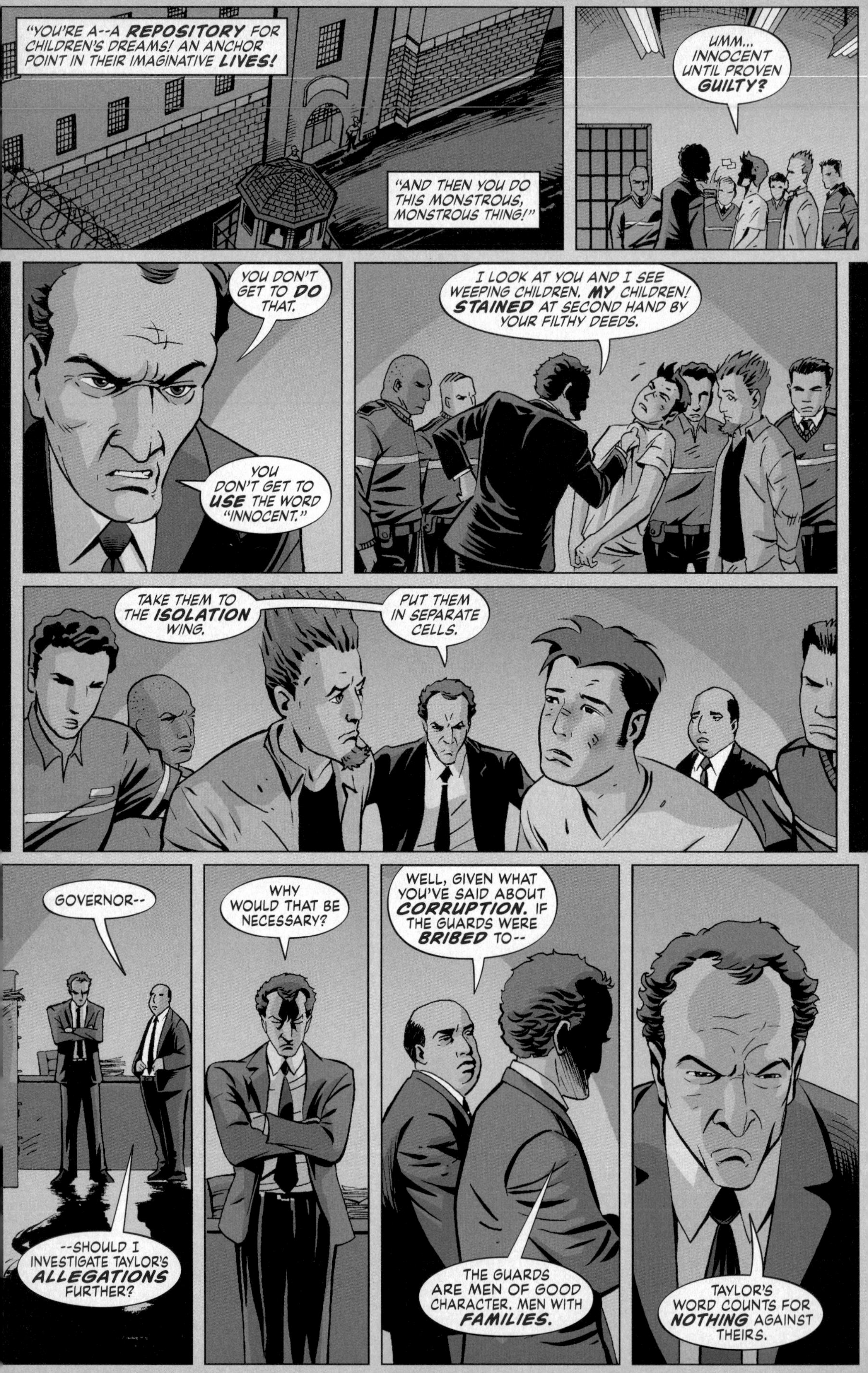
"YOU'RE A--A REPOSITORY FOR CHILDREN'S DREAMS! AN ANCHOR POINT IN THEIR IMAGINATIVE LIVES!
"AND THEN YOU DO THIS MONSTROUS, MONSTROUS THING!"
UMM... INNOCENT UNTIL PROVEN GUILTY?
YOU DON'T GET TO DO THAT.
YOU DON'T GET TO USE THE WORD "INNOCENT."
I LOOK AT YOU AND I SEE WEEPING CHILDREN. MY CHILDREN! STAINED AT SECOND HAND BY YOUR FILTHY DEEDS.
TAKE THEM TO THE ISOLATION WING.
PUT THEM IN SEPARATE CELLS.
GOVERNOR--
--SHOULD I INVESTIGATE TAYLOR'S ALLEGATIONS FURTHER?
WHY WOULD THAT BE NECESSARY?
WELL, GIVEN WHAT YOU'VE SAID ABOUT CORRUPTION. IF THE GUARDS WERE BRIBED TO--
THE GUARDS ARE MEN OF GOOD CHARACTER. MEN WITH FAMILIES.
TAYLOR'S WORD COUNTS FOR NOTHING AGAINST THEIRS.

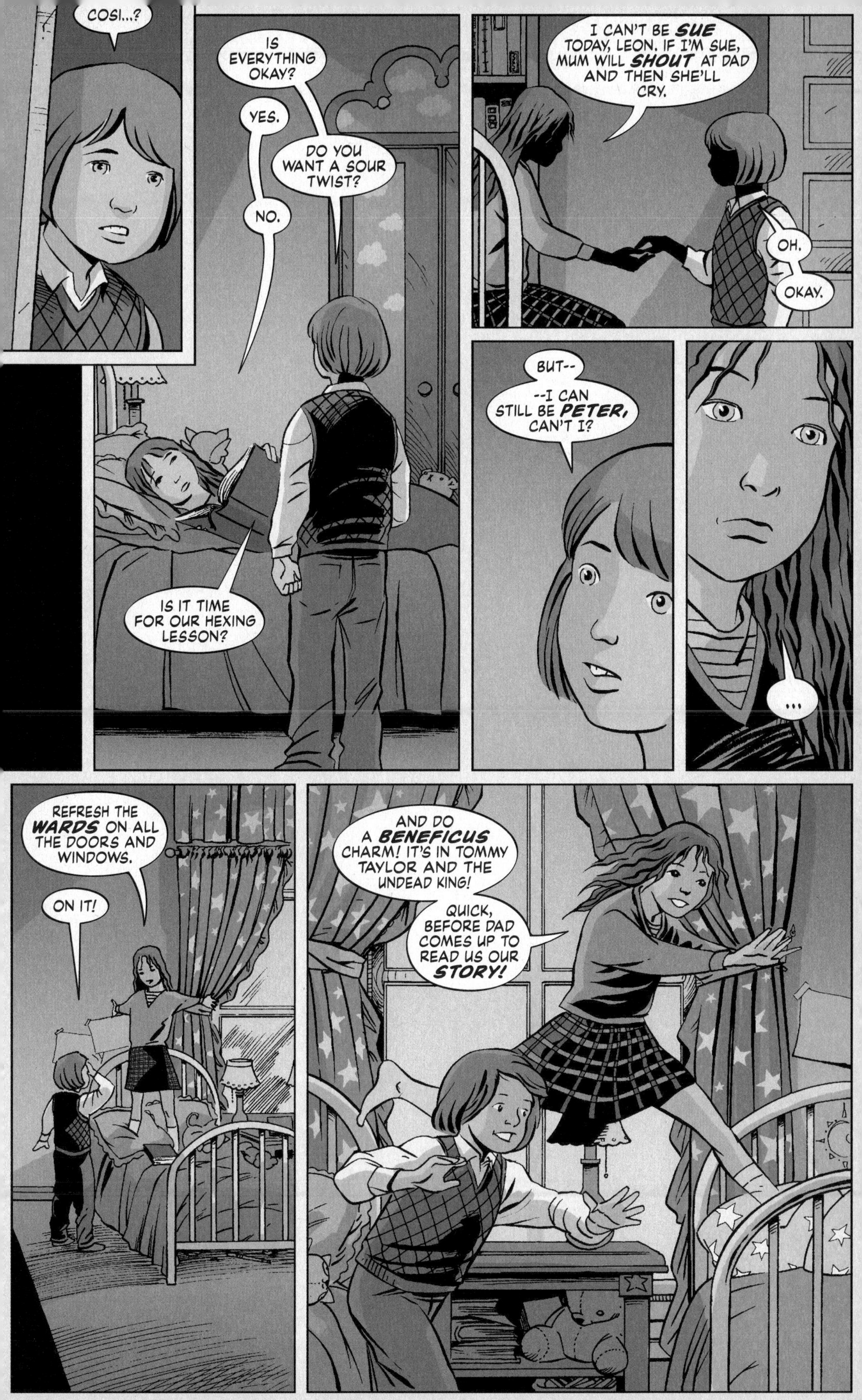
COSI...?
IS EVERYTHING OKAY?
YES.
DO YOU WANT A SOUR TWIST?
NO.
IS IT TIME FOR OUR HEXING LESSON?
I CAN'T BE SUE TODAY, LEON. IF I'M SUE, MUM WILL SHOUT AT DAD AND THEN SHE'LL CRY.
OH.
OKAY.
BUT--
--I CAN STILL BE PETER, CAN'T I?
...
REFRESH THE WARDS ON ALL THE DOORS AND WINDOWS.
ON IT!
AND DO A BENEFICUS CHARM! IT'S IN TOMMY TAYLOR AND THE UNDEAD KING!
QUICK, BEFORE DAD COMES UP TO READ US OUR STORY!

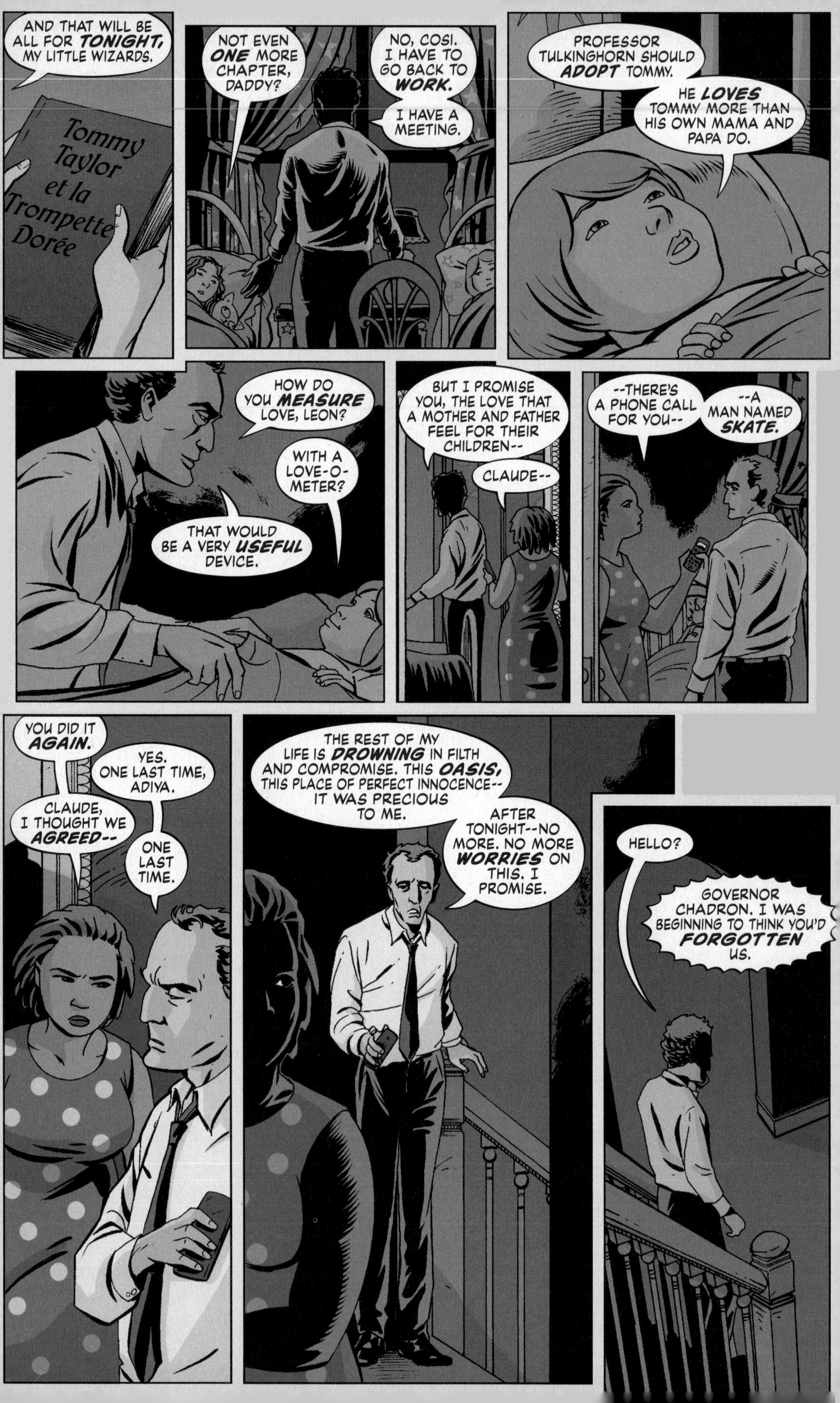
AND THAT WILL BE ALL FOR TONIGHT, MY LITTLE WIZARDS.
Tommy Taylor et la Trompette Dorée
NOT EVEN ONE MORE CHAPTER, DADDY?
NO, COSI. I HAVE TO GO BACK TO WORK.
I HAVE A MEETING.
PROFESSOR TULKINGHORN SHOULD ADOPT TOMMY.
HE LOVES TOMMY MORE THAN HIS OWN MAMA AND PAPA DO.
HOW DO YOU MEASURE LOVE, LEON?
WITH A LOVE-O-METER?
THAT WOULD BE A VERY USEFUL DEVICE.
BUT I PROMISE YOU, THE LOVE THAT A MOTHER AND FATHER FEEL FOR THEIR CHILDREN--
CLAUDE--
--THERE'S A PHONE CALL FOR YOU--
--A MAN NAMED SKATE.
YOU DID IT AGAIN.
YES. ONE LAST TIME, ADIYA.
CLAUDE, I THOUGHT WE AGREED--
ONE LAST TIME.
THE REST OF MY LIFE IS DROWNING IN FILTH AND COMPROMISE. THIS OASIS, THIS PLACE OF PERFECT INNOCENCE--IT WAS PRECIOUS TO ME.
AFTER TONIGHT--NO MORE. NO MORE WORRIES ON THIS. I PROMISE.
HELLO?
GOVERNOR CHADRON. I WAS BEGINNING TO THINK YOU'D FORGOTTEN US.

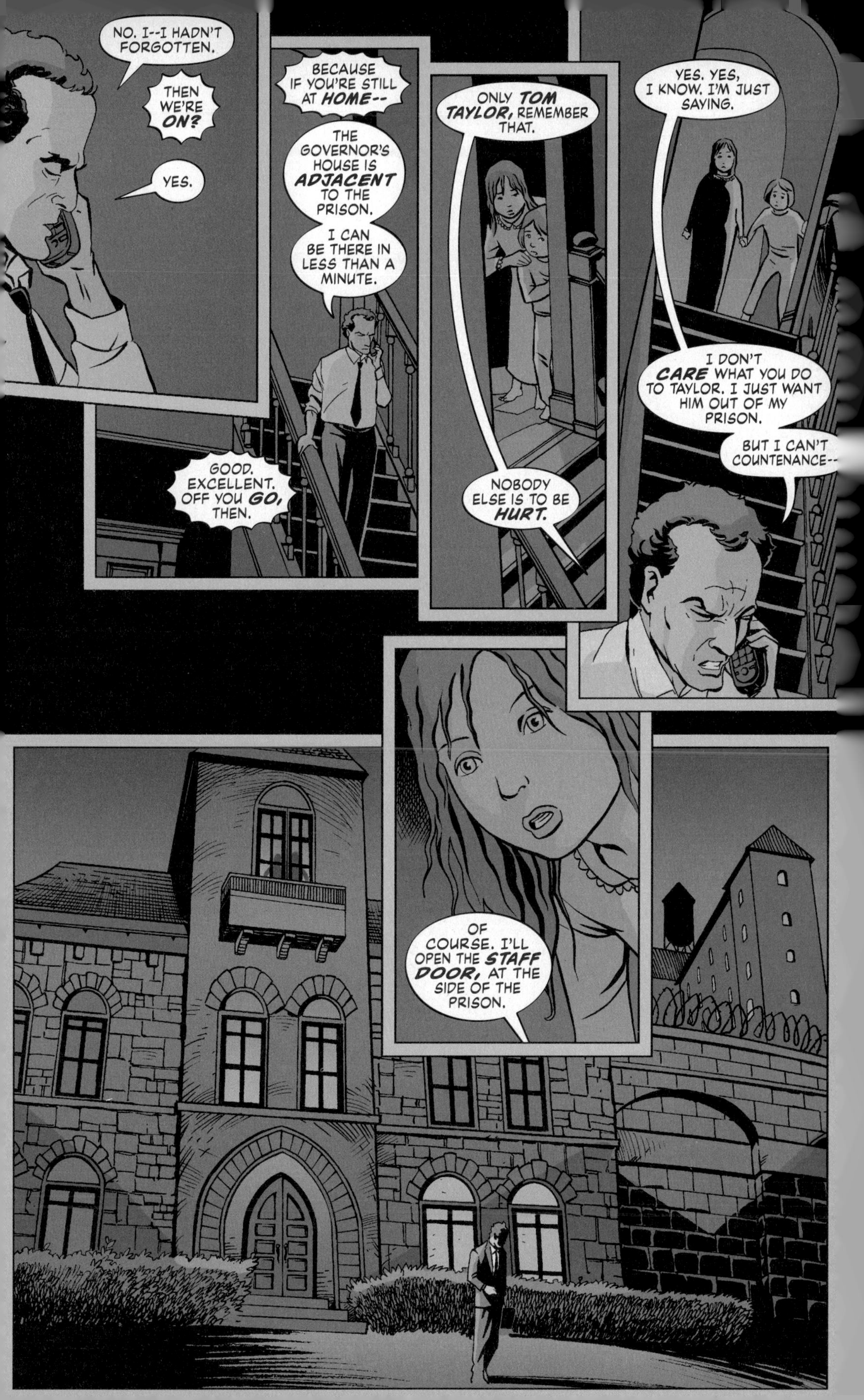
NO. I--I HADN'T FORGOTTEN.
THEN WE'RE ON?
YES.
BECAUSE IF YOU'RE STILL AT HOME--
THE GOVERNOR'S HOUSE IS ADJACENT TO THE PRISON.
I CAN BE THERE IN LESS THAN A MINUTE.
GOOD. EXCELLENT. OFF YOU GO, THEN.
ONLY TOM TAYLOR, REMEMBER THAT.
NOBODY ELSE IS TO BE HURT.
YES. YES, I KNOW. I'M JUST SAYING.
I DON'T CARE WHAT YOU DO TO TAYLOR. I JUST WANT HIM OUT OF MY PRISON.
BUT I CAN'T COUNTENANCE--
OF COURSE. I'LL OPEN THE STAFF DOOR, AT THE SIDE OF THE PRISON.

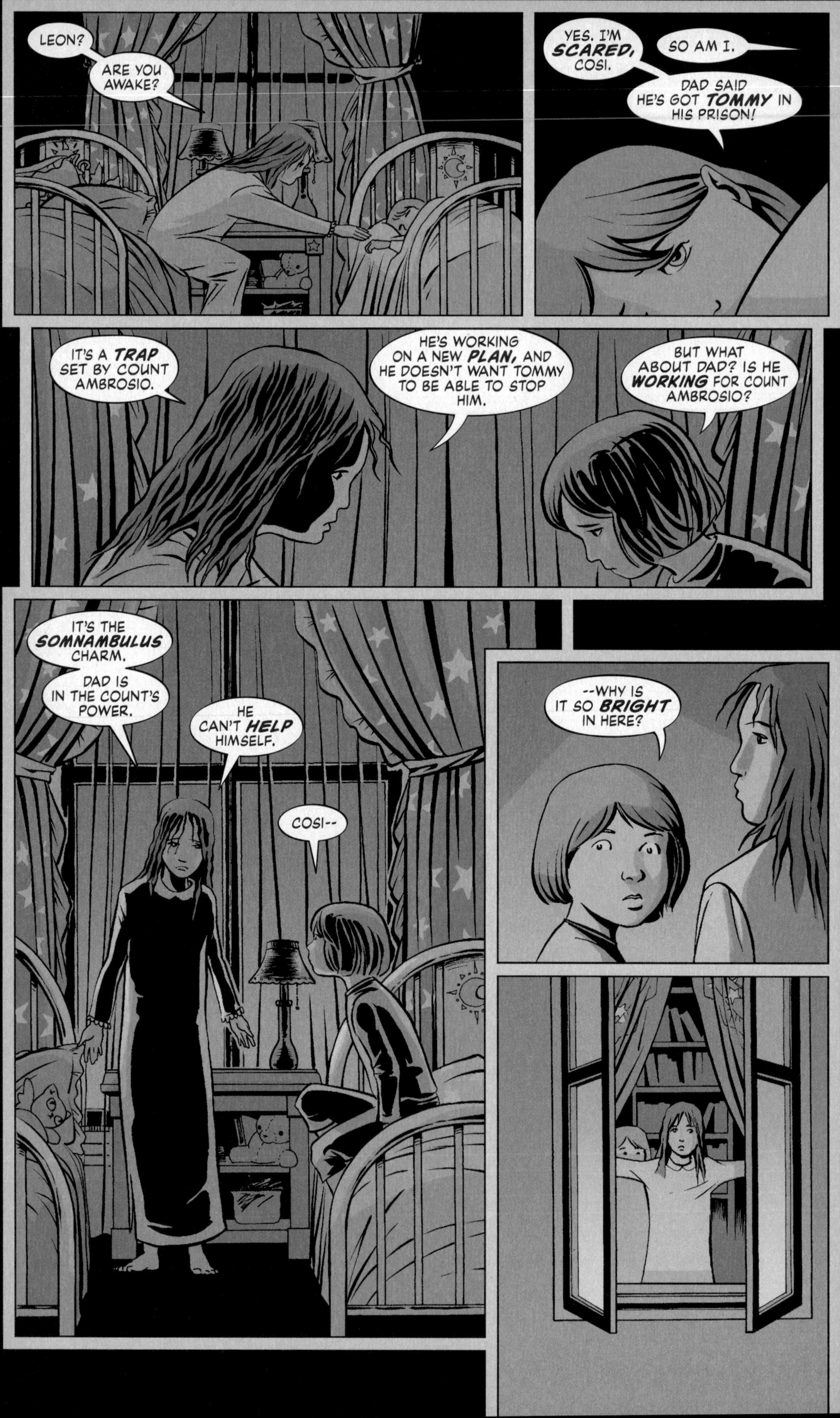
LEON?
ARE YOU AWAKE?
YES. I'M SCARED, COSI.
SO AM I.
DAD SAID HE'S GOT TOMMY IN HIS PRISON!
IT'S A TRAP SET BY COUNT AMBROSIO.
HE'S WORKING ON A NEW PLAN, AND HE DOESN'T WANT TOMMY TO BE ABLE TO STOP HIM.
BUT WHAT ABOUT DAD? IS HE WORKING FOR COUNT AMBROSIO?
IT'S THE SOMNAMBULUS CHARM.
DAD IS IN THE COUNT'S POWER.
HE CAN'T HELP HIMSELF.
COSI--
--WHY IS IT SO BRIGHT IN HERE?

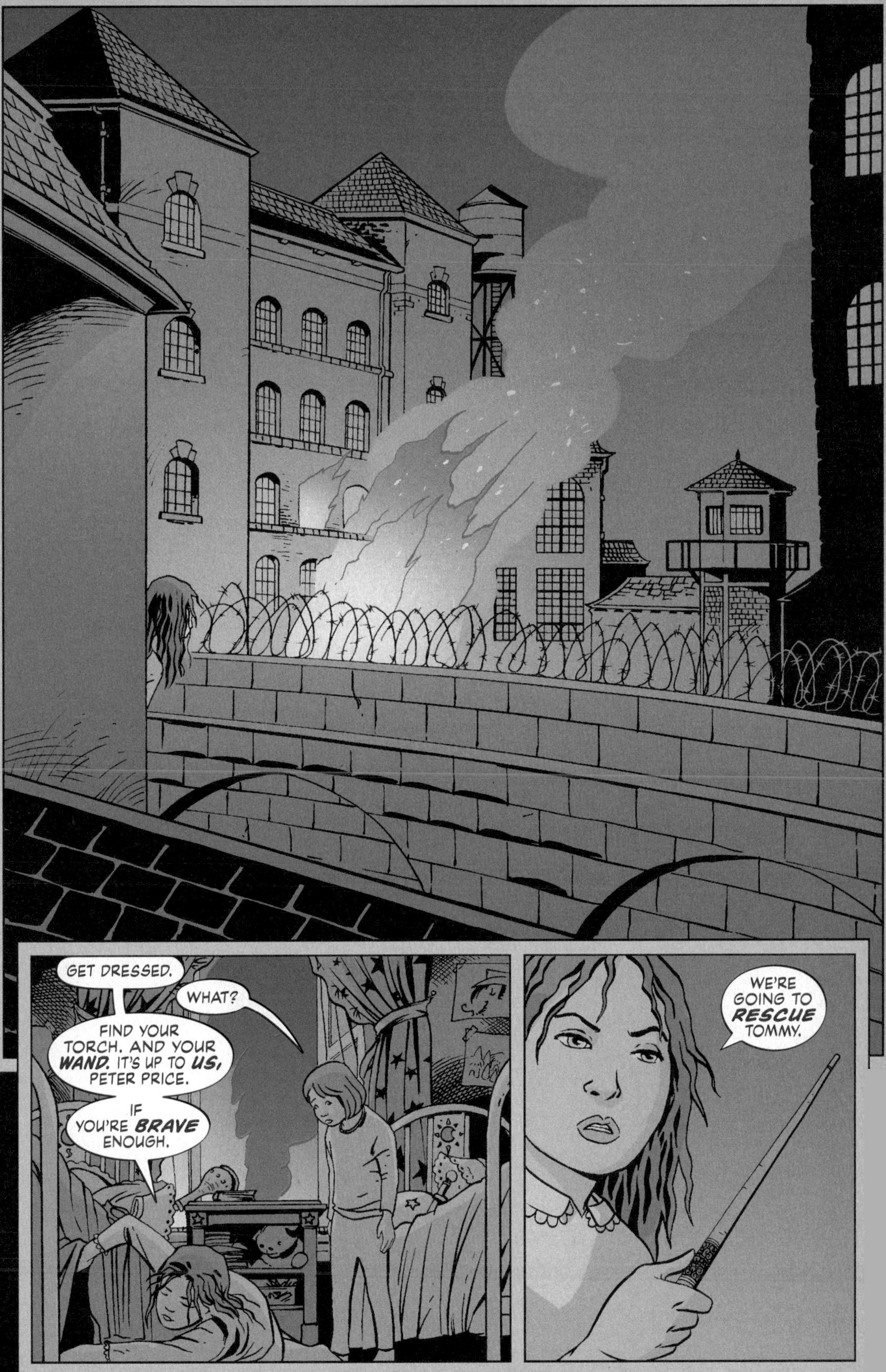
GET DRESSED.
WHAT?
FIND YOUR TORCH. AND YOUR ***WAND.*** IT'S UP TO ***US,*** PETER PRICE.
IF YOU'RE ***BRAVE*** ENOUGH.
WE'RE GOING TO ***RESCUE*** TOMMY.

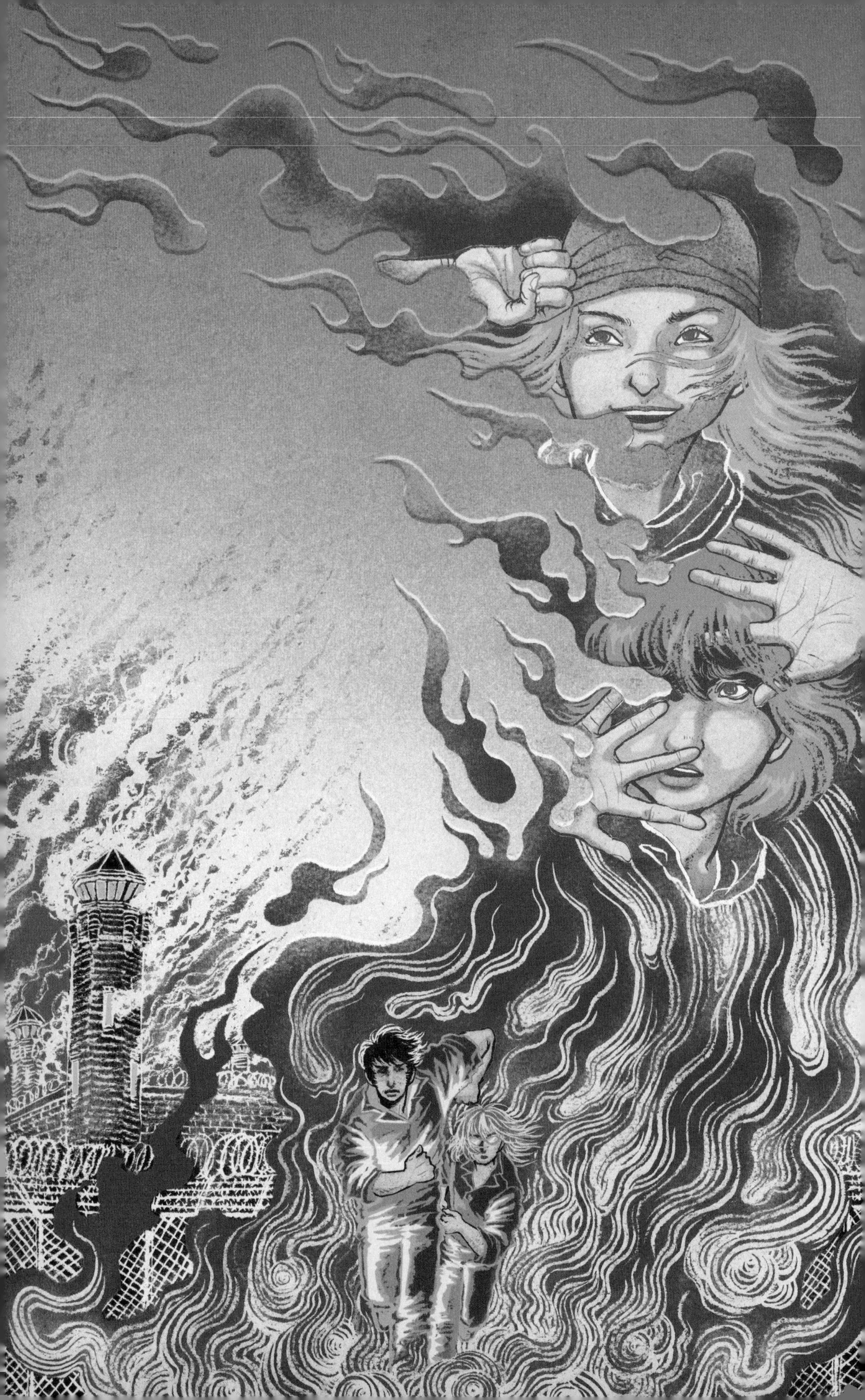

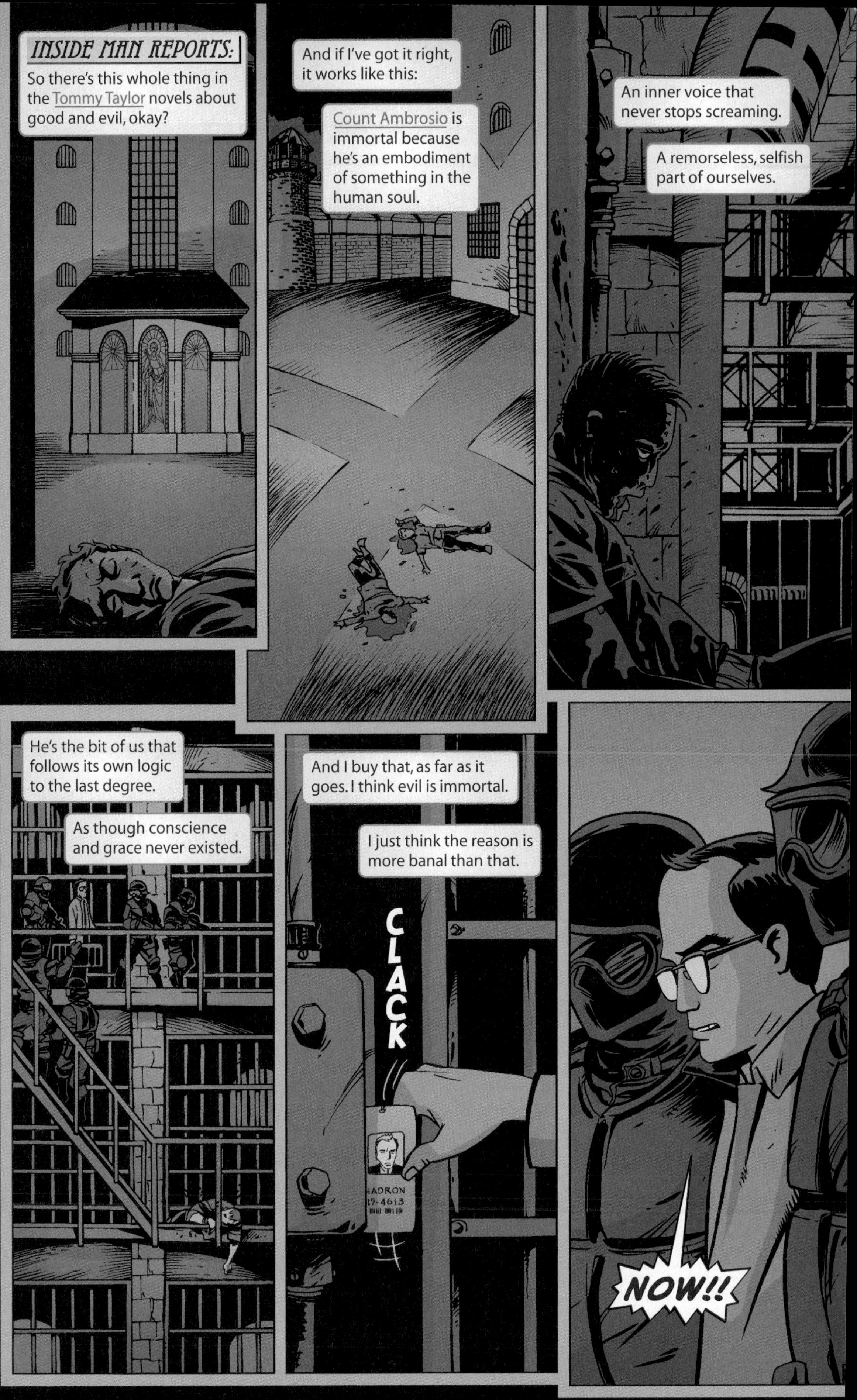
INSIDE MAN REPORTS:
So there's this whole thing in the Tommy Taylor novels about good and evil, okay?
And if I've got it right, it works like this:
Count Ambrosio is immortal because he's an embodiment of something in the human soul.
An inner voice that never stops screaming.
A remorseless, selfish part of ourselves.
He's the bit of us that follows its own logic to the last degree.
As though conscience and grace never existed.
And I buy that, as far as it goes. I think evil is immortal.
I just think the reason is more banal than that.
CLACK
HADRON
19-4613
NOW!!

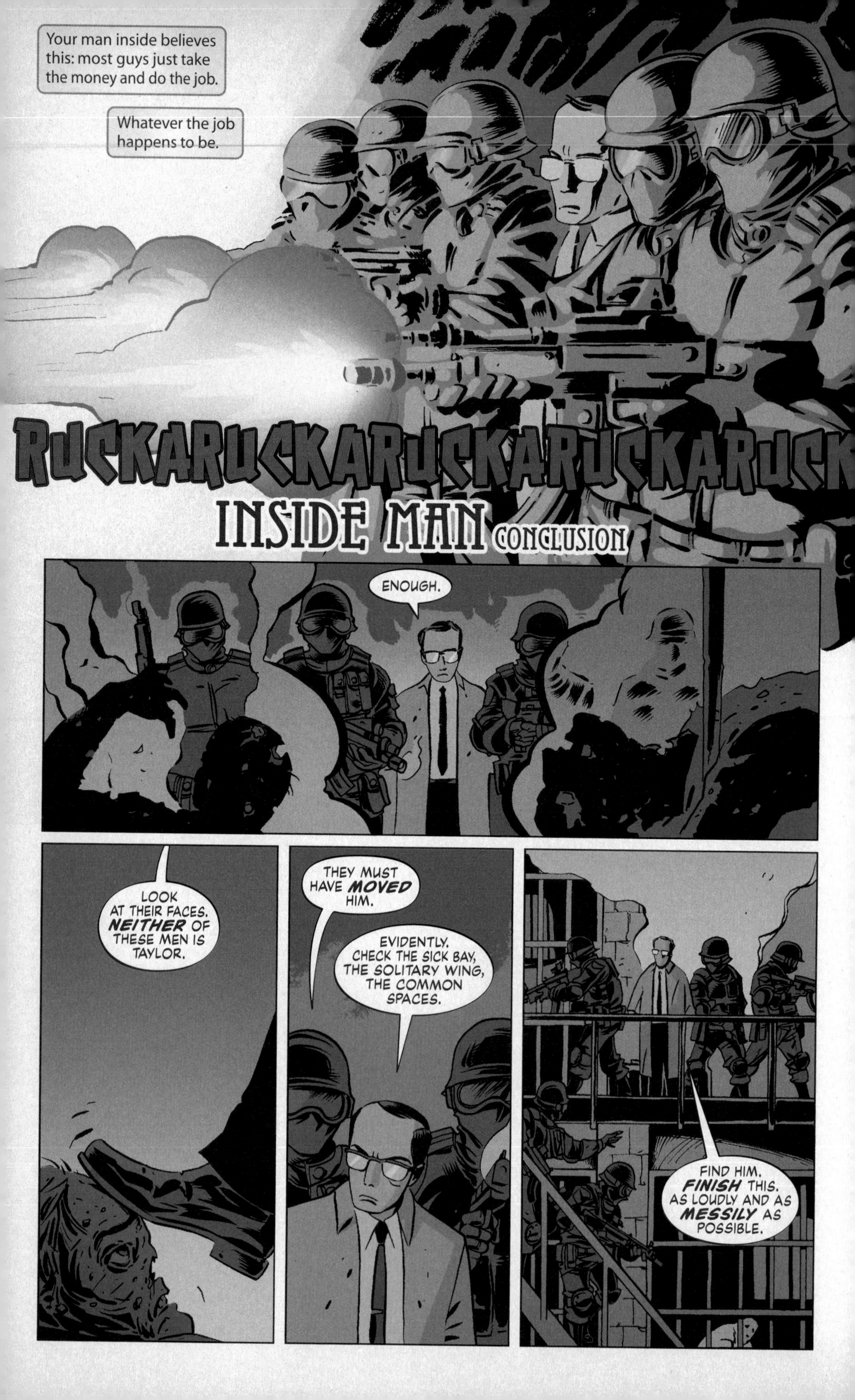
Your man inside believes this: most guys just take the money and do the job.
Whatever the job happens to be.
RUCKARUCKARUCKARUCKARUCK
INSIDE MAN CONCLUSION
ENOUGH.
LOOK AT THEIR FACES. NEITHER OF THESE MEN IS TAYLOR.
THEY MUST HAVE MOVED HIM.
EVIDENTLY. CHECK THE SICK BAY, THE SOLITARY WING, THE COMMON SPACES.
FIND HIM. FINISH THIS. AS LOUDLY AND AS MESSILY AS POSSIBLE.

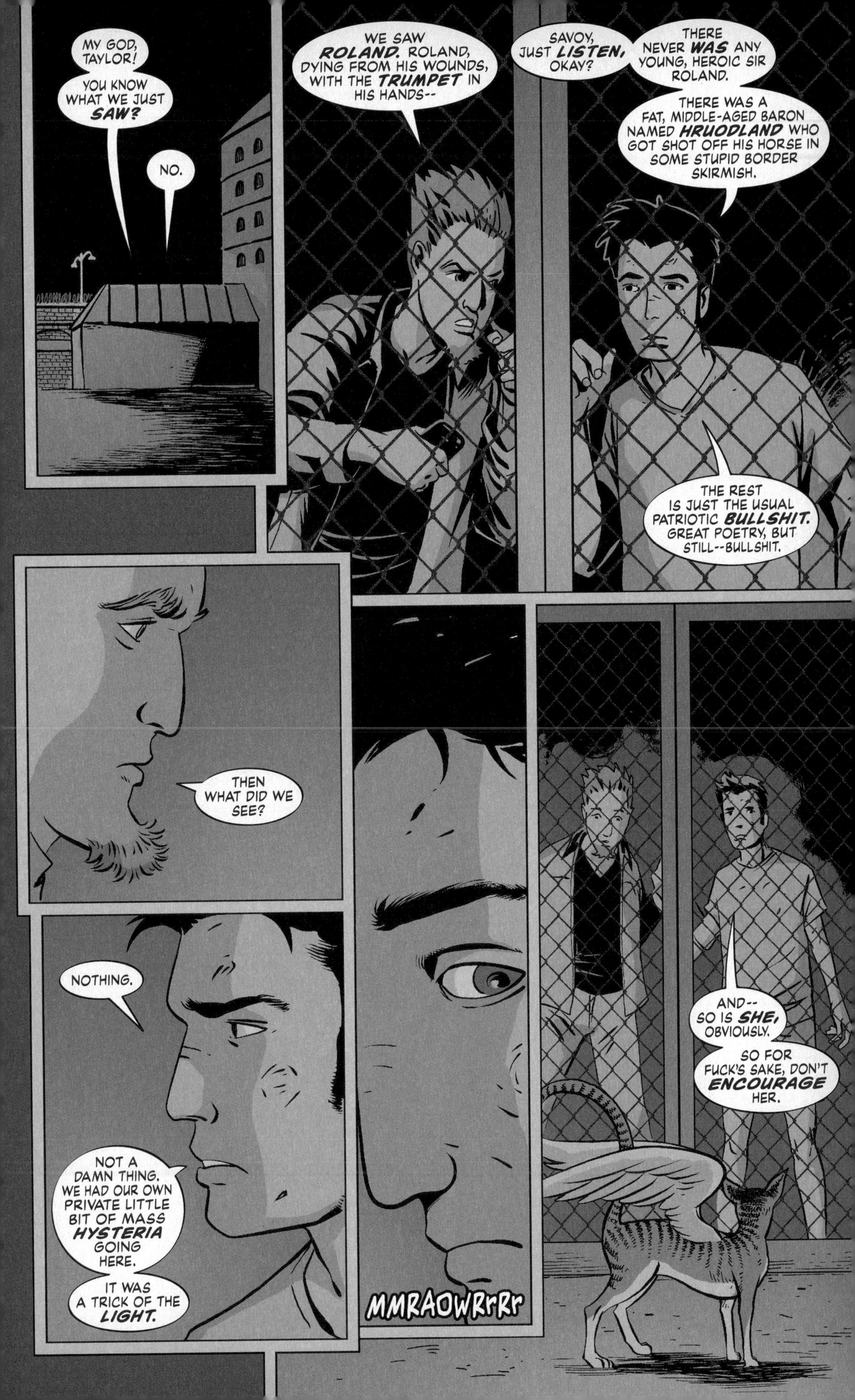
MY GOD, TAYLOR!
YOU KNOW WHAT WE JUST SAW?
NO.
WE SAW ROLAND. ROLAND, DYING FROM HIS WOUNDS, WITH THE TRUMPET IN HIS HANDS--
SAVOY, JUST LISTEN, OKAY?
THERE NEVER WAS ANY YOUNG, HEROIC SIR ROLAND.
THERE WAS A FAT, MIDDLE-AGED BARON NAMED HRUODLAND WHO GOT SHOT OFF HIS HORSE IN SOME STUPID BORDER SKIRMISH.
THE REST IS JUST THE USUAL PATRIOTIC BULLSHIT. GREAT POETRY, BUT STILL--BULLSHIT.
THEN WHAT DID WE SEE?
NOTHING.
NOT A DAMN THING. WE HAD OUR OWN PRIVATE LITTLE BIT OF MASS HYSTERIA GOING HERE.
IT WAS A TRICK OF THE LIGHT.
MMRAOWRrrr
AND-- SO IS SHE, OBVIOUSLY.
SO FOR FUCK'S SAKE, DON'T ENCOURAGE HER.

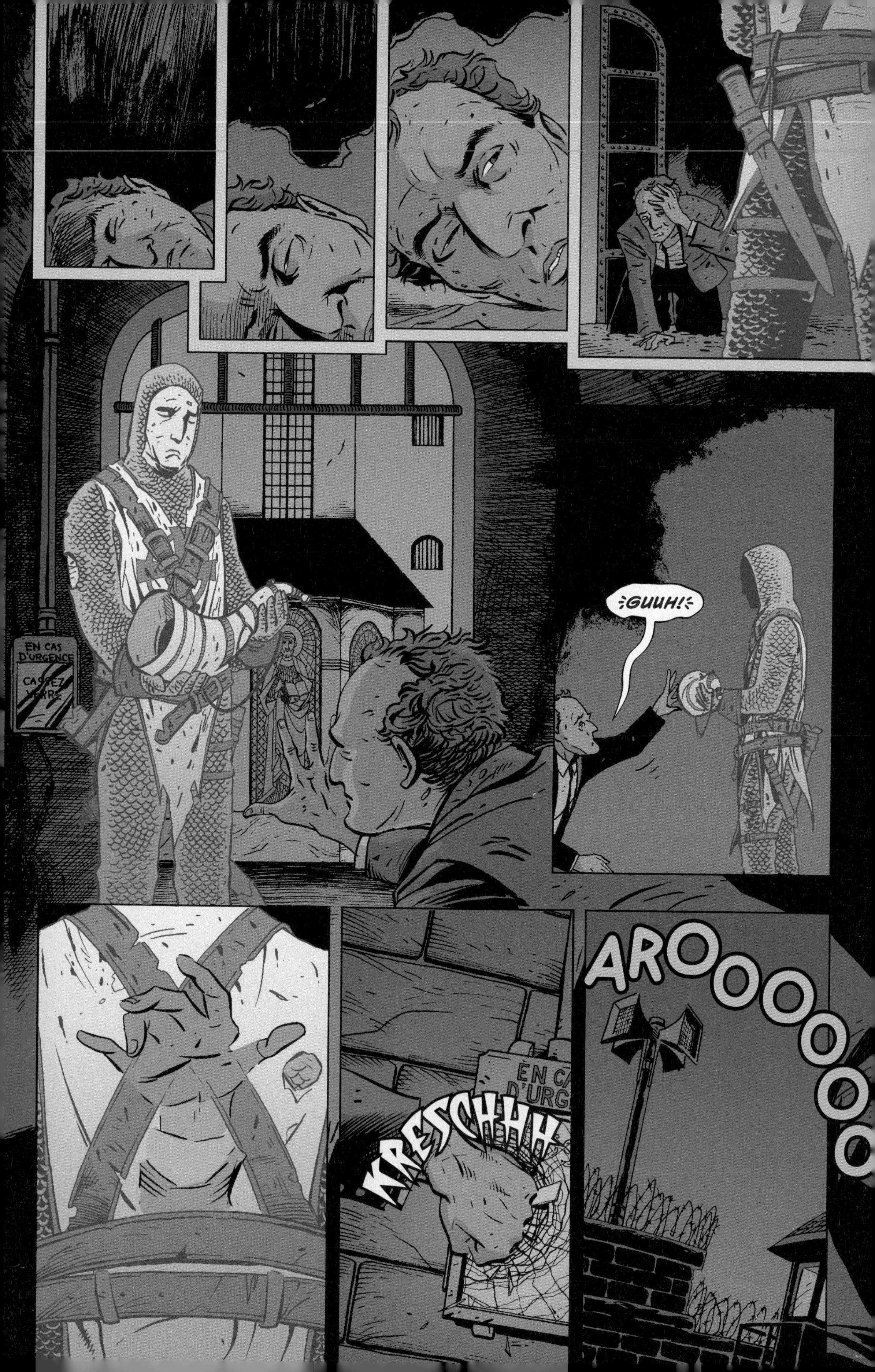
EN CAS D'URGENCE CASSEZ VERRE
¡GUUH!¡
KRESCHHH
AROOOOOOO

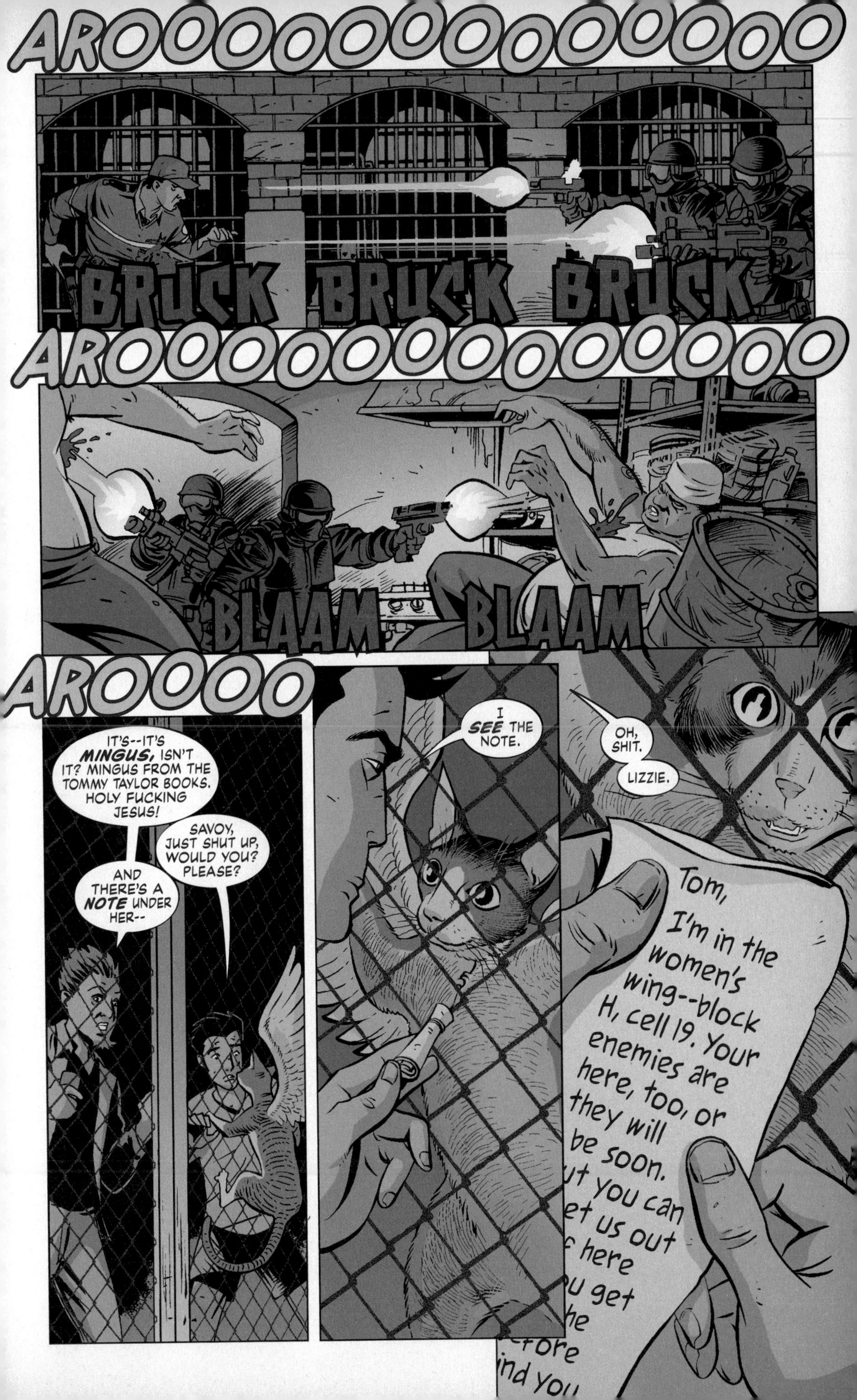
AROOOOOOOOOOOOO
BRUCK BRUCK BRUCK
AROOOOOOOOOOOOOO
BLAAM BLAAM
AROOOO
IT'S--IT'S MINGUS, ISN'T IT? MINGUS FROM THE TOMMY TAYLOR BOOKS. HOLY FUCKING JESUS!
SAVOY, JUST SHUT UP, WOULD YOU? PLEASE?
AND THERE'S A NOTE UNDER HER--
I SEE THE NOTE.
OH, SHIT.
LIZZIE.
Tom,
I'm in the women's wing--block H, cell 19. Your enemies are here, too, or they will be soon.

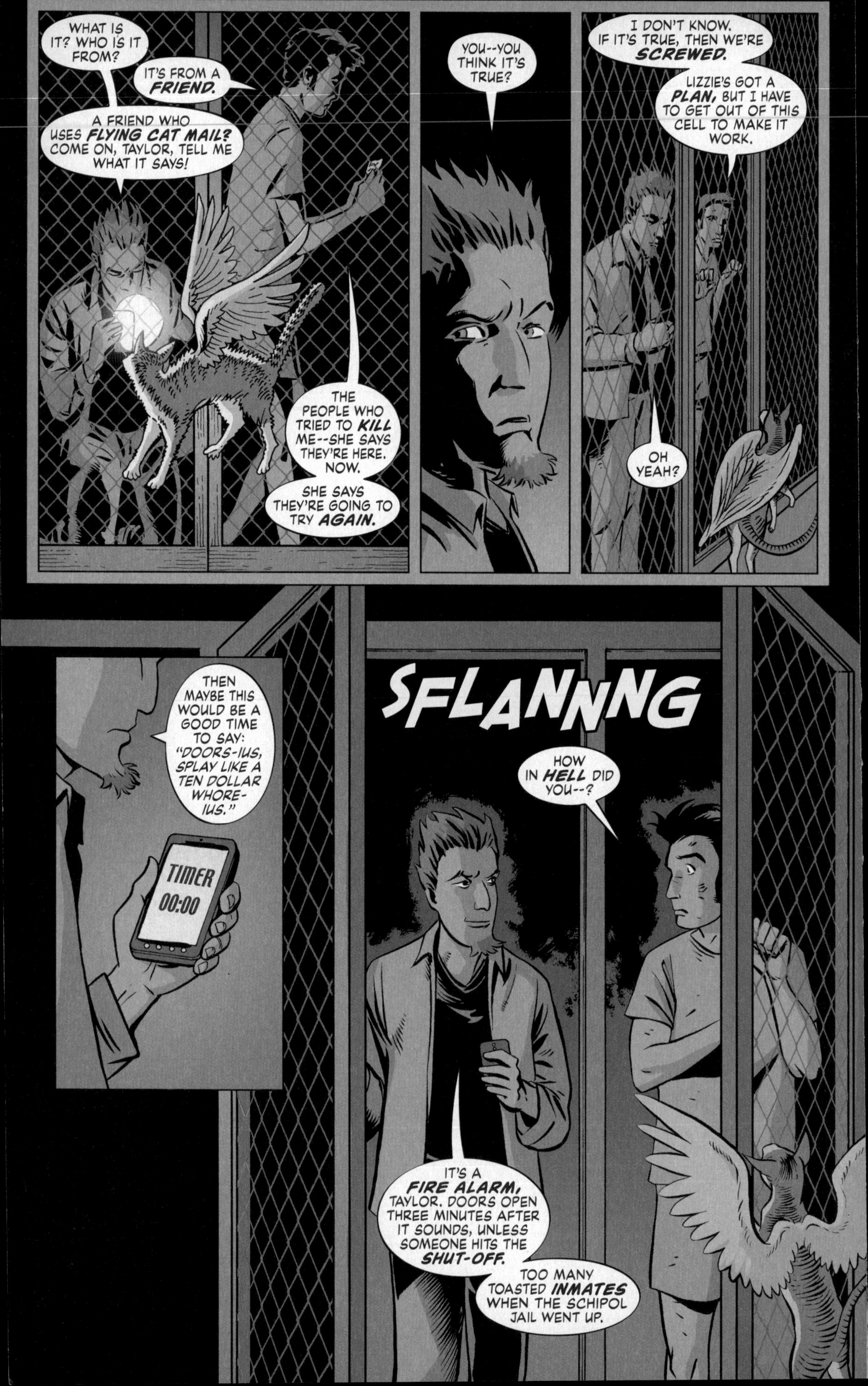
WHAT IS IT? WHO IS IT FROM?
IT'S FROM A FRIEND.
A FRIEND WHO USES FLYING CAT MAIL? COME ON, TAYLOR, TELL ME WHAT IT SAYS!
THE PEOPLE WHO TRIED TO KILL ME--SHE SAYS THEY'RE HERE. NOW.
SHE SAYS THEY'RE GOING TO TRY AGAIN.
YOU--YOU THINK IT'S TRUE?
I DON'T KNOW. IF IT'S TRUE, THEN WE'RE SCREWED.
LIZZIE'S GOT A PLAN, BUT I HAVE TO GET OUT OF THIS CELL TO MAKE IT WORK.
OH YEAH?
THEN MAYBE THIS WOULD BE A GOOD TIME TO SAY: "DOORS-IUS, SPLAY LIKE A TEN DOLLAR WHORE-IUS."
TIMER 00:00
SFLANNNG
HOW IN HELL DID YOU--?
IT'S A FIRE ALARM, TAYLOR. DOORS OPEN THREE MINUTES AFTER IT SOUNDS, UNLESS SOMEONE HITS THE SHUT-OFF.
TOO MANY TOASTED INMATES WHEN THE SCHIPOL JAIL WENT UP.

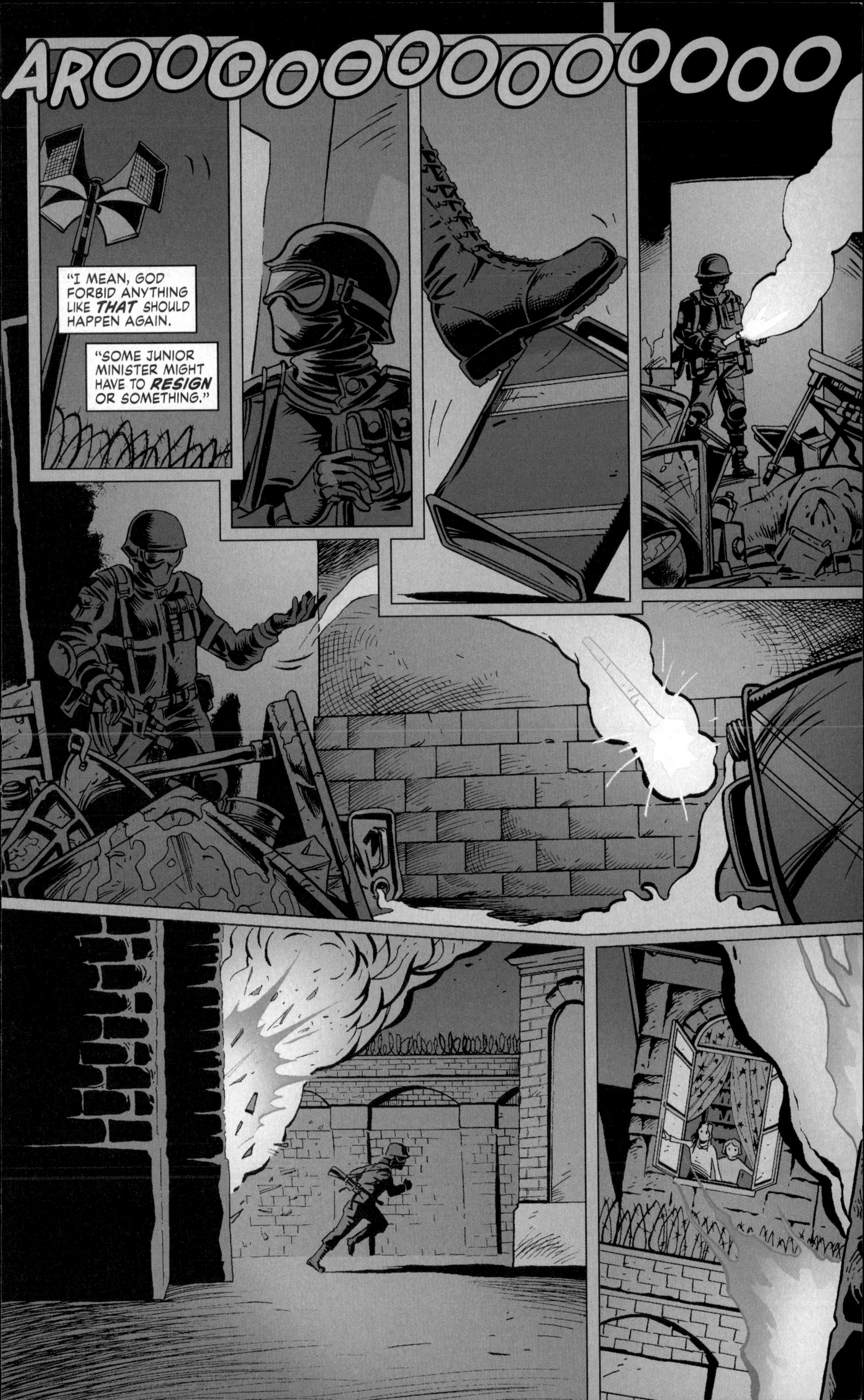
AROOOOOOOOOOOOOOO
"I MEAN, GOD FORBID ANYTHING LIKE THAT SHOULD HAPPEN AGAIN.
"SOME JUNIOR MINISTER MIGHT HAVE TO RESIGN OR SOMETHING."

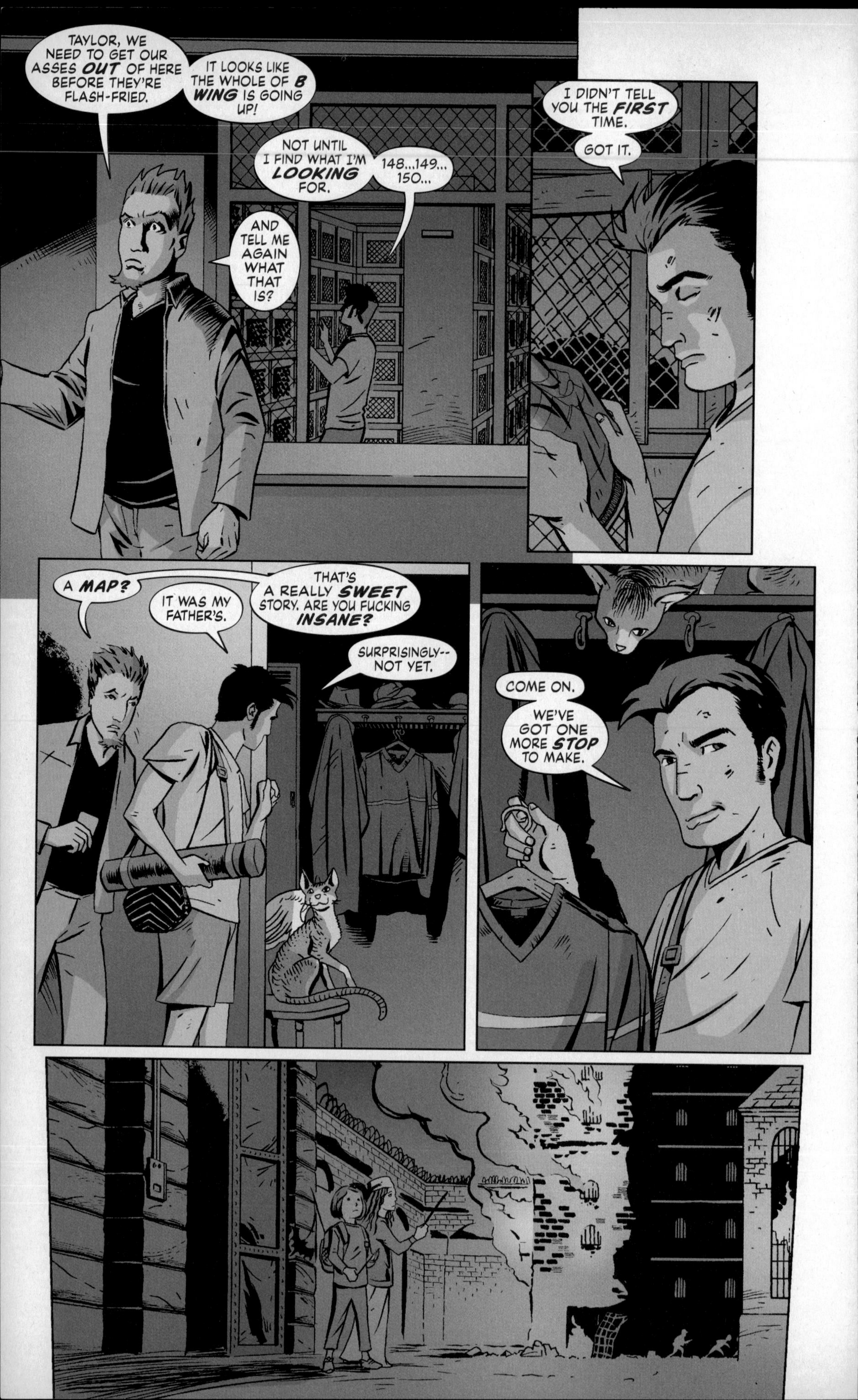
TAYLOR, WE NEED TO GET OUR ASSES OUT OF HERE BEFORE THEY'RE FLASH-FRIED.
IT LOOKS LIKE THE WHOLE OF B WING IS GOING UP!
NOT UNTIL I FIND WHAT I'M LOOKING FOR.
148...149... 150...
AND TELL ME AGAIN WHAT THAT IS?
I DIDN'T TELL YOU THE FIRST TIME.
GOT IT.
A MAP?
IT WAS MY FATHER'S.
THAT'S A REALLY SWEET STORY. ARE YOU FUCKING INSANE?
SURPRISINGLY--NOT YET.
COME ON.
WE'VE GOT ONE MORE STOP TO MAKE.

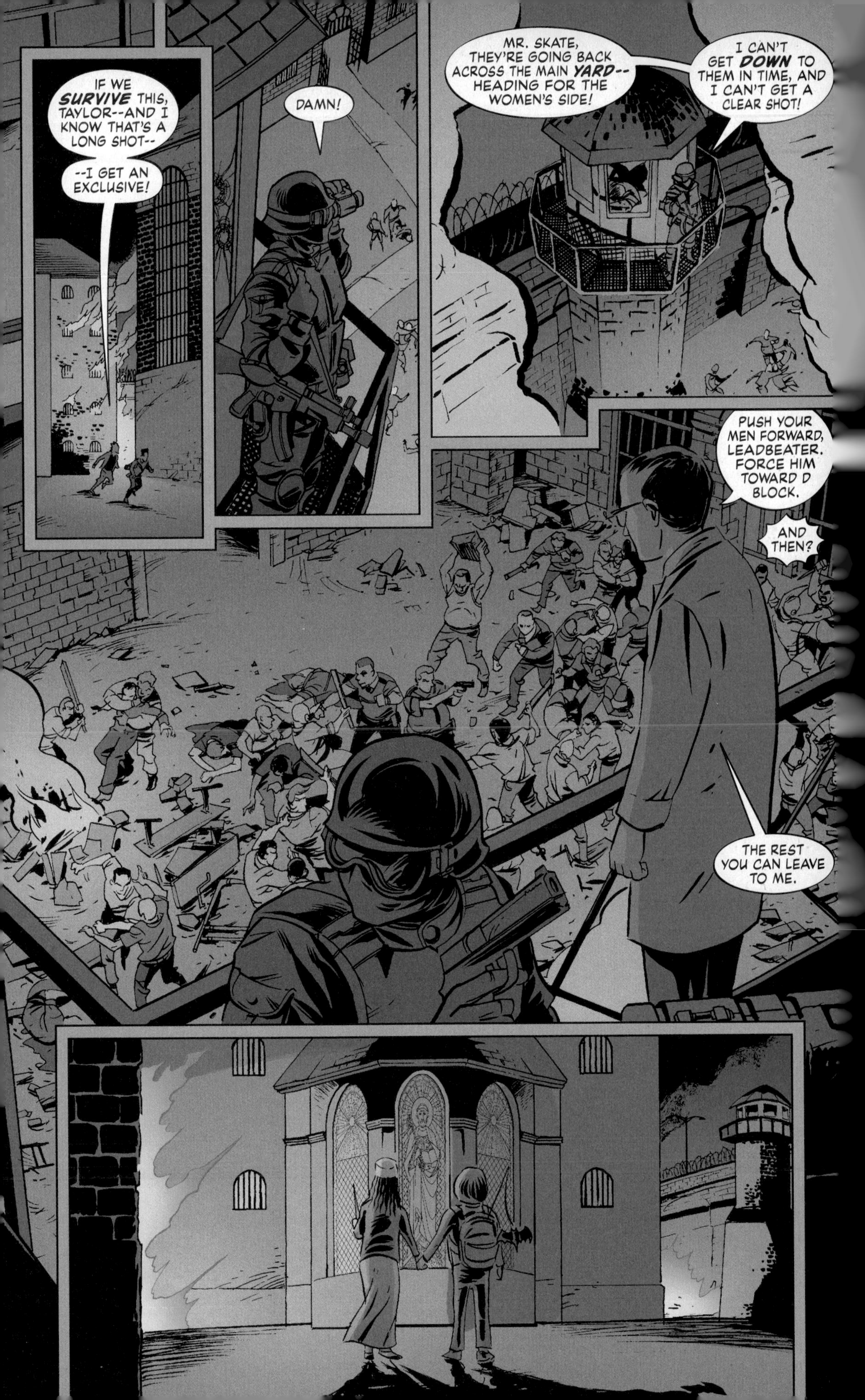
IF WE SURVIVE THIS, TAYLOR--AND I KNOW THAT'S A LONG SHOT--
--I GET AN EXCLUSIVE!
DAMN!
MR. SKATE, THEY'RE GOING BACK ACROSS THE MAIN YARD-- HEADING FOR THE WOMEN'S SIDE!
I CAN'T GET DOWN TO THEM IN TIME, AND I CAN'T GET A CLEAR SHOT!
PUSH YOUR MEN FORWARD, LEADBEATER. FORCE HIM TOWARD D BLOCK.
AND THEN?
THE REST YOU CAN LEAVE TO ME.

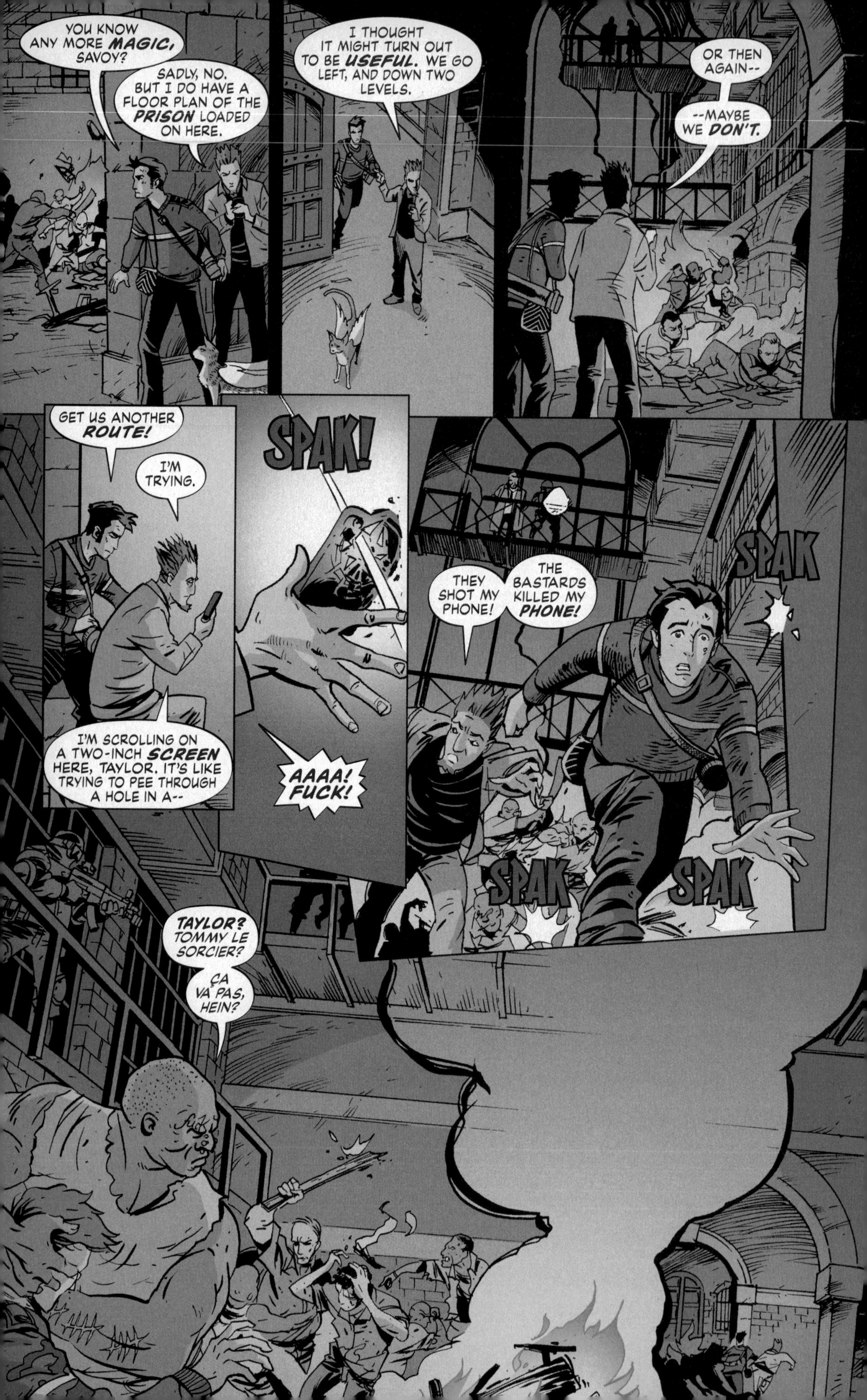
YOU KNOW ANY MORE MAGIC, SAVOY?
SADLY, NO. BUT I DO HAVE A FLOOR PLAN OF THE PRISON LOADED ON HERE.
I THOUGHT IT MIGHT TURN OUT TO BE USEFUL. WE GO LEFT, AND DOWN TWO LEVELS.
OR THEN AGAIN--
--MAYBE WE DON'T.
GET US ANOTHER ROUTE!
I'M TRYING.
I'M SCROLLING ON A TWO-INCH SCREEN HERE, TAYLOR. IT'S LIKE TRYING TO PEE THROUGH A HOLE IN A--
SPAK!
AAAA! FUCK!
THEY SHOT MY PHONE!
THE BASTARDS KILLED MY PHONE!
SPAK
SPAK
SPAK
TAYLOR? TOMMY LE SORCIER?
ÇA VA PAS, HEIN?

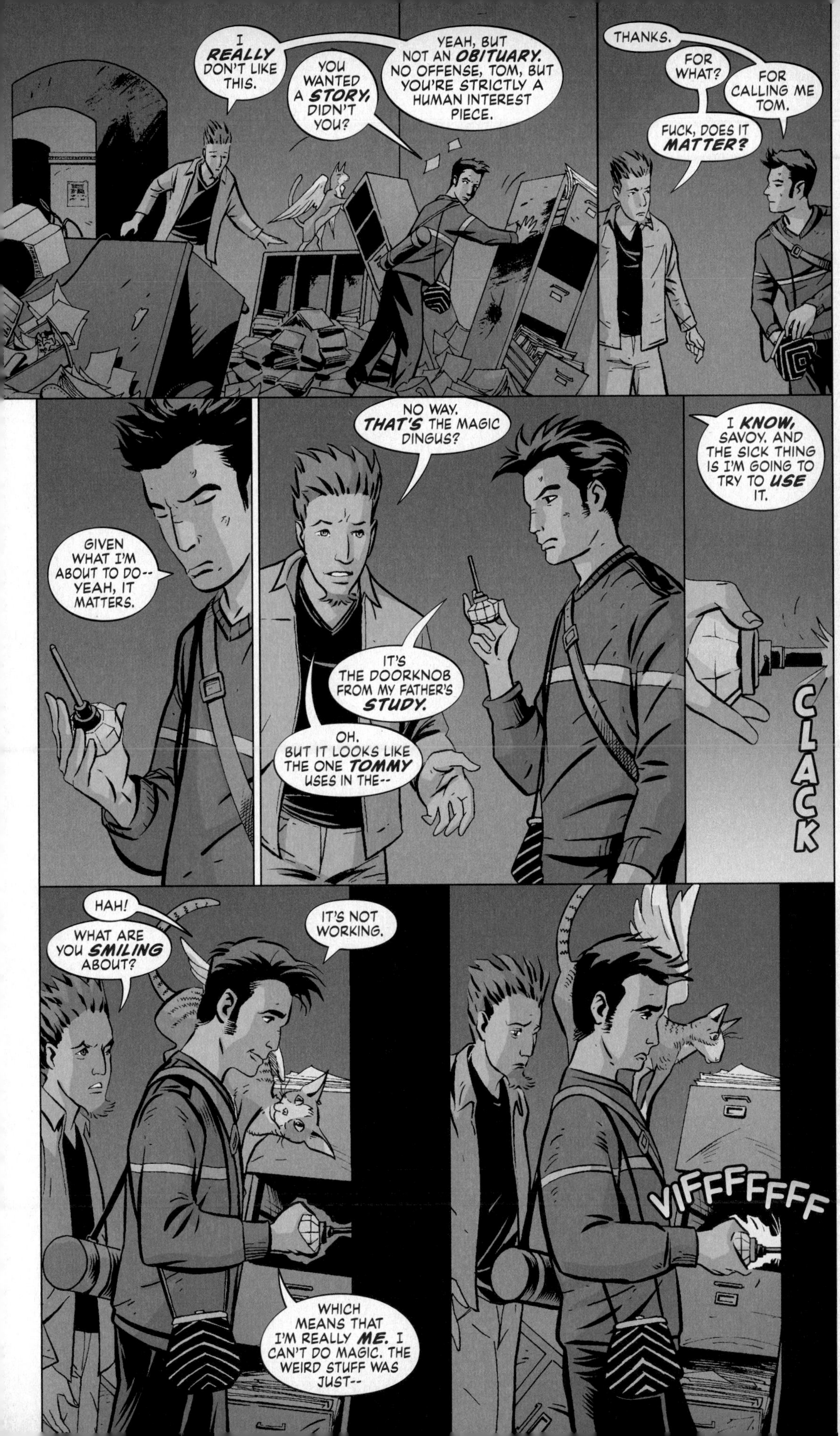
I REALLY DON'T LIKE THIS.
YOU WANTED A STORY, DIDN'T YOU?
YEAH, BUT NOT AN OBITUARY. NO OFFENSE, TOM, BUT YOU'RE STRICTLY A HUMAN INTEREST PIECE.
THANKS.
FOR WHAT?
FOR CALLING ME TOM.
FUCK, DOES IT MATTER?
GIVEN WHAT I'M ABOUT TO DO-- YEAH, IT MATTERS.
NO WAY. THAT'S THE MAGIC DINGUS?
IT'S THE DOORKNOB FROM MY FATHER'S STUDY.
OH. BUT IT LOOKS LIKE THE ONE TOMMY USES IN THE--
I KNOW, SAVOY. AND THE SICK THING IS I'M GOING TO TRY TO USE IT.
CLACK
HAH!
WHAT ARE YOU SMILING ABOUT?
IT'S NOT WORKING.
WHICH MEANS THAT I'M REALLY ME. I CAN'T DO MAGIC. THE WEIRD STUFF WAS JUST--
VIFFFFFFF

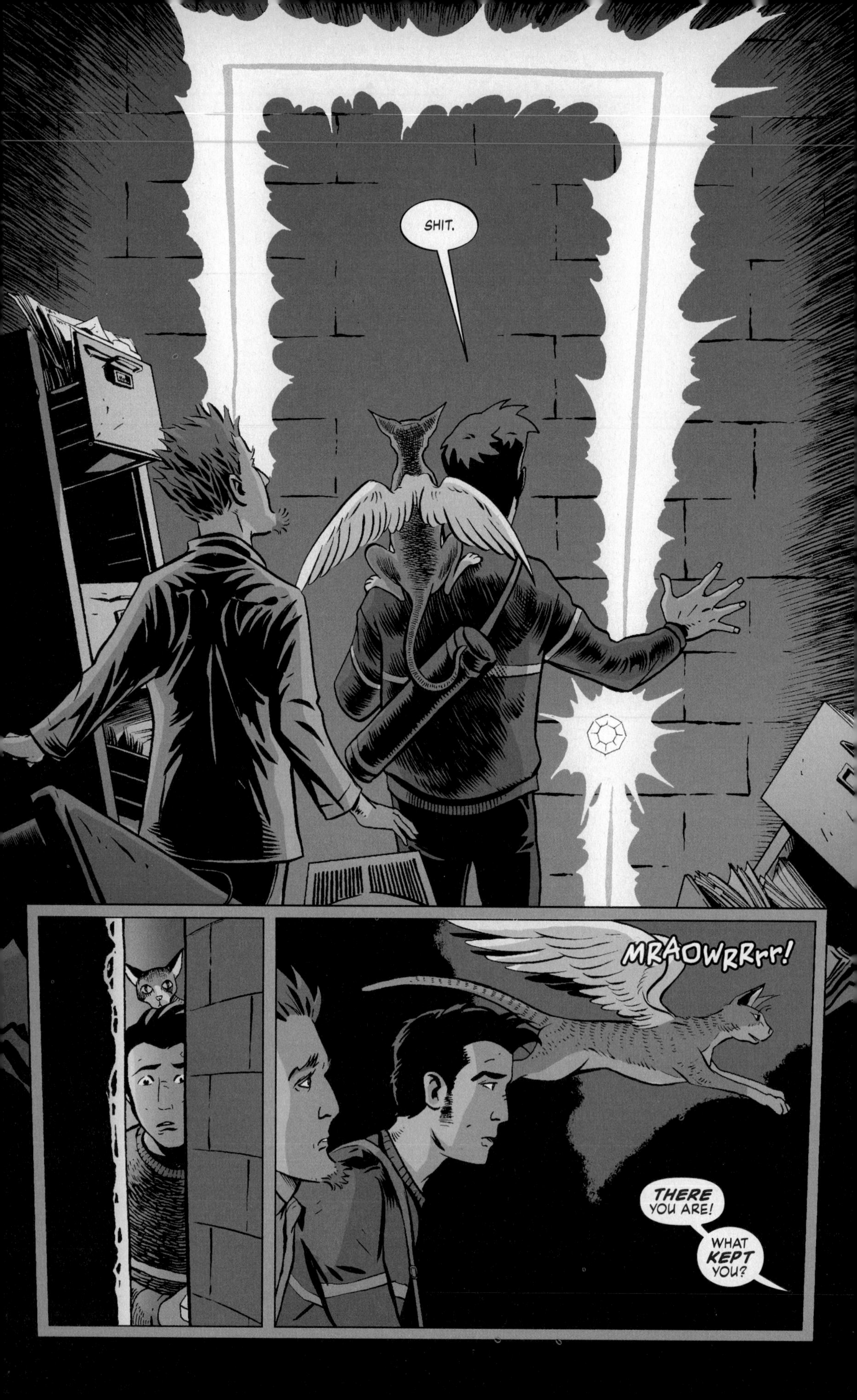
SHIT.
MRAOWRRrr!
THERE YOU ARE!
WHAT KEPT YOU?

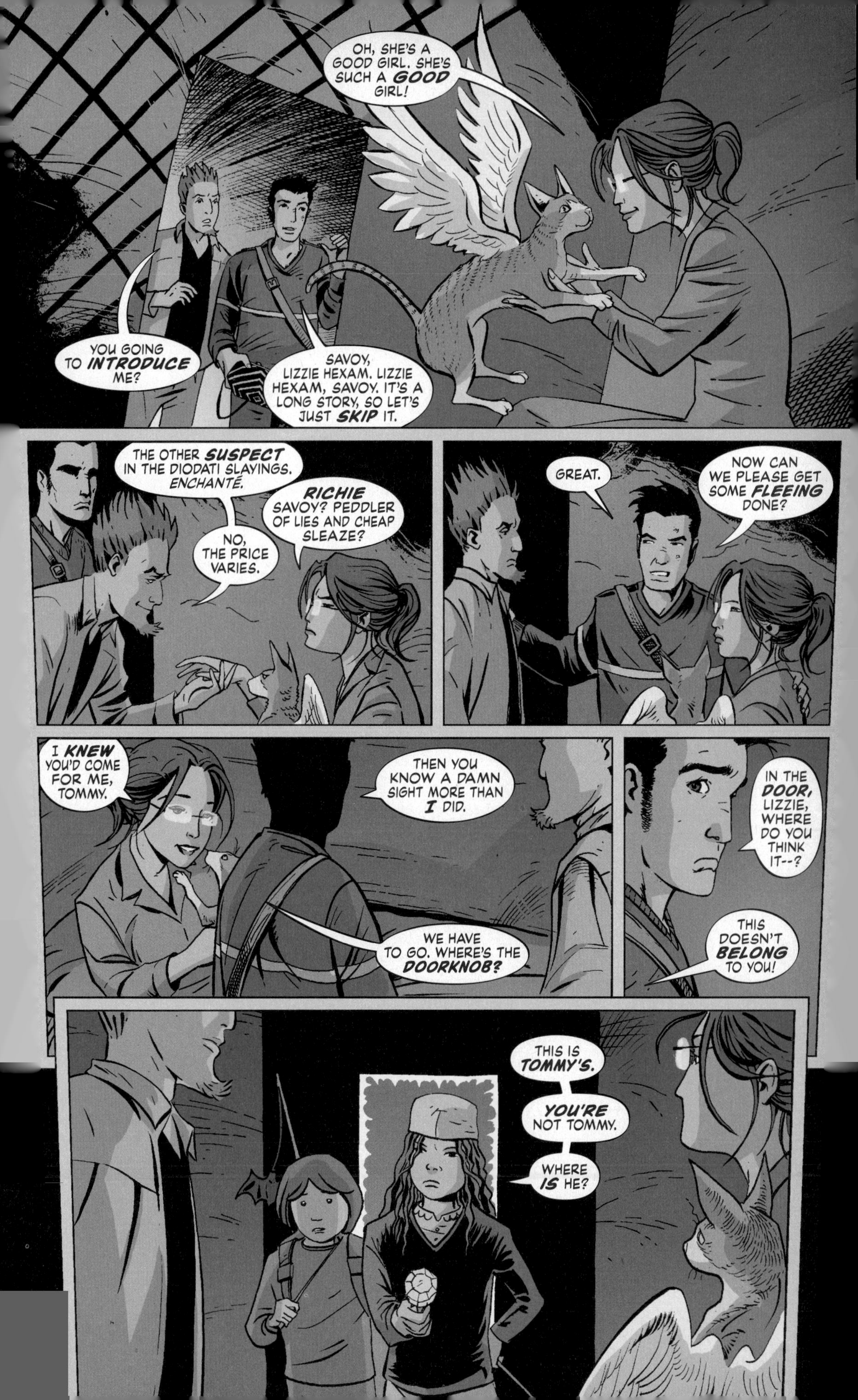

OH, SHE'S A GOOD GIRL. SHE'S SUCH A GOOD GIRL!
YOU GOING TO INTRODUCE ME?
SAVOY, LIZZIE HEXAM. LIZZIE HEXAM, SAVOY. IT'S A LONG STORY, SO LET'S JUST SKIP IT.
THE OTHER SUSPECT IN THE DIODATI SLAYINGS. ENCHANTÉ.
RICHIE SAVOY? PEDDLER OF LIES AND CHEAP SLEAZE?
NO, THE PRICE VARIES.
GREAT.
NOW CAN WE PLEASE GET SOME FLEEING DONE?
I KNEW YOU'D COME FOR ME, TOMMY.
THEN YOU KNOW A DAMN SIGHT MORE THAN I DID.
WE HAVE TO GO. WHERE'S THE DOORKNOB?
IN THE DOOR, LIZZIE, WHERE DO YOU THINK IT--?
THIS DOESN'T BELONG TO YOU!
THIS IS TOMMY'S.
YOU'RE NOT TOMMY.
WHERE IS HE?

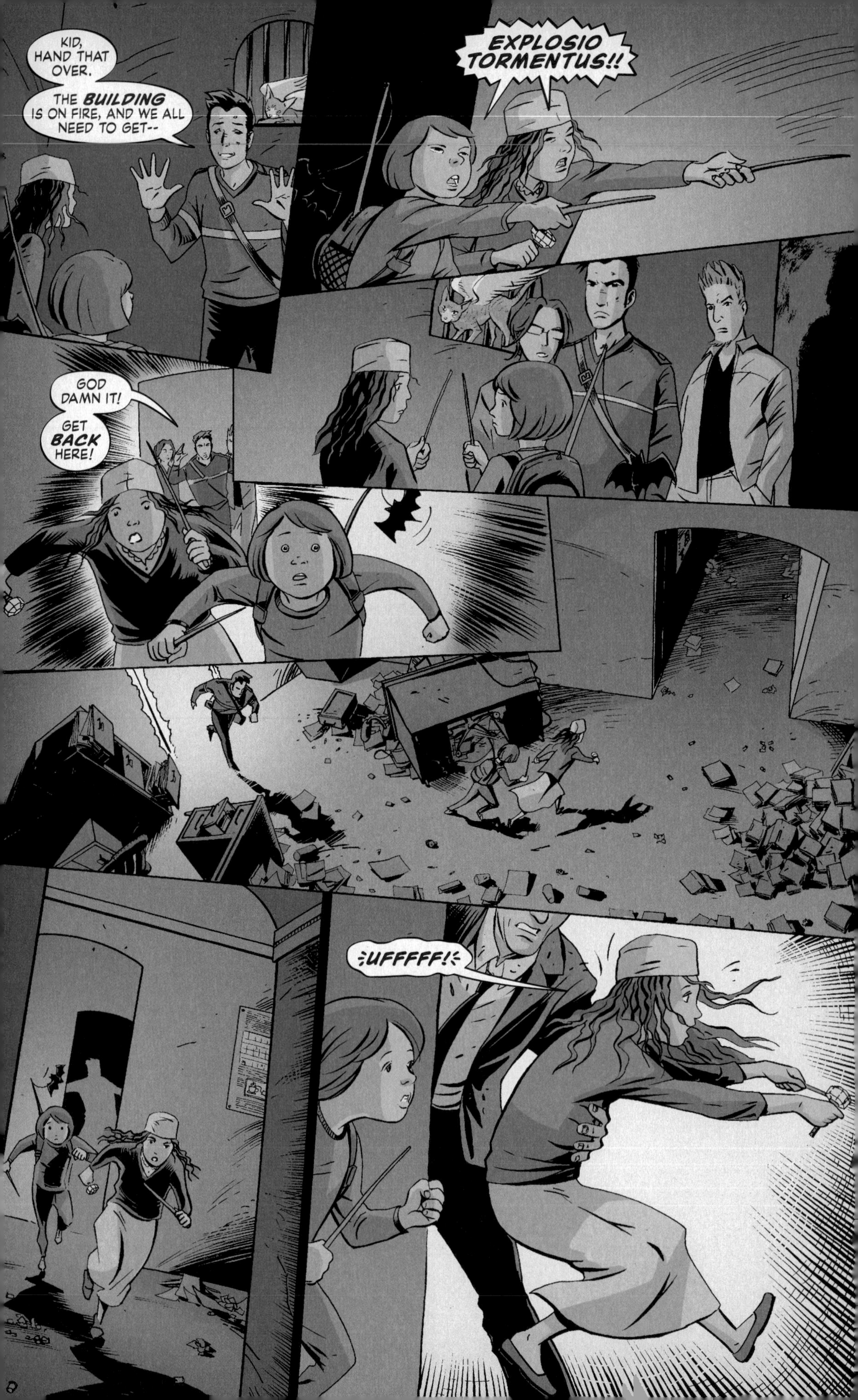
KID, HAND THAT OVER.
THE BUILDING IS ON FIRE, AND WE ALL NEED TO GET--
EXPLOSIO TORMENTUS!!
GOD DAMN IT!
GET BACK HERE!
UFFFFF!

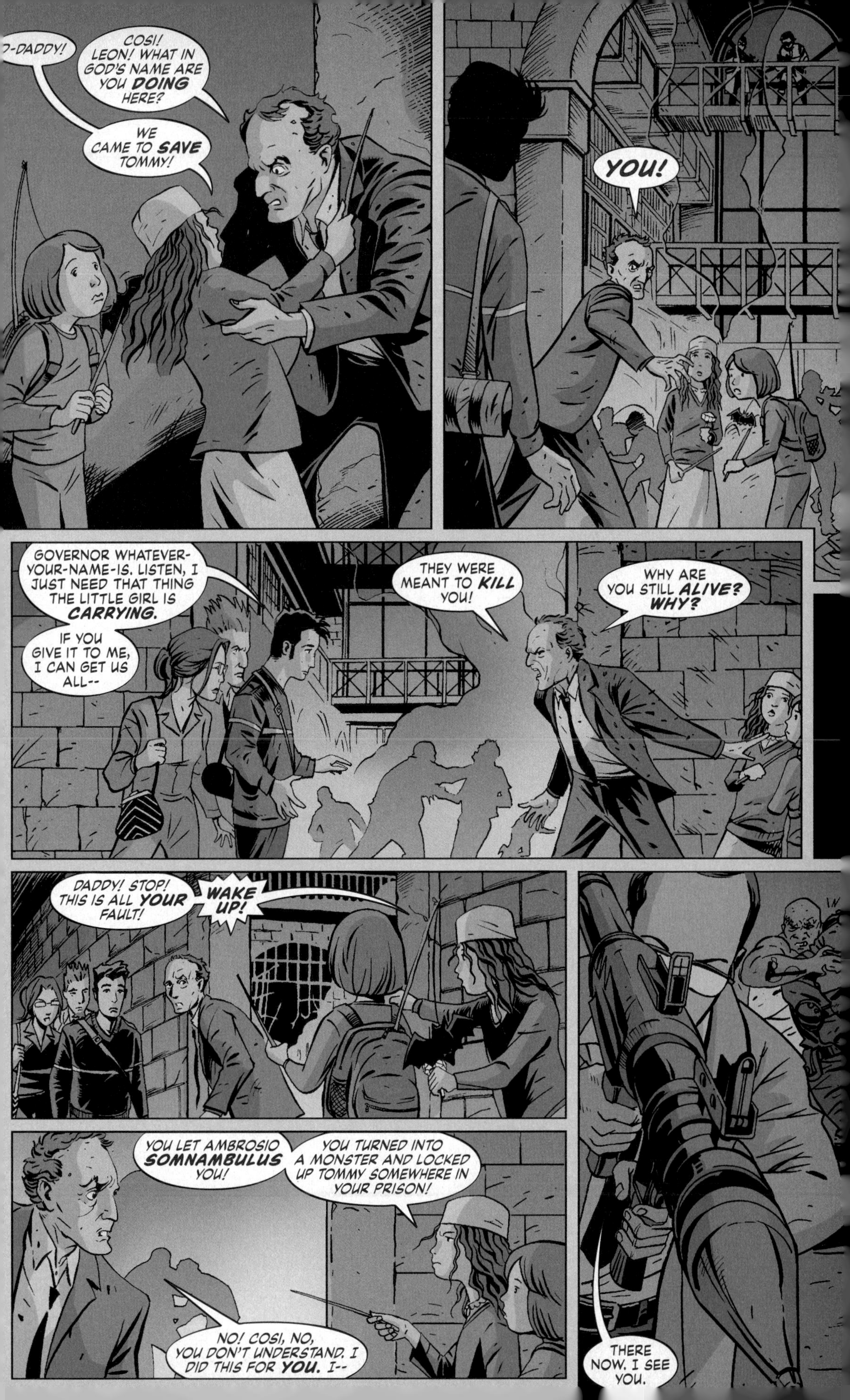
D-DADDY!
COSI! LEON! WHAT IN GOD'S NAME ARE YOU DOING HERE?
WE CAME TO SAVE TOMMY!
YOU!
GOVERNOR WHATEVER-YOUR-NAME-IS. LISTEN, I JUST NEED THAT THING THE LITTLE GIRL IS CARRYING.
IF YOU GIVE IT TO ME, I CAN GET US ALL--
THEY WERE MEANT TO KILL YOU!
WHY ARE YOU STILL ALIVE? WHY?
DADDY! STOP! THIS IS ALL YOUR FAULT!
WAKE UP!
YOU LET AMBROSIO SOMNAMBULUS YOU!
YOU TURNED INTO A MONSTER AND LOCKED UP TOMMY SOMEWHERE IN YOUR PRISON!
NO! COSI, NO, YOU DON'T UNDERSTAND. I DID THIS FOR YOU. I--
THERE NOW. I SEE YOU.

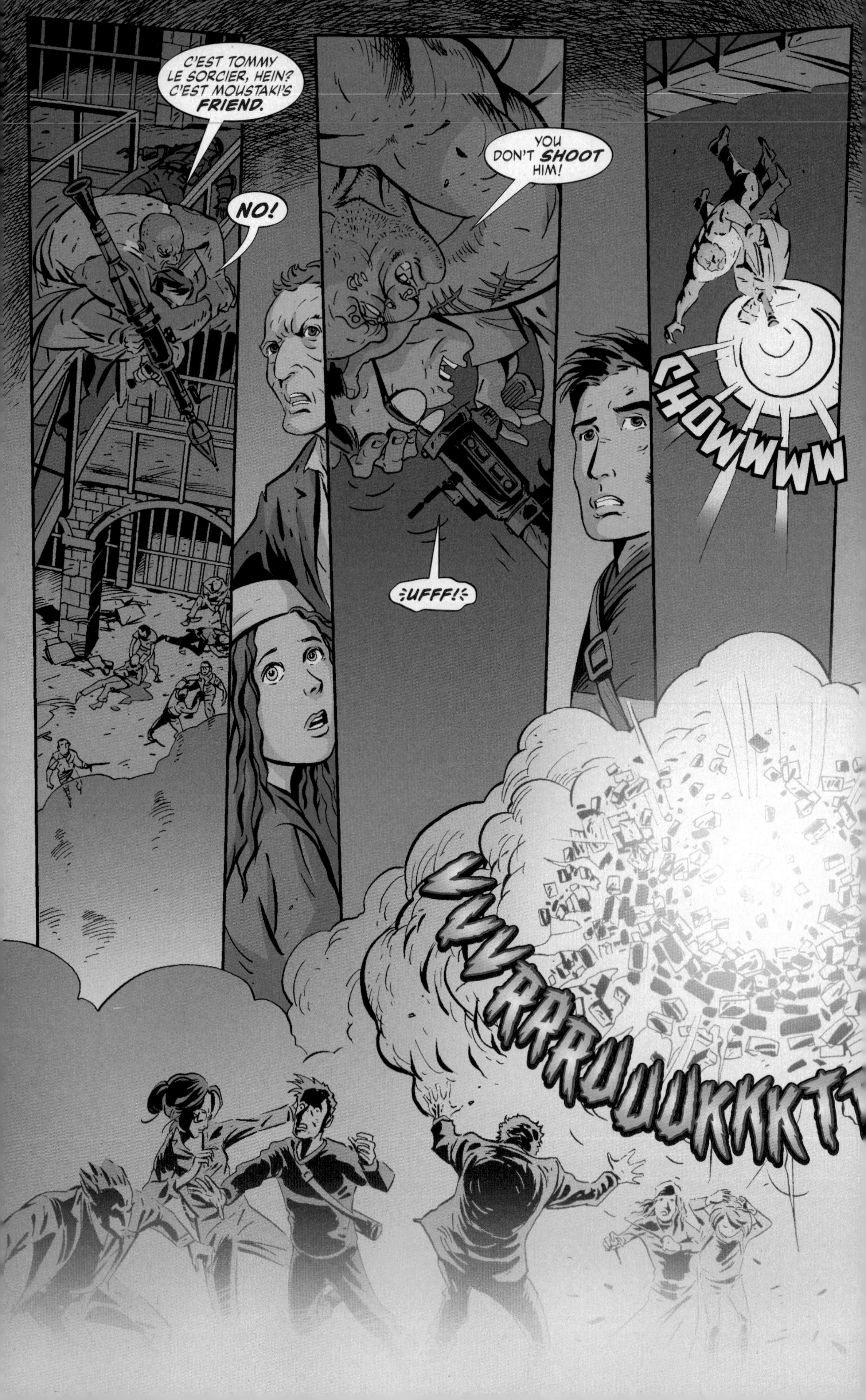
C'EST TOMMY LE SORCIER, HEIN? C'EST MOUSTAKI'S FRIEND.
NO!
YOU DON'T SHOOT HIM!
UFFF!
CHOWWWW
VVVRRRUUUKKKTT

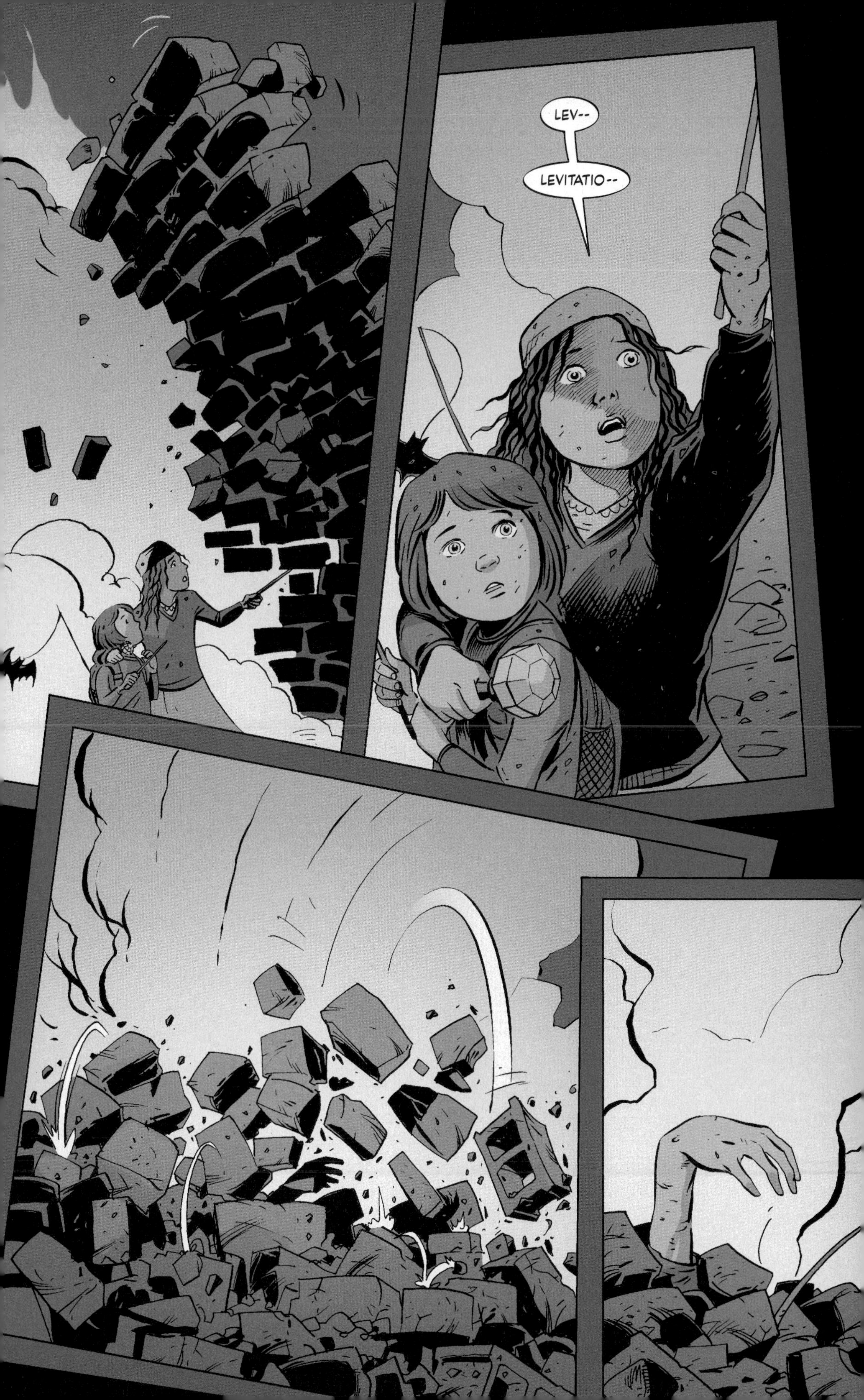
LEV--
LEVITATIO--

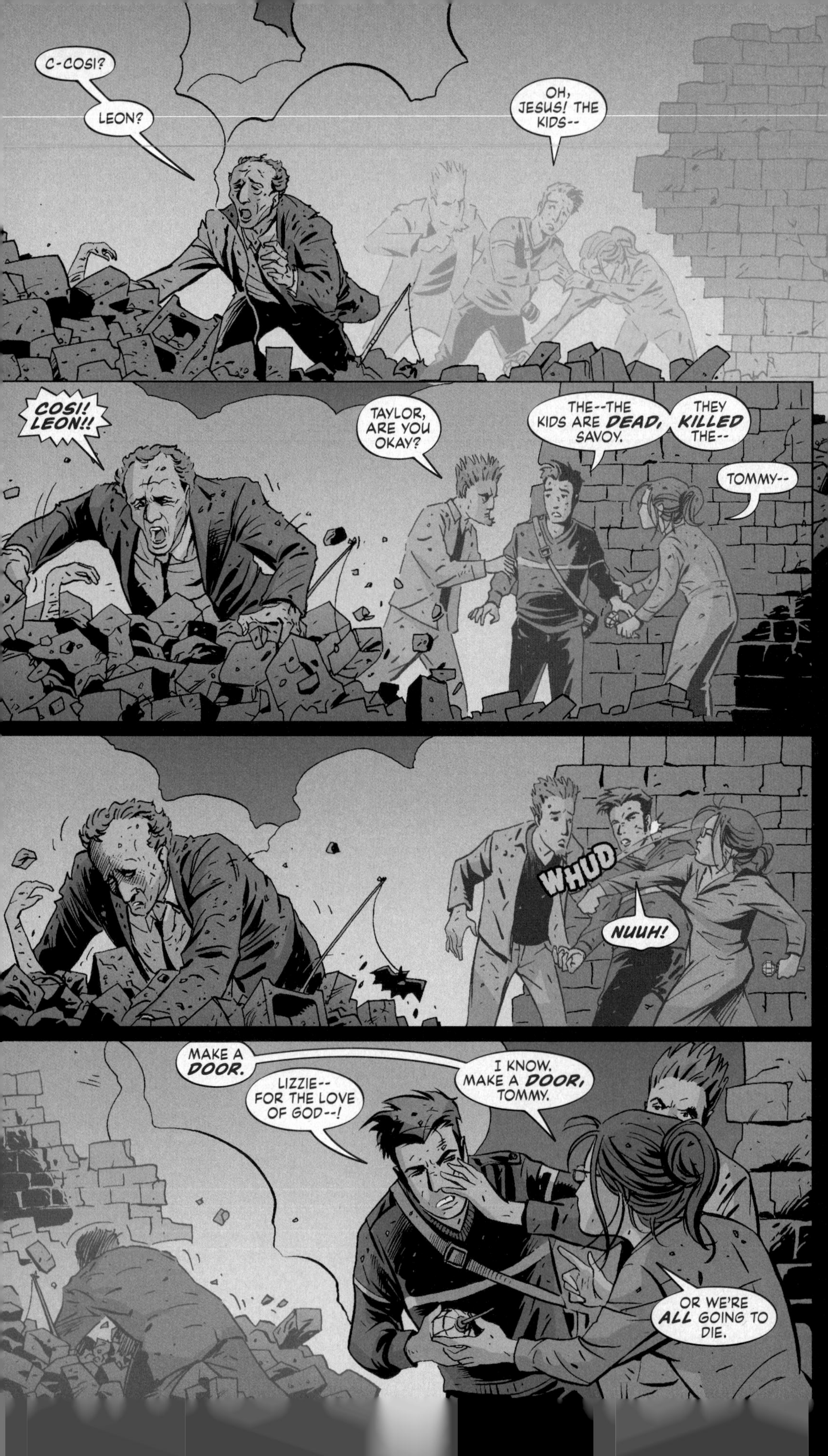
C-COSI?
LEON?
OH, JESUS! THE KIDS--
COSI! LEON!!
TAYLOR, ARE YOU OKAY?
THE--THE KIDS ARE DEAD, SAVOY.
THEY KILLED THE--
TOMMY--
WHUD
NUUH!
MAKE A DOOR.
LIZZIE-- FOR THE LOVE OF GOD--!
I KNOW. MAKE A DOOR, TOMMY.
OR WE'RE ALL GOING TO DIE.

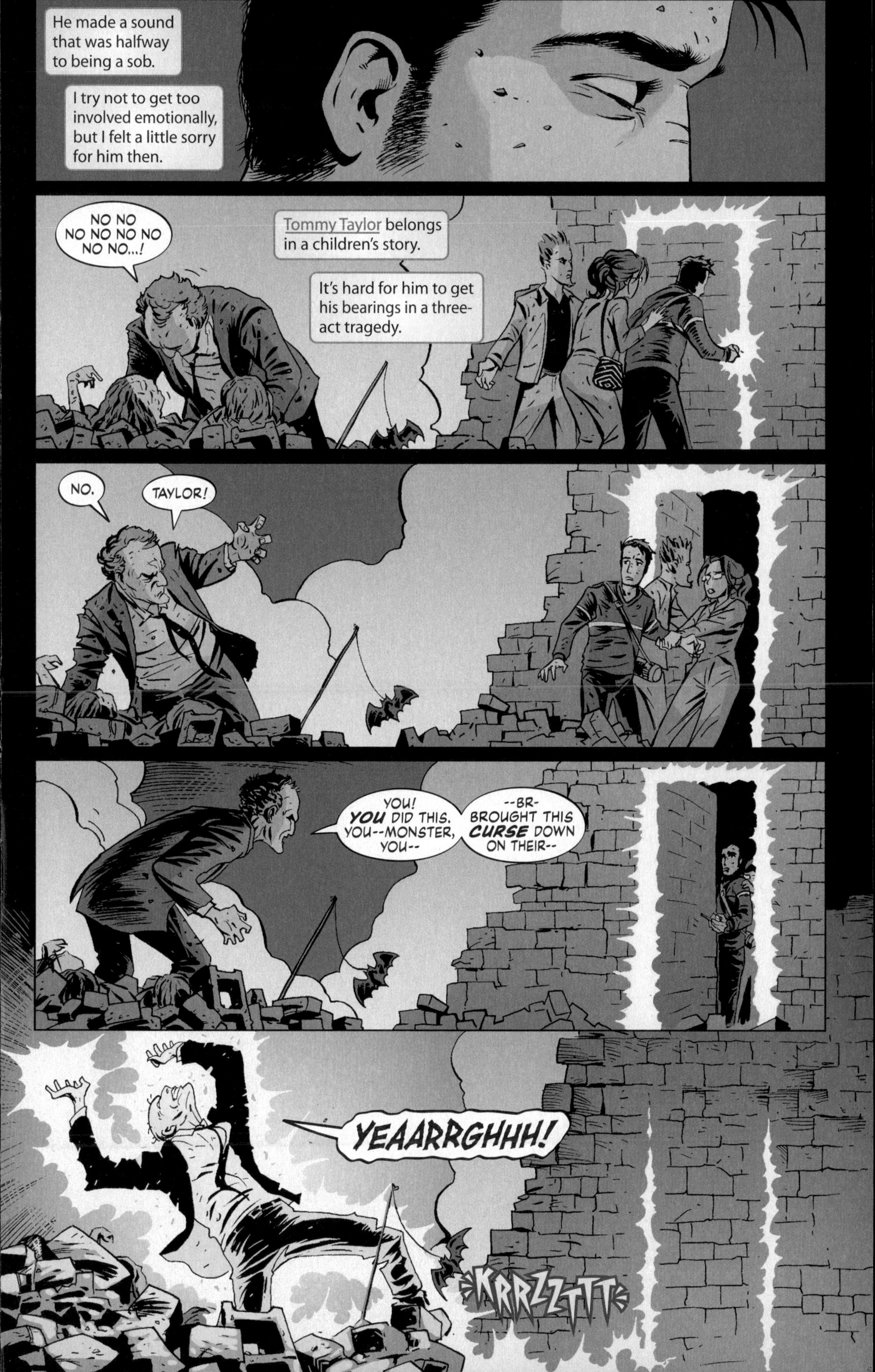
He made a sound that was halfway to being a sob.
I try not to get too involved emotionally, but I felt a little sorry for him then.
NO NO NO NO NO NO NO NO...!
Tommy Taylor belongs in a children's story.
It's hard for him to get his bearings in a three-act tragedy.
NO.
TAYLOR!
YOU! YOU DID THIS. YOU--MONSTER, YOU--
--BR- BROUGHT THIS CURSE DOWN ON THEIR--
YEAARRGHHH!
KRRZZTTT

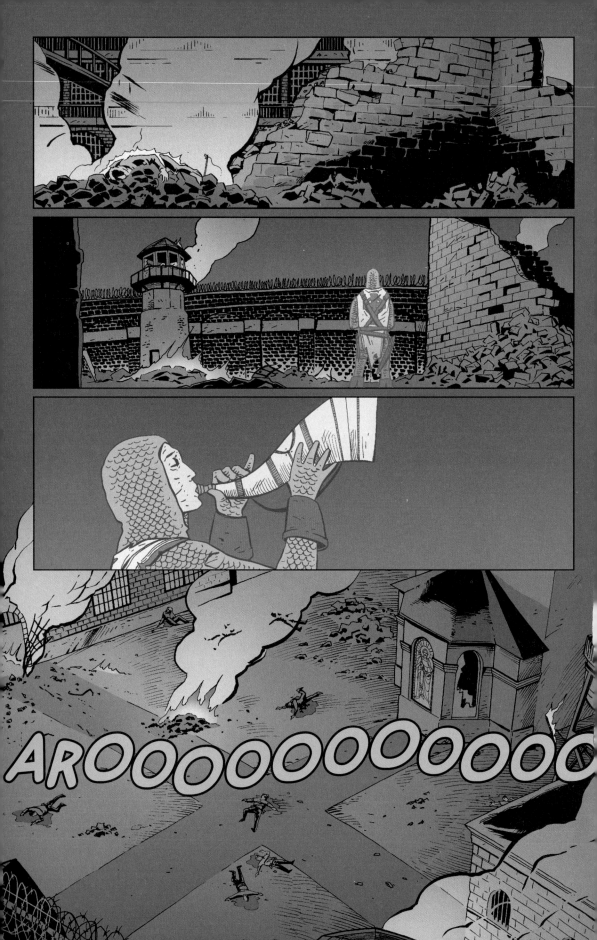

AROOOOOOOOOOOOO

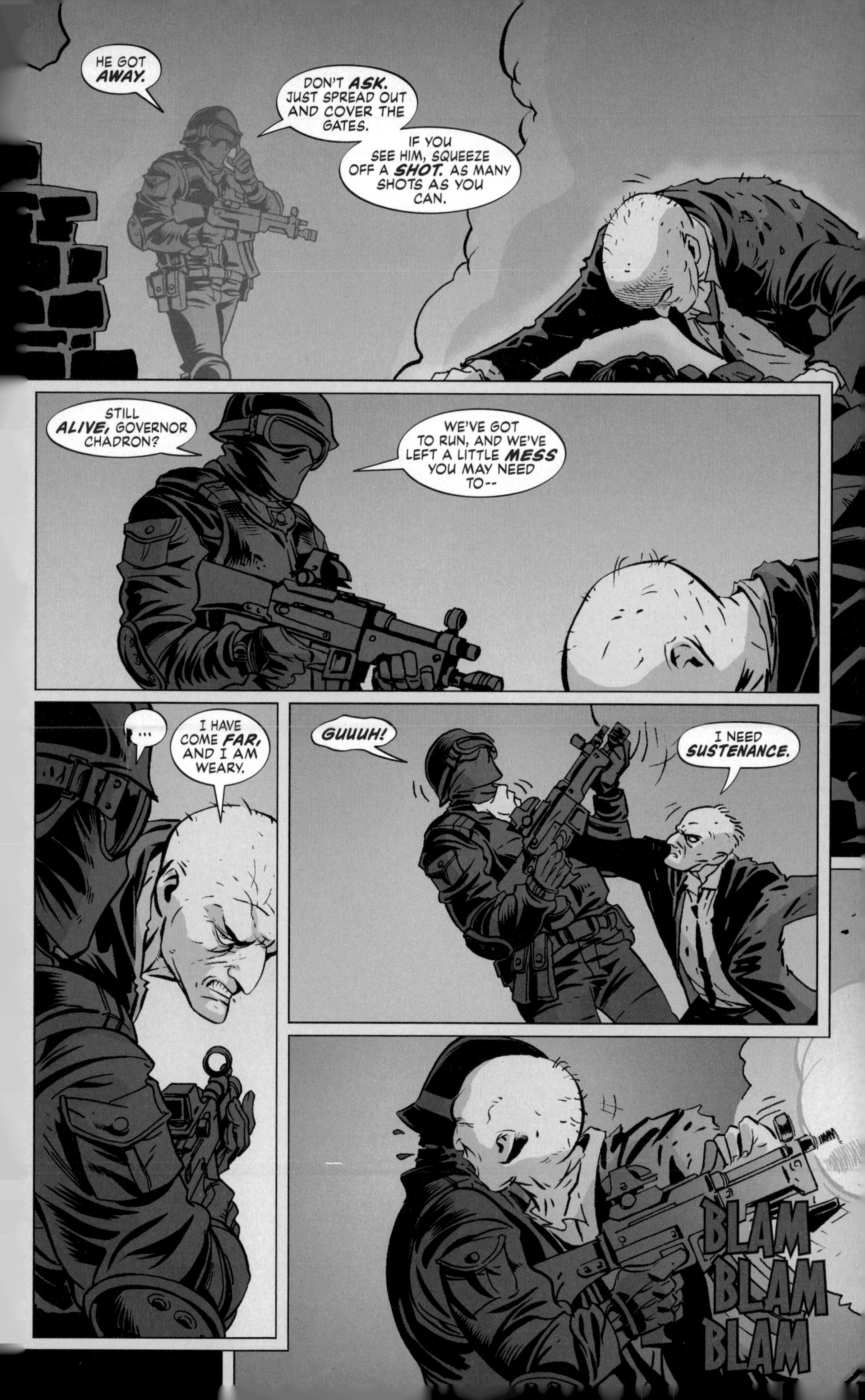
HE GOT AWAY.
DON'T ASK. JUST SPREAD OUT AND COVER THE GATES.
IF YOU SEE HIM, SQUEEZE OFF A SHOT. AS MANY SHOTS AS YOU CAN.
STILL ALIVE, GOVERNOR CHADRON?
WE'VE GOT TO RUN, AND WE'VE LEFT A LITTLE MESS YOU MAY NEED TO--
...
I HAVE COME FAR, AND I AM WEARY.
GUUUH!
I NEED SUSTENANCE.
BLAM BLAM BLAM

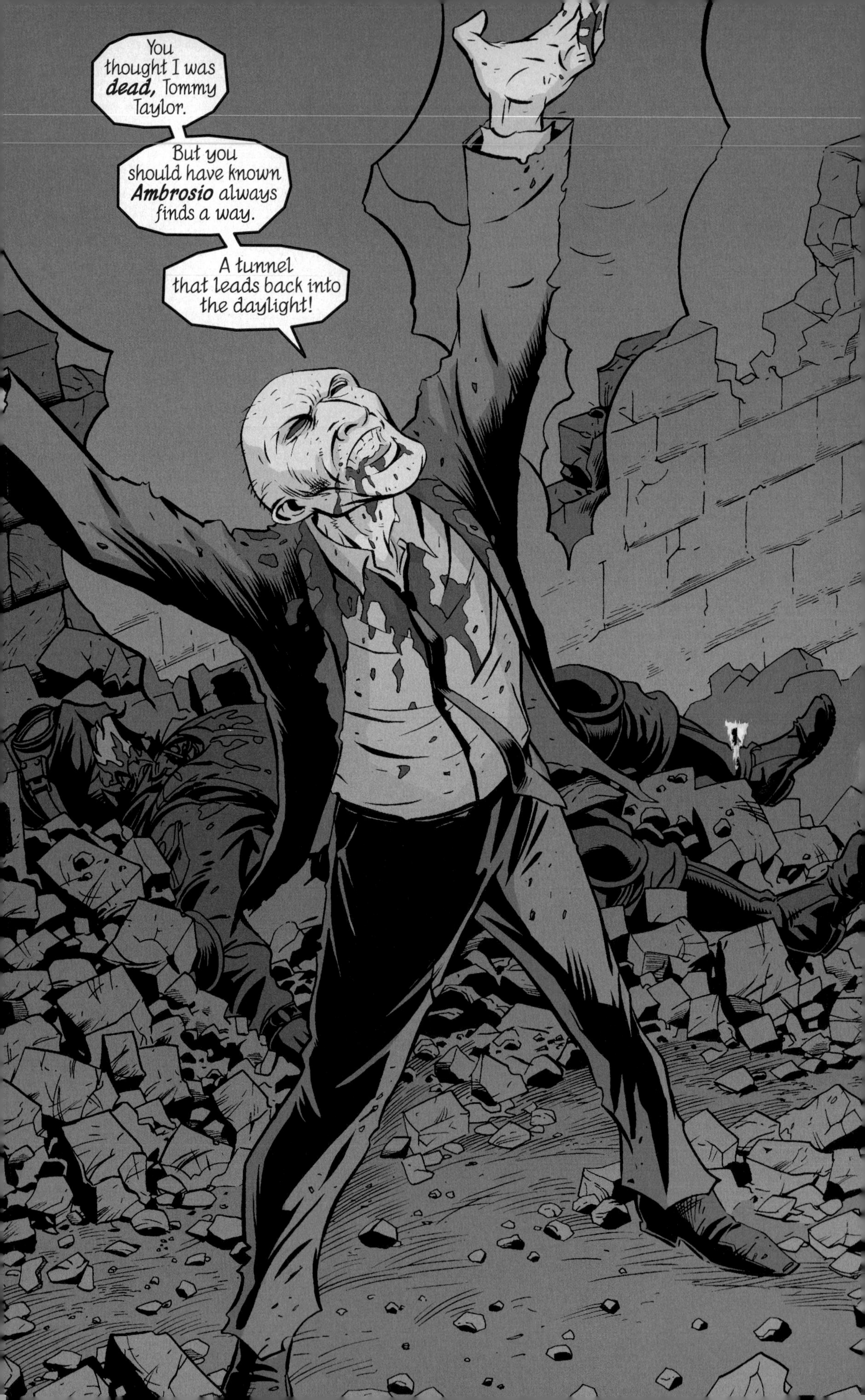
You thought I was **dead,** Tommy Taylor.
But you should have known ***Ambrosio*** always finds a way.
A tunnel that leads back into the daylight!

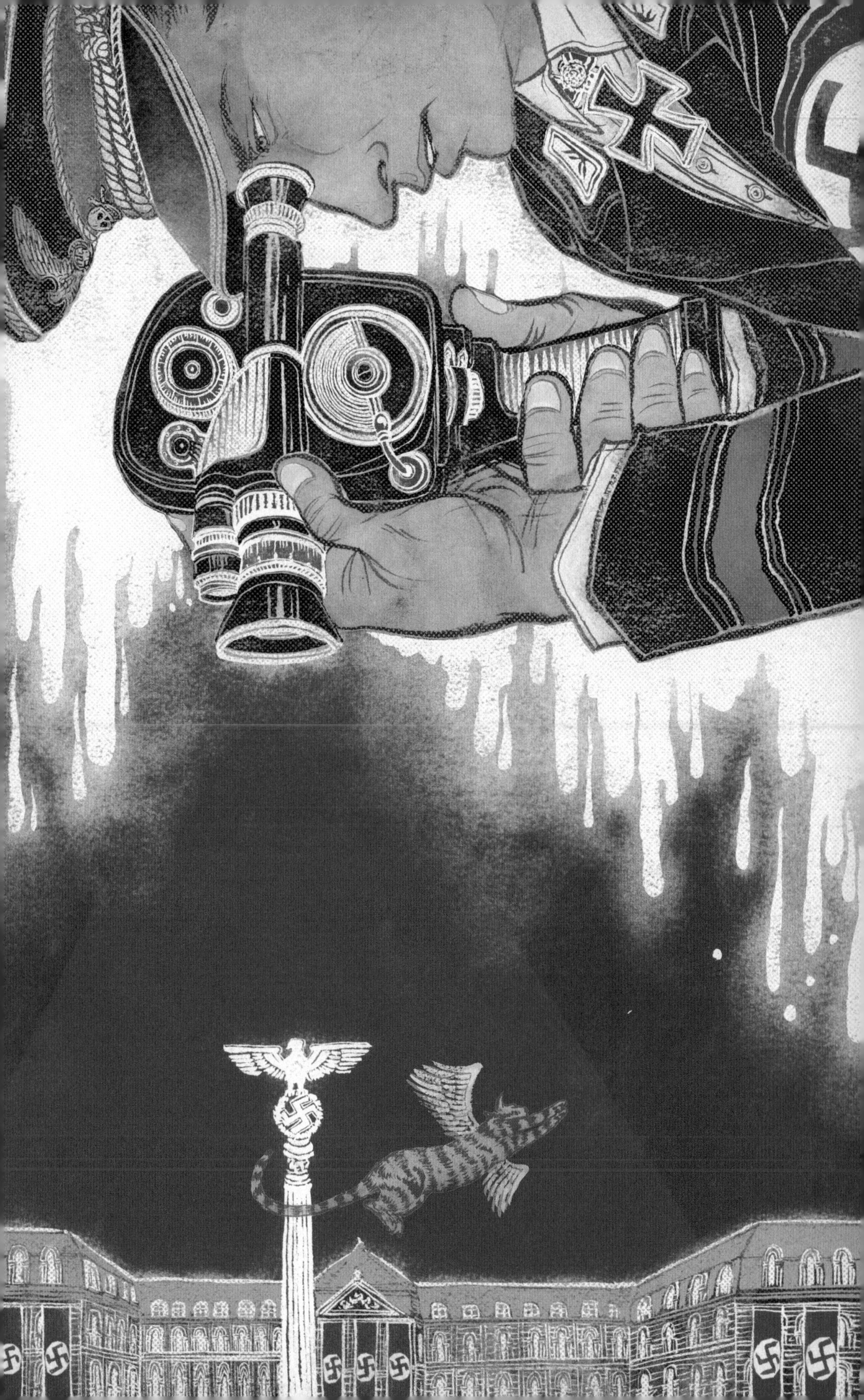

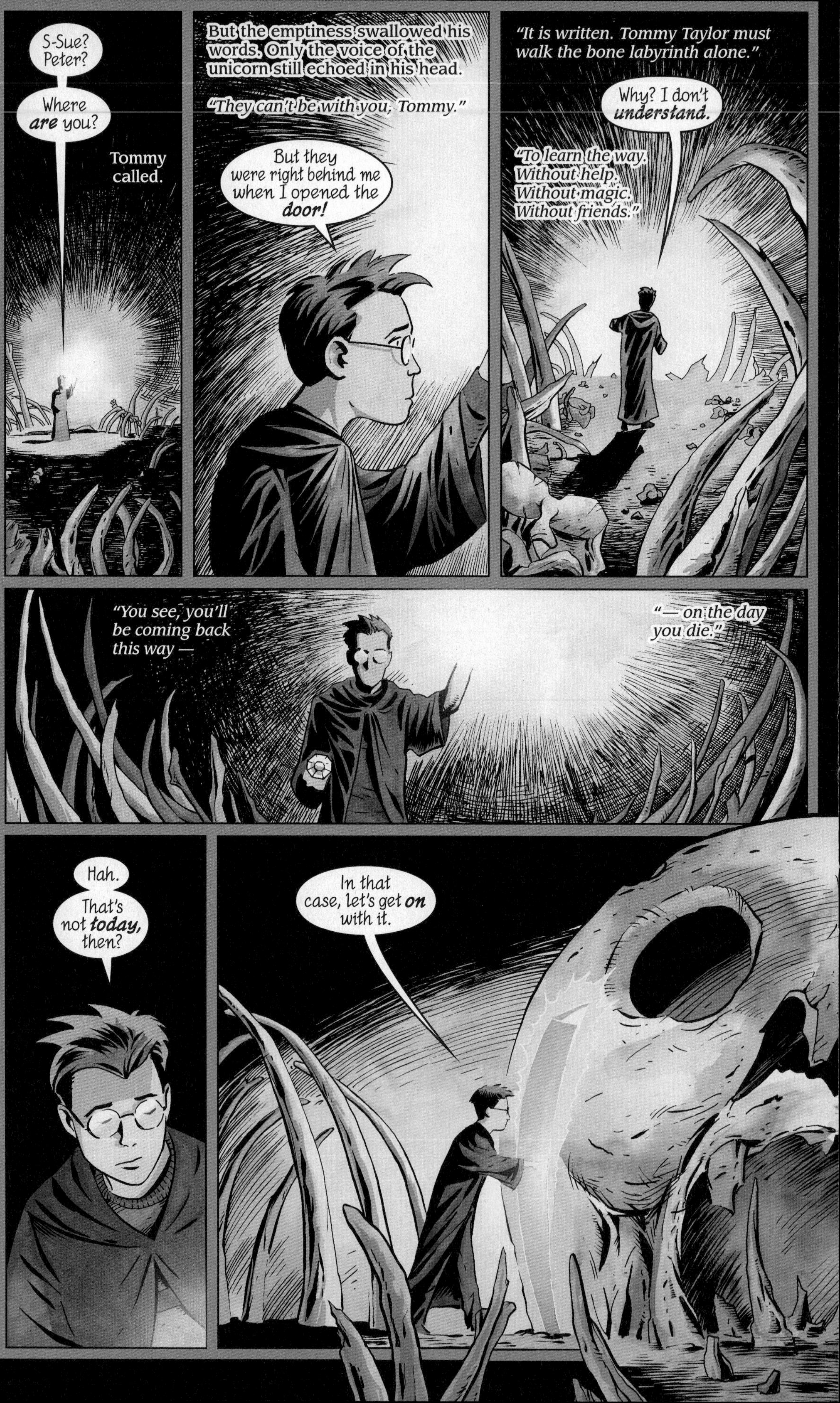
S-Sue? Peter?
Where are you?
Tommy called.
But the emptiness swallowed his words. Only the voice of the unicorn still echoed in his head.
"They can't be with you, Tommy."
But they were right behind me when I opened the door!
"It is written. Tommy Taylor must walk the bone labyrinth alone."
Why? I don't understand.
"To learn the way. Without help. Without magic. Without friends."
"You see, you'll be coming back this way —
"— on the day you die."
Hah.
That's not today, then?
In that case, let's get on with it.

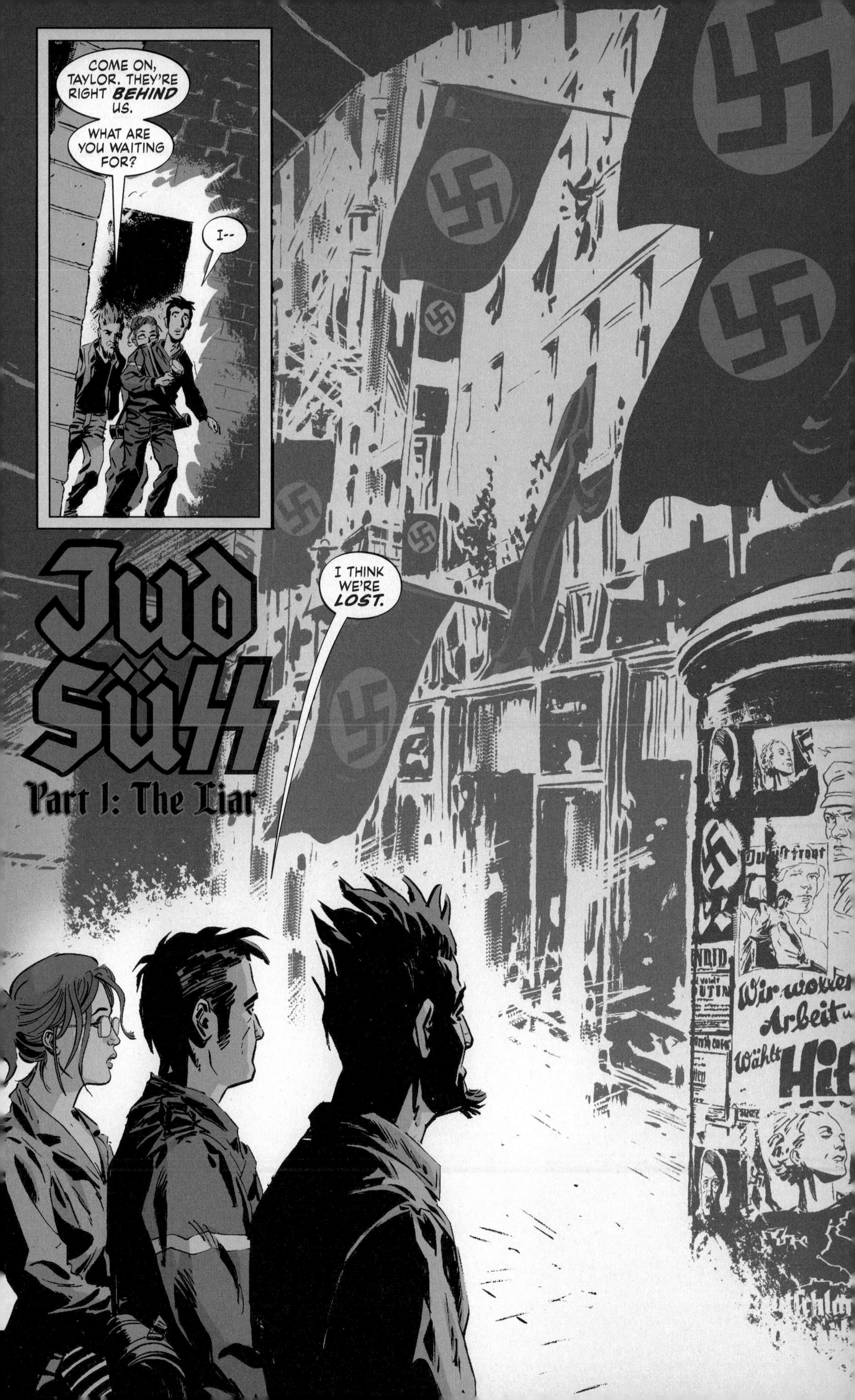

COME ON, TAYLOR. THEY'RE RIGHT BEHIND US.
WHAT ARE YOU WAITING FOR?
I--
Jud Süß
Part 1: The Liar
I THINK WE'RE LOST.

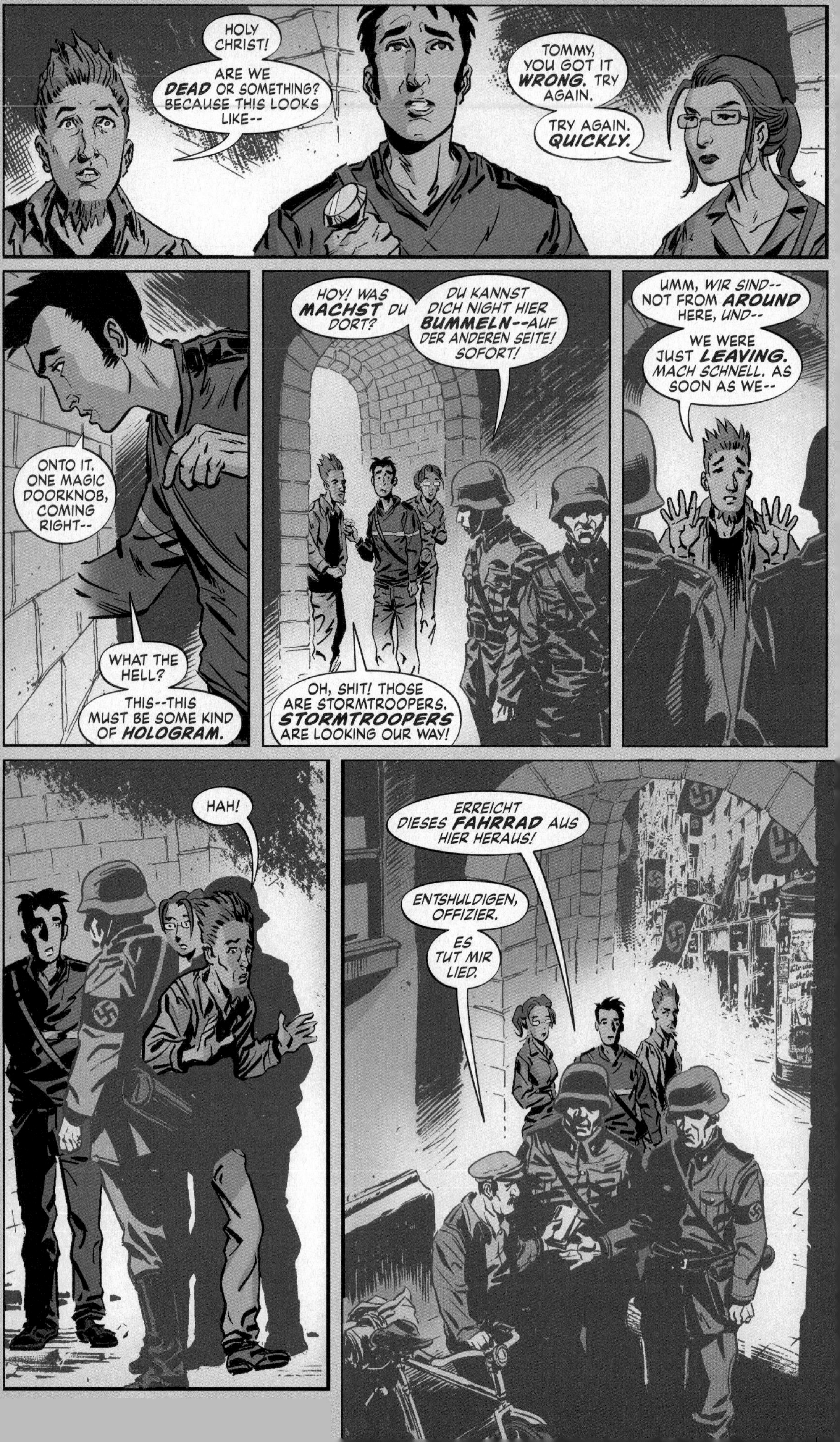
HOLY CHRIST!
ARE WE DEAD OR SOMETHING? BECAUSE THIS LOOKS LIKE--
TOMMY, YOU GOT IT WRONG. TRY AGAIN.
TRY AGAIN. QUICKLY.
ONTO IT. ONE MAGIC DOORKNOB, COMING RIGHT--
WHAT THE HELL?
THIS--THIS MUST BE SOME KIND OF HOLOGRAM.
HOY! WAS MACHST DU DORT?
DU KANNST DICH NIGHT HIER BUMMELN--AUF DER ANDEREN SEITE! SOFORT!
OH, SHIT! THOSE ARE STORMTROOPERS. STORMTROOPERS ARE LOOKING OUR WAY!
UMM, WIR SIND-- NOT FROM AROUND HERE, UND--
WE WERE JUST LEAVING. MACH SCHNELL. AS SOON AS WE--
HAH!
ERREICHT DIESES FAHRRAD AUS HIER HERAUS!
ENTSHULDIGEN, OFFIZIER.
ES TUT MIR LIED.

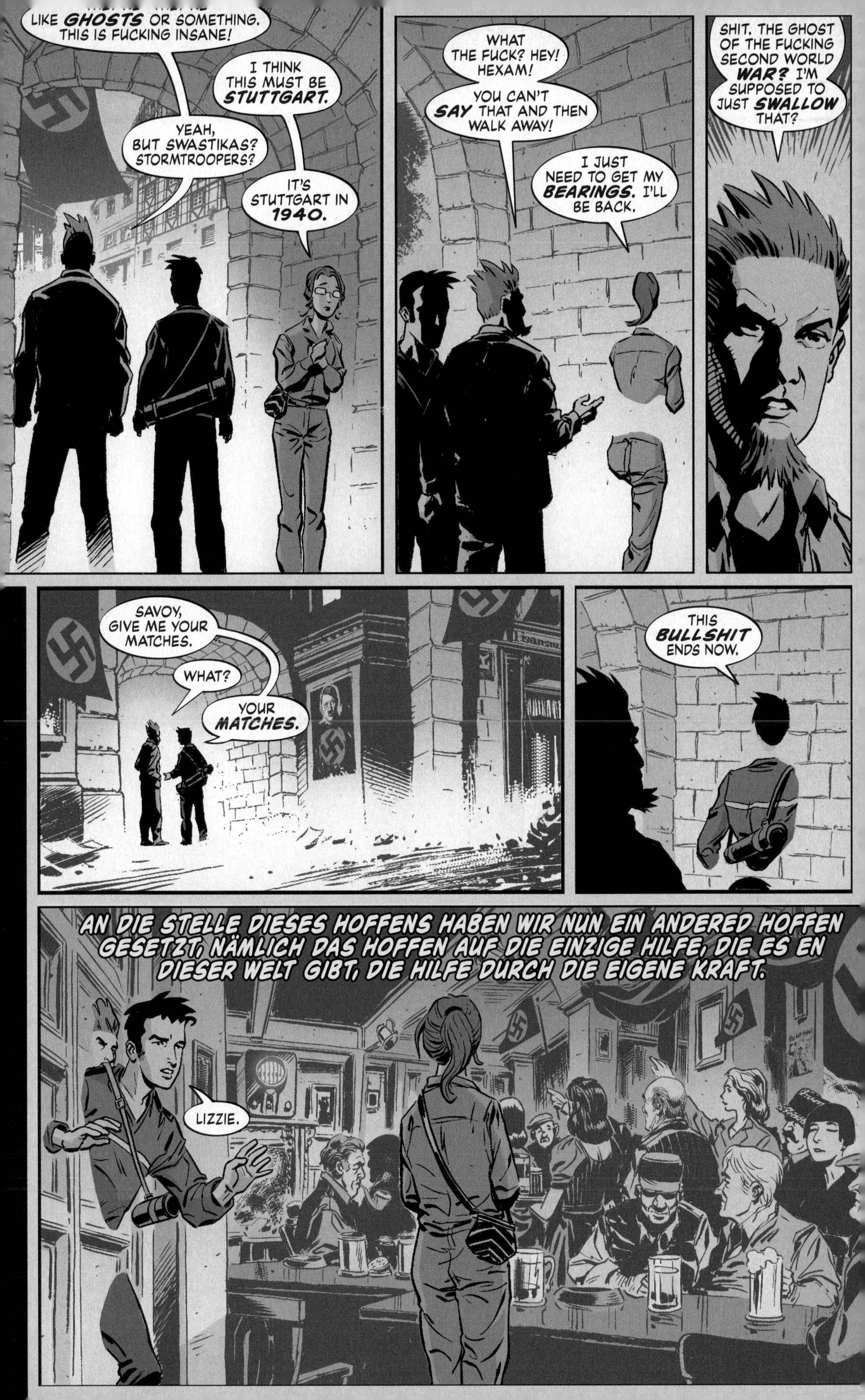
LIKE GHOSTS OR SOMETHING. THIS IS FUCKING INSANE!
I THINK THIS MUST BE STUTTGART.
YEAH, BUT SWASTIKAS? STORMTROOPERS?
IT'S STUTTGART IN 1940.
WHAT THE FUCK? HEY! HEXAM!
YOU CAN'T SAY THAT AND THEN WALK AWAY!
I JUST NEED TO GET MY BEARINGS. I'LL BE BACK.
SHIT. THE GHOST OF THE FUCKING SECOND WORLD WAR? I'M SUPPOSED TO JUST SWALLOW THAT?
SAVOY, GIVE ME YOUR MATCHES.
WHAT?
YOUR MATCHES.
THIS BULLSHIT ENDS NOW.
AN DIE STELLE DIESES HOFFENS HABEN WIR NUN EIN ANDERED HOFFEN GESETZT, NÄMLICH DAS HOFFEN AUF DIE EINZIGE HILFE, DIE ES EN DIESER WELT GIBT, DIE HILFE DURCH DIE EIGENE KRAFT.
LIZZIE.

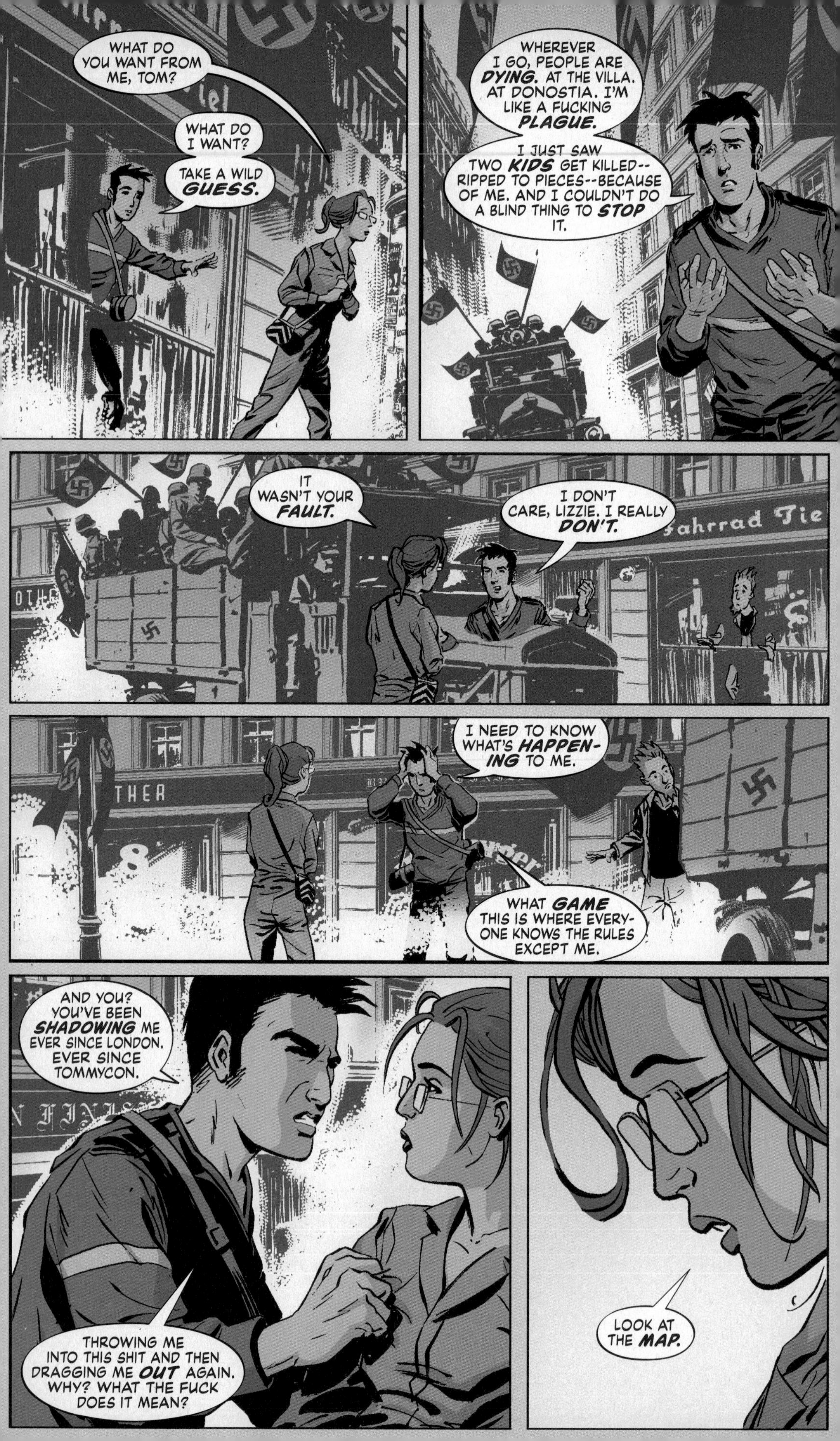

WHAT DO YOU WANT FROM ME, TOM?
WHAT DO I WANT?
TAKE A WILD GUESS.
WHEREVER I GO, PEOPLE ARE DYING. AT THE VILLA. AT DONOSTIA. I'M LIKE A FUCKING PLAGUE.
I JUST SAW TWO KIDS GET KILLED--RIPPED TO PIECES--BECAUSE OF ME. AND I COULDN'T DO A BLIND THING TO STOP IT.
IT WASN'T YOUR FAULT.
I DON'T CARE, LIZZIE. I REALLY DON'T.
I NEED TO KNOW WHAT'S HAPPEN-ING TO ME.
WHAT GAME THIS IS WHERE EVERY-ONE KNOWS THE RULES EXCEPT ME.
AND YOU? YOU'VE BEEN SHADOWING ME EVER SINCE LONDON. EVER SINCE TOMMYCON.
THROWING ME INTO THIS SHIT AND THEN DRAGGING ME OUT AGAIN. WHY? WHAT THE FUCK DOES IT MEAN?
LOOK AT THE MAP.

THE MAP?

YES.

WHY?

BECAUSE THAT'S WHY WE'RE *HERE*, TOMMY.

YOU SEE?

I DON'T SEE *ANYTHING.* MOST OF THESE COASTLINES DON'T EVEN LOOK LIKE--

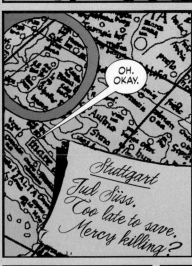

OH. OKAY.

Stuttgart Jud Süss. Too late to save. Mercy killing?

SO *STUTTGART'S* ON THERE. AND THERE'S A NOTE.

"JUD SÜSS? TOO LATE TO SAVE?" I DON'T GET IT.

I CAN'T *EXPLAIN* JUST YET, TOMMY.

PLEASE BELIEVE ME. I CAN'T.

WELL, THAT'S A REAL *PITY.*

BECAUSE IN THAT CASE--

--I'M ABOUT TO MAKE A *BONFIRE* OUT OF WHAT YOU CALLED "MY DESTINY."

TSHRIFFF

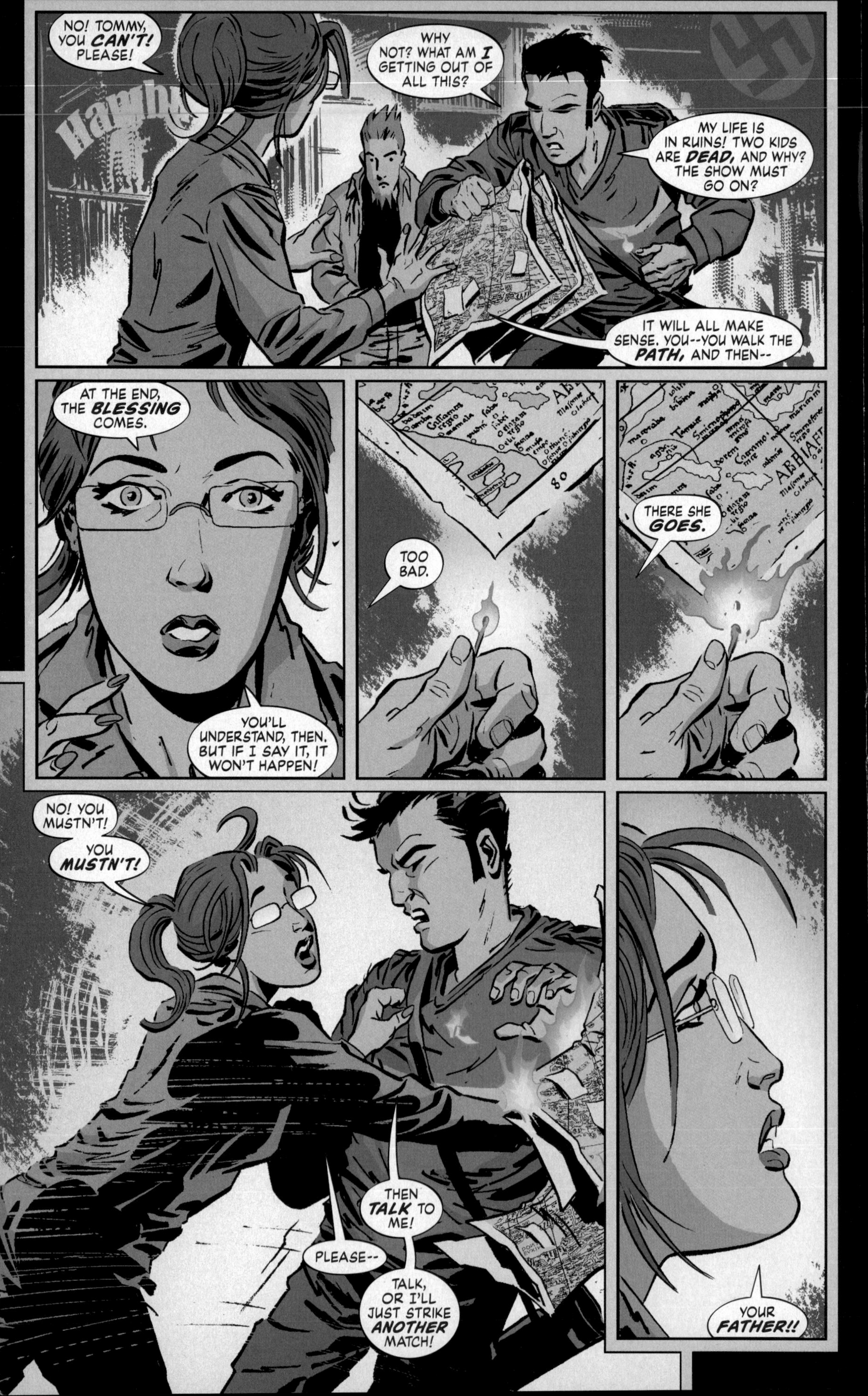

NO! TOMMY, YOU CAN'T! PLEASE!
WHY NOT? WHAT AM I GETTING OUT OF ALL THIS?
MY LIFE IS IN RUINS! TWO KIDS ARE DEAD, AND WHY? THE SHOW MUST GO ON?
IT WILL ALL MAKE SENSE. YOU--YOU WALK THE PATH, AND THEN--
AT THE END, THE BLESSING COMES.
YOU'LL UNDERSTAND, THEN. BUT IF I SAY IT, IT WON'T HAPPEN!
TOO BAD.
THERE SHE GOES.
NO! YOU MUSTN'T!
YOU MUSTN'T!
THEN TALK TO ME!
PLEASE--
TALK, OR I'LL JUST STRIKE ANOTHER MATCH!
YOUR FATHER!!

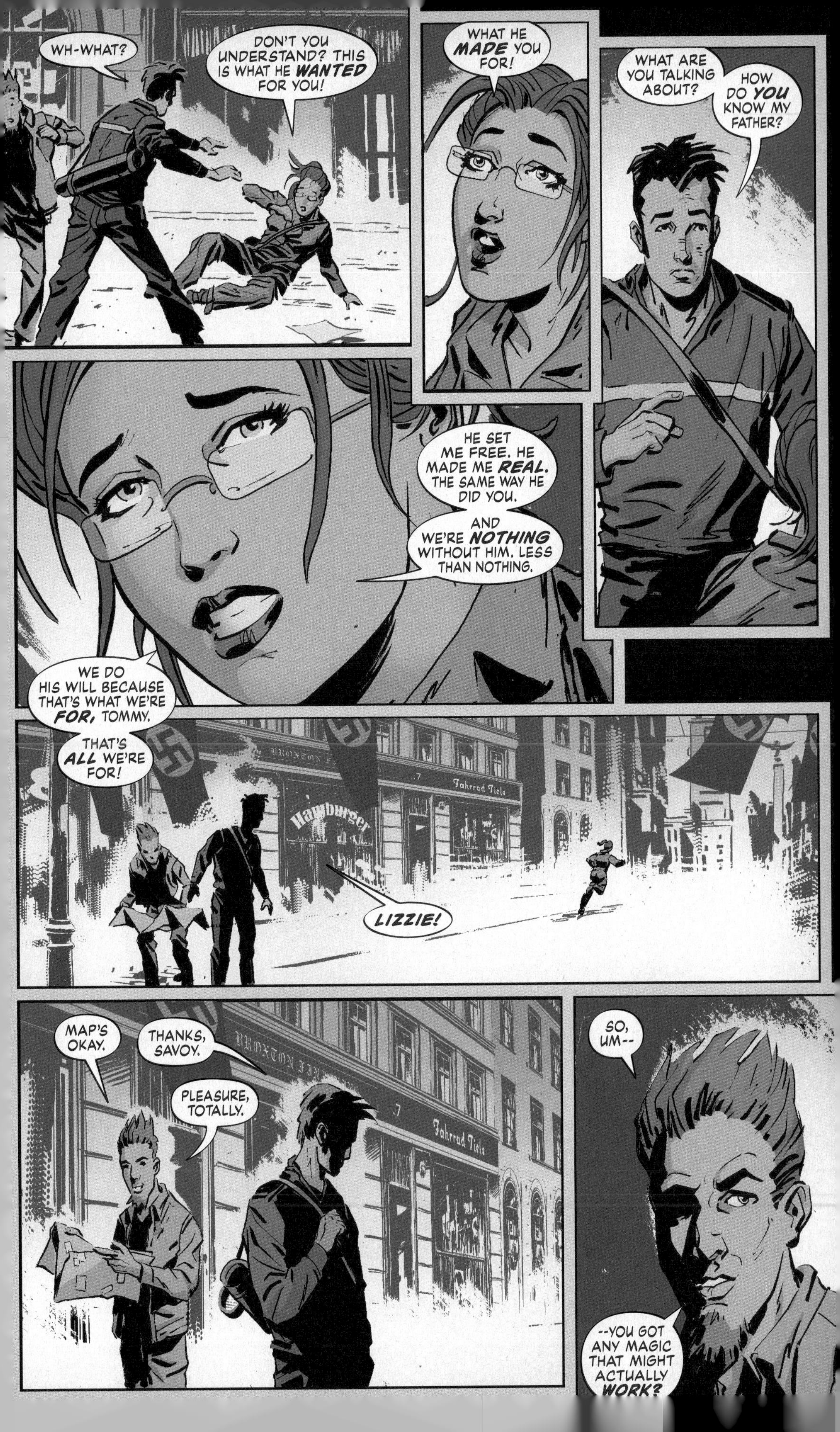
WH-WHAT?
DON'T YOU UNDERSTAND? THIS IS WHAT HE WANTED FOR YOU!
WHAT HE MADE YOU FOR!
WHAT ARE YOU TALKING ABOUT?
HOW DO YOU KNOW MY FATHER?
HE SET ME FREE. HE MADE ME REAL. THE SAME WAY HE DID YOU.
AND WE'RE NOTHING WITHOUT HIM. LESS THAN NOTHING.
WE DO HIS WILL BECAUSE THAT'S WHAT WE'RE FOR, TOMMY.
THAT'S ALL WE'RE FOR!
Hamburger
Fahrrad Tiels
LIZZIE!
MAP'S OKAY.
THANKS, SAVOY.
PLEASURE, TOTALLY.
SO, UM--
--YOU GOT ANY MAGIC THAT MIGHT ACTUALLY WORK?

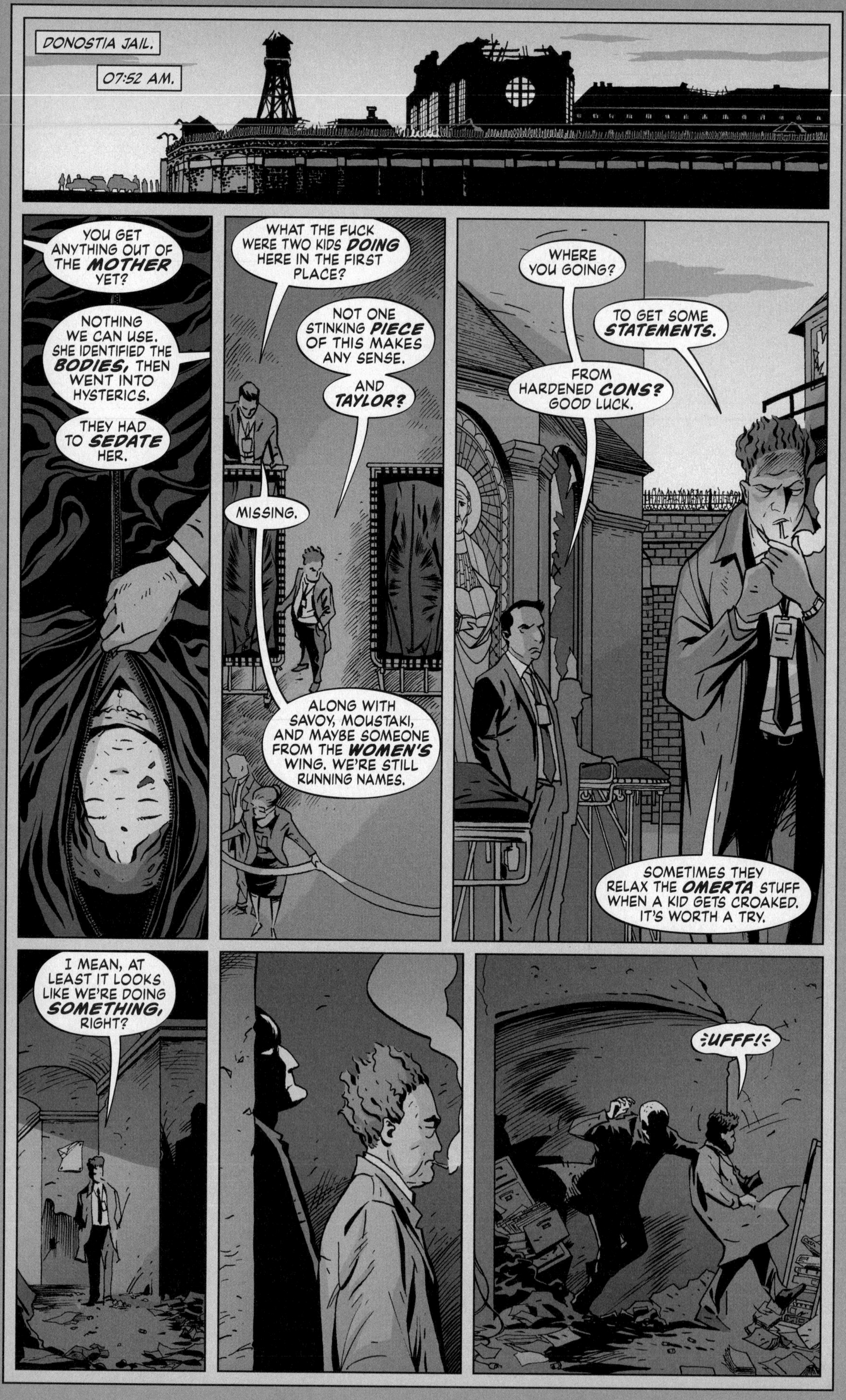
DONOSTIA JAIL.
07:52 AM.
YOU GET ANYTHING OUT OF THE MOTHER YET?
NOTHING WE CAN USE. SHE IDENTIFIED THE BODIES, THEN WENT INTO HYSTERICS.
THEY HAD TO SEDATE HER.
WHAT THE FUCK WERE TWO KIDS DOING HERE IN THE FIRST PLACE?
NOT ONE STINKING PIECE OF THIS MAKES ANY SENSE.
AND TAYLOR?
MISSING.
ALONG WITH SAVOY, MOUSTAKI, AND MAYBE SOMEONE FROM THE WOMEN'S WING. WE'RE STILL RUNNING NAMES.
WHERE YOU GOING?
TO GET SOME STATEMENTS.
FROM HARDENED CONS? GOOD LUCK.
SOMETIMES THEY RELAX THE OMERTA STUFF WHEN A KID GETS CROAKED. IT'S WORTH A TRY.
I MEAN, AT LEAST IT LOOKS LIKE WE'RE DOING SOMETHING, RIGHT?
UFFF!

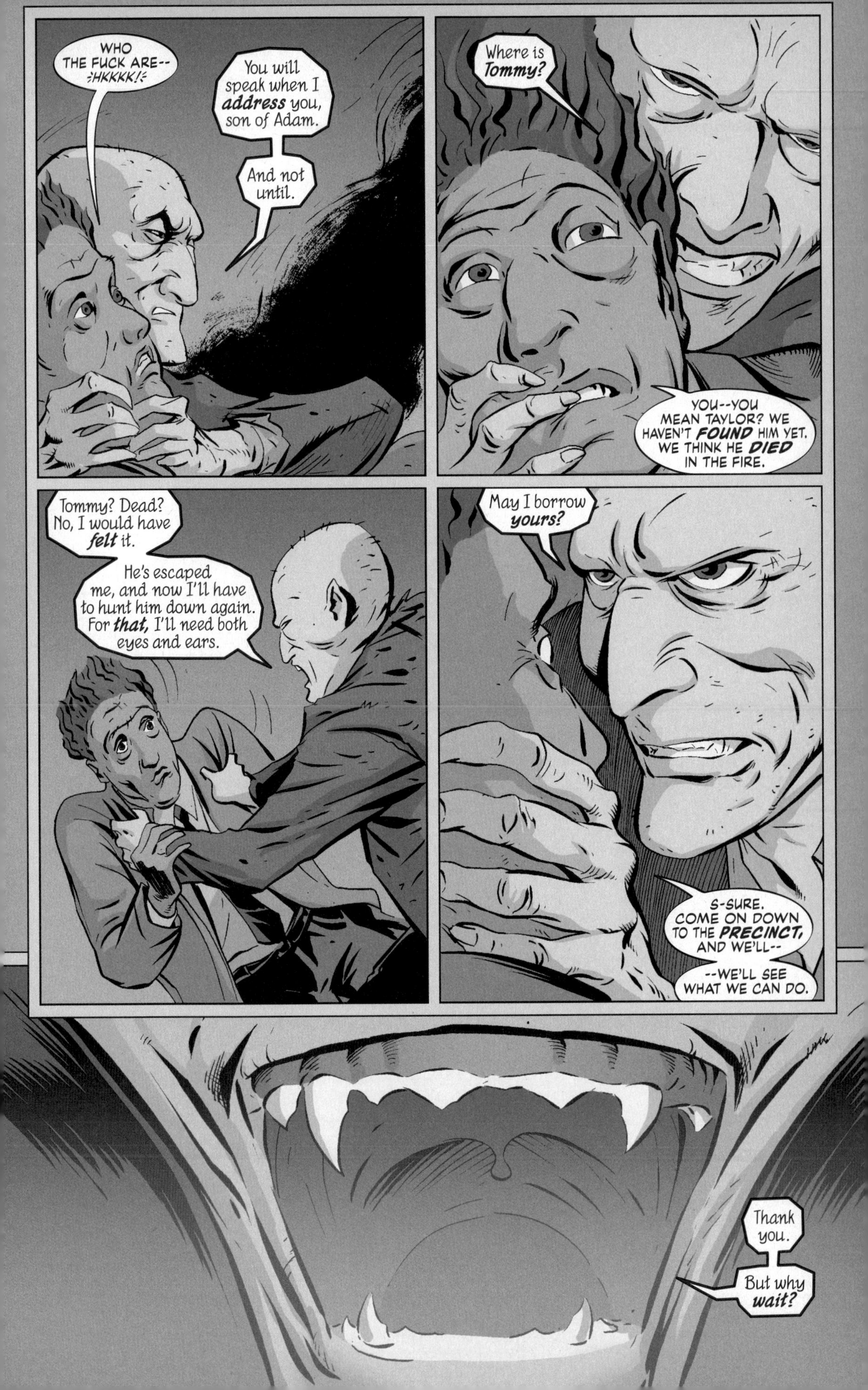
WHO THE FUCK ARE-- HKKKK!
You will speak when I address you, son of Adam.
And not until.
Where is Tommy?
YOU--YOU MEAN TAYLOR? WE HAVEN'T FOUND HIM YET. WE THINK HE DIED IN THE FIRE.
Tommy? Dead? No, I would have felt it.
He's escaped me, and now I'll have to hunt him down again. For that, I'll need both eyes and ears.
May I borrow yours?
S-SURE. COME ON DOWN TO THE PRECINCT, AND WE'LL--
--WE'LL SEE WHAT WE CAN DO.
Thank you.
But why wait?

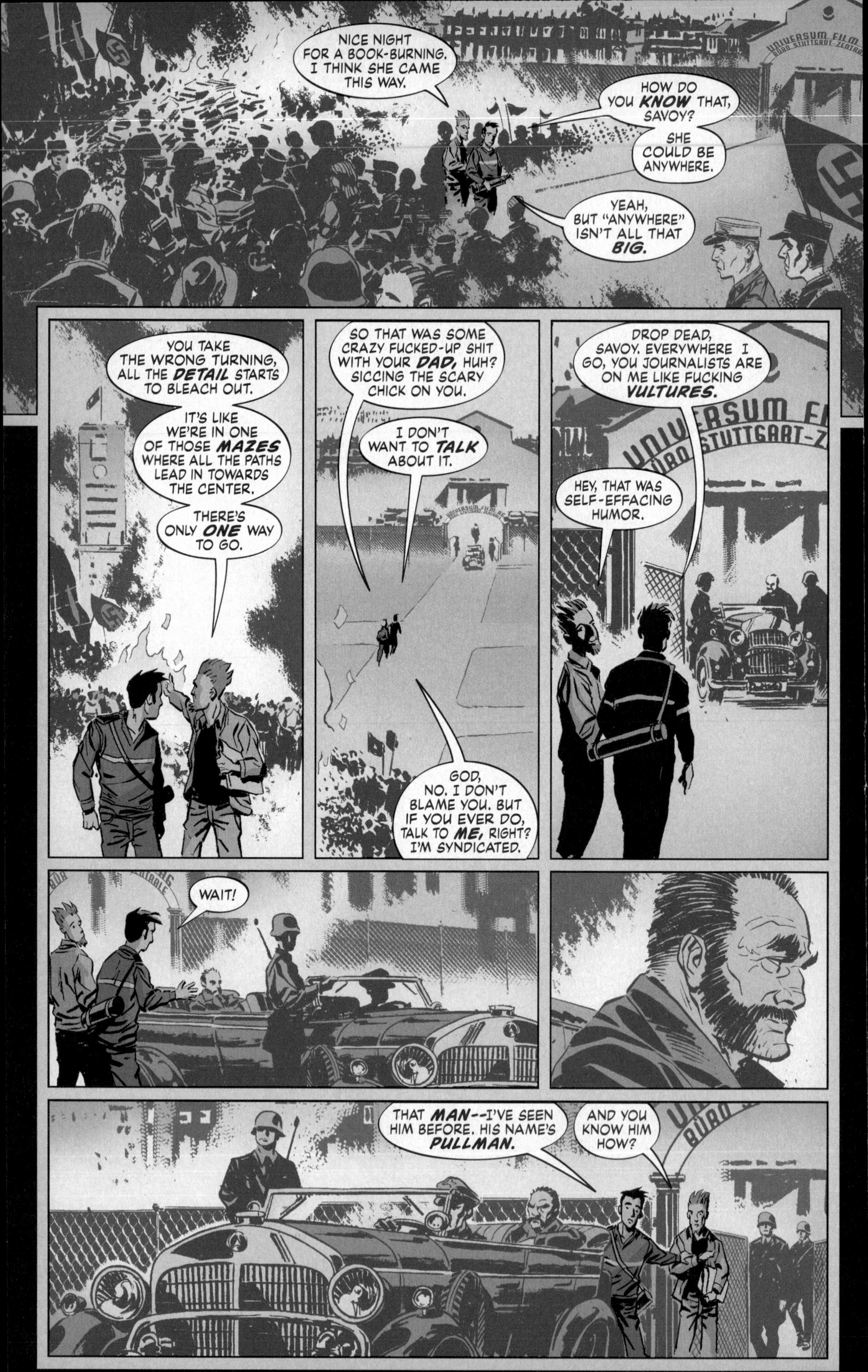

NICE NIGHT FOR A BOOK-BURNING. I THINK SHE CAME THIS WAY.
HOW DO YOU KNOW THAT, SAVOY?
SHE COULD BE ANYWHERE.
YEAH, BUT "ANYWHERE" ISN'T ALL THAT BIG.
UNIVERSUM FILM
YOU TAKE THE WRONG TURNING, ALL THE DETAIL STARTS TO BLEACH OUT.
IT'S LIKE WE'RE IN ONE OF THOSE MAZES WHERE ALL THE PATHS LEAD IN TOWARDS THE CENTER.
THERE'S ONLY ONE WAY TO GO.
SO THAT WAS SOME CRAZY FUCKED-UP SHIT WITH YOUR DAD, HUH? SICCING THE SCARY CHICK ON YOU.
I DON'T WANT TO TALK ABOUT IT.
GOD, NO. I DON'T BLAME YOU. BUT IF YOU EVER DO, TALK TO ME, RIGHT? I'M SYNDICATED.
DROP DEAD, SAVOY. EVERYWHERE I GO, YOU JOURNALISTS ARE ON ME LIKE FUCKING VULTURES.
UNIVERSUM FI
BÜRO STUTTGART-Z
HEY, THAT WAS SELF-EFFACING HUMOR.
WAIT!
THAT MAN--I'VE SEEN HIM BEFORE. HIS NAME'S PULLMAN.
AND YOU KNOW HIM HOW?

HE'S THE REAL *KILLER* FROM THE VILLA *DIODATI.* I THINK WE'VE FOUND THE CENTER OF THE *MAZE.*

YOU'RE SHITTING ME. IF YOU SAW HIM IN *GENEVA,* HE WOULDN'T EVEN HAVE BEEN *BORN* IN 1940.

WE'RE HERE, AREN'T WE? MAYBE HE'S GOT HIS OWN MAGIC DOORKNOB.

IT DOESN'T *MATTER* RIGHT NOW. COME ON, I WANT TO LOOK AROUND THIS PLACE.

FUCK! WHY?

BECAUSE PULLMAN CAME HERE FOR A *REASON.*

AND I WANT TO KNOW WHAT IT *WAS.*

UNIVERSUM FILM
BÜRO STUTTGART-ZENT

AND THAT IS JUD SÜSS. *OUR* JUD SÜSS. YOUR COMMENTS, PLEASE.

IT--I WOULD NOT HAVE *BELIEVED* IT, HERR REICHSMINISTER, GIVEN THE SOURCE...

THIS MOVIE IS A *MASTERPIECE* FOR THE MODERN ERA! EVERY GERMAN CITIZEN AND SOLDIER SHOULD SEE IT.

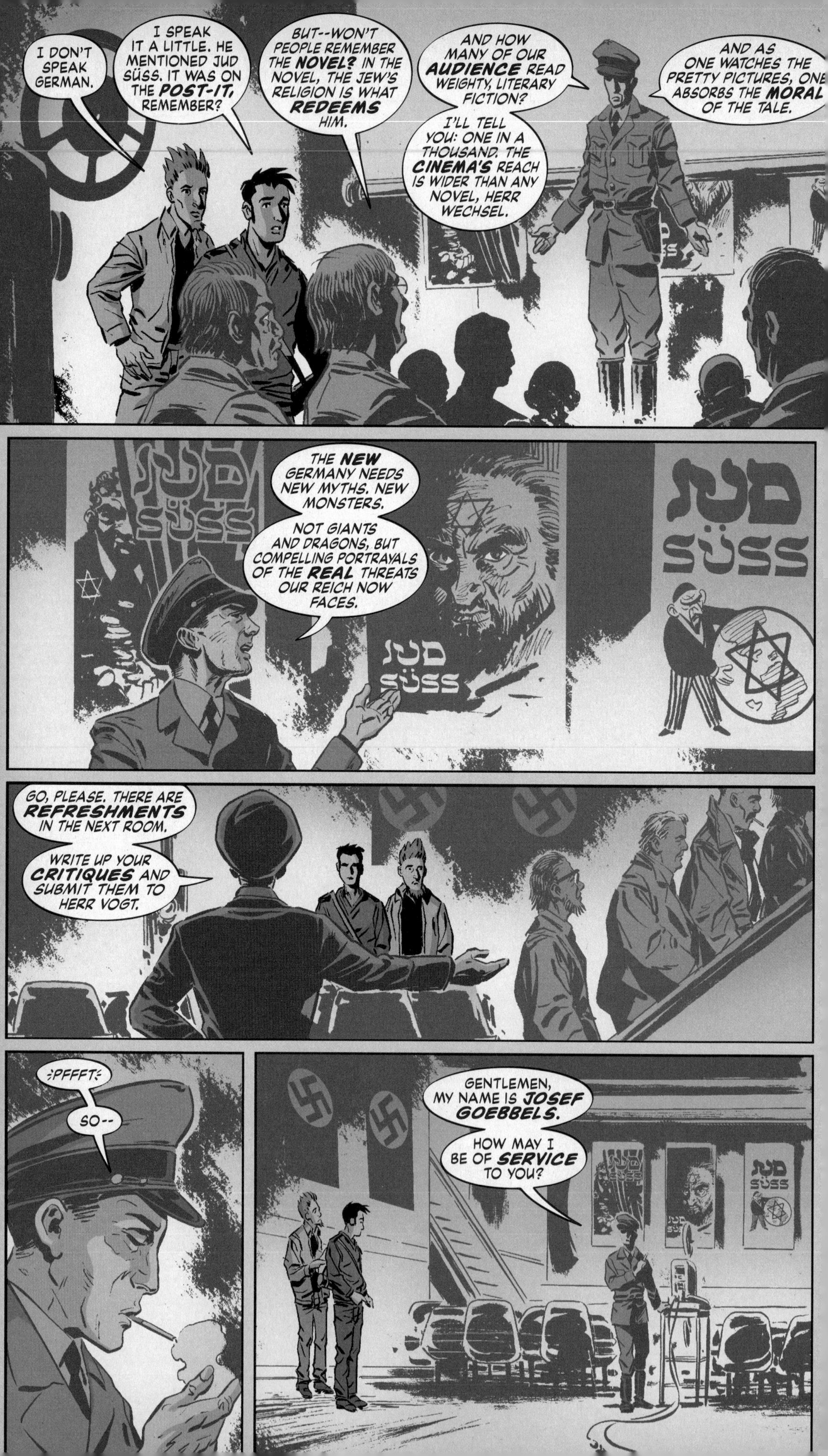
I DON'T SPEAK GERMAN.
I SPEAK IT A LITTLE. HE MENTIONED JUD SÜSS. IT WAS ON THE POST-IT, REMEMBER?
BUT--WON'T PEOPLE REMEMBER THE NOVEL? IN THE NOVEL, THE JEW'S RELIGION IS WHAT REDEEMS HIM.
AND HOW MANY OF OUR AUDIENCE READ WEIGHTY, LITERARY FICTION?
I'LL TELL YOU: ONE IN A THOUSAND. THE CINEMA'S REACH IS WIDER THAN ANY NOVEL, HERR WECHSEL.
AND AS ONE WATCHES THE PRETTY PICTURES, ONE ABSORBS THE MORAL OF THE TALE.
JUD SÜSS
THE NEW GERMANY NEEDS NEW MYTHS. NEW MONSTERS.
NOT GIANTS AND DRAGONS, BUT COMPELLING PORTRAYALS OF THE REAL THREATS OUR REICH NOW FACES.
JUD SÜSS
JUD SÜSS
GO, PLEASE. THERE ARE REFRESHMENTS IN THE NEXT ROOM.
WRITE UP YOUR CRITIQUES AND SUBMIT THEM TO HERR VOGT.
PFFFT
SO--
GENTLEMEN, MY NAME IS JOSEF GOEBBELS.
HOW MAY I BE OF SERVICE TO YOU?
JUD SÜSS

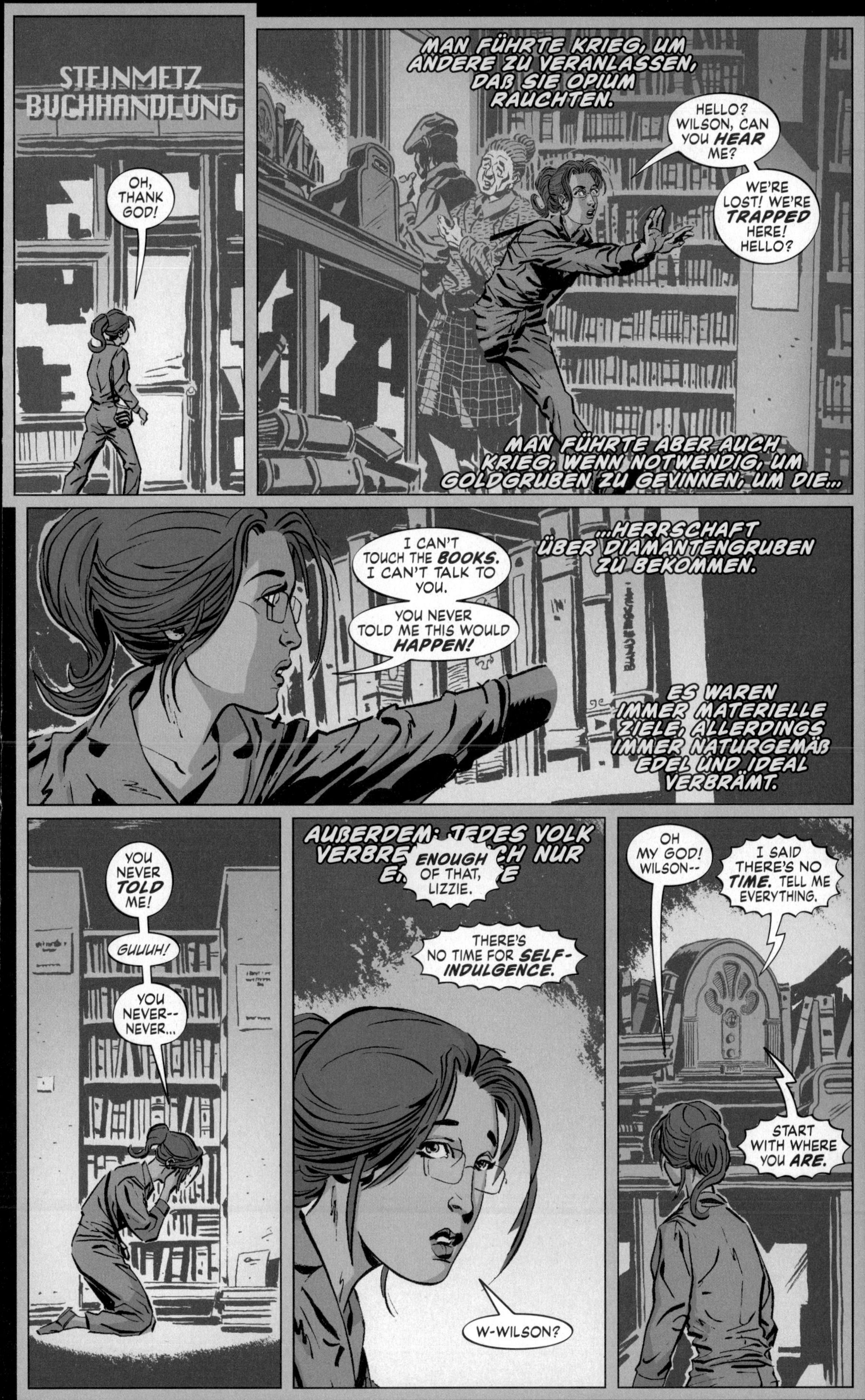
STEINMETZ BUCHHANDLUNG
OH, THANK GOD!
MAN FÜHRTE KRIEG, UM ANDERE ZU VERANLASSEN, DAß SIE OPIUM RAUCHTEN.
HELLO? WILSON, CAN YOU HEAR ME?
WE'RE LOST! WE'RE TRAPPED HERE! HELLO?
MAN FÜHRTE ABER AUCH KRIEG, WENN NOTWENDIG, UM GOLDGRUBEN ZU GEVINNEN, UM DIE...
...HERRSCHAFT ÜBER DIAMANTENGRUBEN ZU BEKOMMEN.
I CAN'T TOUCH THE BOOKS. I CAN'T TALK TO YOU.
YOU NEVER TOLD ME THIS WOULD HAPPEN!
ES WAREN IMMER MATERIELLE ZIELE, ALLERDINGS IMMER NATURGEMÄß EDEL UND IDEAL VERBRÄMT.
YOU NEVER TOLD ME!
GUUUH!
YOU NEVER-- NEVER...
AUßERDEM: JEDES VOLK VERBRE CH NUR
ENOUGH OF THAT, LIZZIE.
THERE'S NO TIME FOR SELF-INDULGENCE.
W-WILSON?
OH MY GOD! WILSON--
I SAID THERE'S NO TIME. TELL ME EVERYTHING.
START WITH WHERE YOU ARE.

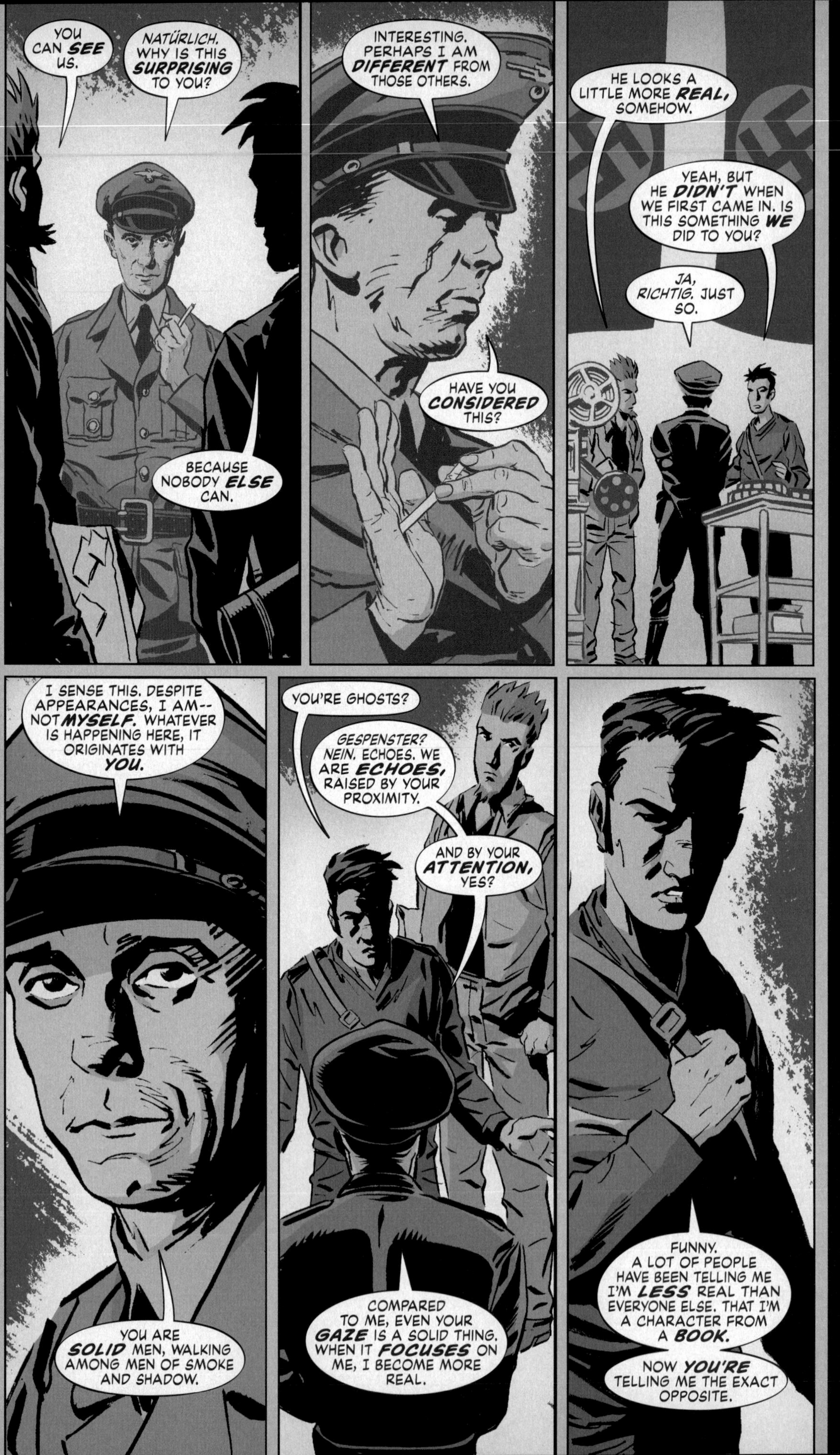
YOU CAN SEE US.
NATÜRLICH. WHY IS THIS SURPRISING TO YOU?
BECAUSE NOBODY ELSE CAN.
INTERESTING. PERHAPS I AM DIFFERENT FROM THOSE OTHERS.
HAVE YOU CONSIDERED THIS?
HE LOOKS A LITTLE MORE REAL, SOMEHOW.
YEAH, BUT HE DIDN'T WHEN WE FIRST CAME IN. IS THIS SOMETHING WE DID TO YOU?
JA, RICHTIG. JUST SO.
I SENSE THIS. DESPITE APPEARANCES, I AM-- NOT MYSELF. WHATEVER IS HAPPENING HERE, IT ORIGINATES WITH YOU.
YOU ARE SOLID MEN, WALKING AMONG MEN OF SMOKE AND SHADOW.
YOU'RE GHOSTS?
GESPENSTER? NEIN. ECHOES. WE ARE ECHOES, RAISED BY YOUR PROXIMITY.
AND BY YOUR ATTENTION, YES?
COMPARED TO ME, EVEN YOUR GAZE IS A SOLID THING. WHEN IT FOCUSES ON ME, I BECOME MORE REAL.
FUNNY. A LOT OF PEOPLE HAVE BEEN TELLING ME I'M LESS REAL THAN EVERYONE ELSE. THAT I'M A CHARACTER FROM A BOOK.
NOW YOU'RE TELLING ME THE EXACT OPPOSITE.

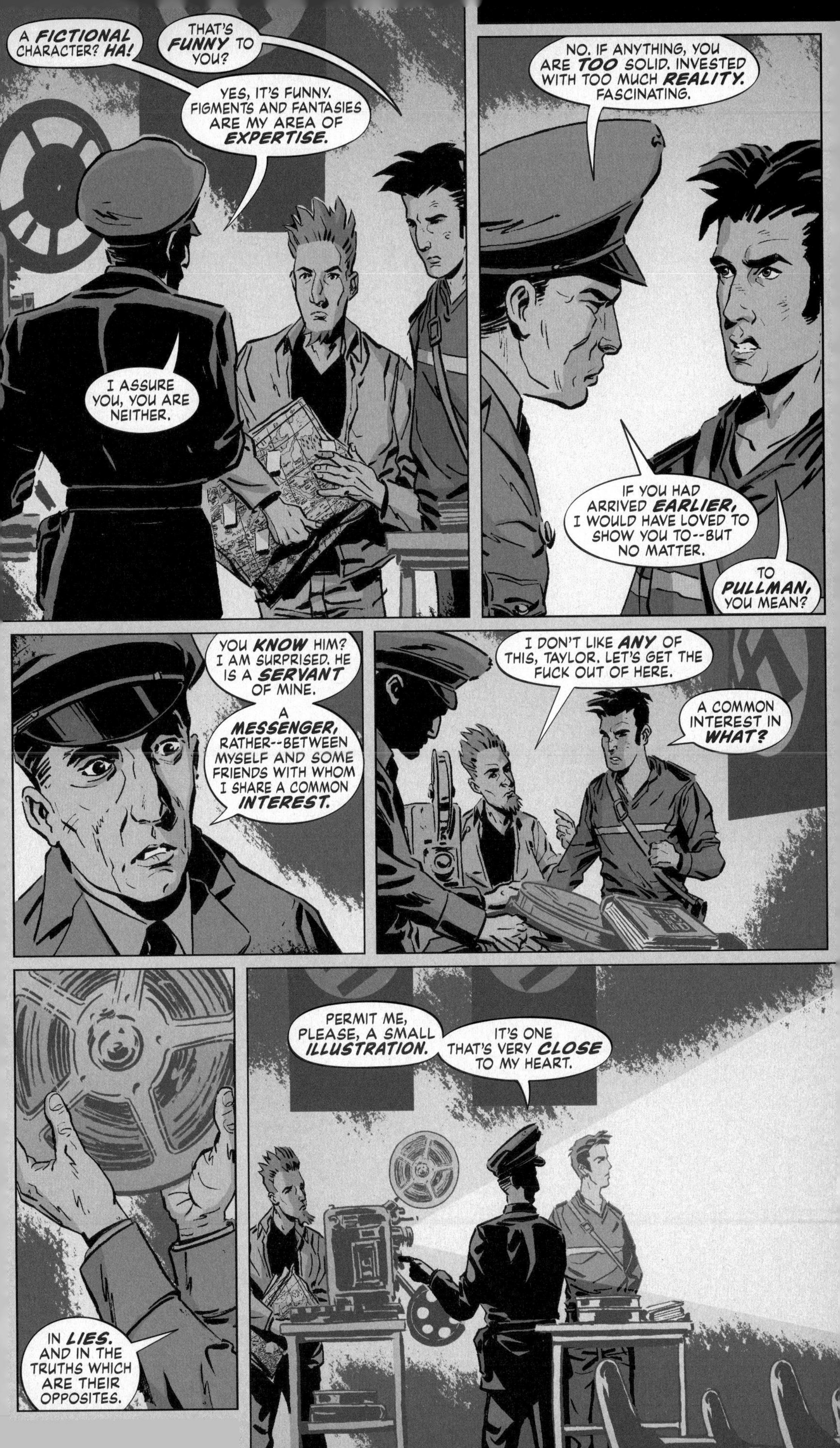

A FICTIONAL CHARACTER? HA!
THAT'S FUNNY TO YOU?
YES, IT'S FUNNY. FIGMENTS AND FANTASIES ARE MY AREA OF EXPERTISE.
I ASSURE YOU, YOU ARE NEITHER.
NO. IF ANYTHING, YOU ARE TOO SOLID. INVESTED WITH TOO MUCH REALITY. FASCINATING.
IF YOU HAD ARRIVED EARLIER, I WOULD HAVE LOVED TO SHOW YOU TO--BUT NO MATTER.
TO PULLMAN, YOU MEAN?
YOU KNOW HIM? I AM SURPRISED. HE IS A SERVANT OF MINE.
A MESSENGER, RATHER--BETWEEN MYSELF AND SOME FRIENDS WITH WHOM I SHARE A COMMON INTEREST.
I DON'T LIKE ANY OF THIS, TAYLOR. LET'S GET THE FUCK OUT OF HERE.
A COMMON INTEREST IN WHAT?
IN LIES. AND IN THE TRUTHS WHICH ARE THEIR OPPOSITES.
PERMIT ME, PLEASE, A SMALL ILLUSTRATION.
IT'S ONE THAT'S VERY CLOSE TO MY HEART.

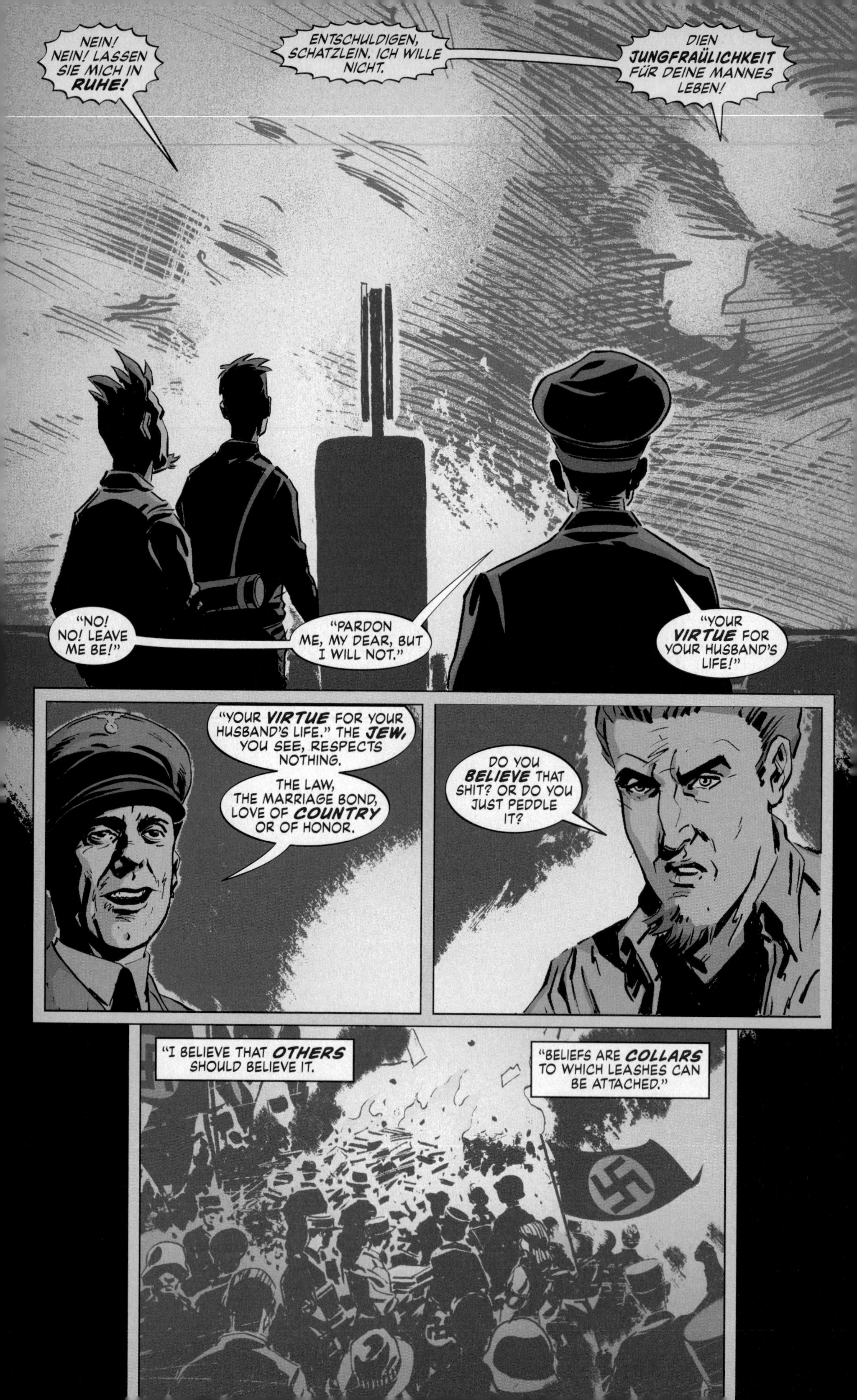
NEIN! NEIN! LASSEN SIE MICH IN RUHE!
ENTSCHULDIGEN, SCHATZLEIN. ICH WILLE NICHT.
DIEN JUNGFRAÜLICHKEIT FÜR DEINE MANNES LEBEN!
"NO! NO! LEAVE ME BE!"
"PARDON ME, MY DEAR, BUT I WILL NOT."
"YOUR VIRTUE FOR YOUR HUSBAND'S LIFE!"
"YOUR VIRTUE FOR YOUR HUSBAND'S LIFE." THE JEW, YOU SEE, RESPECTS NOTHING.
THE LAW, THE MARRIAGE BOND, LOVE OF COUNTRY OR OF HONOR.
DO YOU BELIEVE THAT SHIT? OR DO YOU JUST PEDDLE IT?
"I BELIEVE THAT OTHERS SHOULD BELIEVE IT.
"BELIEFS ARE COLLARS TO WHICH LEASHES CAN BE ATTACHED."

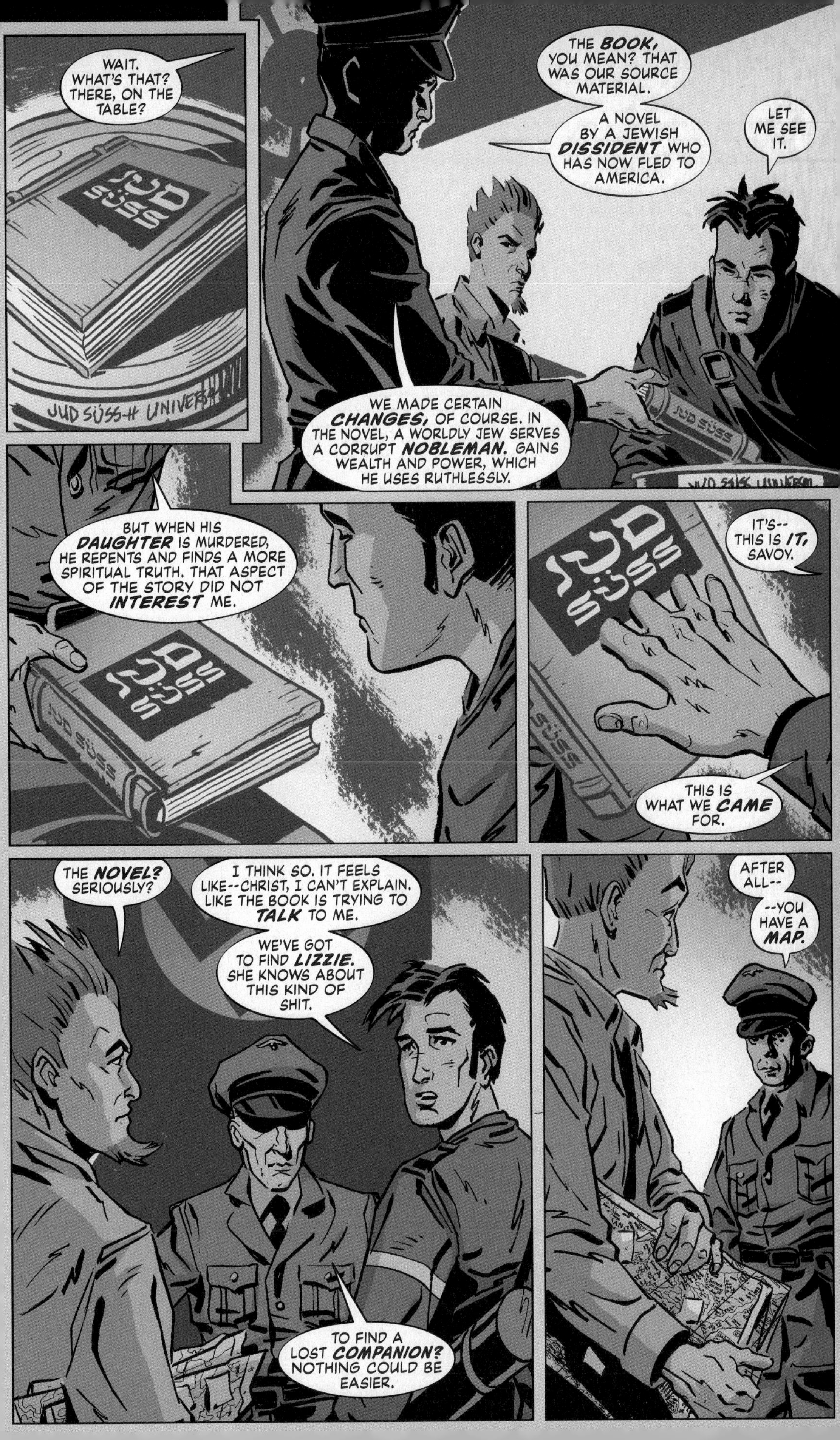
WAIT, WHAT'S THAT? THERE, ON THE TABLE?
JUD SÜSS
JUD SÜSS-H UNIVER
THE BOOK, YOU MEAN? THAT WAS OUR SOURCE MATERIAL.
A NOVEL BY A JEWISH DISSIDENT WHO HAS NOW FLED TO AMERICA.
LET ME SEE IT.
WE MADE CERTAIN CHANGES, OF COURSE. IN THE NOVEL, A WORLDLY JEW SERVES A CORRUPT NOBLEMAN. GAINS WEALTH AND POWER, WHICH HE USES RUTHLESSLY.
JUD SÜSS
BUT WHEN HIS DAUGHTER IS MURDERED, HE REPENTS AND FINDS A MORE SPIRITUAL TRUTH. THAT ASPECT OF THE STORY DID NOT INTEREST ME.
JUD SÜSS
IT'S-- THIS IS IT, SAVOY.
JUD SÜSS
THIS IS WHAT WE CAME FOR.
THE NOVEL? SERIOUSLY?
I THINK SO. IT FEELS LIKE--CHRIST, I CAN'T EXPLAIN. LIKE THE BOOK IS TRYING TO TALK TO ME.
WE'VE GOT TO FIND LIZZIE. SHE KNOWS ABOUT THIS KIND OF SHIT.
TO FIND A LOST COMPANION? NOTHING COULD BE EASIER.
AFTER ALL--
--YOU HAVE A MAP.

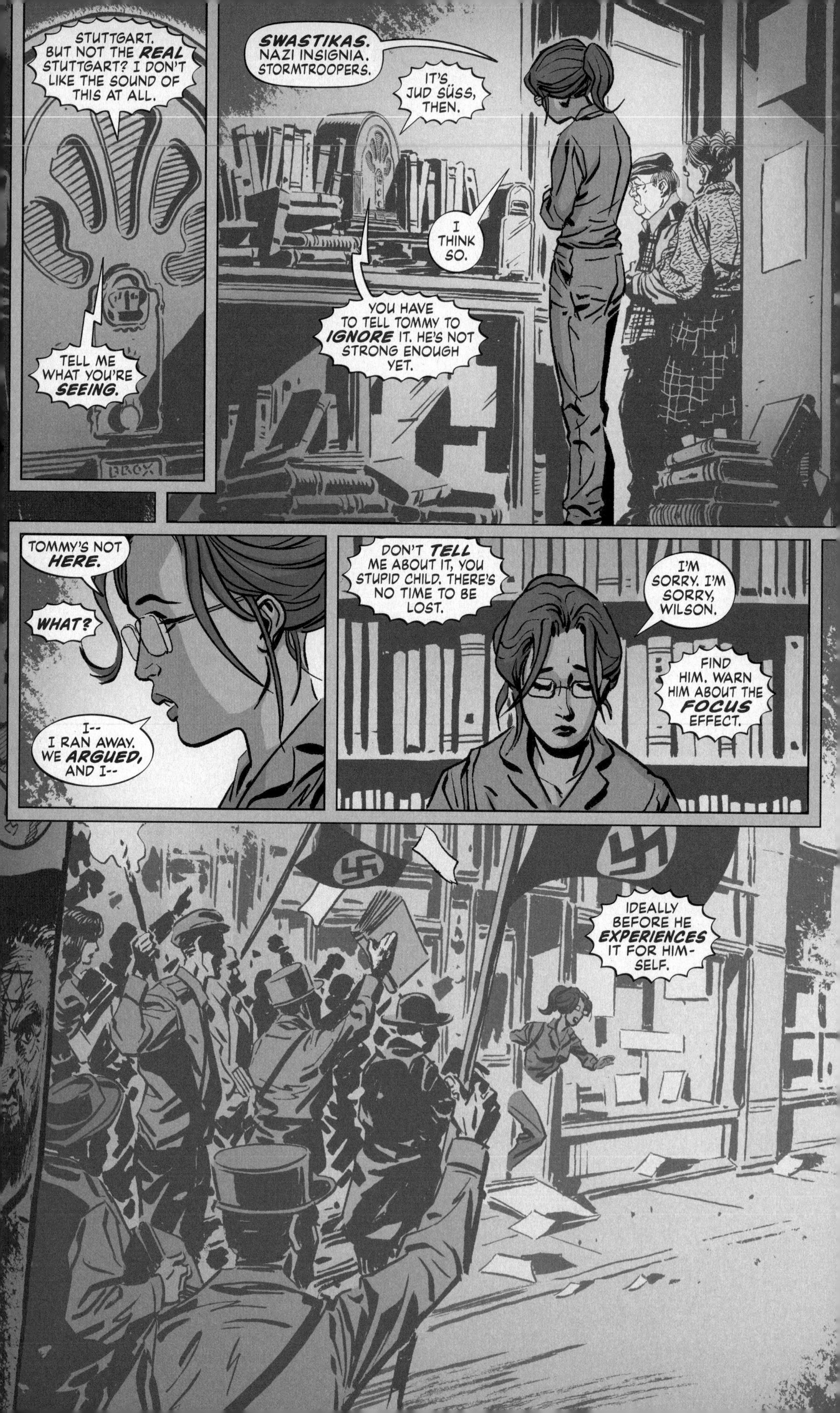

STUTTGART. BUT NOT THE REAL STUTTGART? I DON'T LIKE THE SOUND OF THIS AT ALL.
TELL ME WHAT YOU'RE SEEING.
SWASTIKAS. NAZI INSIGNIA. STORMTROOPERS.
IT'S JUD SÜSS, THEN.
I THINK SO.
YOU HAVE TO TELL TOMMY TO IGNORE IT. HE'S NOT STRONG ENOUGH YET.
BROX
TOMMY'S NOT HERE.
WHAT?
I-- I RAN AWAY. WE ARGUED, AND I--
DON'T TELL ME ABOUT IT, YOU STUPID CHILD. THERE'S NO TIME TO BE LOST.
I'M SORRY. I'M SORRY, WILSON.
FIND HIM. WARN HIM ABOUT THE FOCUS EFFECT.
IDEALLY BEFORE HE EXPERIENCES IT FOR HIM-SELF.

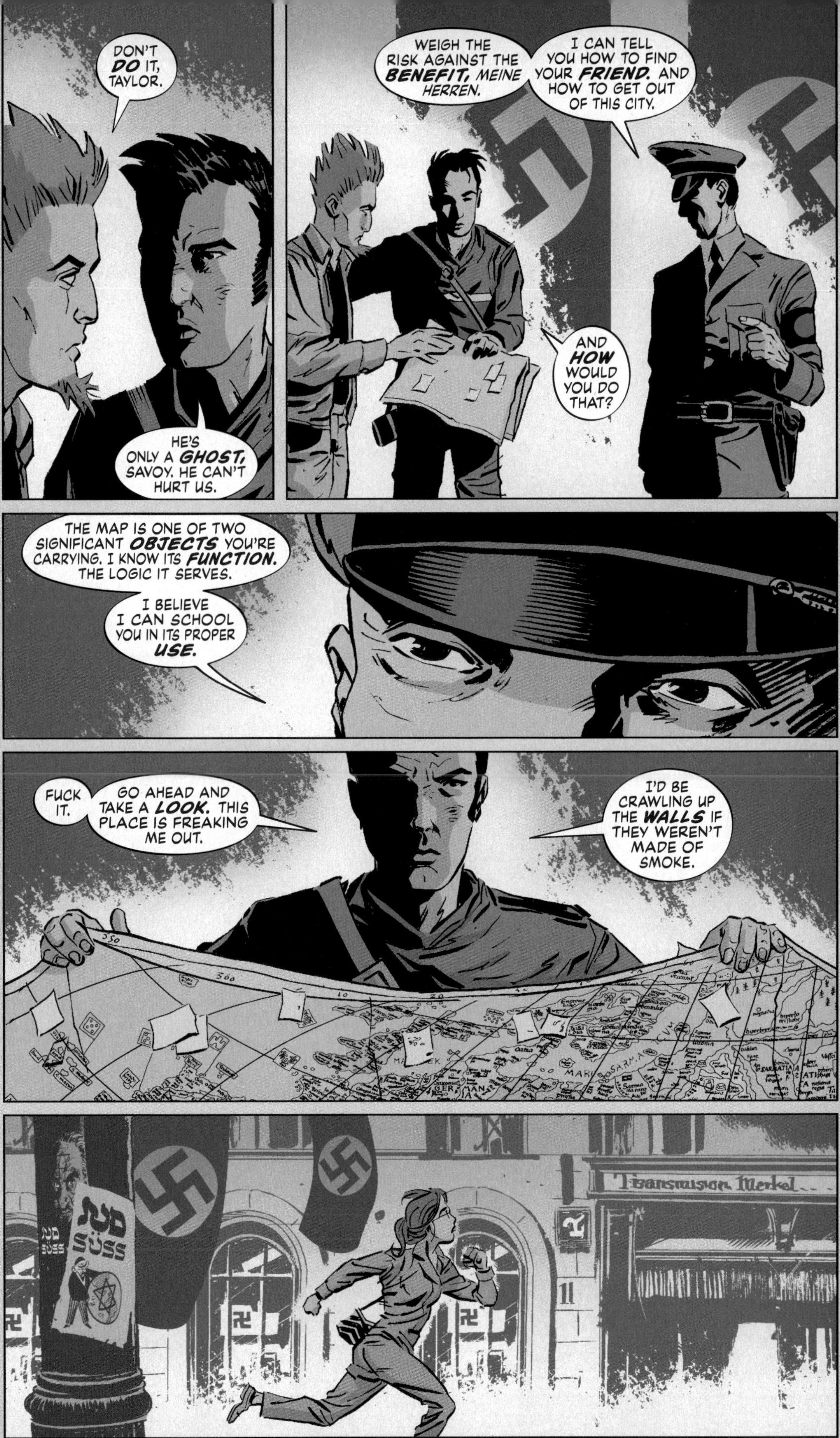
DON'T DO IT, TAYLOR.
HE'S ONLY A GHOST, SAVOY. HE CAN'T HURT US.
WEIGH THE RISK AGAINST THE BENEFIT, MEINE HERREN.
I CAN TELL YOU HOW TO FIND YOUR FRIEND. AND HOW TO GET OUT OF THIS CITY.
AND HOW WOULD YOU DO THAT?
THE MAP IS ONE OF TWO SIGNIFICANT OBJECTS YOU'RE CARRYING. I KNOW ITS FUNCTION. THE LOGIC IT SERVES.
I BELIEVE I CAN SCHOOL YOU IN ITS PROPER USE.
FUCK IT.
GO AHEAD AND TAKE A LOOK. THIS PLACE IS FREAKING ME OUT.
I'D BE CRAWLING UP THE WALLS IF THEY WEREN'T MADE OF SMOKE.
JUD SÜSS
Transmission Merkel
11

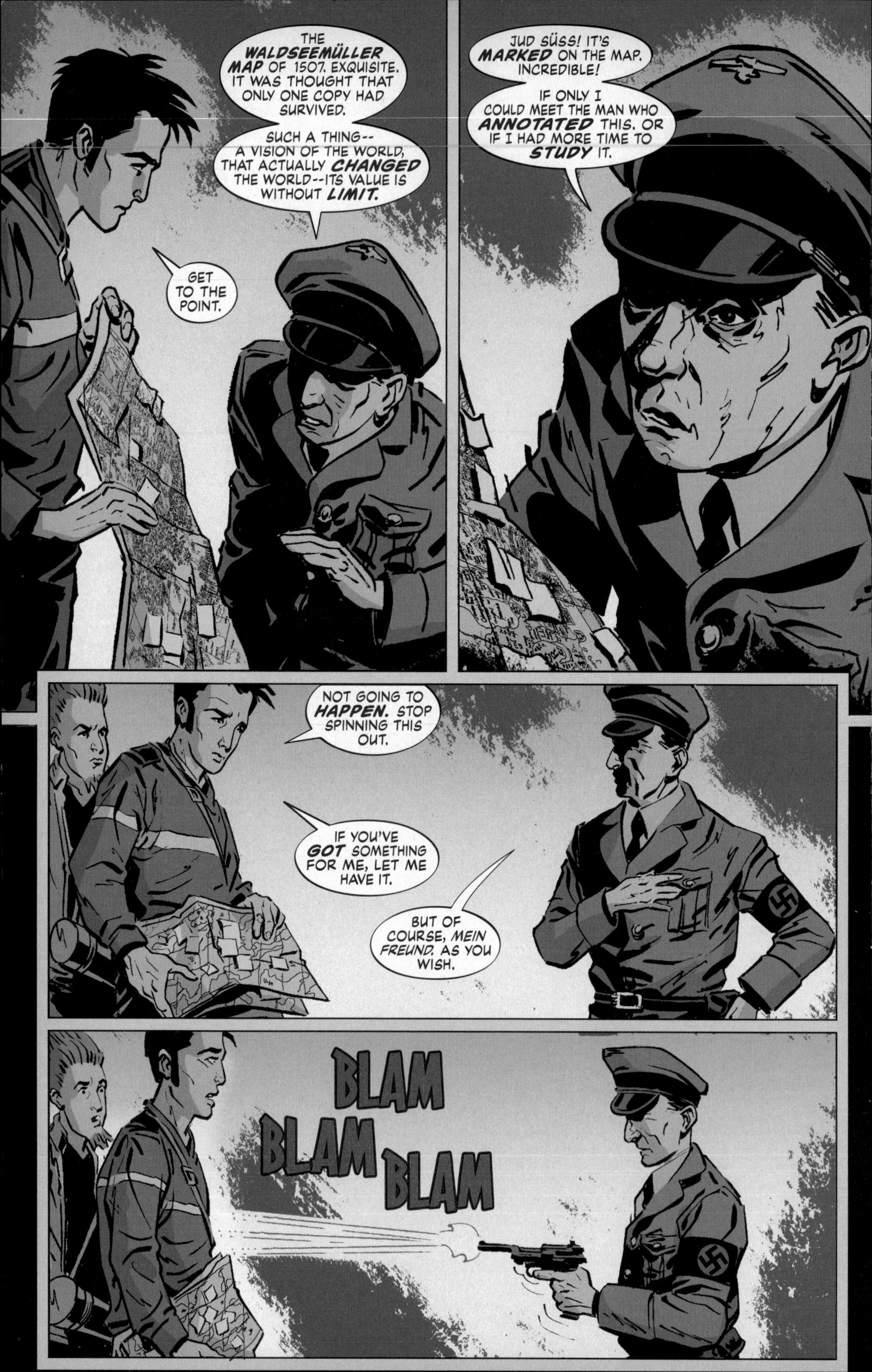
THE WALDSEEMÜLLER MAP OF 1507. EXQUISITE. IT WAS THOUGHT THAT ONLY ONE COPY HAD SURVIVED.
SUCH A THING-- A VISION OF THE WORLD, THAT ACTUALLY CHANGED THE WORLD--ITS VALUE IS WITHOUT LIMIT.
GET TO THE POINT.
JUD SÜSS! IT'S MARKED ON THE MAP. INCREDIBLE!
IF ONLY I COULD MEET THE MAN WHO ANNOTATED THIS. OR IF I HAD MORE TIME TO STUDY IT.
NOT GOING TO HAPPEN. STOP SPINNING THIS OUT.
IF YOU'VE GOT SOMETHING FOR ME, LET ME HAVE IT.
BUT OF COURSE, MEIN FREUND. AS YOU WISH.
BLAM
BLAM
BLAM

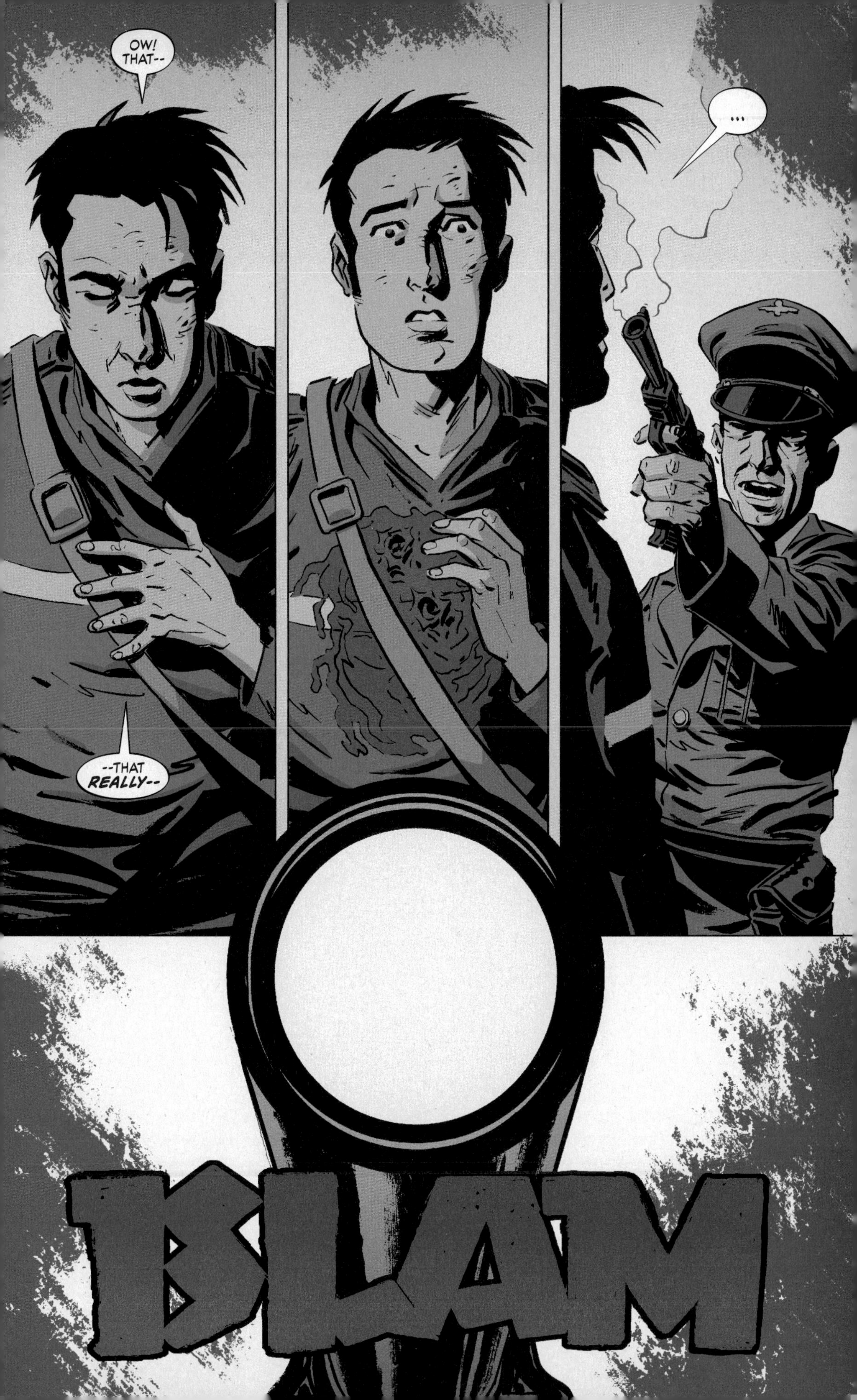
OW! THAT--
--THAT REALLY--
...
BLAM

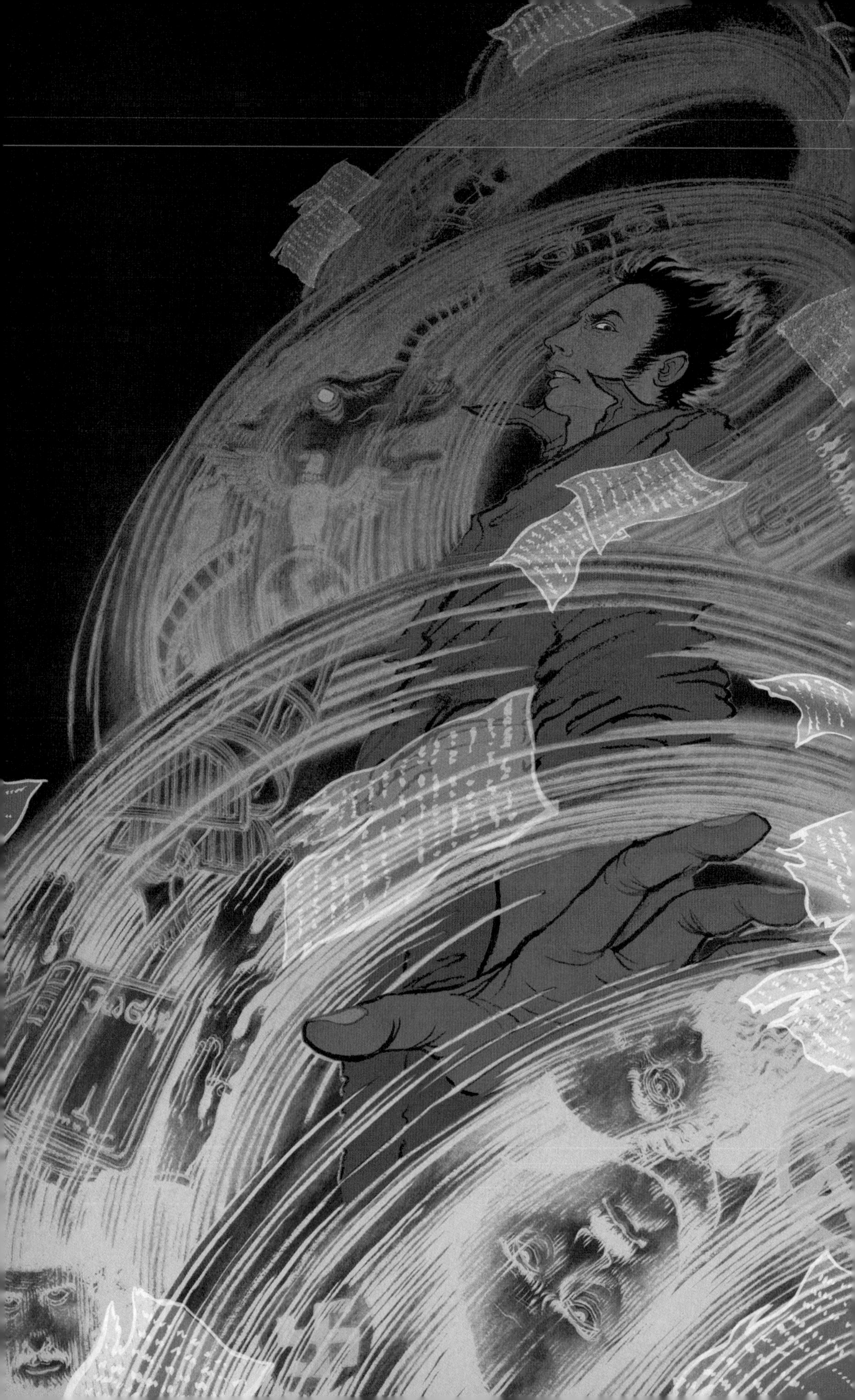

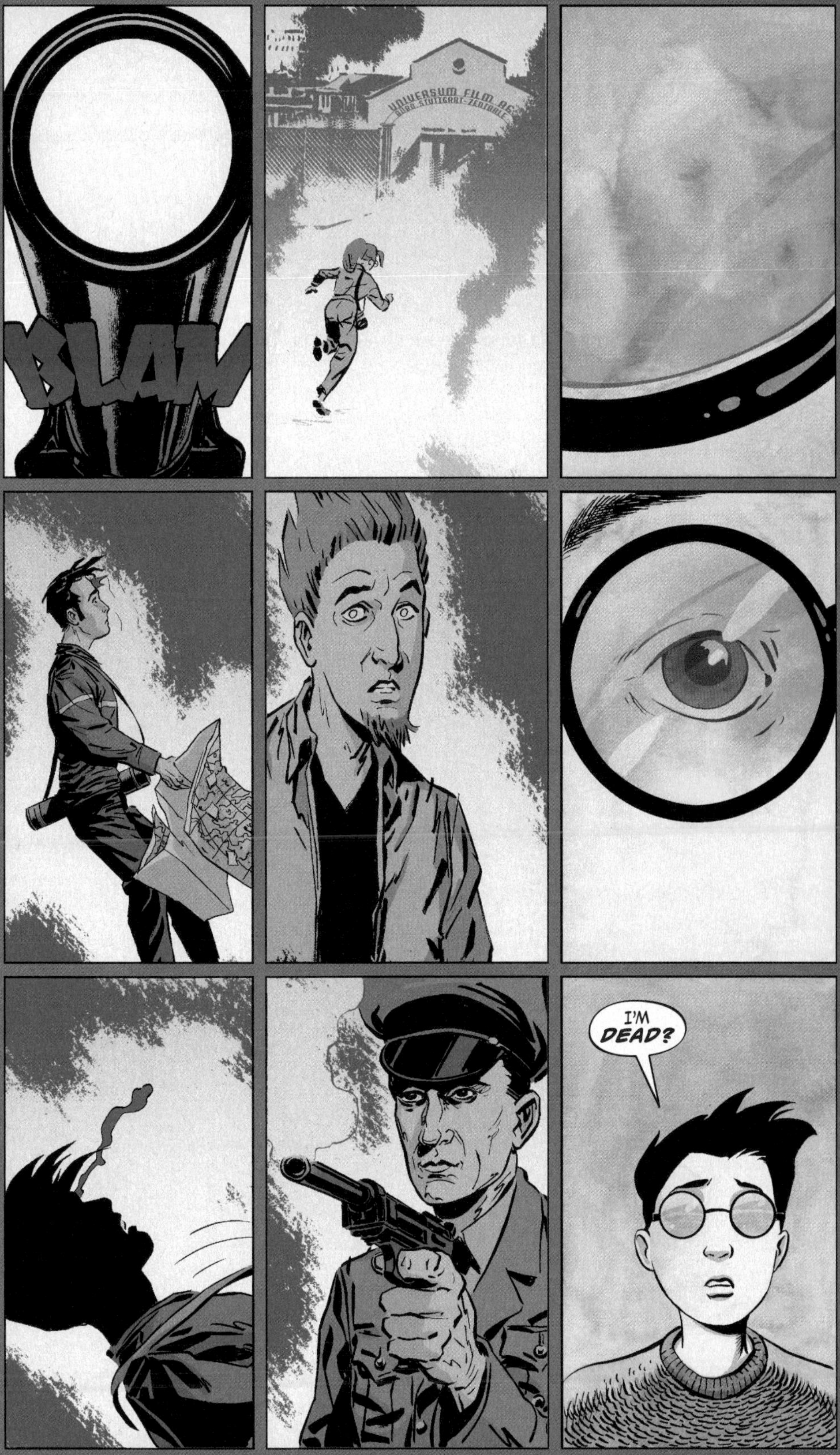
BLAM
UNIVERSUM FILM AG
I'M DEAD?

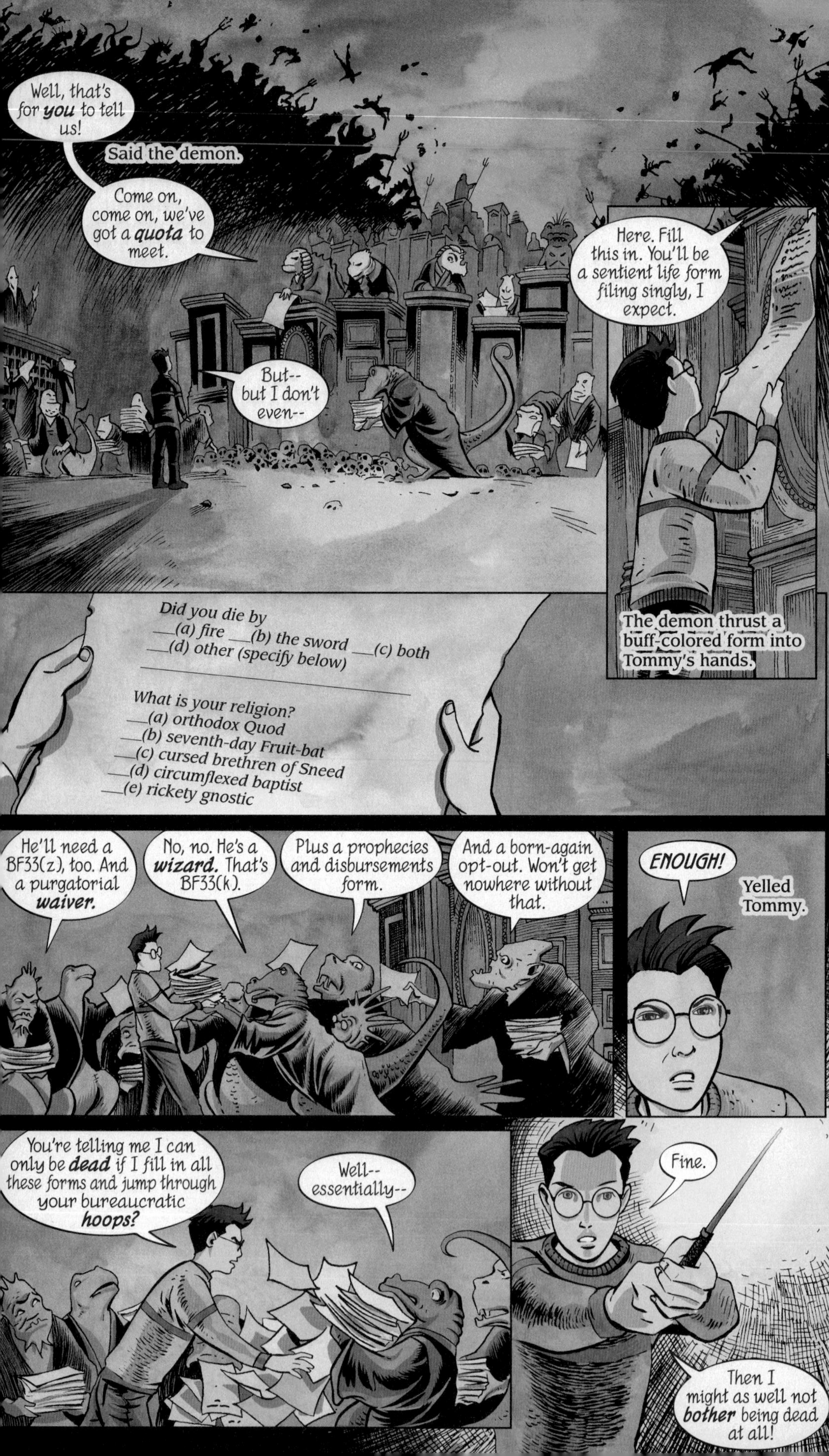

Well, that's for **you** to tell us!
Said the demon.
Come on, come on, we've got a **quota** to meet.
But-- but I don't even--
Here. Fill this in. You'll be a sentient life form filing singly, I expect.
The demon thrust a buff-colored form into Tommy's hands.
Did you die by
___(a) fire ___(b) the sword ___(c) both
___(d) other (specify below)
What is your religion?
___(a) orthodox Quod
___(b) seventh-day Fruit-bat
___(c) cursed brethren of Sneed
___(d) circumflexed baptist
___(e) rickety gnostic
He'll need a BF33(z), too. And a purgatorial **waiver.**
No, no. He's a **wizard.** That's BF33(k).
Plus a prophecies and disbursements form.
And a born-again opt-out. Won't get nowhere without that.
ENOUGH!
Yelled Tommy.
You're telling me I can only be **dead** if I fill in all these forms and jump through your bureaucratic **hoops?**
Well-- essentially--
Fine.
Then I might as well not **bother** being dead at all!

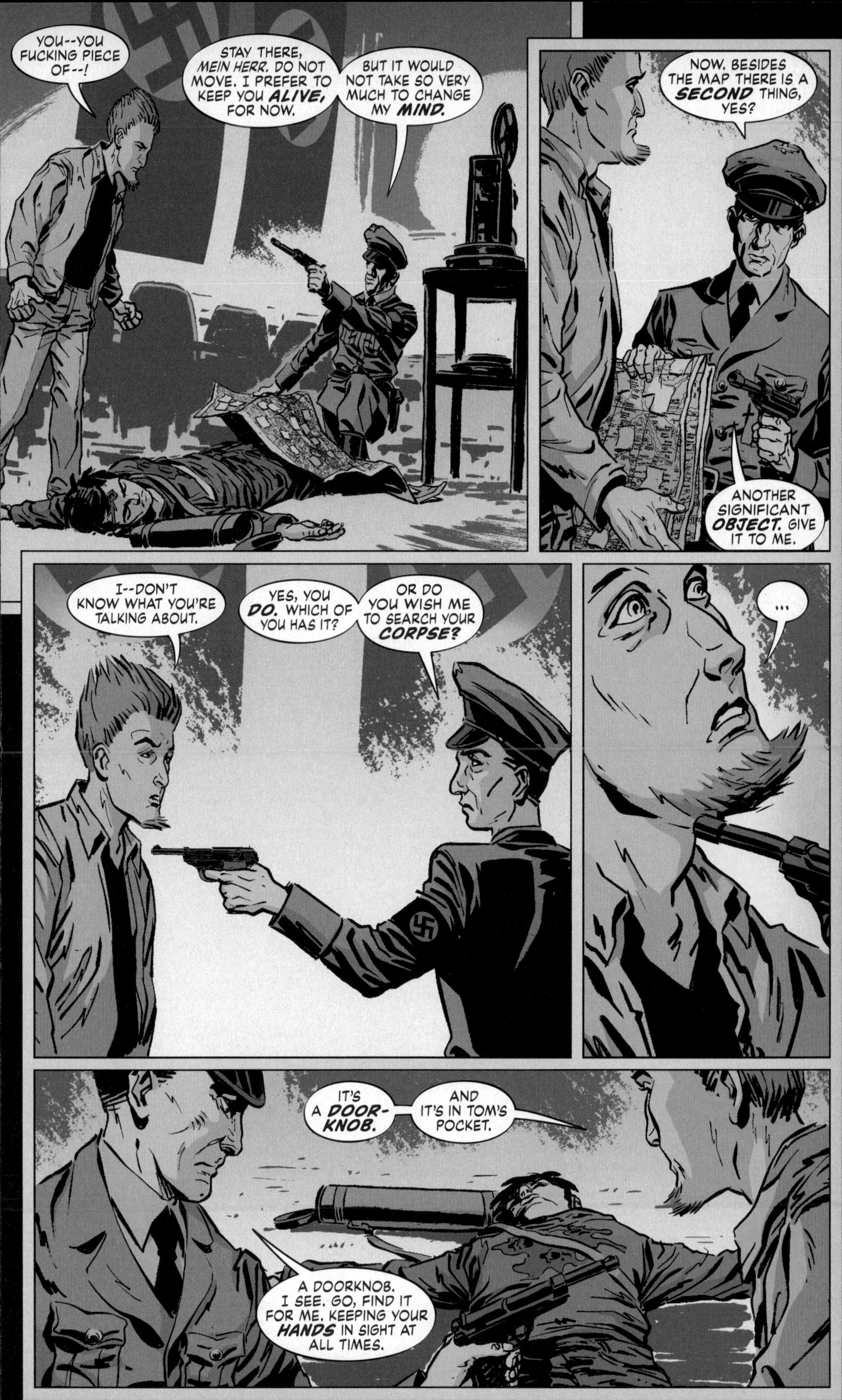
YOU--YOU FUCKING PIECE OF--!
STAY THERE, *MEIN HERR.* DO NOT MOVE. I PREFER TO KEEP YOU **ALIVE,** FOR NOW.
BUT IT WOULD NOT TAKE SO VERY MUCH TO CHANGE MY **MIND.**
NOW. BESIDES THE MAP THERE IS A **SECOND** THING, YES?
ANOTHER SIGNIFICANT **OBJECT.** GIVE IT TO ME.
I--DON'T KNOW WHAT YOU'RE TALKING ABOUT.
YES, YOU **DO.** WHICH OF YOU HAS IT?
OR DO YOU WISH ME TO SEARCH YOUR **CORPSE?**
...
IT'S A **DOOR-KNOB.**
AND IT'S IN TOM'S POCKET.
A DOORKNOB. I SEE. GO, FIND IT FOR ME. KEEPING YOUR **HANDS** IN SIGHT AT ALL TIMES.

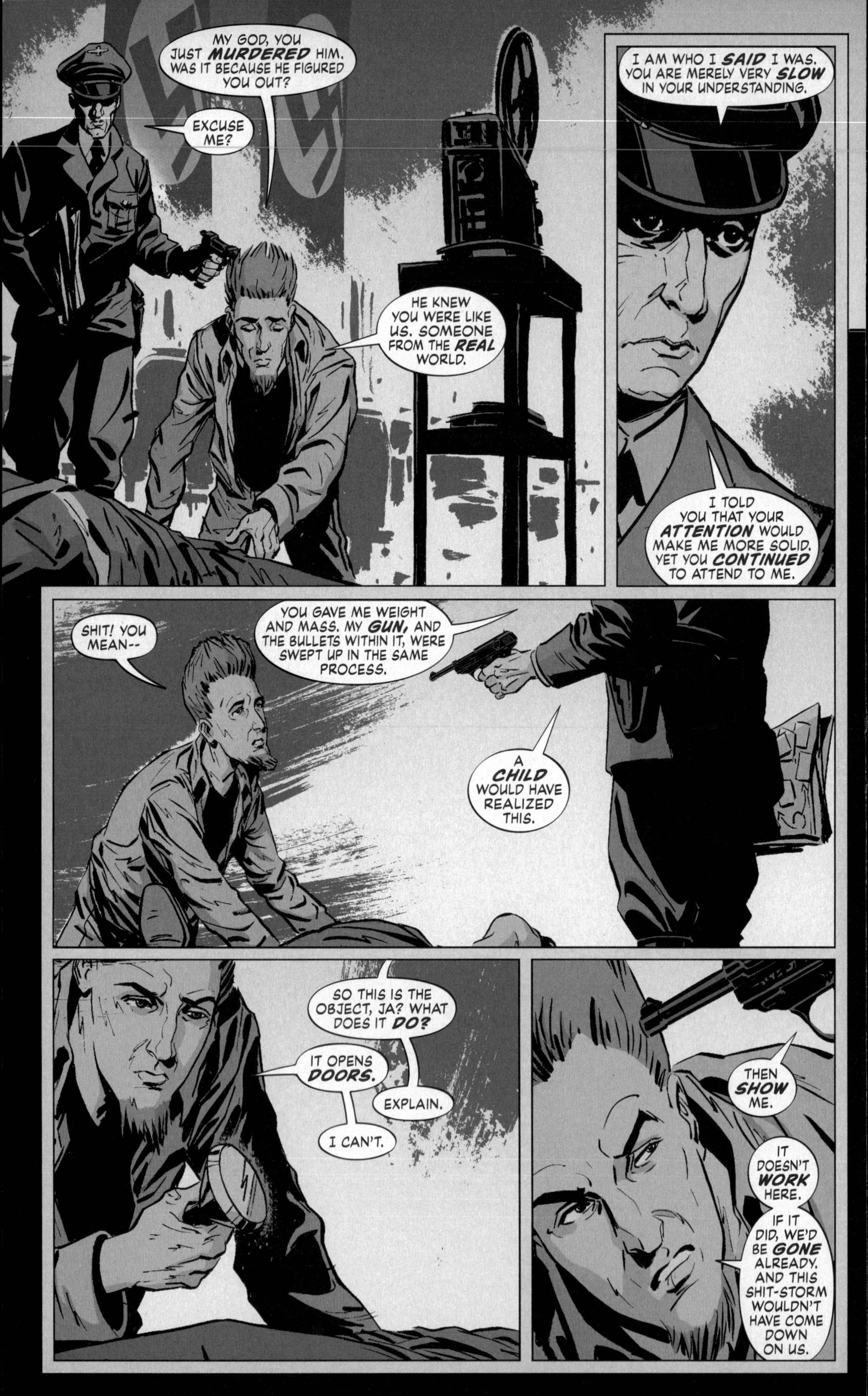
MY GOD, YOU JUST MURDERED HIM. WAS IT BECAUSE HE FIGURED YOU OUT?
EXCUSE ME?
HE KNEW YOU WERE LIKE US. SOMEONE FROM THE REAL WORLD.
I AM WHO I SAID I WAS. YOU ARE MERELY VERY SLOW IN YOUR UNDERSTANDING.
I TOLD YOU THAT YOUR ATTENTION WOULD MAKE ME MORE SOLID. YET YOU CONTINUED TO ATTEND TO ME.
SHIT! YOU MEAN--
YOU GAVE ME WEIGHT AND MASS. MY GUN, AND THE BULLETS WITHIN IT, WERE SWEPT UP IN THE SAME PROCESS.
A CHILD WOULD HAVE REALIZED THIS.
SO THIS IS THE OBJECT, JA? WHAT DOES IT DO?
IT OPENS DOORS.
EXPLAIN.
I CAN'T.
THEN SHOW ME.
IT DOESN'T WORK HERE.
IF IT DID, WE'D BE GONE ALREADY. AND THIS SHIT-STORM WOULDN'T HAVE COME DOWN ON US.

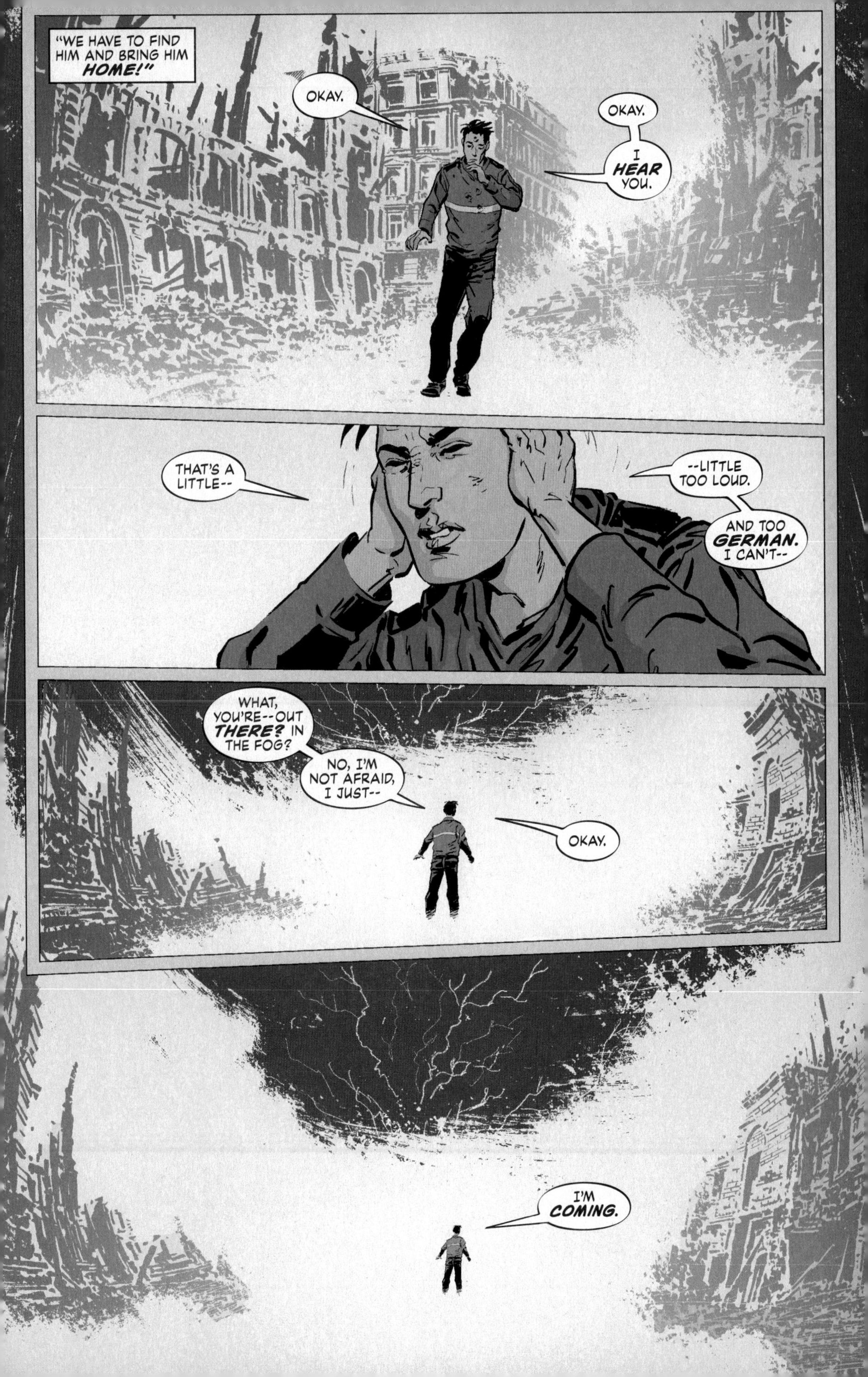
"WE HAVE TO FIND HIM AND BRING HIM HOME!"
OKAY.
OKAY.
I HEAR YOU.
THAT'S A LITTLE--
--LITTLE TOO LOUD.
AND TOO GERMAN. I CAN'T--
WHAT, YOU'RE--OUT THERE? IN THE FOG?
NO, I'M NOT AFRAID, I JUST--
OKAY.
I'M COMING.

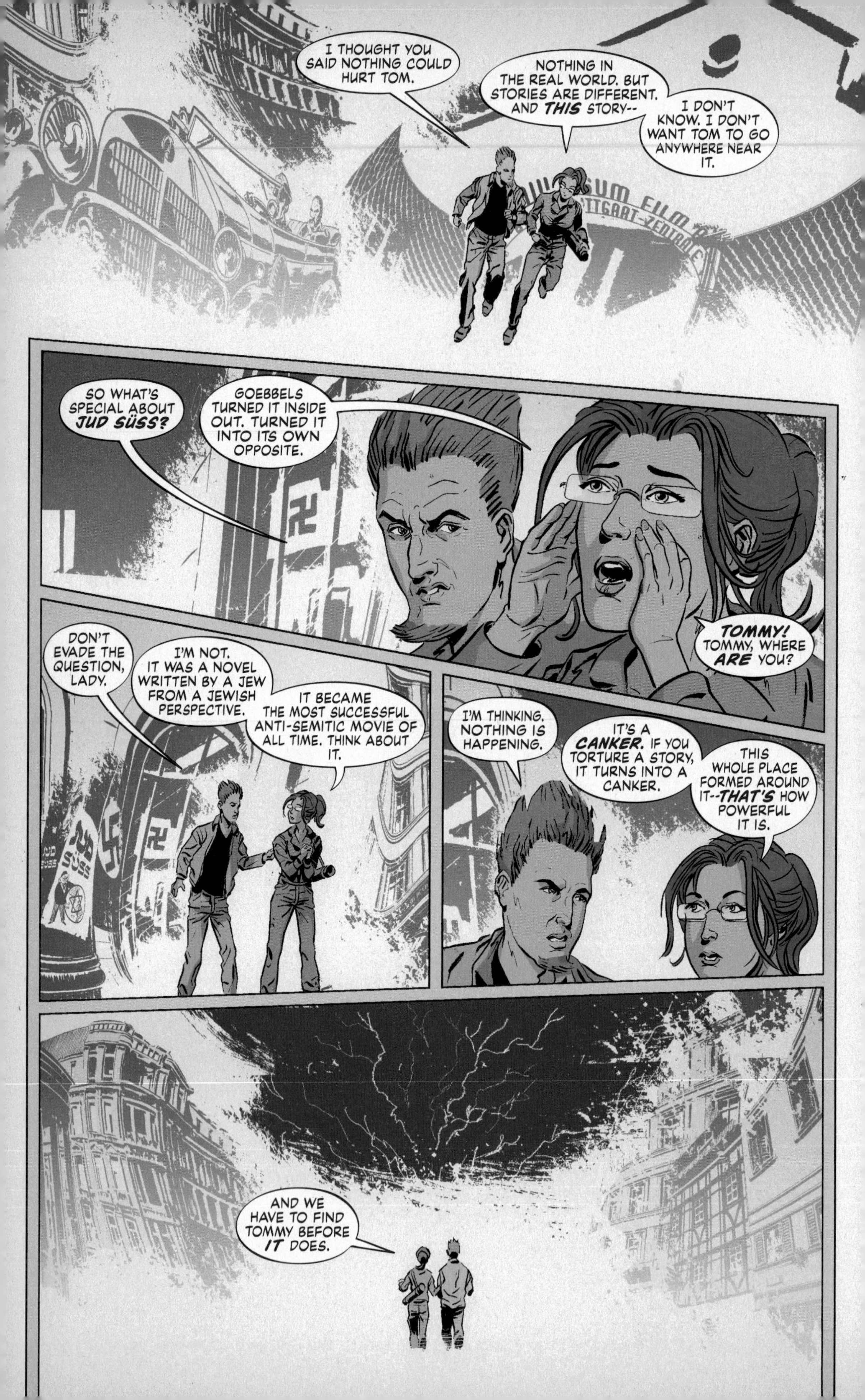
I THOUGHT YOU SAID NOTHING COULD HURT TOM.
NOTHING IN THE REAL WORLD. BUT STORIES ARE DIFFERENT. AND THIS STORY--
I DON'T KNOW. I DON'T WANT TOM TO GO ANYWHERE NEAR IT.
SO WHAT'S SPECIAL ABOUT JUD SÜSS?
GOEBBELS TURNED IT INSIDE OUT. TURNED IT INTO ITS OWN OPPOSITE.
TOMMY! TOMMY, WHERE ARE YOU?
DON'T EVADE THE QUESTION, LADY.
I'M NOT. IT WAS A NOVEL WRITTEN BY A JEW FROM A JEWISH PERSPECTIVE.
IT BECAME THE MOST SUCCESSFUL ANTI-SEMITIC MOVIE OF ALL TIME. THINK ABOUT IT.
JUD SÜSS
I'M THINKING. NOTHING IS HAPPENING.
IT'S A CANKER. IF YOU TORTURE A STORY, IT TURNS INTO A CANKER.
THIS WHOLE PLACE FORMED AROUND IT--THAT'S HOW POWERFUL IT IS.
AND WE HAVE TO FIND TOMMY BEFORE IT DOES.

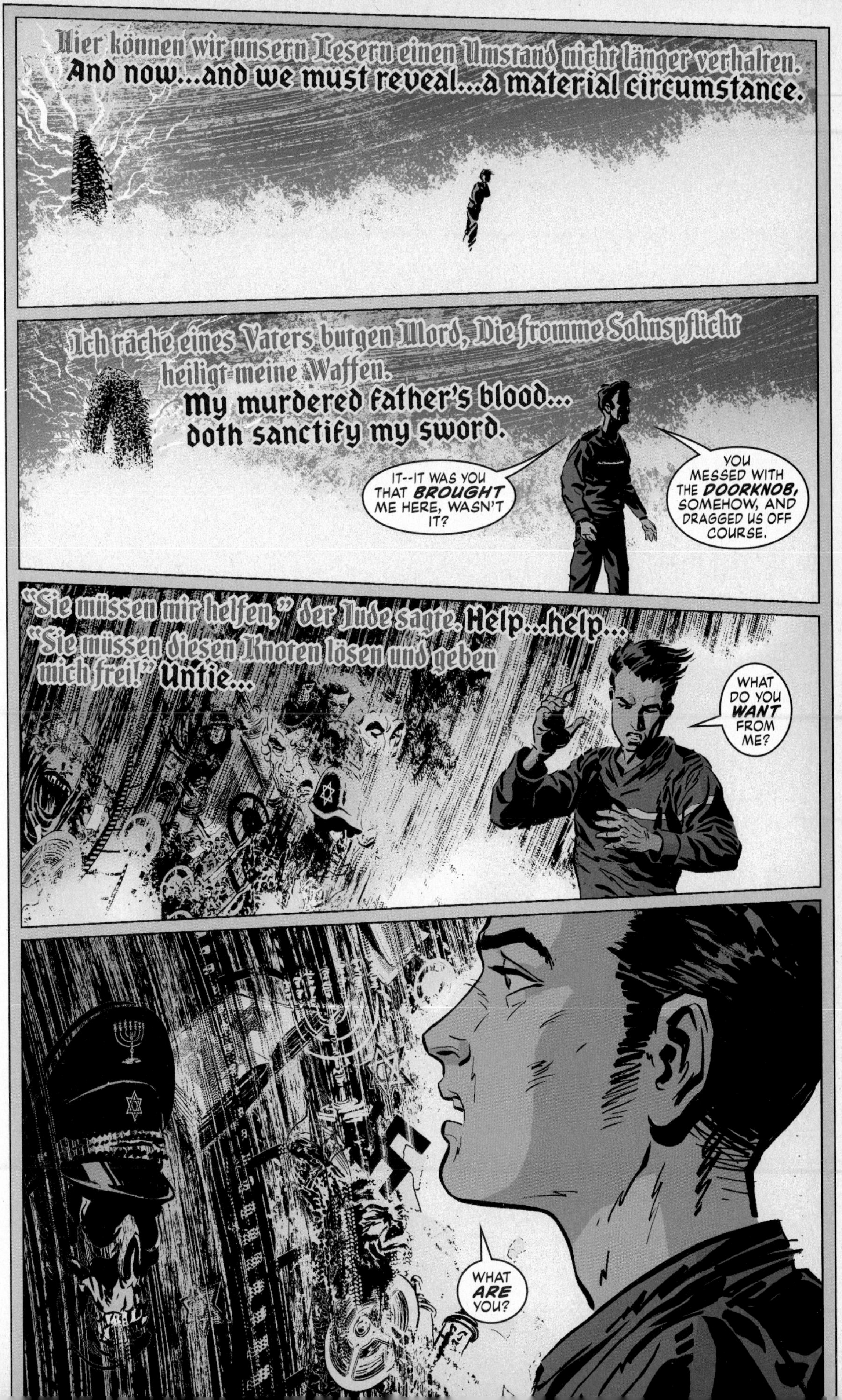

Hier können wir unsern Lesern einen Umstand nicht länger verhalten.
And now...and we must reveal...a material circumstance.
Ich räche eines Vaters butgen Mord, Die fromme Sohnspflicht heiligt meine Waffen.
My murdered father's blood... doth sanctify my sword.
IT--IT WAS YOU THAT **BROUGHT** ME HERE, WASN'T IT?
YOU MESSED WITH THE **DOORKNOB**, SOMEHOW, AND DRAGGED US OFF COURSE.
"Sie müssen mir helfen," der Jude sagte. Help...help...
"Sie müssen diesen Knoten lösen und geben mich frei!" Untie...
WHAT DO YOU **WANT** FROM ME?
WHAT **ARE** YOU?

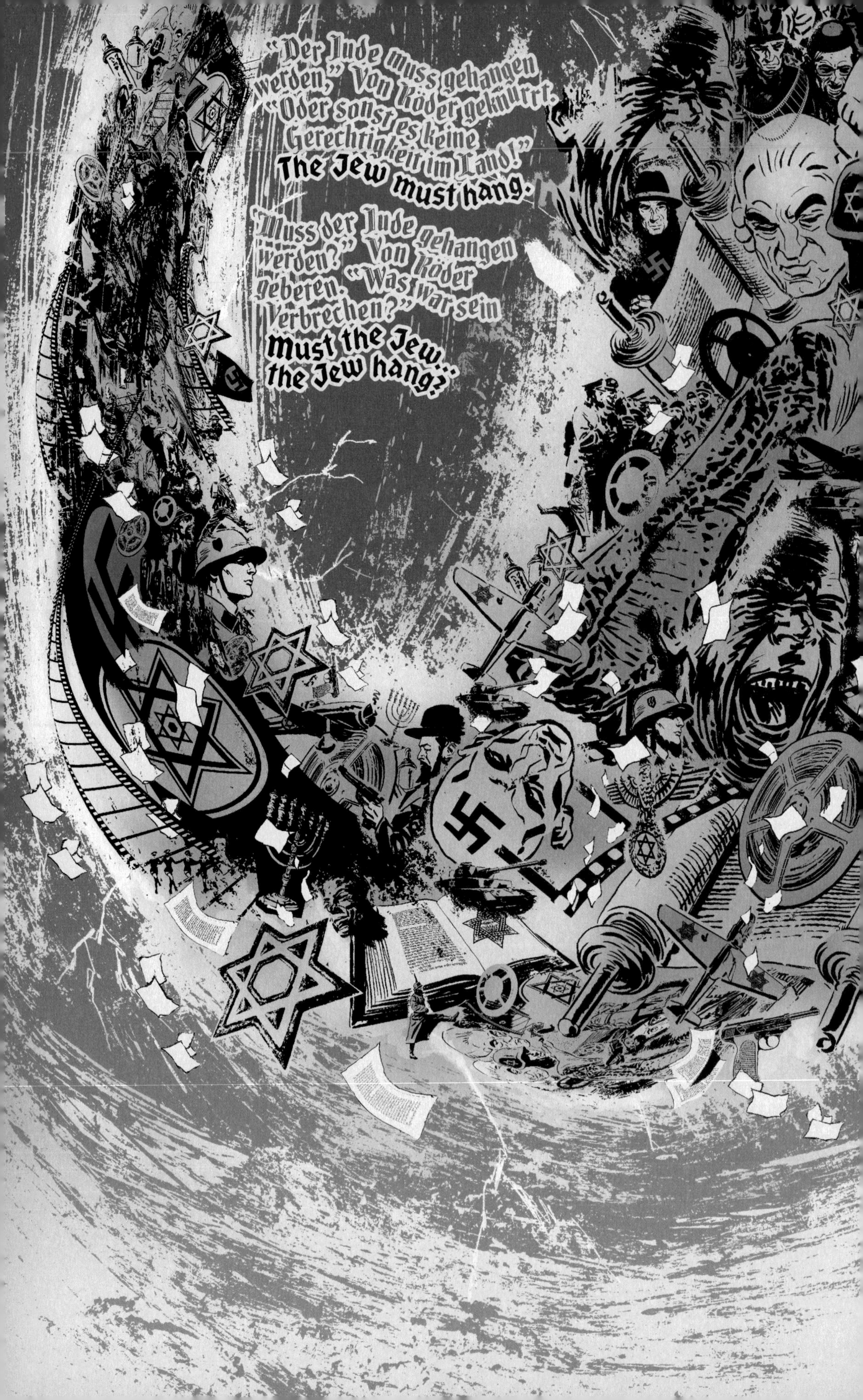
"Der Jude muss gehangen werden," Von Röder geknurrt. "Oder sonst es keine Gerechtigkeit im Land!"
The Jew must hang.
"Muss der Jude gehangen werden?" Von Röder gebeten. "Was war sein Verbrechen?"
Must the Jew... the Jew hang?

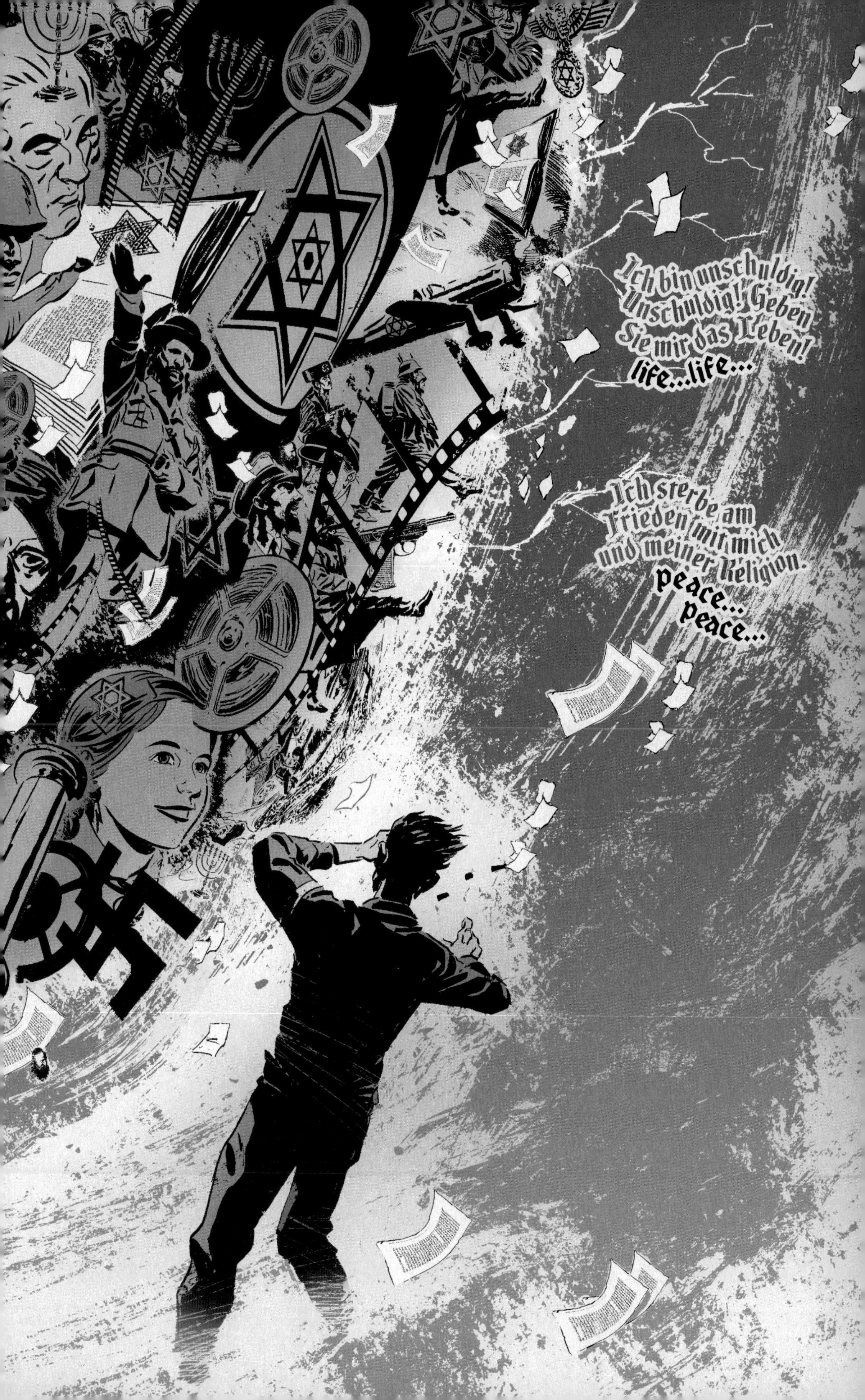
Ich bin unschuldig! Unschuldig! Geben Sie mir das Leben!
life...life...
Ich sterbe am Frieden mit mich und meiner Religion.
peace... peace...

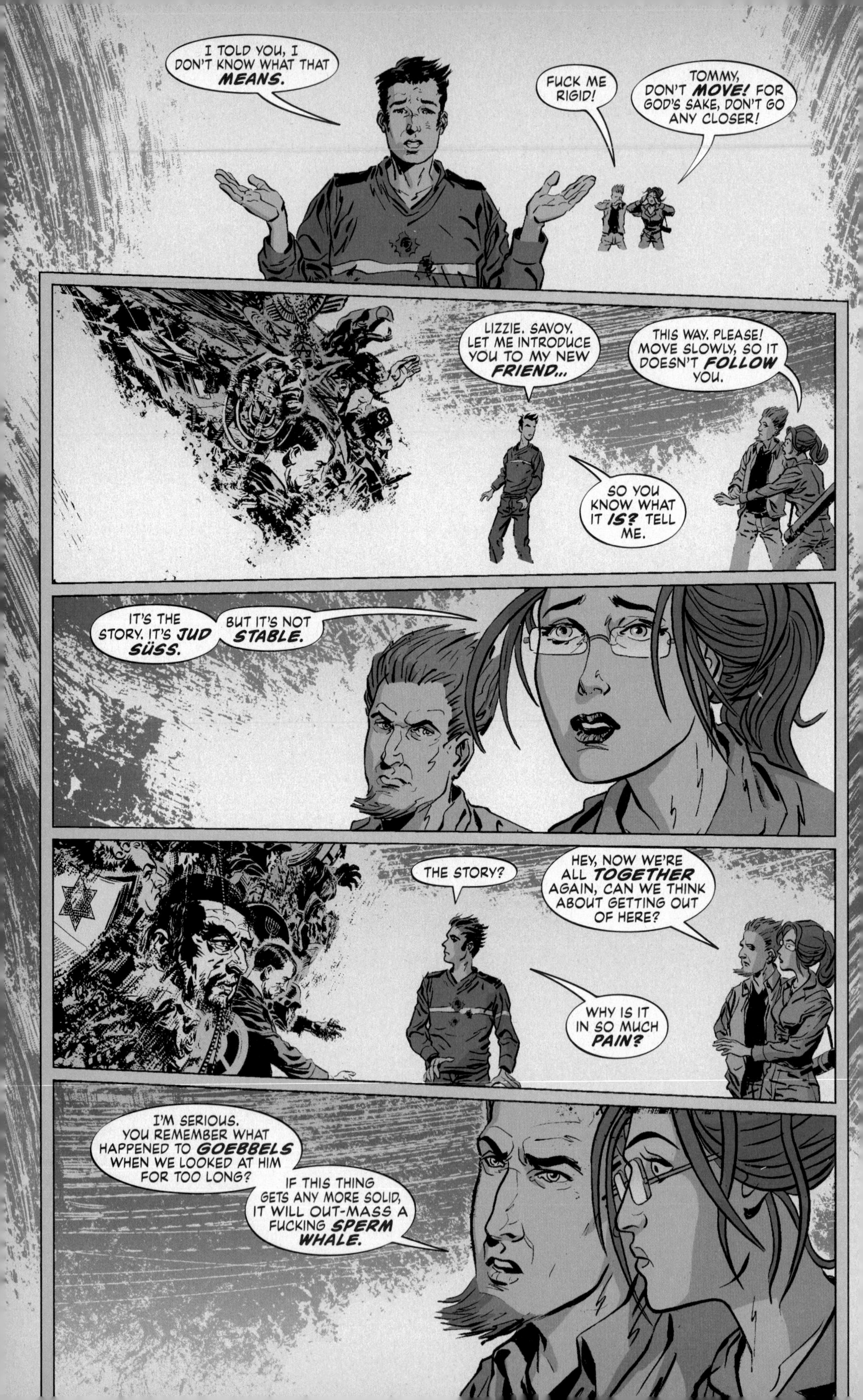
I TOLD YOU, I DON'T KNOW WHAT THAT MEANS.
FUCK ME RIGID!
TOMMY, DON'T MOVE! FOR GOD'S SAKE, DON'T GO ANY CLOSER!
LIZZIE. SAVOY. LET ME INTRODUCE YOU TO MY NEW FRIEND...
THIS WAY. PLEASE! MOVE SLOWLY, SO IT DOESN'T FOLLOW YOU.
SO YOU KNOW WHAT IT IS? TELL ME.
IT'S THE STORY. IT'S JUD SÜSS.
BUT IT'S NOT STABLE.
THE STORY?
HEY, NOW WE'RE ALL TOGETHER AGAIN, CAN WE THINK ABOUT GETTING OUT OF HERE?
WHY IS IT IN SO MUCH PAIN?
I'M SERIOUS. YOU REMEMBER WHAT HAPPENED TO GOEBBELS WHEN WE LOOKED AT HIM FOR TOO LONG?
IF THIS THING GETS ANY MORE SOLID, IT WILL OUT-MASS A FUCKING SPERM WHALE.

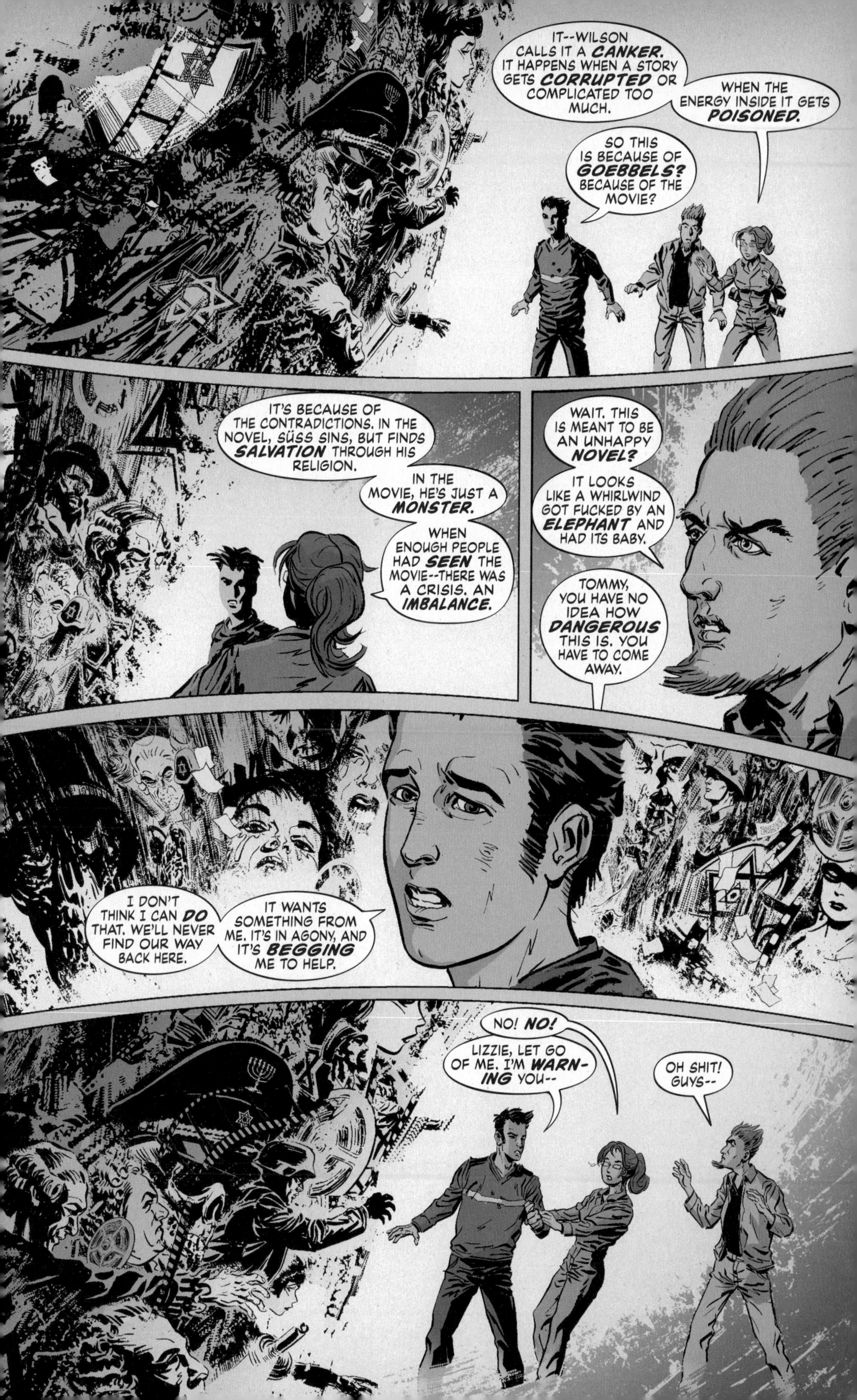
IT--WILSON CALLS IT A CANKER. IT HAPPENS WHEN A STORY GETS CORRUPTED OR COMPLICATED TOO MUCH.
WHEN THE ENERGY INSIDE IT GETS POISONED.
SO THIS IS BECAUSE OF GOEBBELS? BECAUSE OF THE MOVIE?
IT'S BECAUSE OF THE CONTRADICTIONS. IN THE NOVEL, SÜSS SINS, BUT FINDS SALVATION THROUGH HIS RELIGION.
IN THE MOVIE, HE'S JUST A MONSTER.
WHEN ENOUGH PEOPLE HAD SEEN THE MOVIE--THERE WAS A CRISIS. AN IMBALANCE.
WAIT. THIS IS MEANT TO BE AN UNHAPPY NOVEL?
IT LOOKS LIKE A WHIRLWIND GOT FUCKED BY AN ELEPHANT AND HAD ITS BABY.
TOMMY, YOU HAVE NO IDEA HOW DANGEROUS THIS IS. YOU HAVE TO COME AWAY.
I DON'T THINK I CAN DO THAT. WE'LL NEVER FIND OUR WAY BACK HERE.
IT WANTS SOMETHING FROM ME. IT'S IN AGONY, AND IT'S BEGGING ME TO HELP.
NO! NO!
LIZZIE, LET GO OF ME. I'M WARN-ING YOU--
OH SHIT! GUYS--

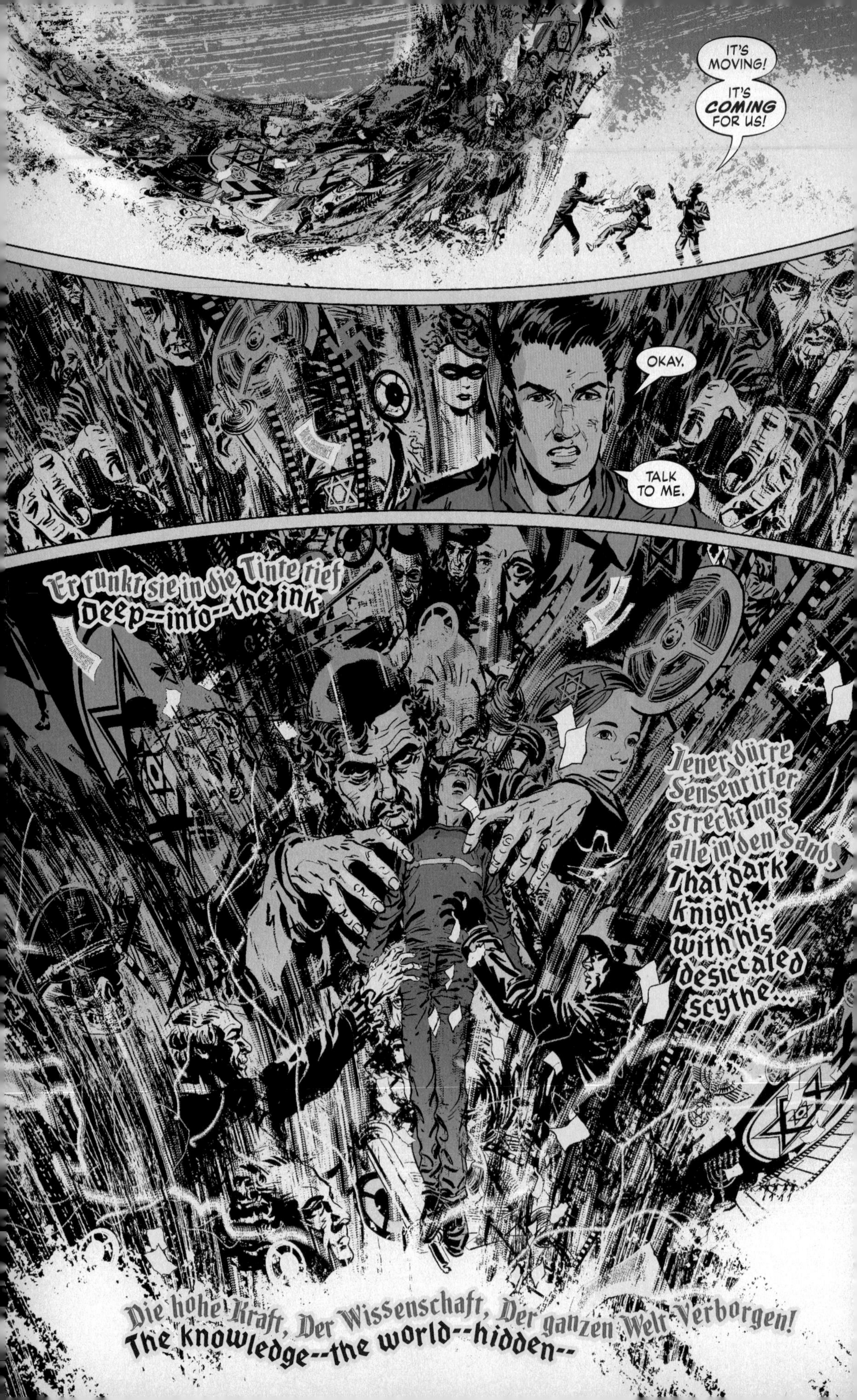
IT'S MOVING!
IT'S COMING FOR US!
OKAY.
TALK TO ME.
Er tunkt sie in die Tinte tief
Deep--into--the ink
Jener dürre Sensenritter streckt uns alle in den Sand.
That dark knight... with his desiccated scythe...
Die hohe Kraft, Der Wissenschaft, Der ganzen Welt Verborgen!
The knowledge--the world--hidden--

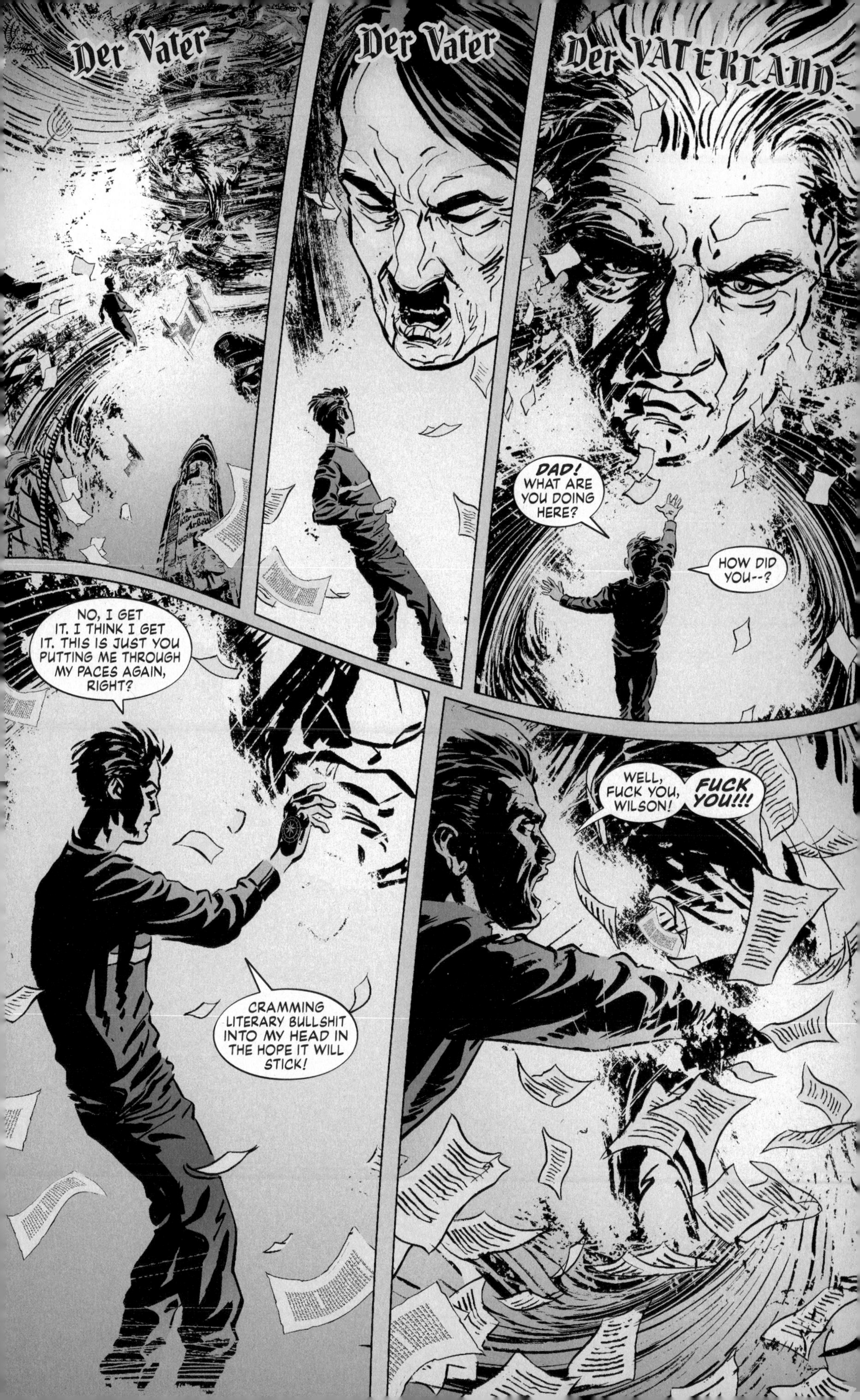
Der Vater
Der Vater
Der VATERLAND
DAD! WHAT ARE YOU DOING HERE?
HOW DID YOU--?
NO, I GET IT. I THINK I GET IT. THIS IS JUST YOU PUTTING ME THROUGH MY PACES AGAIN, RIGHT?
CRAMMING LITERARY BULLSHIT INTO MY HEAD IN THE HOPE IT WILL STICK!
WELL, FUCK YOU, WILSON!
FUCK YOU!!!

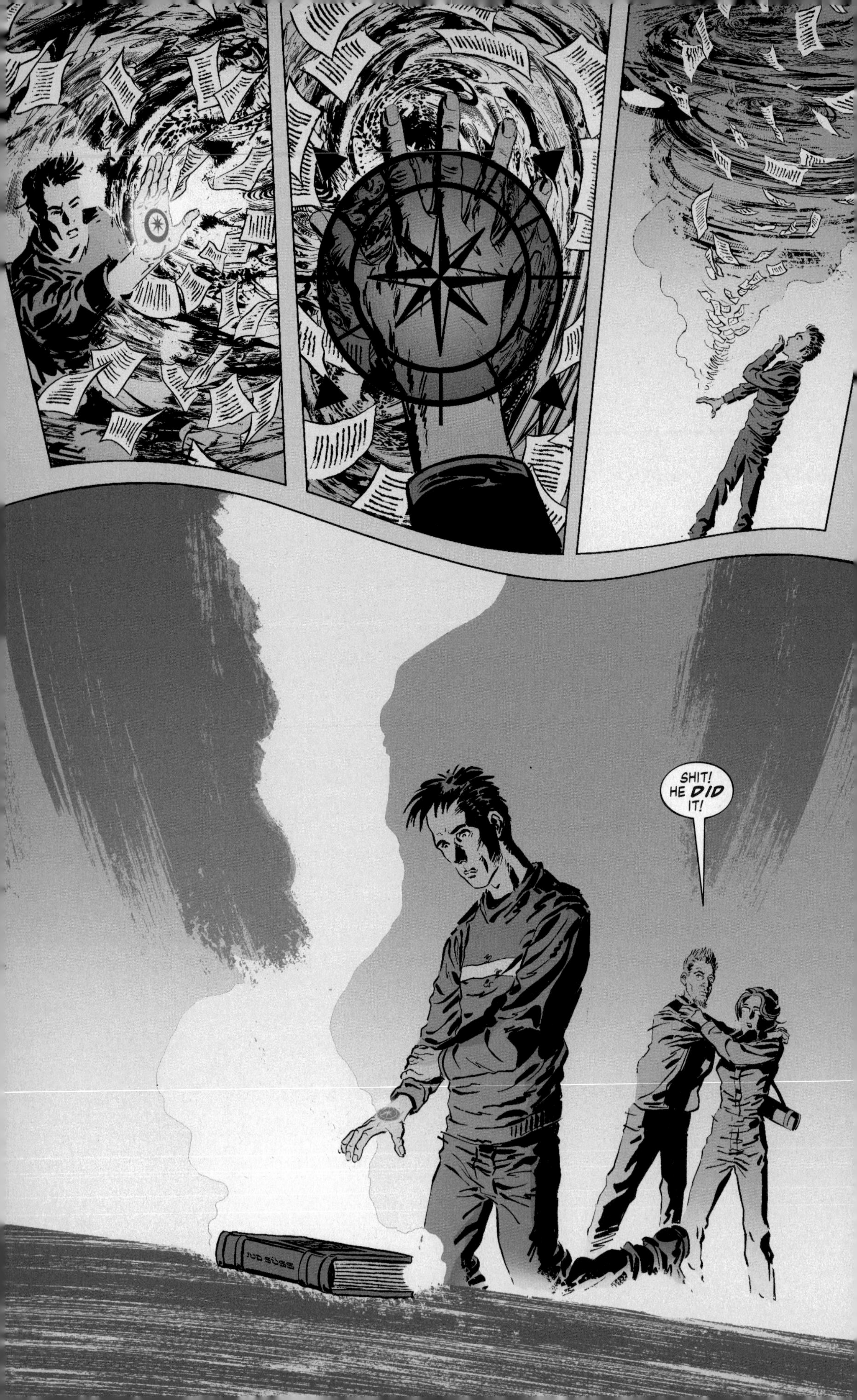
SHIT! HE *DID* IT!
JUD SÜSS

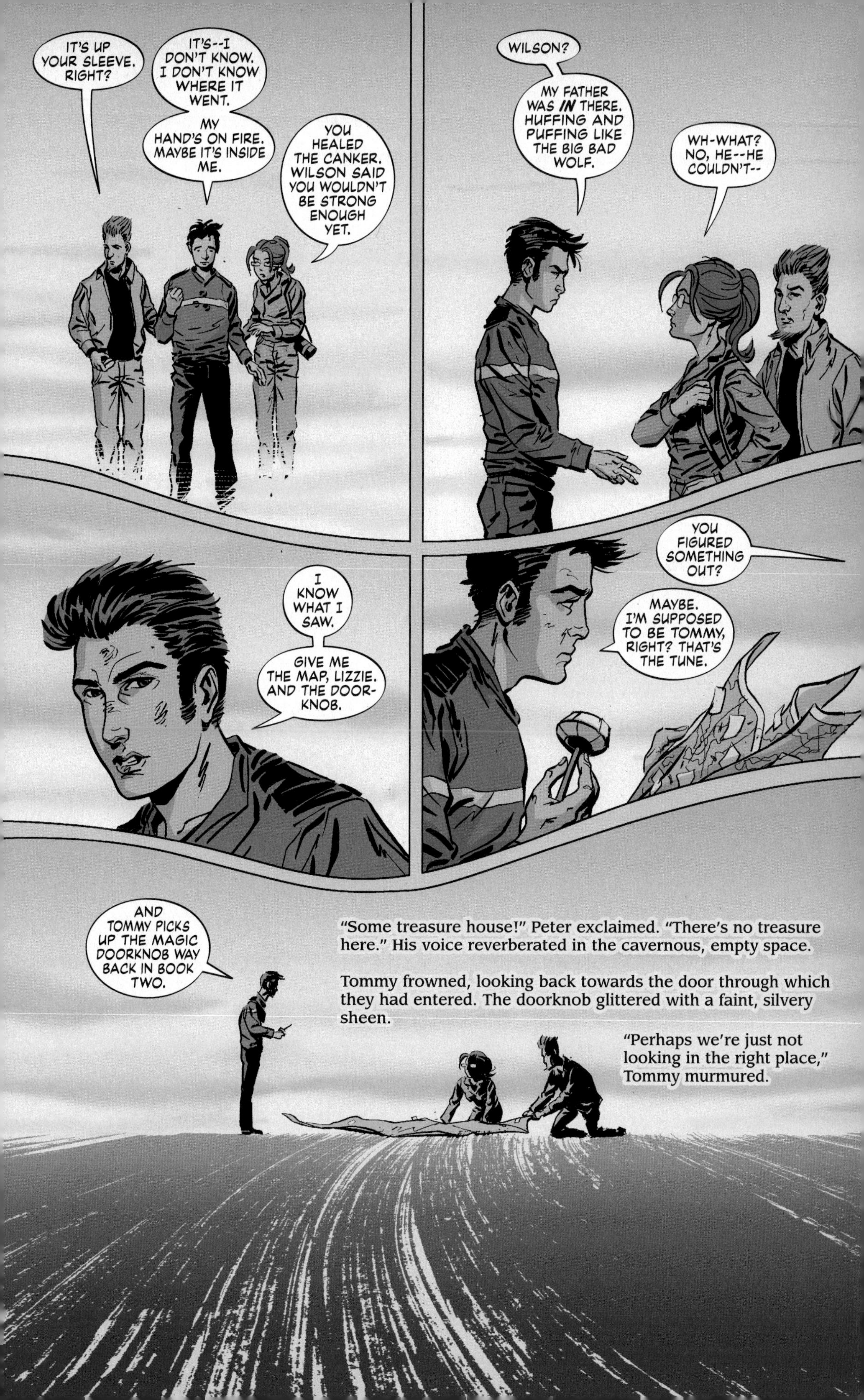
IT'S UP YOUR SLEEVE. RIGHT?
IT'S--I DON'T KNOW. I DON'T KNOW WHERE IT WENT.
MY HAND'S ON FIRE. MAYBE IT'S INSIDE ME.
YOU HEALED THE CANKER. WILSON SAID YOU WOULDN'T BE STRONG ENOUGH YET.
WILSON?
MY FATHER WAS *IN* THERE. HUFFING AND PUFFING LIKE THE BIG BAD WOLF.
WH-WHAT? NO, HE--HE COULDN'T--
I KNOW WHAT I SAW.
GIVE ME THE MAP, LIZZIE. AND THE DOOR-KNOB.
YOU FIGURED SOMETHING OUT?
MAYBE. I'M SUPPOSED TO BE TOMMY, RIGHT? THAT'S THE TUNE.
AND TOMMY PICKS UP THE MAGIC DOORKNOB WAY BACK IN BOOK TWO.
"Some treasure house!" Peter exclaimed. "There's no treasure here." His voice reverberated in the cavernous, empty space.
Tommy frowned, looking back towards the door through which they had entered. The doorknob glittered with a faint, silvery sheen.
"Perhaps we're just not looking in the right place," Tommy murmured.

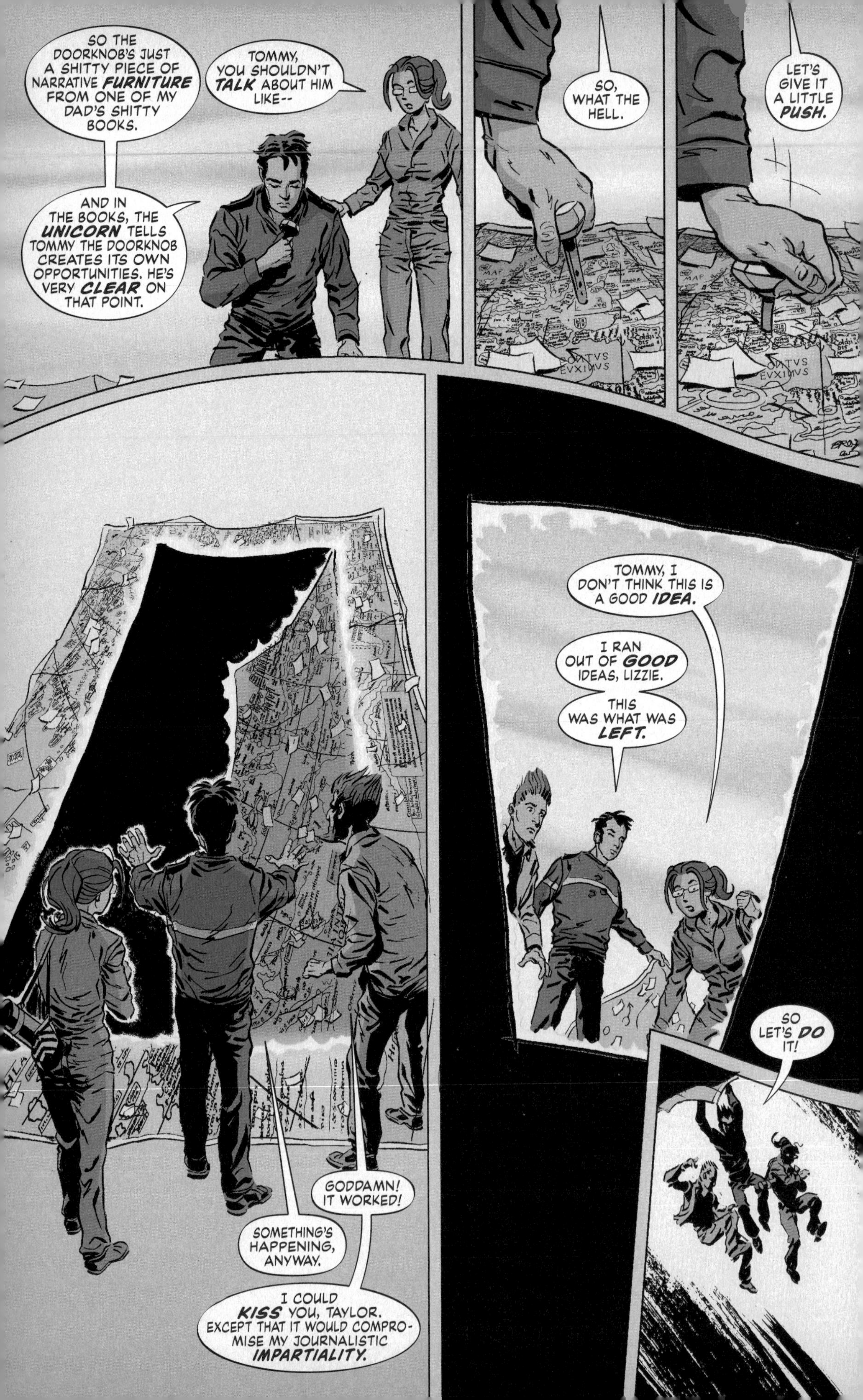

SO THE DOORKNOB'S JUST A SHITTY PIECE OF NARRATIVE FURNITURE FROM ONE OF MY DAD'S SHITTY BOOKS.
TOMMY, YOU SHOULDN'T TALK ABOUT HIM LIKE--
AND IN THE BOOKS, THE UNICORN TELLS TOMMY THE DOORKNOB CREATES ITS OWN OPPORTUNITIES. HE'S VERY CLEAR ON THAT POINT.
SO, WHAT THE HELL.
LET'S GIVE IT A LITTLE PUSH.
TOMMY, I DON'T THINK THIS IS A GOOD IDEA.
I RAN OUT OF GOOD IDEAS, LIZZIE.
THIS WAS WHAT WAS LEFT.
GODDAMN! IT WORKED!
SOMETHING'S HAPPENING, ANYWAY.
I COULD KISS YOU, TAYLOR. EXCEPT THAT IT WOULD COMPROMISE MY JOURNALISTIC IMPARTIALITY.
SO LET'S DO IT!

JESUS!

OW!

¡UFFF!

THIS **ISN'T** THE VILLA DIODATI.

NO. IT LOOKS MORE LIKE **LONDON.** BUT WHAT THE FUCK.

WE'RE OUT OF THAT **SHIT-HOLE,** ANYWAY. THAT'S WHAT COUNTS.

LIZZIE, THIS THING--WHAT WILSON IS DOING--IT'S A LOT **BIGGER** THAN ME, ISN'T IT?

WHAT DO YOU MEAN?

I MEAN IT GOES BACK BEFORE I WAS **BORN.** PEOPLE HAVE BEEN DYING FOR IT, **KILLING** FOR IT, SINCE THE SECOND WORLD WAR.

OH SHIT! LOOK AT THE DATE...

WE'RE OFFICIALLY **OLD** NEWS. WE WERE IN THERE FOR **THREE MONTHS.**

I'M THREE MONTHS PAST MY FUCKING **DEADLINE!**

THE POST

EW TOMMY TAYLOR
O SHATTER RECORDS

Will Wilson Taylor reappear

UK-based Queensberry Publish
are bracing themselves for the
biggest book launch the world has
ever seen
Millions of fans all over the world
have responded with delight to the
news that their favorite fictional
hero is about to get a new outing
will finally be answered after
and that questions as to his fate,
hiatus of more than ten
Speculation as to the
of long missing
ry in costume,
up in droves to
outside country
ly in country

NO, THAT'S GOOD. IT MEANS THEY'LL HAVE STOPPED **LOOKING** FOR US.

I'VE GOT TO FIND MY DAD. FIND OUT WHAT'S REALLY GOING ON. WHO **PULLMAN** AND HIS FRIENDS ARE, AND WHAT THEY WANT.

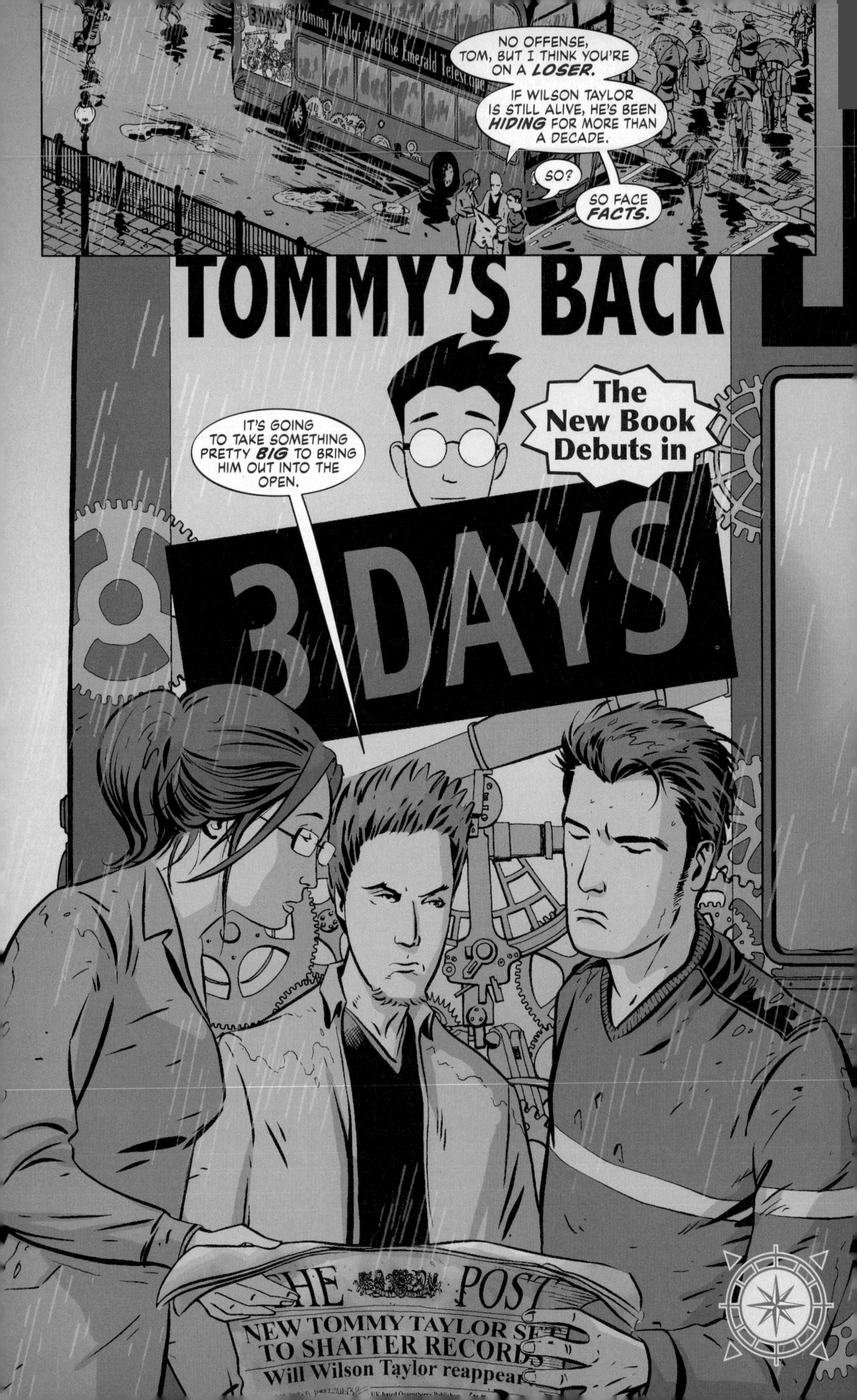
3 DAYS
Tommy Taylor and the Emerald Telescope
NO OFFENSE, TOM, BUT I THINK YOU'RE ON A *LOSER*.
IF WILSON TAYLOR IS STILL ALIVE, HE'S BEEN *HIDING* FOR MORE THAN A DECADE.
SO?
SO FACE *FACTS*.
TOMMY'S BACK
The New Book Debuts in
3 DAYS
IT'S GOING TO TAKE SOMETHING PRETTY *BIG* TO BRING HIM OUT INTO THE OPEN.
THE POST
NEW TOMMY TAYLOR SET TO SHATTER RECORDS
Will Wilson Taylor reappear

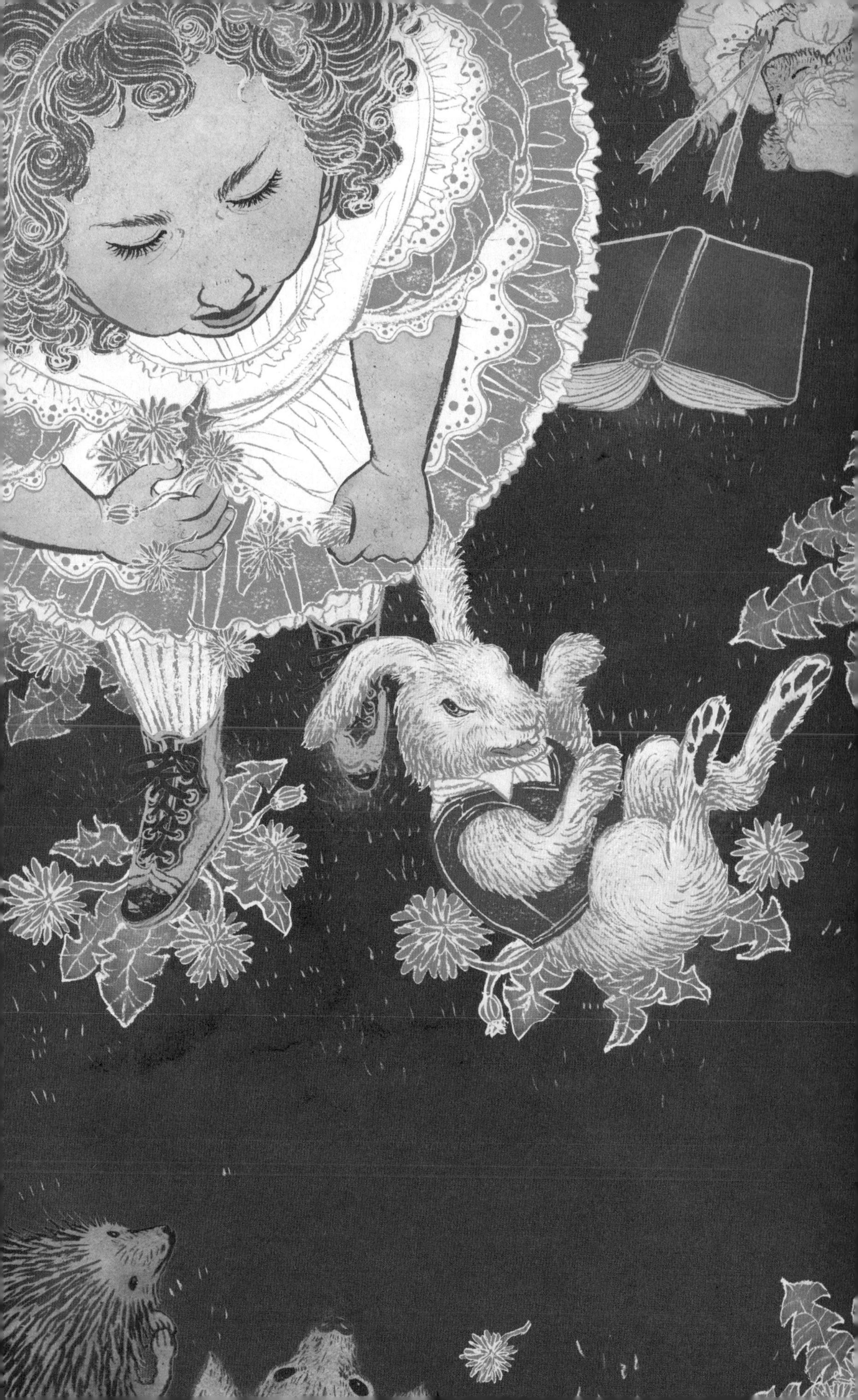

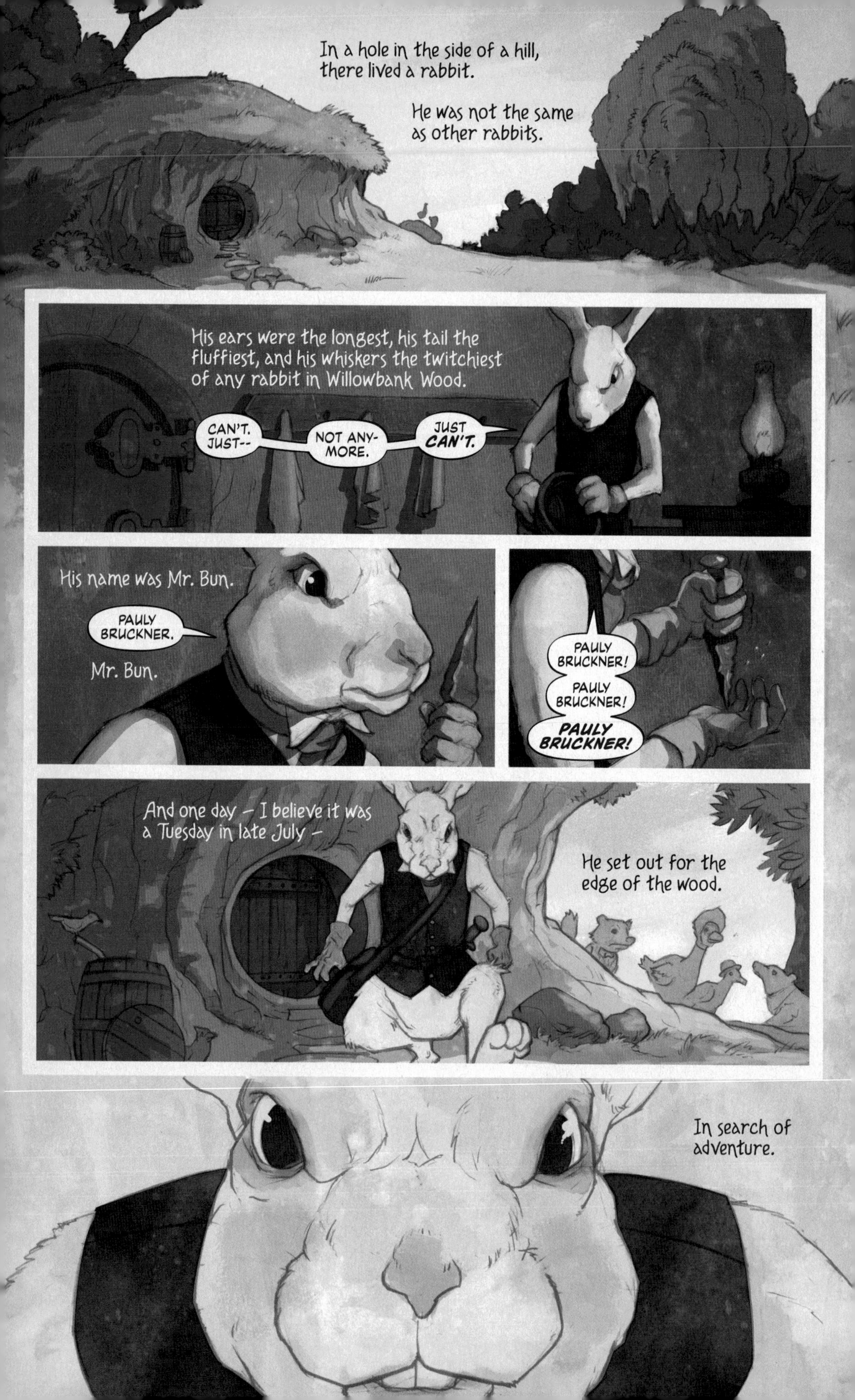
In a hole in the side of a hill, there lived a rabbit.
He was not the same as other rabbits.
His ears were the longest, his tail the fluffiest, and his whiskers the twitchiest of any rabbit in Willowbank Wood.
CAN'T. JUST--
NOT ANY-MORE.
JUST CAN'T.
His name was Mr. Bun.
PAULY BRUCKNER.
Mr. Bun.
PAULY BRUCKNER!
PAULY BRUCKNER!
PAULY BRUCKNER!
And one day – I believe it was a Tuesday in late July –
He set out for the edge of the wood.
In search of adventure.

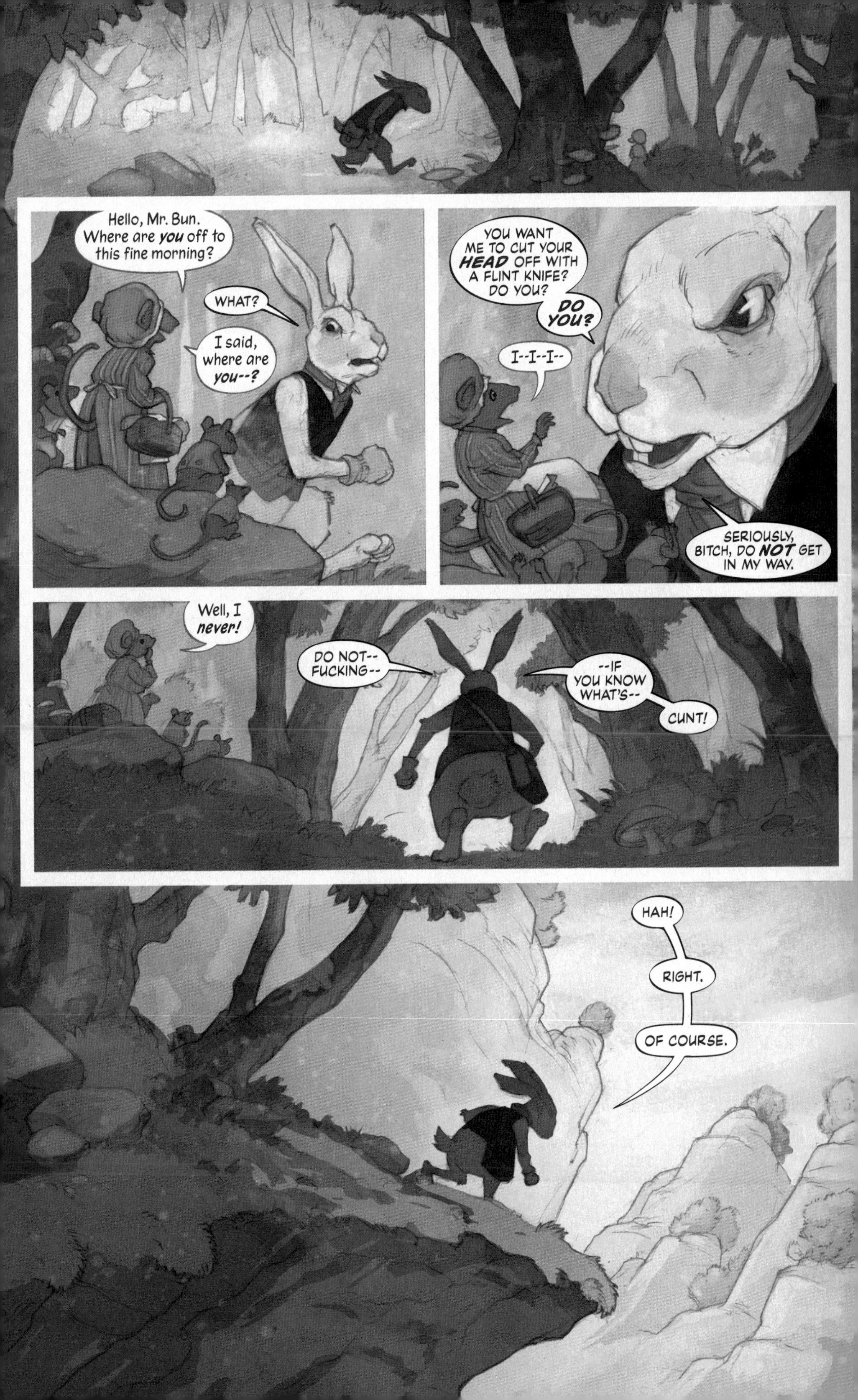
Hello, Mr. Bun. Where are *you* off to this fine morning?
WHAT?
I said, where are *you--?*
YOU WANT ME TO CUT YOUR ***HEAD*** OFF WITH A FLINT KNIFE? DO YOU? ***DO YOU?***
I--I--I--
SERIOUSLY, BITCH, DO ***NOT*** GET IN MY WAY.
Well, I ***never!***
DO NOT-- FUCKING--
--IF YOU KNOW WHAT'S--
CUNT!
HAH!
RIGHT.
OF COURSE.

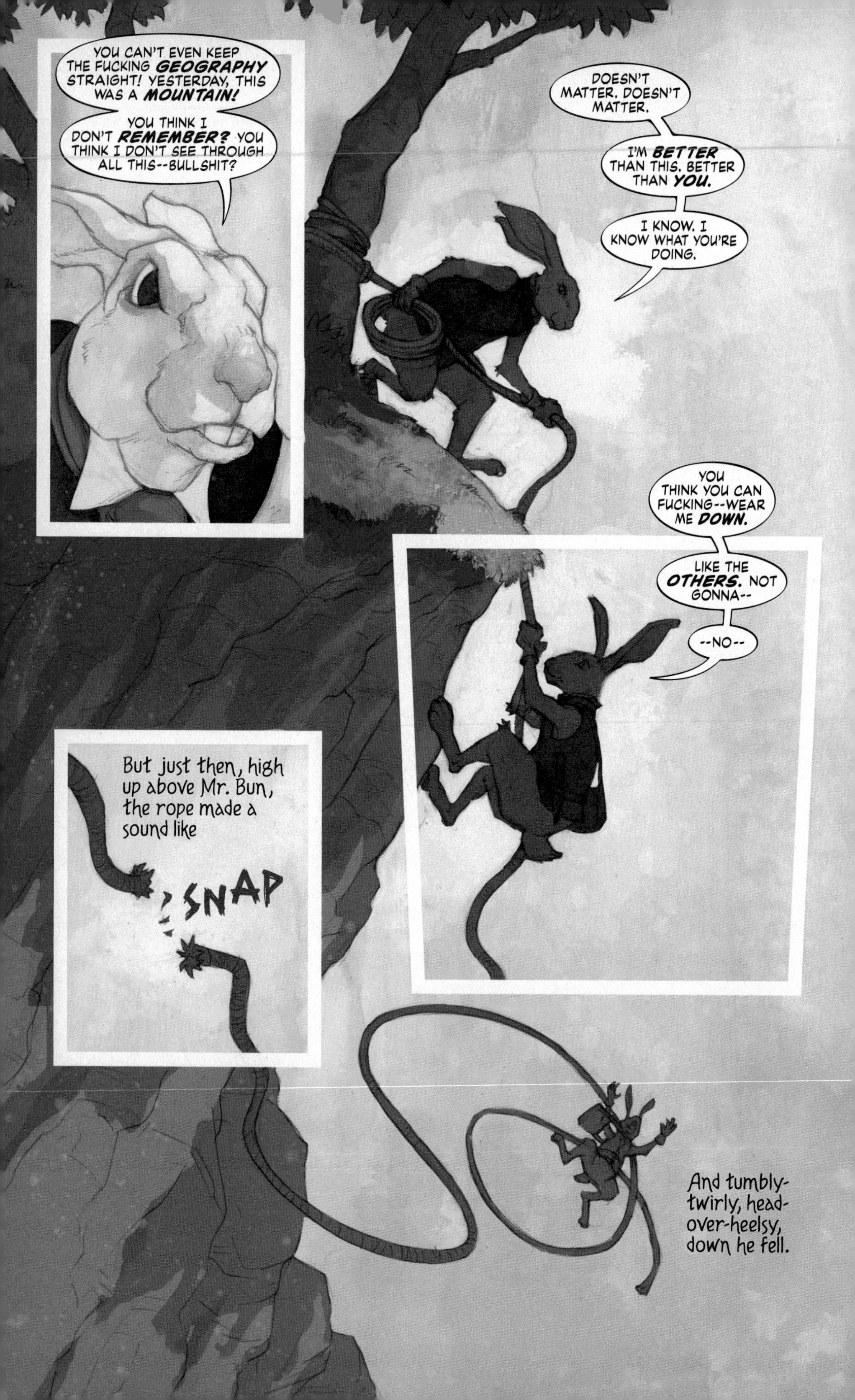
YOU CAN'T EVEN KEEP THE FUCKING GEOGRAPHY STRAIGHT! YESTERDAY, THIS WAS A MOUNTAIN!
YOU THINK I DON'T REMEMBER? YOU THINK I DON'T SEE THROUGH ALL THIS--BULLSHIT?
DOESN'T MATTER. DOESN'T MATTER.
I'M BETTER THAN THIS. BETTER THAN YOU.
I KNOW. I KNOW WHAT YOU'RE DOING.
YOU THINK YOU CAN FUCKING--WEAR ME DOWN.
LIKE THE OTHERS. NOT GONNA--
--NO--
But just then, high up above Mr. Bun, the rope made a sound like
SNAP
And tumbly-twirly, head-over-heelsy, down he fell.

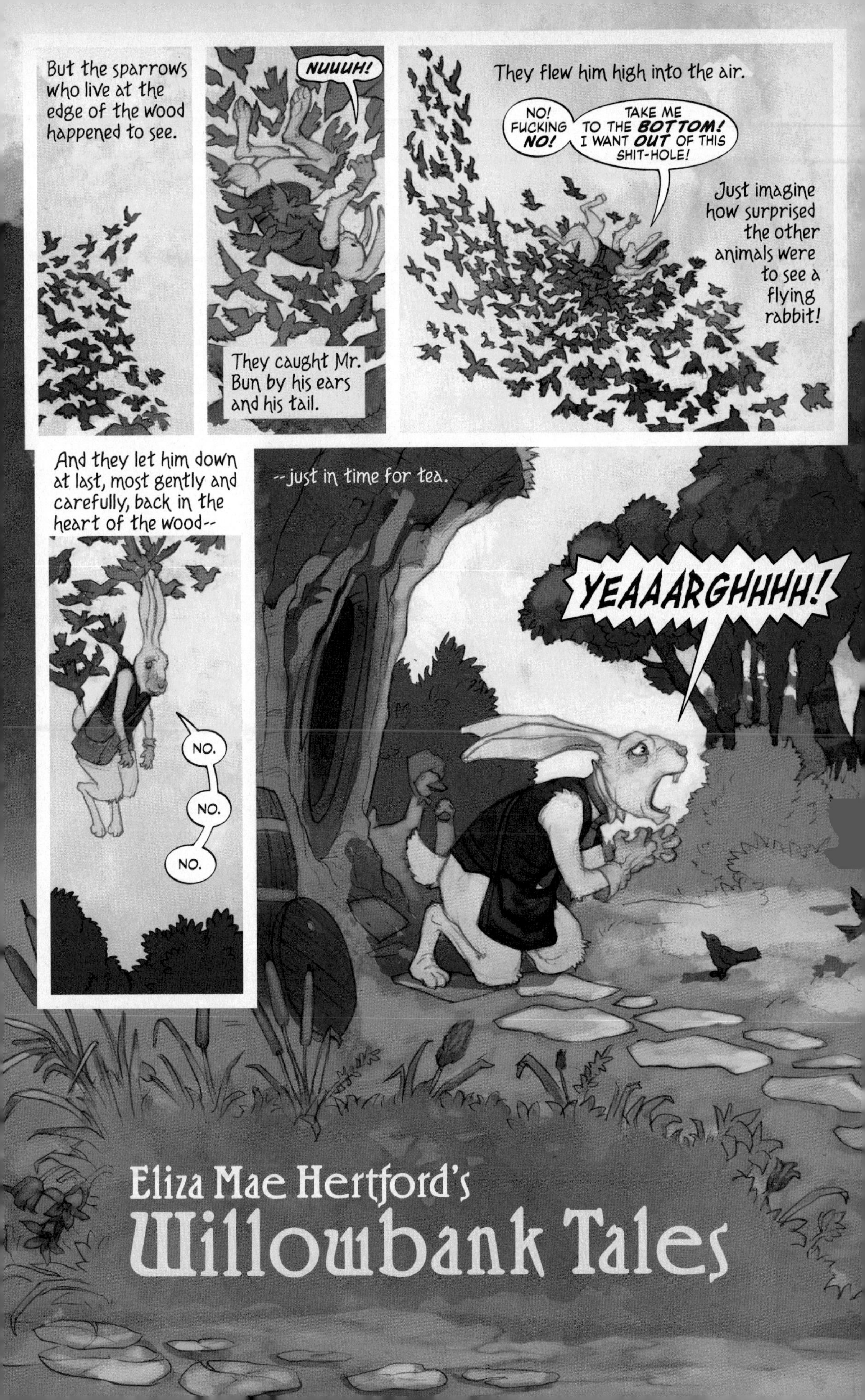
But the sparrows who live at the edge of the wood happened to see.
NUUUH!
They caught Mr. Bun by his ears and his tail.
They flew him high into the air.
NO! FUCKING NO!
TAKE ME TO THE BOTTOM! I WANT OUT OF THIS SHIT-HOLE!
Just imagine how surprised the other animals were to see a flying rabbit!
And they let him down at last, most gently and carefully, back in the heart of the wood--
NO.
NO.
NO.
--just in time for tea.
YEAAARGHHHH!
Eliza Mae Hertford's
Willowbank Tales

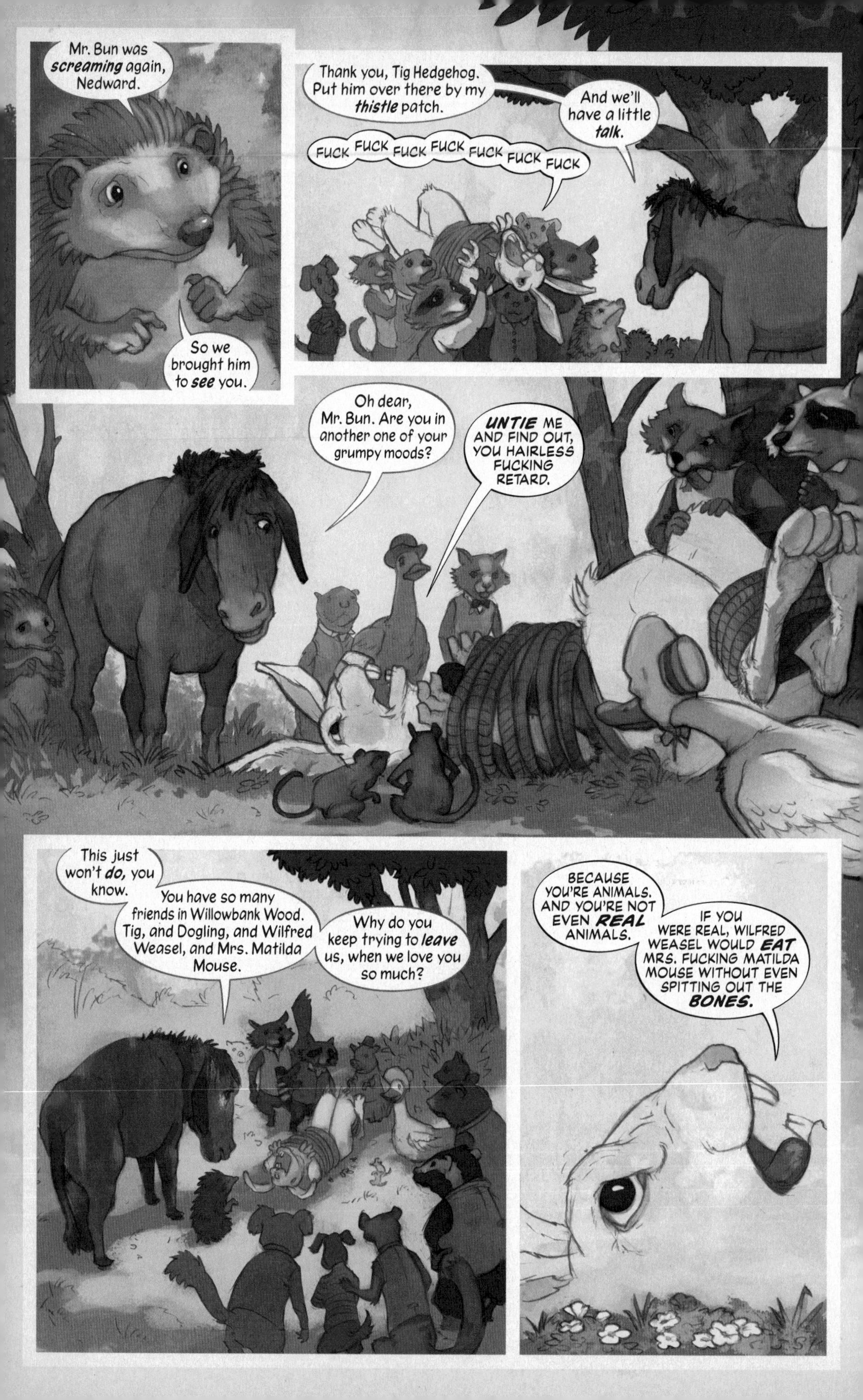

Mr. Bun was *screaming* again, Nedward.
So we brought him to *see* you.
Thank you, Tig Hedgehog. Put him over there by my *thistle* patch.
And we'll have a little *talk*.
FUCK FUCK FUCK FUCK FUCK FUCK FUCK
Oh dear, Mr. Bun. Are you in another one of your grumpy moods?
UNTIE ME AND FIND OUT, YOU HAIRLESS FUCKING RETARD.
This just won't *do,* you know.
You have so many friends in Willowbank Wood. Tig, and Dogling, and Wilfred Weasel, and Mrs. Matilda Mouse.
Why do you keep trying to *leave* us, when we love you so much?
BECAUSE YOU'RE ANIMALS. AND YOU'RE NOT EVEN *REAL* ANIMALS.
IF YOU WERE REAL, WILFRED WEASEL WOULD *EAT* MRS. FUCKING MATILDA MOUSE WITHOUT EVEN SPITTING OUT THE *BONES.*

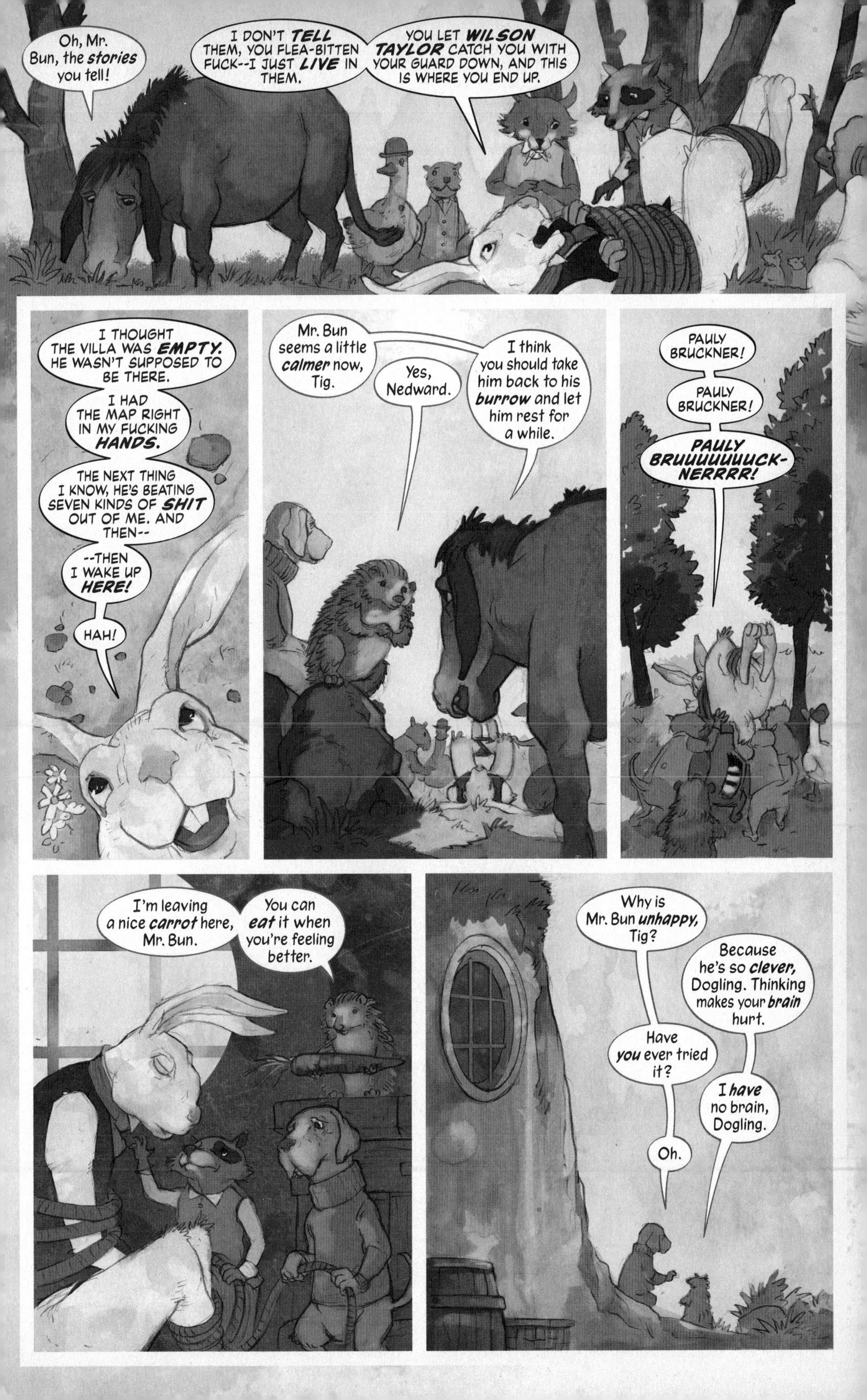
Oh, Mr. Bun, the stories you tell!
I DON'T TELL THEM, YOU FLEA-BITTEN FUCK--I JUST LIVE IN THEM.
YOU LET WILSON TAYLOR CATCH YOU WITH YOUR GUARD DOWN, AND THIS IS WHERE YOU END UP.
I THOUGHT THE VILLA WAS EMPTY. HE WASN'T SUPPOSED TO BE THERE.
I HAD THE MAP RIGHT IN MY FUCKING HANDS.
THE NEXT THING I KNOW, HE'S BEATING SEVEN KINDS OF SHIT OUT OF ME. AND THEN--
--THEN I WAKE UP HERE!
HAH!
Mr. Bun seems a little calmer now, Tig.
I think you should take him back to his burrow and let him rest for a while.
Yes, Nedward.
PAULY BRUCKNER!
PAULY BRUCKNER!
PAULY BRUUUUUUCK-NERRRR!
I'm leaving a nice carrot here, Mr. Bun.
You can eat it when you're feeling better.
Why is Mr. Bun unhappy, Tig?
Because he's so clever, Dogling. Thinking makes your brain hurt.
Have you ever tried it?
I have no brain, Dogling.
Oh.

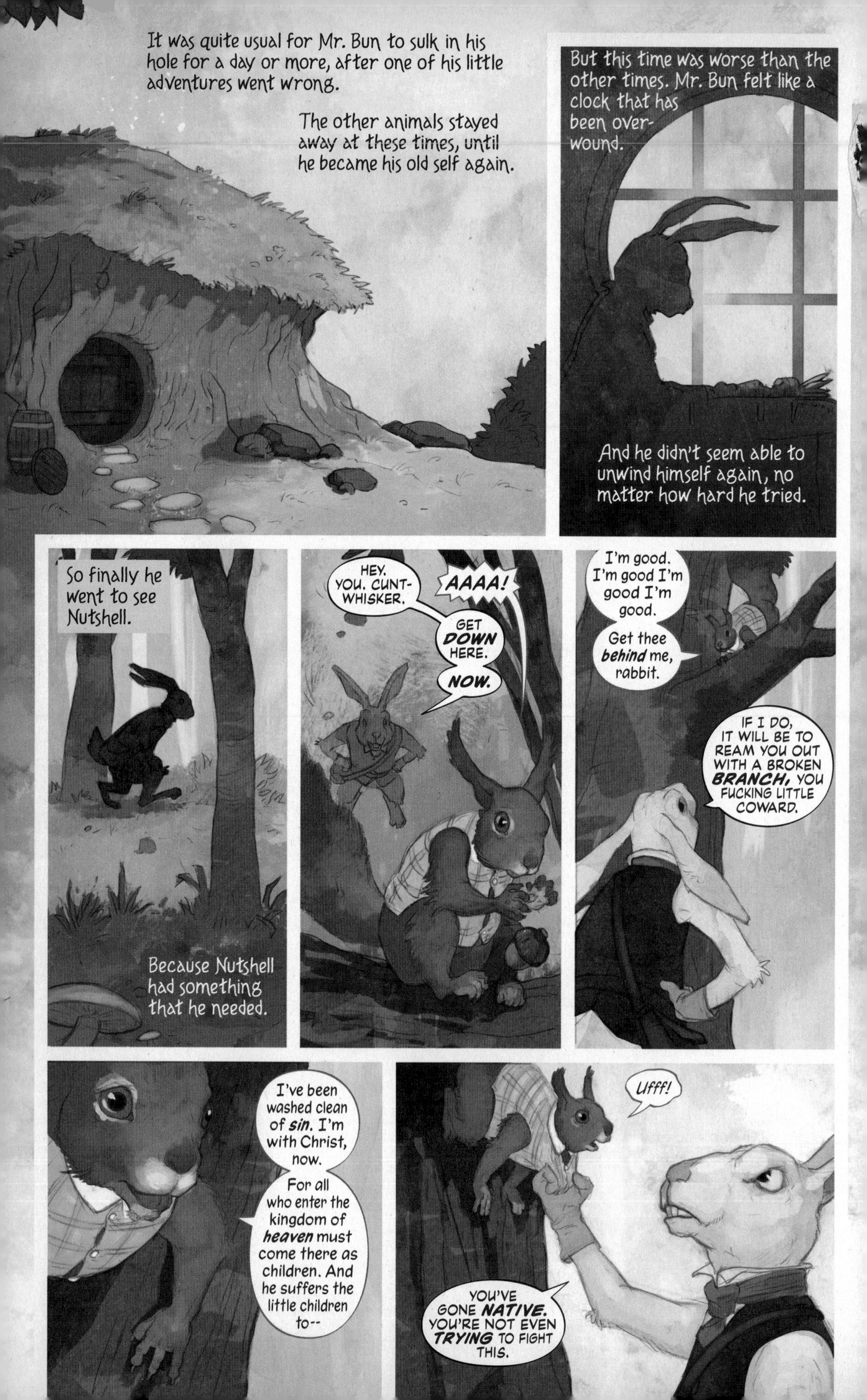

It was quite usual for Mr. Bun to sulk in his hole for a day or more, after one of his little adventures went wrong.
The other animals stayed away at these times, until he became his old self again.
But this time was worse than the other times. Mr. Bun felt like a clock that has been over-wound.
And he didn't seem able to unwind himself again, no matter how hard he tried.
So finally he went to see Nutshell.
Because Nutshell had something that he needed.
HEY. YOU. CUNT-WHISKER.
AAAA!
GET DOWN HERE. NOW.
I'm good. I'm good I'm good I'm good.
Get thee behind me, rabbit.
IF I DO, IT WILL BE TO REAM YOU OUT WITH A BROKEN BRANCH, YOU FUCKING LITTLE COWARD.
I've been washed clean of sin. I'm with Christ, now.
For all who enter the kingdom of heaven must come there as children. And he suffers the little children to--
Ufff!
YOU'VE GONE NATIVE. YOU'RE NOT EVEN TRYING TO FIGHT THIS.

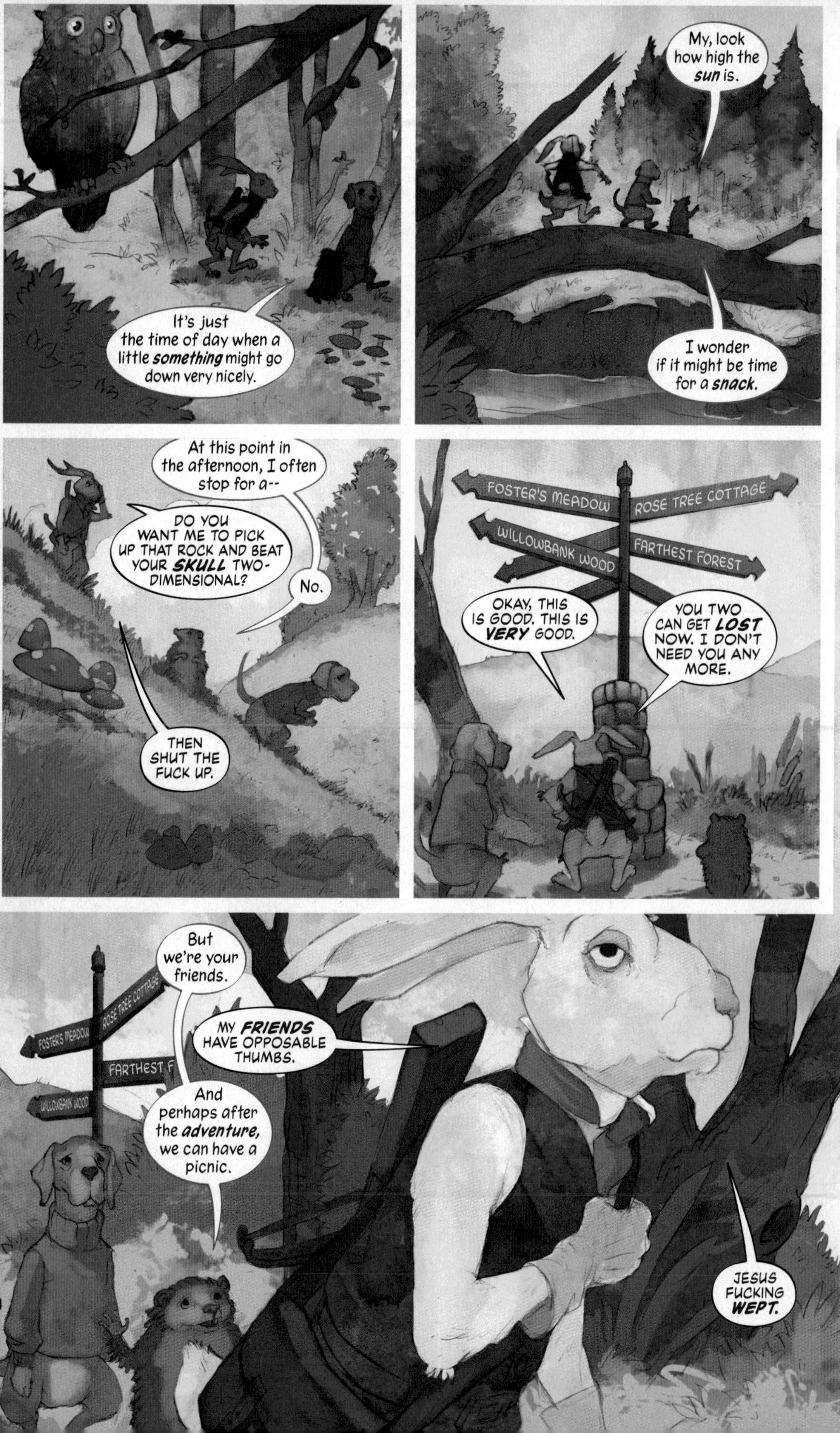
It's just the time of day when a little *something* might go down very nicely.
My, look how high the *sun* is.
I wonder if it might be time for a *snack*.
At this point in the afternoon, I often stop for a--
DO YOU WANT ME TO PICK UP THAT ROCK AND BEAT YOUR *SKULL* TWO-DIMENSIONAL?
No.
THEN SHUT THE FUCK UP.
FOSTER'S MEADOW
ROSE TREE COTTAGE
WILLOWBANK WOOD
FARTHEST FOREST
OKAY, THIS IS GOOD. THIS IS *VERY* GOOD.
YOU TWO CAN GET *LOST* NOW. I DON'T NEED YOU ANY MORE.
But we're your friends.
MY *FRIENDS* HAVE OPPOSABLE THUMBS.
And perhaps after the *adventure,* we can have a picnic.
JESUS FUCKING *WEPT.*

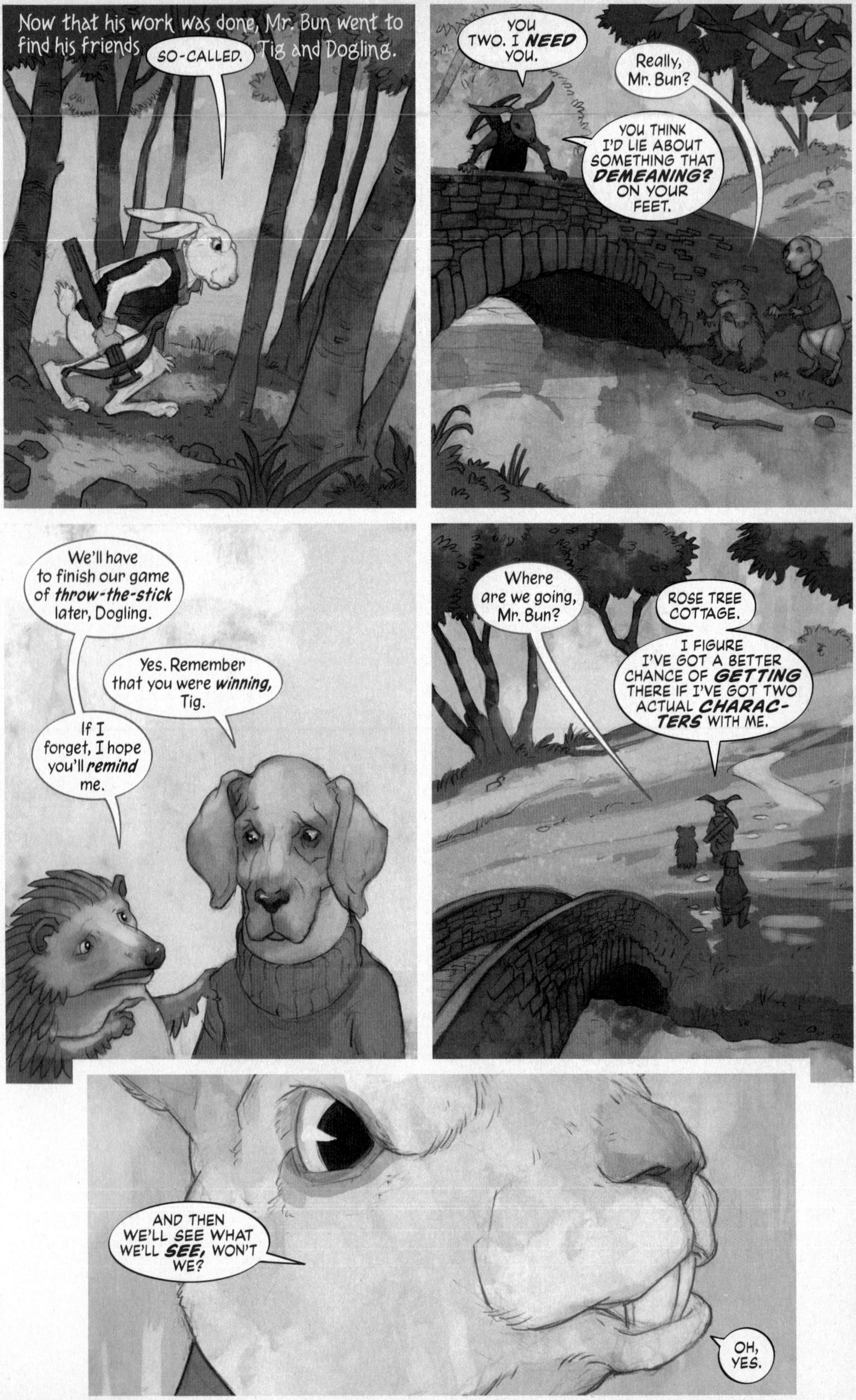
Now that his work was done, Mr. Bun went to find his friends
SO-CALLED.
Tig and Dogling.
YOU TWO. I **NEED** YOU.
Really, Mr. Bun?
YOU THINK I'D LIE ABOUT SOMETHING THAT ***DEMEANING?*** ON YOUR FEET.
We'll have to finish our game of ***throw-the-stick*** later, Dogling.
Yes. Remember that you were ***winning,*** Tig.
If I forget, I hope you'll ***remind*** me.
Where are we going, Mr. Bun?
ROSE TREE COTTAGE.
I FIGURE I'VE GOT A BETTER CHANCE OF ***GETTING*** THERE IF I'VE GOT TWO ACTUAL ***CHARAC-TERS*** WITH ME.
AND THEN WE'LL SEE WHAT WE'LL ***SEE,*** WON'T WE?
OH, YES.

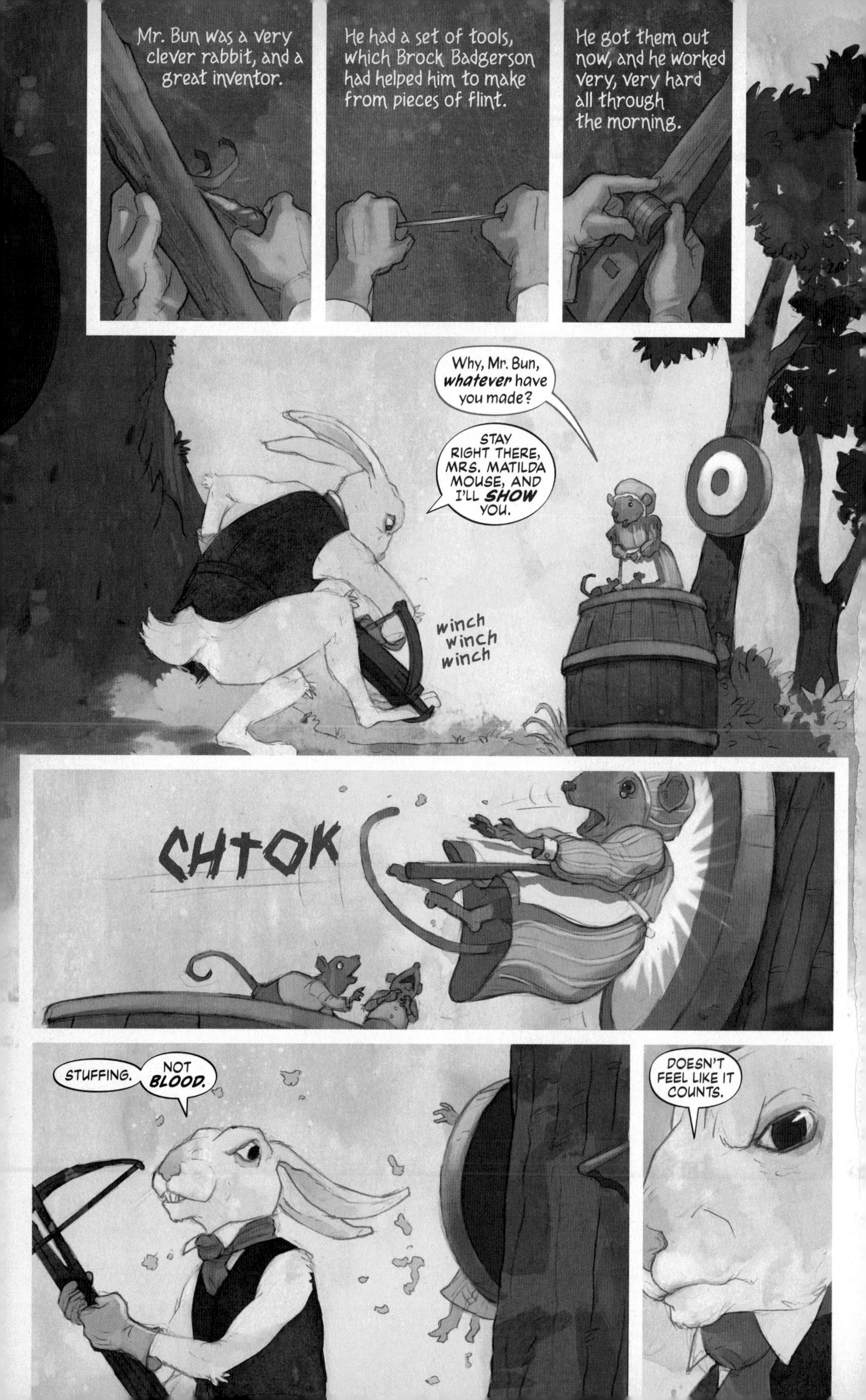
Mr. Bun was a very clever rabbit, and a great inventor.
He had a set of tools, which Brock Badgerson had helped him to make from pieces of flint.
He got them out now, and he worked very, very hard all through the morning.
Why, Mr. Bun, *whatever* have you made?
STAY RIGHT THERE, MRS. MATILDA MOUSE, AND I'LL ***SHOW*** YOU.
winch winch winch
CHTOK
STUFFING.
NOT ***BLOOD.***
DOESN'T FEEL LIKE IT COUNTS.

YOU FUCKING *DISGUST* ME, NIELSON!

THEN LEAVE ME *ALONE*, PAULY.

I--I DON'T EVER *THINK* ABOUT THOSE DAYS, EXCEPT WHEN I SEE *YOU*. PLEASE, JUST LEAVE ME ALONE.

I'D LOVE TO. BUT YOU READ THE *BOOKS*, DIDN'T YOU? TALES OF THE WILLOWBANK WOOD, BY ELIZA MAE HERTFORD.

I--YEAH, I KNOW THEM. I HAD THE WHOLE *SET*. FIRST EDITIONS.

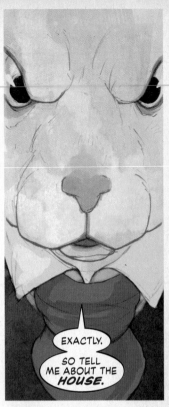

EXACTLY. SO TELL ME ABOUT THE *HOUSE*.

THE HOUSE? *ROSE TREE COTTAGE?* THAT WAS WHERE ELIZA MAE HERTFORD LIVED AS A KID.

IN THE BOOKS, *"MISS LIZA"* LIVES THERE. BUT THE ANIMALS DON'T GET TO *SEE* HER ALL THAT MUCH.

AND WHERE DO I *FIND* IT?

THERE'S-- UHH!--THERE'S A *PATH*.

FROM THE BIG OAK, OVER THE MILL RACE *BRIDGE*, TO THE COTTAGE.

PAULY, YOU SHOULD JUST *FORGET* IT.

I'M GOING TO FINISH THE JOB. GET THE MAP. FIND THE *MAANIM*, AND BLOW IT THE FUCK UP.

DO UNTO OTHERS, NIELSON. CHECK IT OUT.

IT'S IN THE *BIBLE*.

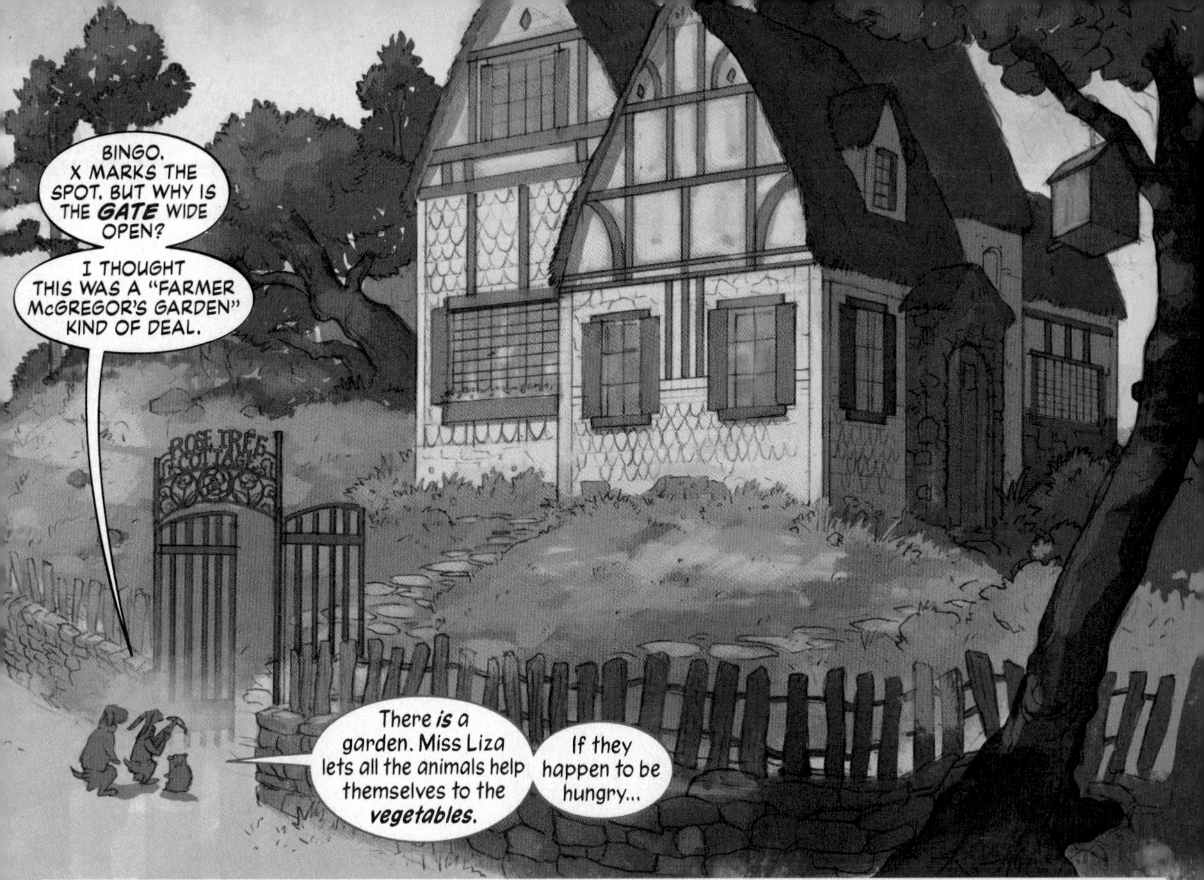
BINGO. X MARKS THE SPOT. BUT WHY IS THE **GATE** WIDE OPEN?
I THOUGHT THIS WAS A "FARMER McGREGOR'S GARDEN" KIND OF DEAL.
ROSE TREE COTTAGE
There *is* a garden. Miss Liza lets all the animals help themselves to the ***vegetables***.
If they happen to be hungry...

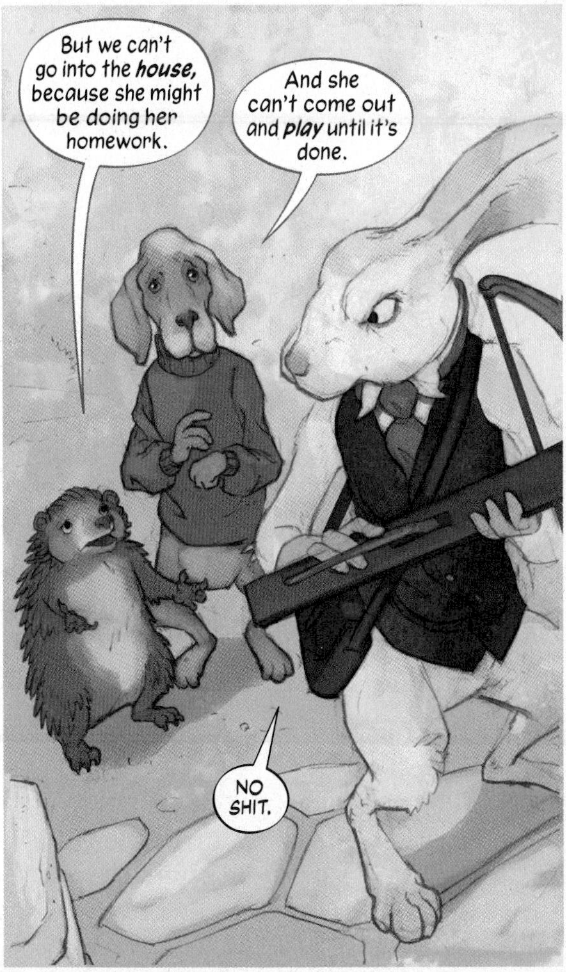
But we can't go into the ***house,*** because she might be doing her homework.
And she can't come out and ***play*** until it's done.
NO SHIT.

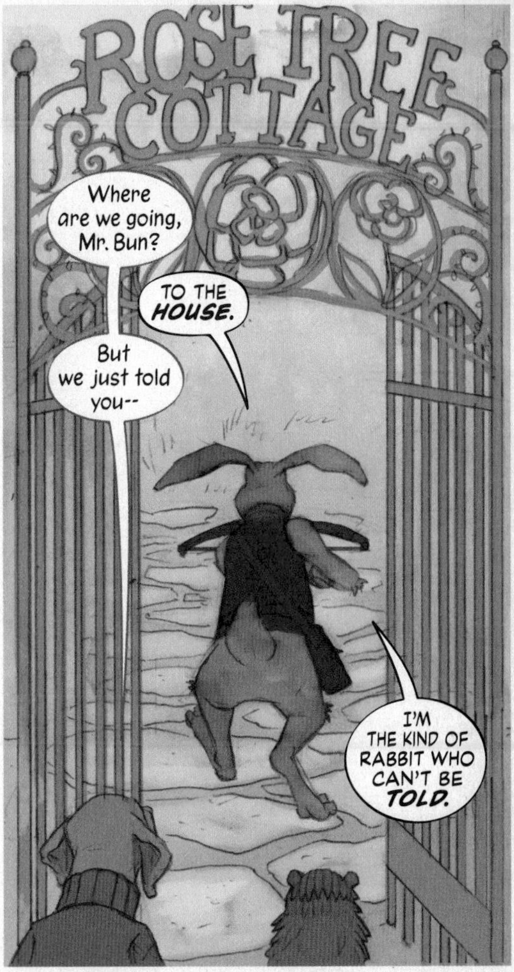
ROSE TREE COTTAGE
Where are we going, Mr. Bun?
TO THE ***HOUSE***.
But we just told you--
I'M THE KIND OF RABBIT WHO CAN'T BE ***TOLD***.

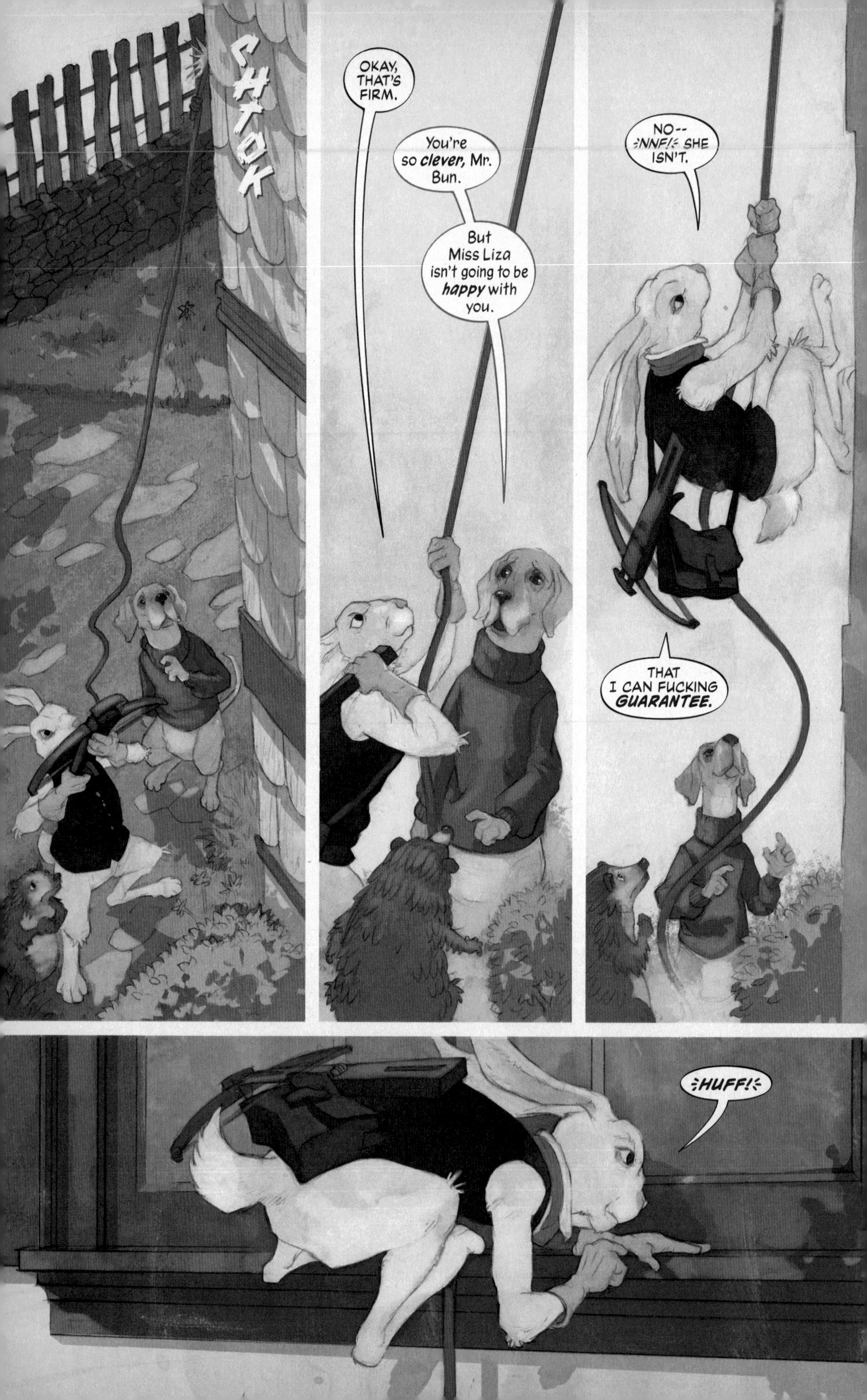
CHTOK
OKAY, THAT'S FIRM.
You're so *clever,* Mr. Bun.
But Miss Liza isn't going to be *happy* with you.
NO-- ⁝NNF!⁝ SHE ISN'T.
THAT I CAN FUCKING **GUARANTEE.**
⁝HUFF!⁝

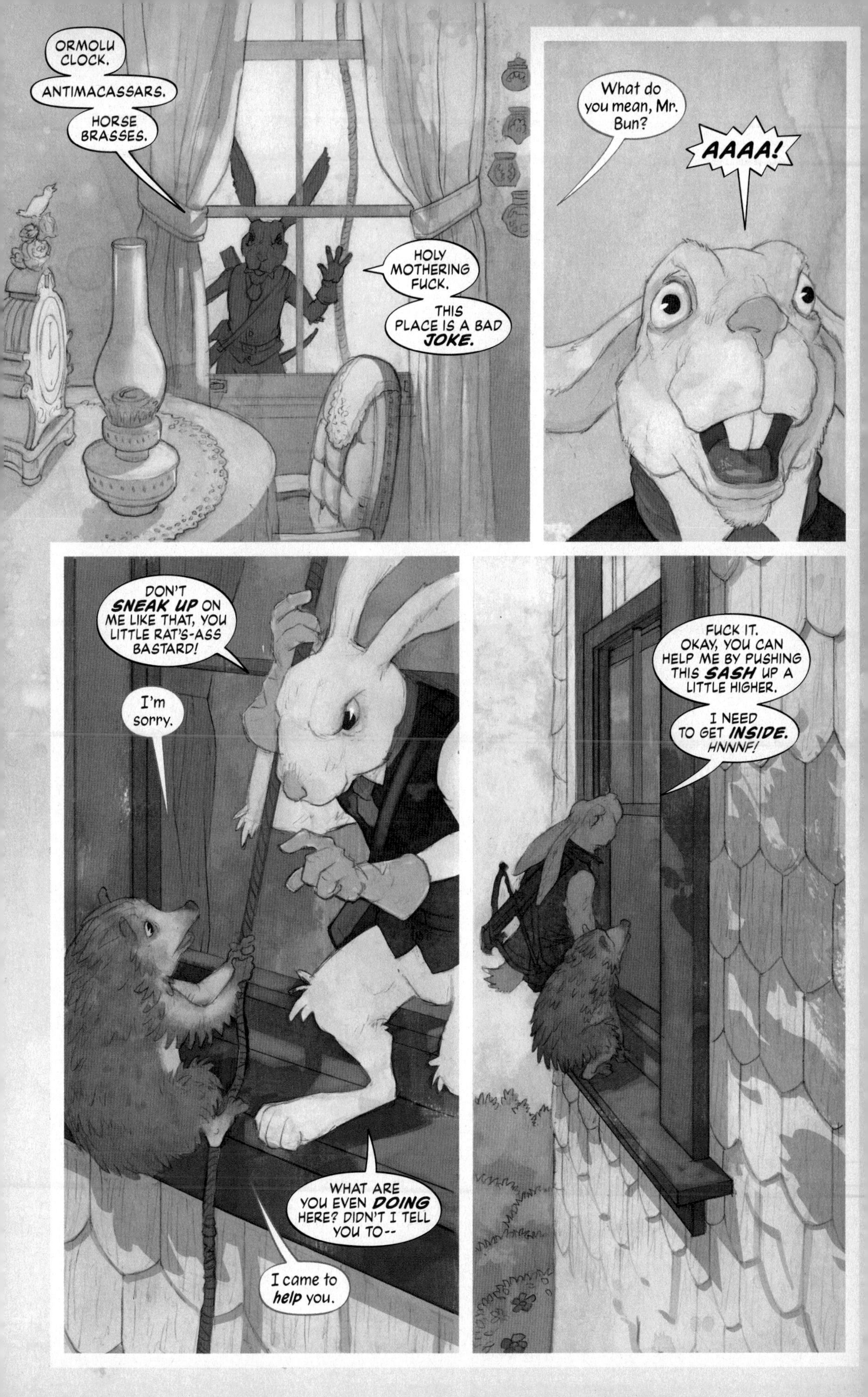
ORMOLU CLOCK.
ANTIMACASSARS.
HORSE BRASSES.
HOLY MOTHERING FUCK.
THIS PLACE IS A BAD **JOKE.**
What do you mean, Mr. Bun?
AAAA!
DON'T **SNEAK UP** ON ME LIKE THAT, YOU LITTLE RAT'S-ASS BASTARD!
I'm sorry.
WHAT ARE YOU EVEN **DOING** HERE? DIDN'T I TELL YOU TO--
I came to **help** you.
FUCK IT. OKAY, YOU CAN HELP ME BY PUSHING THIS **SASH** UP A LITTLE HIGHER.
I NEED TO GET **INSIDE.** *HNNNF!*

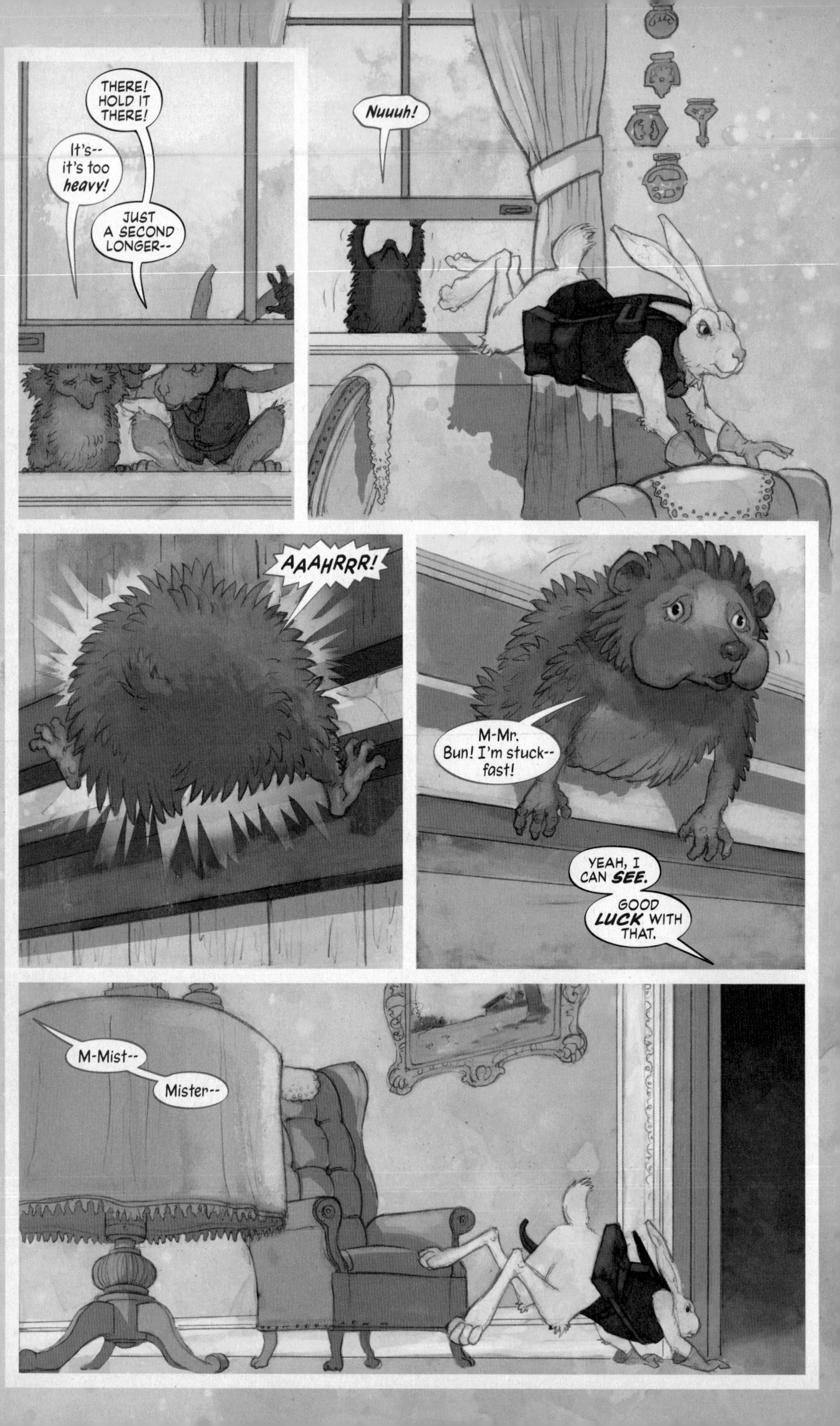
THERE! HOLD IT THERE!
It's-- it's too *heavy!*
JUST A SECOND LONGER--
Nuuuh!
AAAHRRR!
M-Mr. Bun! I'm stuck-- fast!
YEAH, I CAN **SEE.**
GOOD **LUCK** WITH THAT.
M-Mist--
Mister--

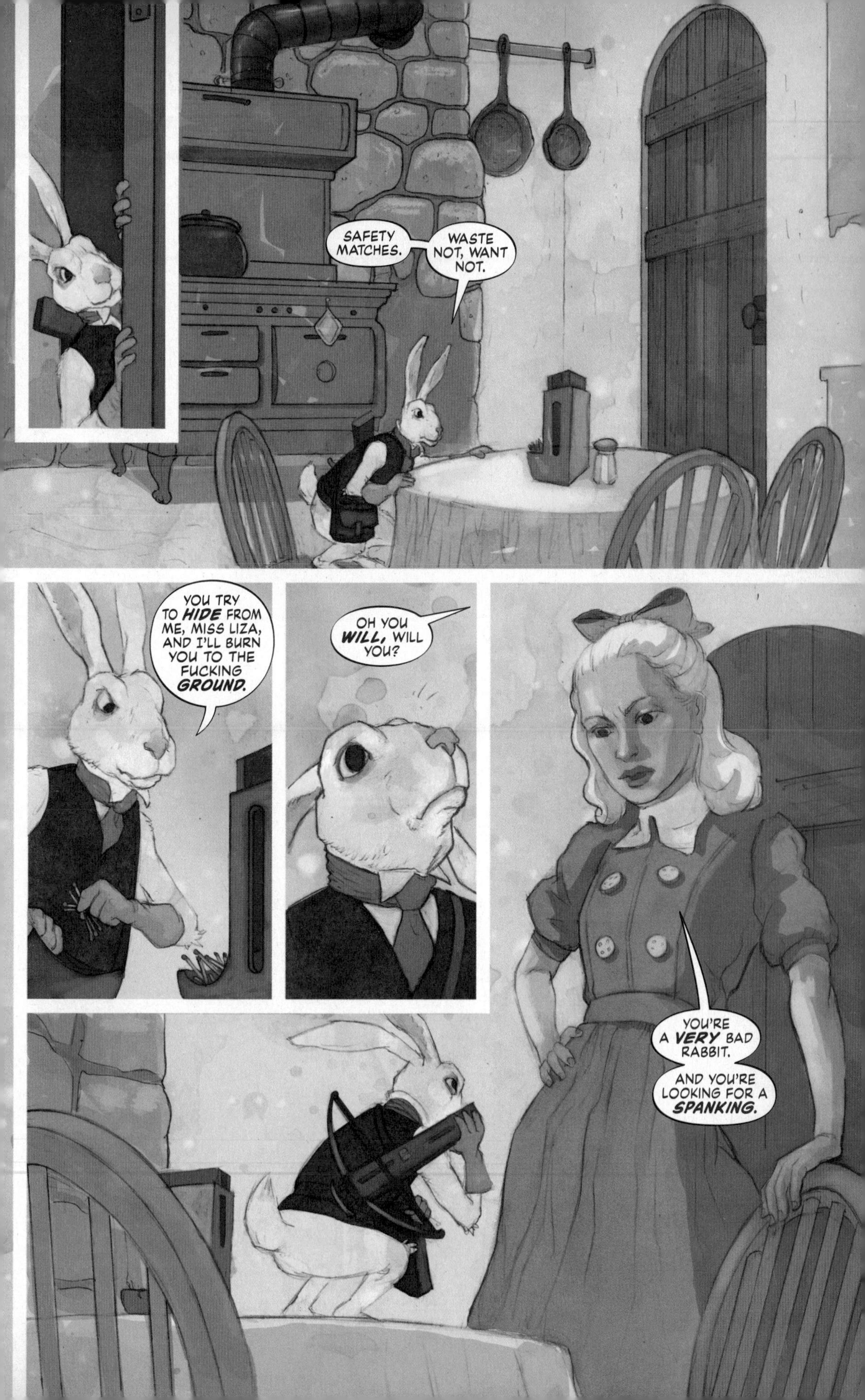
SAFETY MATCHES.
WASTE NOT, WANT NOT.
YOU TRY TO **HIDE** FROM ME, MISS LIZA, AND I'LL BURN YOU TO THE FUCKING **GROUND.**
OH YOU **WILL,** WILL YOU?
YOU'RE A **VERY** BAD RABBIT.
AND YOU'RE LOOKING FOR A **SPANKING.**

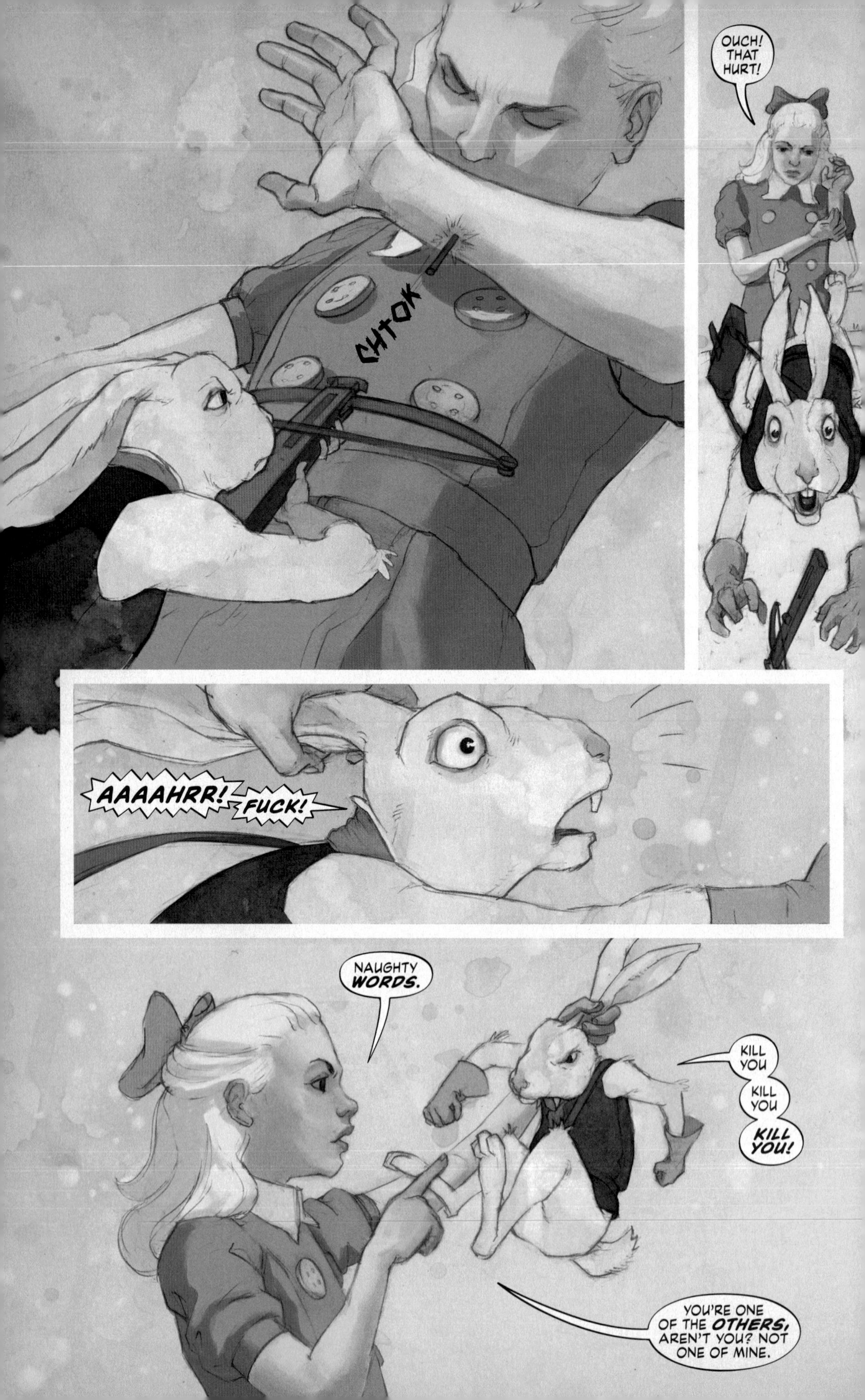
CHTOK
OUCH! THAT HURT!
AAAAHRR!
FUCK!
NAUGHTY WORDS.
KILL YOU
KILL YOU
KILL YOU!
YOU'RE ONE OF THE OTHERS, AREN'T YOU? NOT ONE OF MINE.

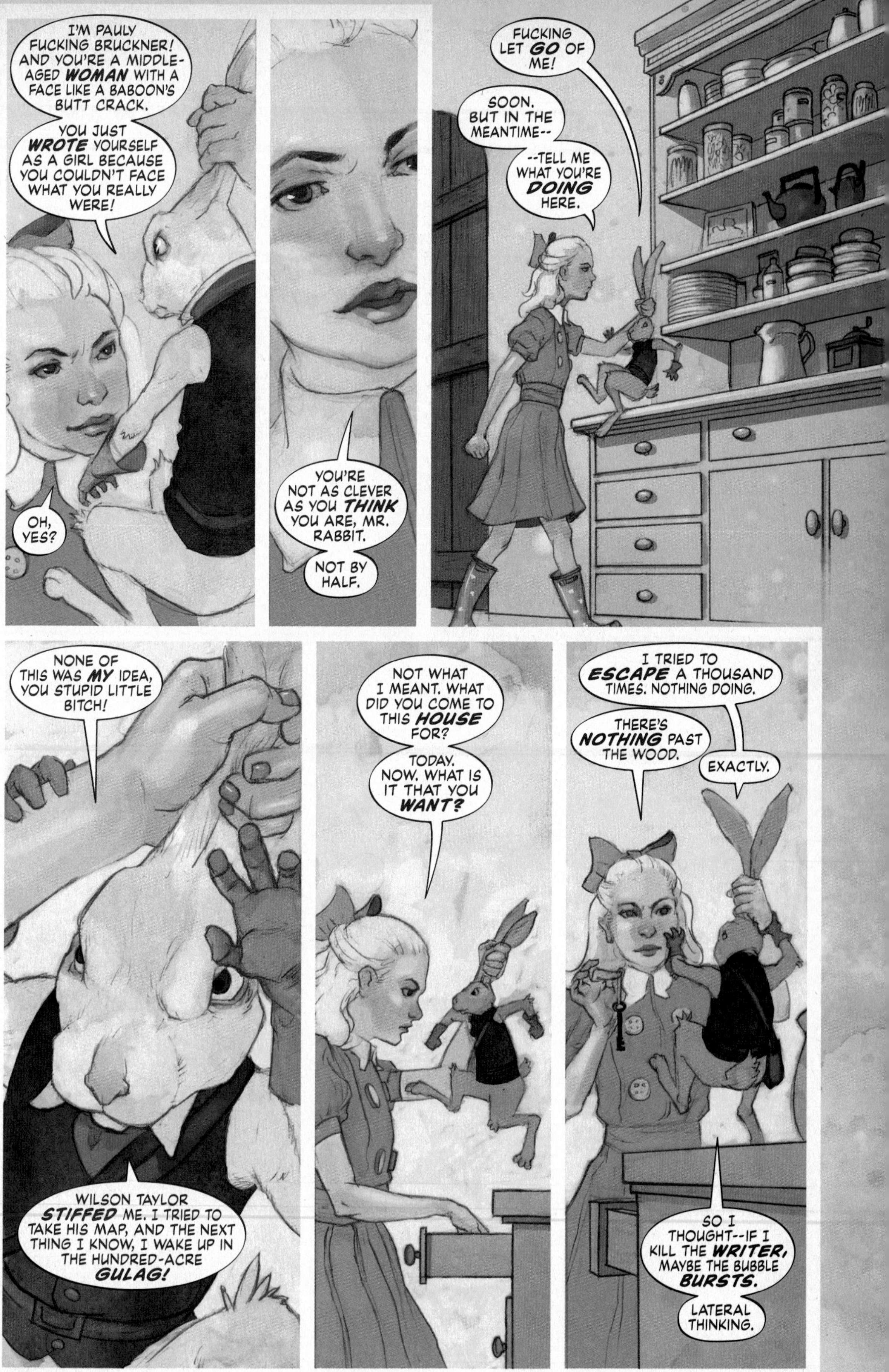
I'M PAULY FUCKING BRUCKNER! AND YOU'RE A MIDDLE-AGED WOMAN WITH A FACE LIKE A BABOON'S BUTT CRACK.
YOU JUST WROTE YOURSELF AS A GIRL BECAUSE YOU COULDN'T FACE WHAT YOU REALLY WERE!
OH, YES?
YOU'RE NOT AS CLEVER AS YOU THINK YOU ARE, MR. RABBIT.
NOT BY HALF.
FUCKING LET GO OF ME!
SOON. BUT IN THE MEANTIME--
--TELL ME WHAT YOU'RE DOING HERE.
NONE OF THIS WAS MY IDEA, YOU STUPID LITTLE BITCH!
WILSON TAYLOR STIFFED ME. I TRIED TO TAKE HIS MAP, AND THE NEXT THING I KNOW, I WAKE UP IN THE HUNDRED-ACRE GULAG!
NOT WHAT I MEANT. WHAT DID YOU COME TO THIS HOUSE FOR?
TODAY. NOW. WHAT IS IT THAT YOU WANT?
I TRIED TO ESCAPE A THOUSAND TIMES. NOTHING DOING.
THERE'S NOTHING PAST THE WOOD.
EXACTLY.
SO I THOUGHT--IF I KILL THE WRITER, MAYBE THE BUBBLE BURSTS.
LATERAL THINKING.

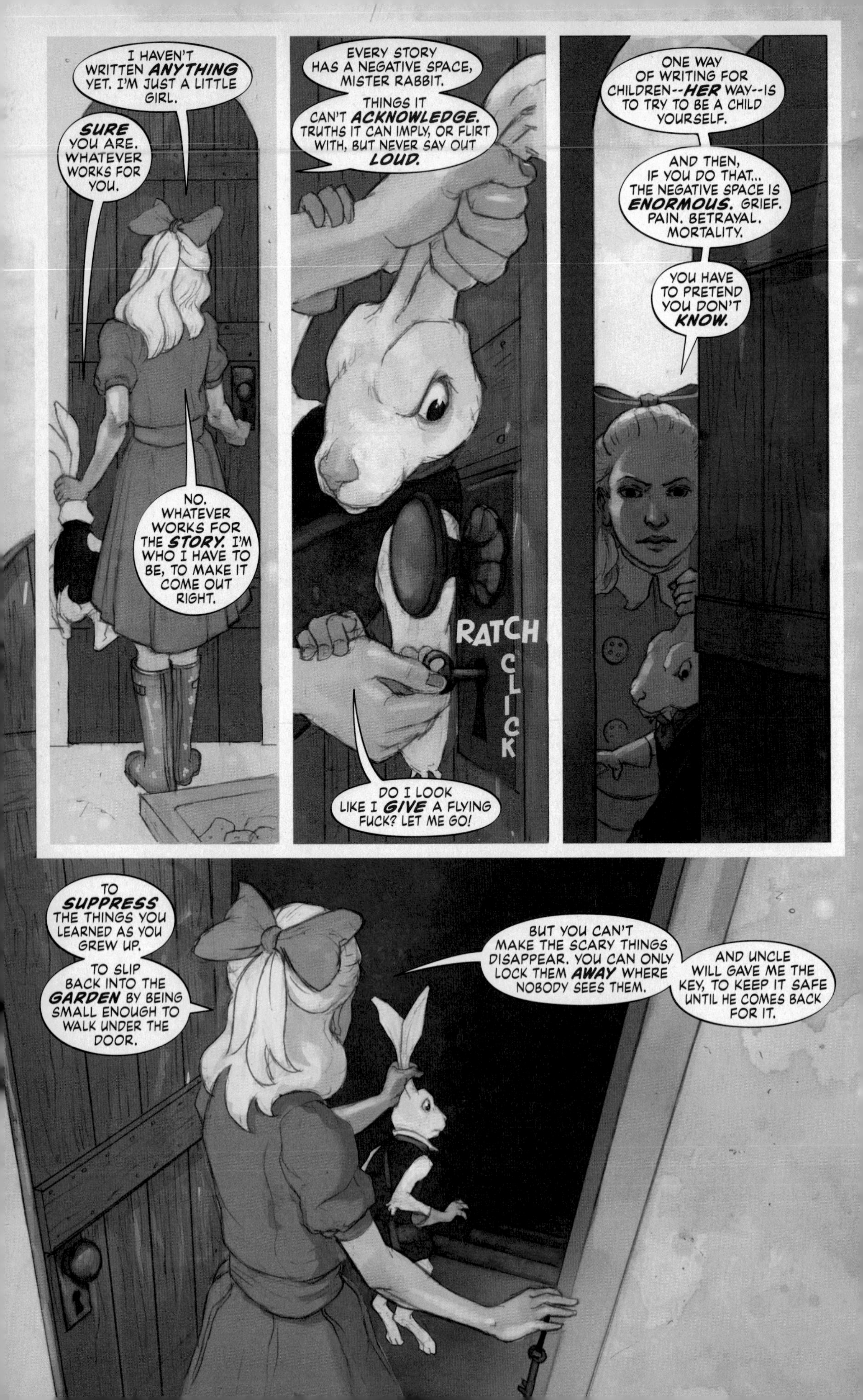
I HAVEN'T WRITTEN ANYTHING YET. I'M JUST A LITTLE GIRL.
SURE YOU ARE. WHATEVER WORKS FOR YOU.
NO. WHATEVER WORKS FOR THE STORY. I'M WHO I HAVE TO BE, TO MAKE IT COME OUT RIGHT.
EVERY STORY HAS A NEGATIVE SPACE, MISTER RABBIT.
THINGS IT CAN'T ACKNOWLEDGE. TRUTHS IT CAN IMPLY, OR FLIRT WITH, BUT NEVER SAY OUT LOUD.
RATCH
CLICK
DO I LOOK LIKE I GIVE A FLYING FUCK? LET ME GO!
ONE WAY OF WRITING FOR CHILDREN--HER WAY--IS TO TRY TO BE A CHILD YOURSELF.
AND THEN, IF YOU DO THAT... THE NEGATIVE SPACE IS ENORMOUS. GRIEF. PAIN. BETRAYAL. MORTALITY.
YOU HAVE TO PRETEND YOU DON'T KNOW.
TO SUPPRESS THE THINGS YOU LEARNED AS YOU GREW UP.
TO SLIP BACK INTO THE GARDEN BY BEING SMALL ENOUGH TO WALK UNDER THE DOOR.
BUT YOU CAN'T MAKE THE SCARY THINGS DISAPPEAR. YOU CAN ONLY LOCK THEM AWAY WHERE NOBODY SEES THEM.
AND UNCLE WILL GAVE ME THE KEY, TO KEEP IT SAFE UNTIL HE COMES BACK FOR IT.

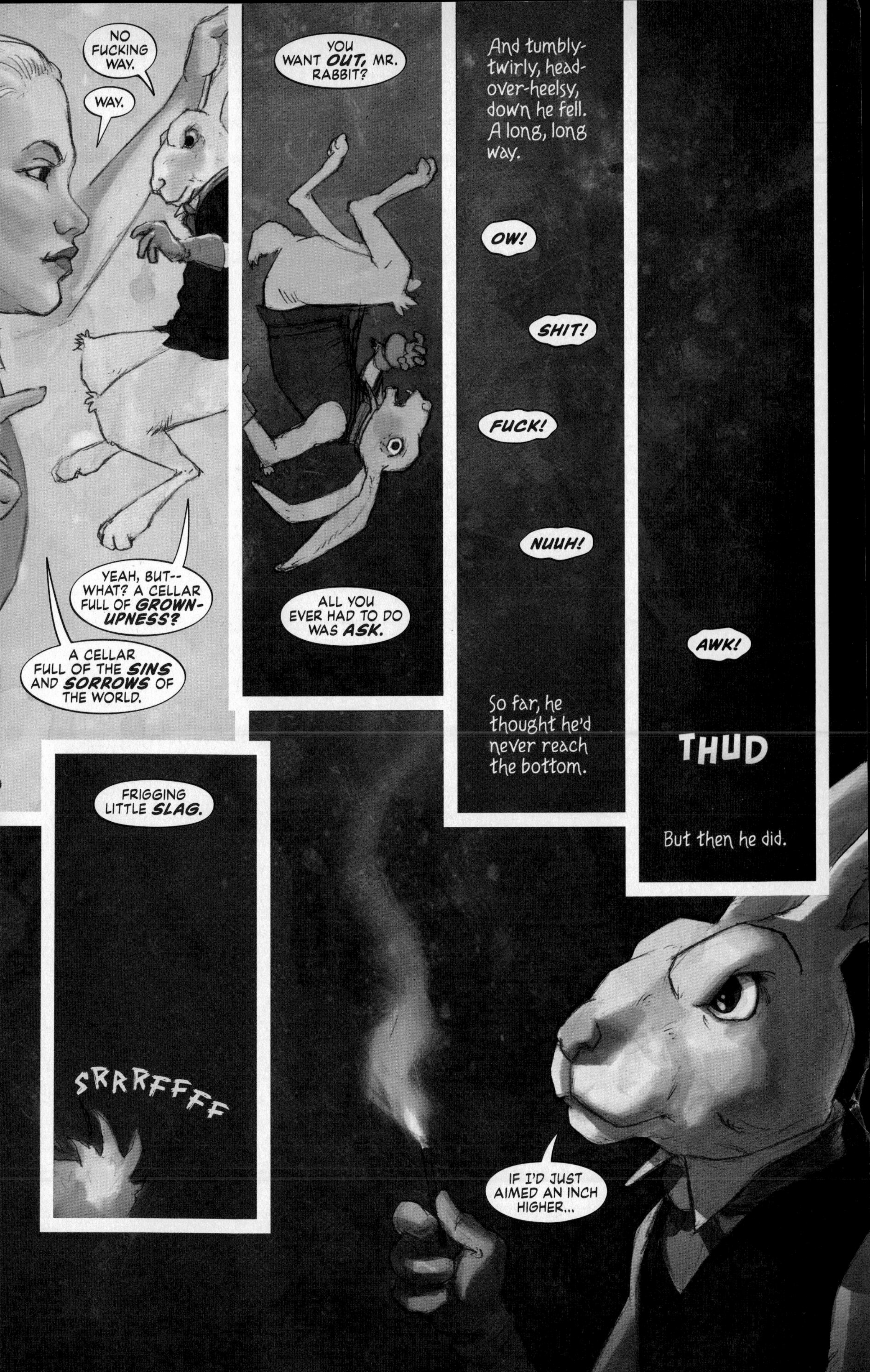
NO FUCKING WAY.
WAY.
YEAH, BUT-- WHAT? A CELLAR FULL OF GROWN-UPNESS?
A CELLAR FULL OF THE SINS AND SORROWS OF THE WORLD.
YOU WANT OUT, MR. RABBIT?
ALL YOU EVER HAD TO DO WAS ASK.
And tumbly-twirly, head-over-heelsy, down he fell. A long, long way.
OW!
SHIT!
FUCK!
NUUH!
So far, he thought he'd never reach the bottom.
AWK!
THUD
But then he did.
FRIGGING LITTLE SLAG.
SRRRFFFF
IF I'D JUST AIMED AN INCH HIGHER...

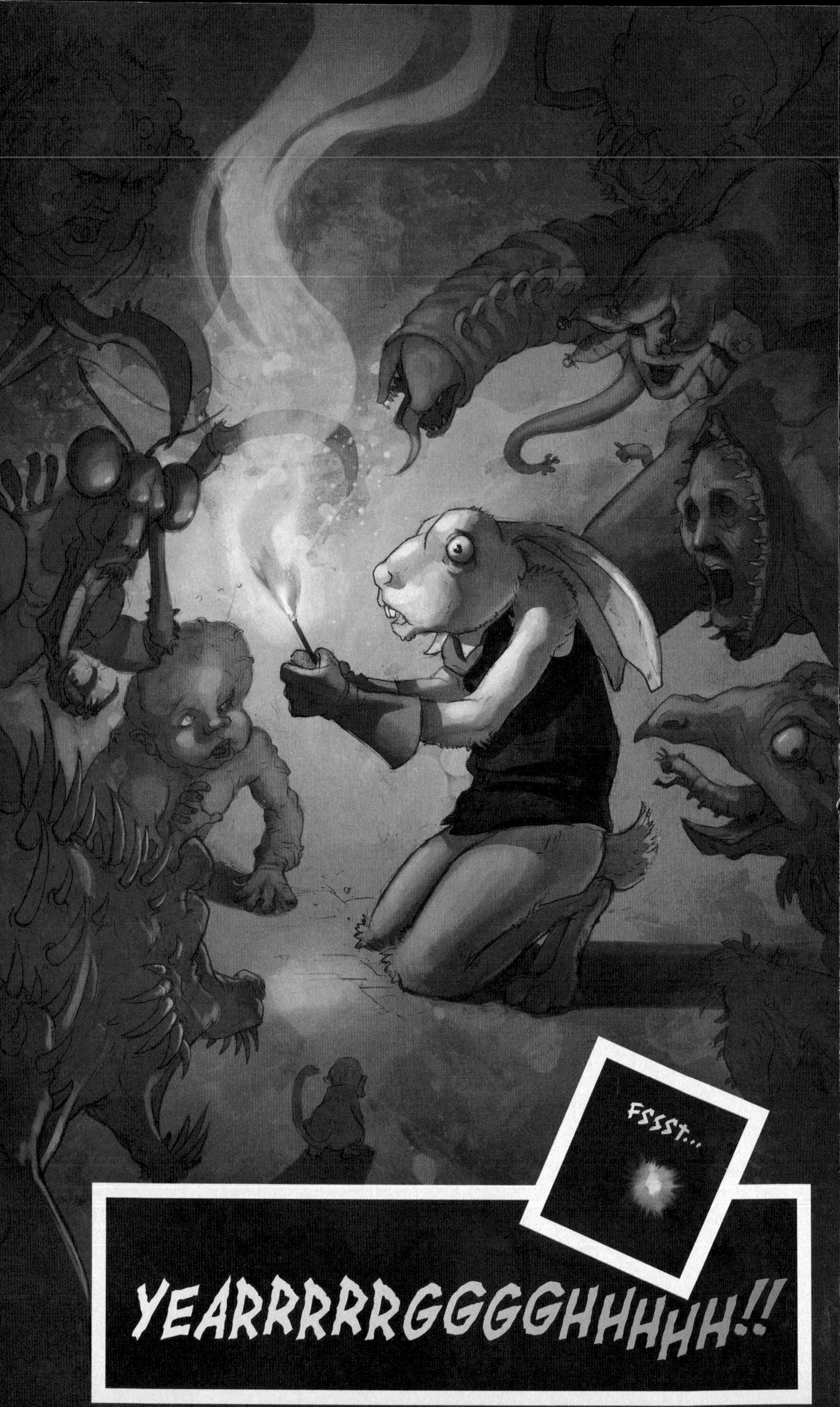
FSSST...
YEARRRRRRGGGGHHHHH!!

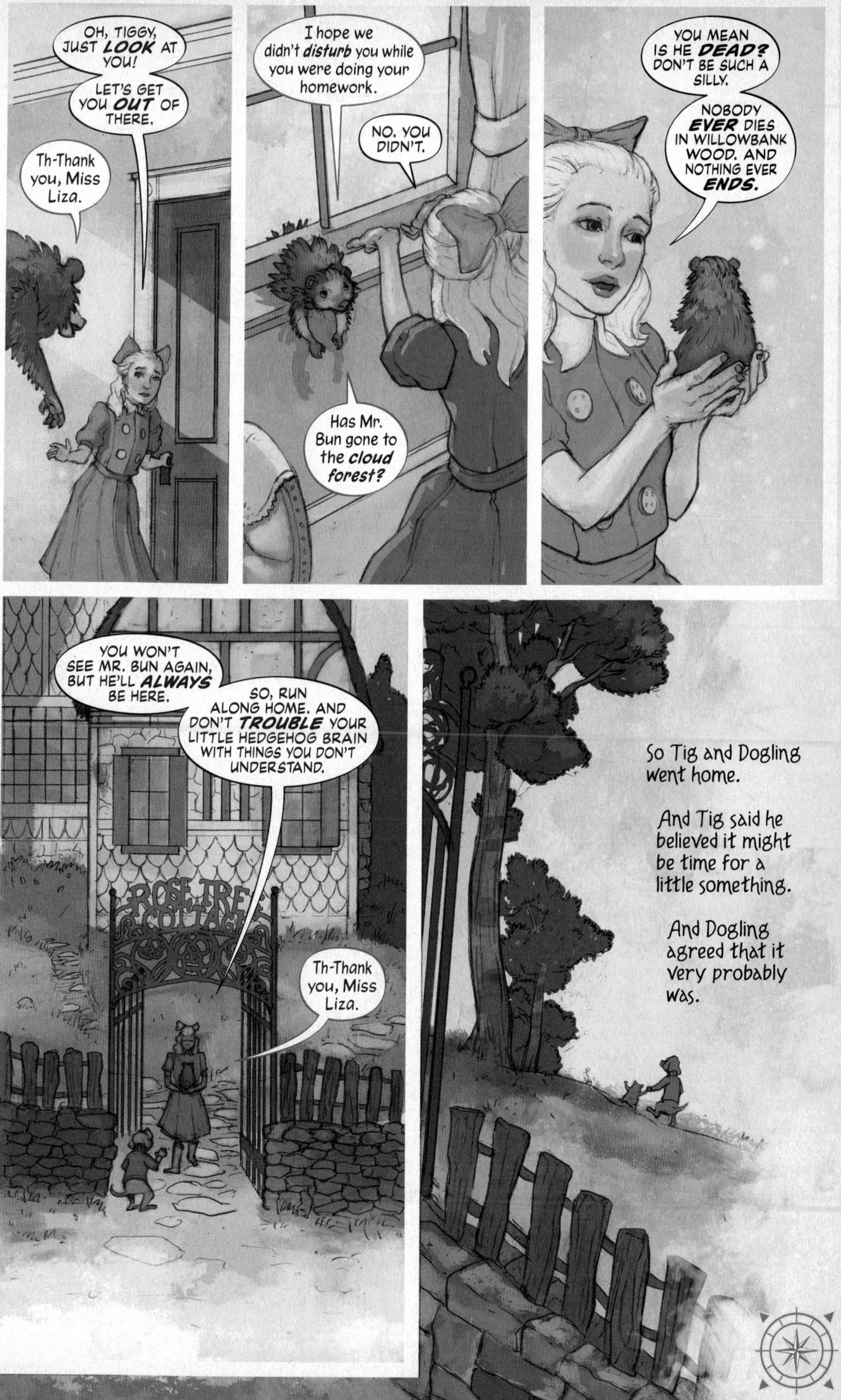

OH, TIGGY, JUST LOOK AT YOU!
LET'S GET YOU OUT OF THERE.
Th-Thank you, Miss Liza.
I hope we didn't disturb you while you were doing your homework.
NO. YOU DIDN'T.
Has Mr. Bun gone to the cloud forest?
YOU MEAN IS HE DEAD? DON'T BE SUCH A SILLY.
NOBODY EVER DIES IN WILLOWBANK WOOD. AND NOTHING EVER ENDS.
YOU WON'T SEE MR. BUN AGAIN, BUT HE'LL ALWAYS BE HERE.
SO, RUN ALONG HOME. AND DON'T TROUBLE YOUR LITTLE HEDGEHOG BRAIN WITH THINGS YOU DON'T UNDERSTAND.
ROSE TREE COTTAGE
Th-Thank you, Miss Liza.
So Tig and Dogling went home.
And Tig said he believed it might be time for a little something.
And Dogling agreed that it very probably was.

...ES is an excellent series in the tradition of ...MAN, one that rewards careful attention ...oyalty." – ENTERTAINMENT WEEKLY

BILL WILLINGHAM

"[A] wonderfully twisted concept... features fairy tale characters banished to the noirish world of present-day New York."
–THE WASHINGTON POST

"An epic, beautifully written story that places 'Fables,' familiar characters from folklore, in the mundane world after a mysterious Adversary conquers their homelands."
– THE ONION

"Great fun."– BOOKLIST

VERTIGO
"FABLES is a must-read for any aficionado of fantasy in a contemporary setting."
— The Magazine of Fantasy and Science Fiction
"We hope this series lasts happily ever after."
— WIZARD
FABLES
LEGENDS IN EXILE
Willingham • Medina
Leialoha • Hamilton

VOL. 1: LEGENDS IN EXILE
VOL. 2: ANIMAL FARM
VOL. 3: STORYBOOK LOVE
VOL. 4: MARCH OF THE WOODEN SOLDIERS
VOL. 5: THE MEAN SEASONS
VOL. 6: HOMELANDS
VOL. 7: ARABIAN NIGHTS (AND DAYS)
VOL. 8: WOLVES
VOL. 9: SONS OF EMPIRE
VOL. 10: THE GOOD PRINCE
VOL. 11: WAR AND PIECES
1001 NIGHTS OF SNOWFALL

FABLES VOL. 3:
STORYBOOK LOVE

WINNER OF TWO EISNER AWARDS
FABLES
STORYBOOK LOVE
Bill Willingham
Mark Buckingham
Steve Leialoha
VERTIGO

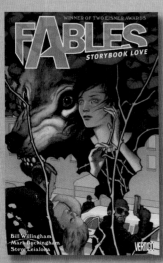

FABLES VOL. 6:
HOMELANDS

VERTIGO
"Great fun." —Booklist
WINNER OF FIVE EISNER AWARDS
FABLES
HOMELANDS
Bill Willingham
Mark Buckingham
David Hahn
Steve Leialoha

FABLES:
1001 NIGHTS OF SNOWFALL

FABLES
1001 NIGHTS of SNOWFALL
AN ORIGINAL GRAPHIC NOVEL BY
BILL WILLINGHAM

GO TO
VERTIGOBOOKS.COM
FOR FREE SAMPLES OF THE FIRST ISSUES OF OUR GRAPHIC NOVELS

Suggested for Mature Readers